How Literature Comes to Matter

New Materialisms
Series editors: Iris van der Tuin and Rosi Braidotti

New Materialisms asks how materiality permits representation, actualises ethical subjectivities and innovates the political. The series will provide a discursive hub and an institutional home to this vibrant emerging field and open it up to a wider readership.

Editorial Advisory board
Marie-Luise Angerer, Karen Barad, Corinna Bath, Barbara Bolt, Felicity Colman, Manuel DeLanda, Richard Grusin, Vicki Kirby, Gregg Lambert, Nina Lykke, Brian Massumi, Henk Oosterling, Arun Saldanha

Books available
What if Culture was Nature all Along?
Edited by Vicki Kirby
Critical and Clinical Cartographies: Architecture, Robotics, Medicine, Philosophy
Edited by Andrej Radman and Heidi Sohn
Architectural Materialisms: Non-Human Creativity
Edited by Maria Voyatzaki
Placemaking: A New Materialist Theory of Pedagogy
Tara Page
Queer Defamiliarisation: Writing, Mattering, Making Strange
Helen Palmer
Biopolitics, Materiality and Meaning in Modern European Drama
Hedwig Fraunhofer
How Literature Comes to Matter: Post-Anthropocentric Approaches to Fiction
Edited by Sten Pultz Moslund, Marlene Karlsson Marcussen and Martin Karlsson Pedersen

Visit the series web page at: edinburghuniversitypress.com/series/nmat

How Literature Comes to Matter

Post-Anthropocentric Approaches to Fiction

Edited by Sten Pultz Moslund, Marlene Karlsson Marcussen and Martin Karlsson Pedersen

EDINBURGH
University Press

Edinburgh University Press is one of the leading university presses in the UK. We publish academic books and journals in our selected subject areas across the humanities and social sciences, combining cutting-edge scholarship with high editorial and production values to produce academic works of lasting importance. For more information visit our website: edinburghuniversitypress.com

© editorial matter and organisation Sten Pultz Moslund, Marlene Karlsson Marcussen and Martin Karlsson Pedersen, 2021, 2022
© the chapters their several authors, 2021, 2022

Edinburgh University Press Ltd
The Tun – Holyrood Road
12(2f) Jackson's Entry
Edinburgh EH8 8PJ

First published in hardback by Edinburgh University Press 2021

Typeset in 11/13 Adobe Sabon by
IDSUK (DataConnection) Ltd

A CIP record for this book is available from the British Library

ISBN 978 1 4744 6131 3 (hardback)
ISBN 978 1 4744 6132 0 (paperback)
ISBN 978 1 4744 6134 4 (webready PDF)
ISBN 978 1 4744 6133 7 (epub)

The right of Sten Pultz Moslund, Marlene Karlsson Marcussen and Martin Karlsson Pedersen to be identified as the editor of this work has been asserted in accordance with the Copyright, Designs and Patents Act 1988, and the Copyright and Related Rights Regulations 2003 (SI No. 2498).

Contents

Acknowledgements vii
Preface viii
Notes on Contributors x

Introduction 1
    Sten Pultz Moslund, Marlene Karlsson Marcussen and
    Martin Karlsson Pedersen

I. **Matter-Oriented Perspectives on Literary Techniques, Language and Representation**

  1. The Abundance of Things in the Midst of Writing: A Post-Anthropocentric View on Description and Georges Perec's 'Still Life/Style Leaf' 31
     Marlene Karlsson Marcussen

  2. Slow Narrative and the Perception of Material Forms 49
     Marco Caracciolo

II. **Object Intrusions in Subject-Centric Texts**

  3. Aisthetic Realities in Ayi Kwei Armah's *The Beautyful Ones Are Not Yet Born*: A Matter-Oriented Reading of Postcolonial Literature 73
     Sten Pultz Moslund

  4. Sylvia Plath's 'Tulips': On the Hostile Nature of Things 93
     Michael Karlsson Pedersen

  5. 'We have nothing to be arrogant about' – Hans Christian Andersen and Anti-Anthropocentrism 109
     Torsten Bøgh Thomsen

III. Carnal Realities: Lively Flesh in Feminist and Queer Readings

6. Feminist New Materialism and Literary Studies: Methodological Meditations on the Tradition of Feminist Literary Criticism and (Post)Critique   131
   Tobias Skiveren

7. Djuna Barnes and Queer Interiorities   153
   Laura Oulanne

8. Corporeal Creativity and Queer Gaps in Time   172
   Karin Sellberg

IV. Capitalism, Crisis and the Anthropocene

9. Putting the Earth to Use: Reading Resources in the End Times (Through Science Fiction)   193
   Rune Graulund

10. Dry Ontology and Finance Capitalism: A Material–Affective Reading of Financial Crisis Fiction   214
    Martin Karlsson Pedersen

11. The Work of Art in the Age of Capitalist Realism: Materiality/Aura/Apocalypse   236
    Maurizia Boscagli

Afterword: Woodenness – The (Palm) Heart of the Matter   257
   Timothy Morton

Index   266

Acknowledgements

The editors wish to thank everyone in the *Materiality, Literature and Aesthetics* research programme at the University of Southern Denmark for our exciting discussions and peer feedback on several chapters in the book.

We thank Iris van der Tuin and Rosi Braidotti for their suggestions of contributors to the book.

We would also like to thank Nobrow Press for granting us permission to include four images from Jon McNaught's *Kingdom* in Marco Caracciolo's Chapter 2.

While working on Chapter 2, 'Slow Narrative and the Perception of Material Forms', Marco Caracciolo received funding from the European Research Council (ERC) under the European Union's Horizon 2020 research and innovation programme (grant agreement No 714166). Laura Oulanne would like to thank the Alfred Kordelin Foundation for supporting the research from which her contribution, 'Djuna Barnes and Queer Interiorities', stems.

Preface

The making of this book began in the small collective research programme *Materiality, Literature and Aesthetics*, at the Institute for the Study of Culture at the University of Southern Denmark (SDU). The three-year programme (running from September 2015 to August 2018) was chaired by Sten Moslund and numbered twenty-plus participants at its peak, with various degrees of affiliation, and a steady core group of twelve members. *Materiality, Literature and Aesthetics* was a programme whose aim was to bring together scholars at the University of Southern Denmark who were interested in the material turn and post-anthropocentric theory and the way they continue to significantly impact contemporary developments in the humanities.

From the outset, the main ambition of the programme was to explore ways in which post-anthropocentric theory might create new and innovative approaches to literature and, vice versa, how the ontological and epistemological complexities of art and literature might contribute to theoretical explorations of matter, objects and all sorts of entanglements between the non-human and human histories, cultures and societies.

Our meetings will be remembered for their lively discussions of texts by Jane Bennett, Diane Coole and Samantha Frost, Maurizia Boscagli, Bruno Latour, Karen Barad, Vicki Kirby, Rosi Braidotti, Stacy Alaimo, Graham Harman, Timothy Morton, Bill Brown, all in combination with literary texts by writers such as Virginia Woolf, H. P. Lovecraft, Francis Ponge, Jeff VanderMeer and Paolo Bacigalupi. Although such theoretical voices represent a very broad spectrum of post-anthropocentric theory with very different conceptualisations – and contextualisations – of matter and objects and more-than-human realities, the programme appreciated their common ground as a radical reappraisal of phenomena, such as place, nature, the body and material manifestations of reality, whether it happens in examinations of such phenomena in themselves or the ways in which they influence, condition and co-create human ways of being-in-the-world.

However, as we ploughed through one text after another, which would often refer to the significance of literature and offer more or less sketchy illustrations of post-anthropocentric philosophy with literary examples, we kept being struck by the absence of more sustained and in-depth analyses of literary works or close readings that would try out and experiment with various ways of reading literature through post-anthropocentric lenses. The wish for a book that would do such a thing is what brought us to make the present volume, half of which consists of contributions by participants in the programme while the other half is made up of contributions by scholars from around the world who were personally invited to write a chapter in their particular areas of expertise.

Another central ambition of the SDU research programme that should be mentioned, because it has made its mark on the book, is the aim of assisting young scholars in their careers. Several PhD students were among the core participants as well as great talents in pursuit of PhD stipends, which, in Denmark as elsewhere in the world, are increasingly hard to come by in the field of literature. Several of these young scholars have given shape to the book with chapters that significantly contribute to the present task of developing the study of literature with the expansion of realities that is brought about by post-anthropocentric theory.

When the *Materiality, Literature and Aesthetics* research programme ended in 2018, a new programme, *Anthropocene Aesthetics*, took its place, chaired by Rune Graulund, which now carries on some of the work on New Materialism and matter realities that has laid the foundation of the current book, but, as the name of the programme suggests, with a special focus on literary studies in relation to global warming, ecocriticism, posthuman and animal studies and genres such as weird fiction, nature writing and climate fiction.

The last thing we wish to say before the book begins, and speaking on behalf of all the authors in the book, is that the work offered here is not to be seen as an arrival but rather as a contribution to the beginning of the expansion of the study of literature with the increased reality perspectives of post-anthropocentric theory – and vice versa – which, in our view, is still at a pioneering stage. In that light, we hope that the book will bring a spark to that general endeavour, trigger new questions and help open new avenues for future research.

Notes on Contributors

Maurizia Boscagli is Professor of English and Feminist Studies at the University of California, Santa Barbara. Her research and teaching focus on twentieth- and twenty-first-century anglophone literature and culture; modernism; contemporary critical theory; feminist and queer theory; materialism, Marxism and Autonomism; the environmental humanities, as well as migration, globalisation, and cosmopolitanism. She is the author of *Eye on the Flesh: Fashions of Masculinity in the Early Twentieth Century* (Routledge, 1996) and *Stuff Theory: Everyday Objects, Radical Materialism* (Bloomsbury, 2014). She is the translator of Antonio Negri's book *Insurgencies: Constituent Power and the Modern State* (2009). Boscagli is also the director of COMMA, the Center on Modern Culture, Materialism and Aesthetics at UC Santa Barbara. Her current research includes a new manuscript on the refusal of work and the politics of not doing.

Marco Caracciolo is Associate Professor of English and Literary Theory at Ghent University in Belgium, where he leads the ERC Starting Grant project 'Narrating the Mesh'. Marco's work explores the phenomenology of narrative, or the structure of the experiences afforded by literary fiction and other narrative media. He is the author of four books, including most recently *Embodiment and the Cosmic Perspective in Twentieth-Century Fiction* (Routledge, 2020).

Rune Graulund is Associate Professor in American Literature and Culture at the Institute of Literature, Media and Cultural Studies, University of Southern Denmark. His research centres on American popular culture and literature (especially Gothic studies, science fiction, and post-apocalyptic film, literature and games). He also writes about political fiction (migrant and postcolonial novels) and non-fiction (nature writing and travel writing) relating to questions of migration, empire, ecology and the Anthropocene. He has written books, chapters and articles on a variety of subjects ranging from zombies to nanotechnology, from the American desert to the Arctic, digital art and experimental prose. His current research focuses on the question of resources and the manner in which literature has grappled with pollution and resource depletion from the Industrial Revolution onwards. He is director of the research group 'Anthropocene Aesthetics' at the University of Southern Denmark.

Marlene Karlsson Marcussen holds a PhD in Comparative Literature from the University of Southern Denmark. Her research explores spatial representation in modern fiction through a combination of narrative theory and New Materialism.

She is the co-editor (with Marco Caracciolo and David Rodriguez) of *Narrating Nonhuman Spaces: Form, Story, and Experience Beyond Anthropocentrism* (forthcoming). Publications with post-anthropocentric themes include 'Floating Air – Solid Furniture: Vibrant Spaces in Virginia Woolf's "Time Passes"' (forthcoming), 'The Postapocalyptic Motherhood' (*Passage*, 2019) and 'Reading for Space: Foregrounding the Sensuous Experience of Space in the French Modern Novel' (*GCSC*, Verlag Trier, 2014).

Timothy Morton is Rita Shea Guffey Chair in English at Rice University. He has collaborated with Björk, Laurie Anderson, Jennifer Walshe, Jeff Bridges, Sabrina Scott, Olafur Eliasson and Pharrell Williams. He co-wrote and appears in *Living in the Future's Past*, a 2018 film about global warming with Jeff Bridges. He is the author of *Being Ecological* (Penguin, 2018), *Humankind: Solidarity with Nonhuman People* (Verso, 2017), *Dark Ecology: For a Logic of Future Coexistence* (Columbia University Press, 2016), *Nothing: Three Inquiries in Buddhism* (Chicago University Press, 2015), *Hyperobjects: Philosophy and Ecology after the End of the World* (University of Minnesota Press, 2013), *Realist Magic: Objects, Ontology, Causality* (Open Humanities Press, 2013), *The Ecological Thought* (Harvard University Press, 2010), *Ecology without Nature* (Harvard University Press, 2007), eight other books and two hundred essays on philosophy, ecology, literature, music, art, architecture, design and food. His work has been translated into ten languages. In 2014 Morton gave the Wellek Lectures in Theory.

Sten Pultz Moslund is Associate Professor in Comparative Literature at the University of Southern Denmark. His research focuses on postcolonial literature and theory. Apart from a range of books and articles on literature and issues of migration, hybridity, place and geocriticism, publications with particular interest in post-anthropocentric perspectives include *Literature's Sensuous Geographies: Postcolonial Matters of Place* (Palgrave Macmillan, 2015) and 'Postcolonialism, Nonhuman Theory and the Anthropocene. A Postanthropocentric Reading of *Robinson Crusoe*' (ARIEL, forthcoming).

Laura Oulanne is a postdoctoral researcher at the University of Helsinki. Her research focuses on material things and environments particularly in anglophone modernist literature, as well as embodied approaches to reading and enactivist philosophy of mind. Her doctoral dissertation is titled 'Lived Things: Materialities of Agency, Affect, and Meaning in the Short Fiction of Djuna Barnes and Jean Rhys' (University of Helsinki/Justus Liebig University, Giessen 2018), while her forthcoming publications study the relationships between mind, subjectivity and the material world in the works of writers such as Jane Bowles, Katherine Mansfield, Gertrude Stein and Virginia Woolf.

Martin Karlsson Pedersen holds a Master of Arts in Literature from the University of Southern Denmark. He has taught several courses in Comparative Literature. His main research area lies in the intersection between economic and financial theory, Marxist criticism and literary realism and he is currently pursuing a PhD on the topic of 'The Realist Financial Novel as an Ideological Battlefield – Critique and Legitimization of Homo Economicus in Times of Crisis for Neoliberal Rationality'. His recent publication is an article on economic science fiction, class and critical anti-utopia (*Passage* 82).

Michael Karlsson Pedersen holds a PhD in Comparative Literature from the University of Southern Denmark. His research focuses on the literary aesthetics of different nonhuman ontologies as especially found in twentieth-century German literature. Publications with post-anthropocentric themes include 'Firm Grips and Light Touches: An Essay on Things and Halfthings in Postwar German Nature Poetry' (Aalborg University Press, 2017), 'Enemy of Stone, Lover of Music: Toward a Material Modernity of *Stimmung*' (*The Germanic Review*, vol. 93, no. 4) and 'The Descriptive Turn in German Nature-Oriented *Neue Sachlichkeit* (1913–1933): An Essay on Nonhuman Literary Genres' (forthcoming).

Karin Sellberg is a lecturer in humanities at the School of Historical and Philosophical Inquiry, University of Queensland. She is primarily a literary scholar with research interests in feminist philosophy, gender studies, medical humanities and historiography. She has a forthcoming book on constructions of transgender embodiment in late twentieth-century feminist and queer theory and new historicist criticism of early modern drama. She has published extensively on queer and feminist conceptions of history and time.

Tobias Skiveren holds a PhD in Scandinavian literature from Aarhus University, Denmark. He is an editorial member of the journals *Women, Gender & Research* and *Passage*. Among his recent publications are 'On Good Listening, Postcritique, and Ta-Nehisi Coates' Affective Testimony' in *Affect Theory and Literary Critical Practice* (Palgrave Macmillan, 2019, ed. Stephen Ahern) and the monograph *Den materielle drejning. Natur, teknologi og (nyere) dansk litteratur* (University Press of Southern Denmark, 2016, co-written with Martin Gregersen). His current research is situated in the cross-section between feminist New Materialism, affect theory and (post)critique.

Torsten Bøgh Thomsen is Assistant Professor in Comparative Literature at the University of Southern Denmark. His research focuses on ecocriticism and romantic literature. For the past ten years he has worked with art and literature in ecocritical, New Materialist and post-humanist perspectives and published extensively on these subjects. He has published a monograph on the diverse understandings of nature in the writings of Hans Christian Andersen (*Skyggepunkter*, Spring 2019) and translated Timothy Morton's *Ecology Without Nature* (2007) into Danish (Spring 2019).

Introduction

Sten Pultz Moslund, Marlene Karlsson Marcussen and Martin Karlsson Pedersen

> *Now, too, the rising sun came in at the window, touching the red-edged curtain, and began to bring out circles and lines. Now in the growing light its whiteness settled in the plate; the blade condensed its gleam. Chairs and cupboards loomed behind so that though each was separate they seemed inextricably involved. The looking-glass whitened its pool upon the wall. The real flower on the window-sill was attended by a phantom flower. Yet the phantom was part of the flower, for when a bud broke free the paler flower in the glass opened a bud too.*
> Virginia Woolf, *The Waves*, 1931

Virginia Woolf is perhaps mostly known for her depiction of reality as a stream of consciousness, but there is another side to the story. It begins with a change of perspective: suspending hermeneutic and interpretive presuppositions, Woolf's novels also bear witness to a profound interest in 'things in themselves' (*A Room of One's Own*) and the way objects interact with each other independently of human characters.

In the quoted passage above, things and phenomena are not rendered merely as passive or symbolic backgrounds, they attract attention in their own right. The passage describes how that which we commonly perceive as the background is foregrounded as a complex network of object-relations. Without any human characters present, the passage describes a meeting between the sun, furniture and everyday objects in a room. The meeting is described through the gesture of *touching*. The touch of sunlight changes the appearance of the curtains as it moves across their lines, folds and curves. Yet, as the passage continues, it becomes clear that the privilege of agency is not only ascribed to moving bodies like the sun, but to all objects. The plate and the blade of the knife translate the porous materiality of sunlight by lending their solidity to the rays: a whiteness of light *settles* in the plate and the gleam is *condensed* by the blade. Objects are transforming and translating each other – *chairs and cupboards, a looking-glass* and *a flower* all translate the light of the sun, each in their own particular mode.

Even if the objects in the passage may still be said to be perceived by some kind of human subject (an impersonal but human narrative stance) and even if the objects are given shape by a human mode of perception, Woolf's mode of representation still manages to call forth their appearance as a reality without any inherent semantic human-made meaning, including the habitual meaning ascribed to objects by everyday human use.

Woolf resists any semantic framing of the objects and their interaction: the passage describes something happening in a *now* where no meaning or explanation unfolds other than the event of objects exchanging agencies. Her mode of representation never lays the objects to rest (as explained or knowable by our use of them). The blade changes from a human utensil into an object interacting with sunlight and the sun is precisely not turned into a symbol of human feeling or enlightened human reason clarifying and giving life to dead matter. The sun figures forth as a material force of light acting on and itself being affected by other objects. The event discloses an immanent 'thing-power': the power of objects to affect other objects.

In this manner, Woolf engages in a rethinking and re-evaluation of the relationship between the human and the nonhuman, between subject and object, agency and non-agency; not to reverse the ontological hierarchy between subject and object in favour of the object, but to open an inquiry into different realities or different modes of being. By allowing objects their own passages, or, in fact, their own chapters in *The Waves* – the 'Interludes' – Woolf presents an unruly juxtaposition between subject and object that flattens the hierarchy between human reality and realities that exist independently from human will or determination.

In this light, the quotation ultimately illuminates how reality is not only made up by streams of human consciousness but also by streams of nonhuman agencies: immanent streams of other-than-human-agencies in which human reality is immersed. Moreover, to distinguish the 'Interludes' from the human-centred episodes in other parts of the novel, Woolf has italicised every word as if to signal that language works differently here; that it no longer communicates a reality that is necessarily human. On yet another level of reading, the italics call attention to a material textuality existing independently from the otherwise purely signifying concept of text and sign: the appearance of marks on paper (or screen). Vibrant matter is here also vibrant textuality: a material vibration of textual appearances or typographical forms.

The short preliminary reflection on materiality and object relations in the passage from Virginia Woolf condenses a rethinking of the traditional relationship between the human and the nonhuman; between subject and object. We might say, accordingly, that Woolf's text anticipates and invites the kind of rethinking of reality that is now offered by the renewed theoretical interest in the reality of matter and objects that has surged since the turn of the millennium. A wide range of new intersecting theories, like Thing Theory, Actor Network Theory (ANT), New Materialism, Speculative Realism, Object-Oriented Ontology (OOO) and Assemblage Theory, work precisely to disrupt our habitual humanisation of reality in order to uncover more-than-human realities and the ways in which the human is shaped by and co-evolves with nonhuman matter and object agencies. This renewed interest in matter and objects is commonly referred to under general headings like 'the material turn', 'the ontological turn', 'the speculative turn', 'the nonhuman turn' or 'the post-anthropocentric turn', none of them really catching the theoretical heterogeneity that characterises the 'turn'. Presently, we choose to stick to 'post-anthropocentric' as the least inadequate umbrella term, since all of the theories are interested in renewing our thinking in ways that displace the human from the centre of reality even if the significance of the human may differ from one theory to the other.

For good reason the general shift in theoretical attention to the nonhuman has stirred up the humanities in new ways. The critical practices and time-honoured intellectual assumptions of the linguistic and cultural turns have come to be seen as insufficient or lacking in explanatory power. Longstanding preoccupations with text, discourse, cultural identity, subjectivity – all kinds of linguistic and historical constructions of the real – are shaken up, modified and rearranged as post-anthropocentric theories embark on reappraisals of nonhuman realities and matter-beings. Things and objects, all kinds of matter and natural phenomena, climate, geology and the otherness of the body are re-understood as nonhuman dimensions in human life whose reality-shaping significance has been overlooked, obscured or ignored – by our everyday utilisations and objectifications of mute matter and objects as well as by the history of thought and theorisations of life and reality.

The theoretical turn resonates through and, indeed, blends a great diversity of disciplines and fields of study: from neuroscience and quantum physics to philosophy, ecocriticism, feminism and gender studies, anthropology, space and place studies, performance studies and the arts. What emerges is not only a heightened awareness of the fact that nonhuman forces shape and condition human life and realities – from electrons and quarks to earthquakes, tsunamis and global warming – but a transformation and expansion of the ways we intellectualise and imagine nature, culture, the environment, society, the subject, objects, language and representation, and so on. A host of new theoretical propositions, perspectives and analytical vocabularies are offered through which we may re-engage our studies of reality and human–world relations, not only in philosophy, environmental studies and the social and natural sciences, but in anthropology, history, art, drama, and in literature as well. Everything is in a way reopened by the current theoretical expansion of reality dimensions.

Although post-anthopocentric theory is increasingly incorporated in readings of fiction, the new theoretical developments are still in their early stages in the field of literary studies and therefore two basic questions are still up for critical discussion. First, what does literature have to offer in the broader rethinking of ontology and matter realities? Second, what new perspectives are offered to the study of literature by the post-anthropocentric turn? The first question has been theorised by some of the prominent thinkers particularly in the fields of New Materialism and OOO, such as Graham Harman and Jane Bennett, though mostly from a philosophical point of view, while the second question still leaves much interesting work to be done, despite noteworthy work by Bill Brown, Timothy Morton, Timothy Clark, Maurizia Boscagli, Grant Hamilton and Brian Willems, among others. The aim of this book is primarily to further the discussion of the second question. How may the new theories expand the study of literature, reveal new sides to it, uncover unexplored dimensions of the literary work and uncharted ways in which matter comes to matter in its representation of life and reality? How, for instance, may post-anthropocentric readings throw new light on the reception of postcolonial literature, feminist writers like Sylvia Plath or deconstructive texts by Georges Perec. And what do these texts say about the relationship between thing and word or between the experiencing subject and its surroundings? And more broadly, how does a focus on the nonhuman in texts challenge well-established textual concepts such as narrator, plot and characters? What new perspectives does a de-anthropocisation of the human subject bring to the study of the author and autobiographical literature? What happens to our reading of the (fleshy) body in literature if we read with a feminist New Materialist like Elizabeth Grosz rather than Judith Butler? How does literature imagine and reimagine the relation between matter and human 'resources' in the age of the Anthropocene; in fact, how does the age of the Anthropocene change our reading of matter as represented in literature? These are only some of the questions that the present chapters will explore.

However, before we present an overview of how literature has been engaged so far by post-anthropocentric theory, and before we introduce the new contributions in the current collection, we will make a brief sketch of the philosophical backdrop and motivation of the overall theoretical turn (which is of course just as much a theoretical re-turn, or re-engagement with prior theory and philosophy). Since most of the chapters in this volume crisscross mainly between New Materialism and OOO, these will also be the main focus in the introduction. The main reason for this focus is quite plain. New Materialism and OOO often use literature and explicitly reflect on it as a mode of encountering nonhuman realities and objects. Finally, the introduction also offers a brief discussion to newcomers to the field of the most significant differences between these two central exponents of post-anthropocentric theory and how these differences affect the ways in which they engage with literature.

The Philosophical Backdrop

Spearheaded by researchers like Jane Bennett, Rosi Braidotti, Karen Barad, Bill Brown, Graham Harman, Vicky Kirby, Timothy Morton, Brian Massumi and Steven Shaviro (to name but a few), the new complex of post-anthropocentric theories embarks on an alternative adventure in thought and analytical approaches. New concepts and theoretical vocabularies are offered to grasp and rethink matter, objects and nonhuman agencies: Bennett's 'thing-power', Barad's 'agential realism', Braidotti's 'matter-realisms', Morton's 'hyperobjects', Boscagli's 'stuff' and Harman's 'immaterialism' all seek to address the underexplored significance of more-than-human realities. In doing so they typically work to disrupt the anthropocentric outlook on reality that has dominated (particularly) the Western production of knowledge since its antique beginnings – to disrupt 'the narcissistic reflex of human language and thought', as summarised by Bennett (2010: xvi), that rests on (false) presumptions of humans as their own and the world's rational, free and autonomous sovereigns. In the following, we will draw a brief overview of how this disruption falls in three steps: first, in the form a post-anthropocentric critique (but also redeployment) of the dominant philosophical tradition from Descartes and Kant; and onwards (the second step) to the linguistic turn represented by Saussure and by Derrida's deconstruction; and, third, in the form of a revival of an alternative philosophical tradition from Spinoza to Deleuze.

One way of framing post-antropocentric theories is to note their common critique of what they see as, in fact, the 'anti-realist' (Harman) tradition that has dominated Western thought up until the present. The philosophical heritage from Descartes, Kant, Saussure and Derrida is often targeted in this regard. Descartes and Kant are interpreted as representing a disembodied idealist and subject-centred tradition that is continued and expanded upon by linguistic, poststructuralist and semiotic theories in the twentieth century. The Cartesian view on nature and matter as extended, unified and inert substance, consisting of discrete quantifiable and measurable objects (identities), is commonly pointed out as having established an entirely human-centred understanding of life and reality. Equally, the Cartesian subject that exists primarily because it *thinks*, along with Platonic and Kantian devaluations of bodily and sensate experience, are seen as having sustained an entirely conceptual frame of inquiry and theorisation of the world, resting on presumptions of mind, consciousness, linguistic representation and disembodied conceptual meaning investments as superior to or at least independent from mute matter and the nonhuman. In all this, Kant's Copernican revolution and critical thinking are acknowledged for having discovered an independent reality outside human knowledge and perception, but Kant is equally criticised for also discouraging and directing all critical inquiry away from this nonhuman sphere by thoroughly sealing it off from what is humanly perceivable and knowable. The only reality we have access to, the only reality we can study, in the Kantian analysis, is reality as it appears to us through our human faculties of thought and perception, which are inherently governed by conceptual categories that impose human intention and purpose on everything. As expounded by Bryant, Srnicek and Harman in their introduction to *The Speculative Turn*:

> In Kant's famous Copernican revolution, it is no longer the mind that conforms to objects, but rather objects that conform to the mind. Experience is structured by a priori categories and forms of intuition that comprise the necessary and universal basis for all knowledge. Yet the price to be paid for securing this basis is the renunciation of any knowledge beyond how things appear to us. Reality-in-itself is cordoned off, at least in its cognitive aspects. (2011: 4)

However, new theories like New Materialism and object-oriented philosophy do not propose an outright rejection of concepts inherited from the dominant strands of Western thought. As much as they criticise them, they also try to rethink inherited concepts. As for Kant, for instance,

Harman (the founder of Objected-Oriented Ontology) sees it as a necessity not to reject but to re-engage the inheritance from Kant's philosophy. As Harman asserts, 'an important feature of object-oriented philosophy is its insistence on the unpopular *thing-in-itself* as a crucial ingredient in intellectual life' (2016: 27). In *Immaterialism* (2016) it is through the Kantian concept of the thing-in-itself that Harman poignantly formulates the basic (nonhuman) understanding of an object in OOO:

> If we reduce an object downward to its pieces, we cannot explain its emergence; if we reduce it upward to its effects, we cannot explain change. From here it is easy to see why we need the thing-in-itself as the reality that cannot be converted into either of the two basic forms of knowledge: what a thing is made of, what a thing does. (2016: 28)

What is pursued by object-oriented philosophers is the nonhuman 'surplus of reality' in every object (Harman 2016: 10). In order to do so, we need to oppose two traditional ways of knowing an object that reduce it to something other than itself in each their way. As Harman explains, objects have traditionally been reduced either by what he calls *undermining*: a dissolution that reduces the object to its smaller physical subcomponents as is the methodological practice of physics, ultimately reducing it to subatomic particles; or by *overmining*: a reduction of the object 'upward' to the functional effects of its relations only, that is, its relations to other objects or its relations to humans and human uses of the object, as practised, for instance, by cultural or social theorists. The task is thus to think the reality of an object as something that is both irreducibly more than its parts *and* more than its relations (Harman 2012: 199).

Regardless of rival readings of towering and complex figures like Descartes and Kant and their philosophical nuances, there is an obviously dominant strand in Western philosophy and knowledge production which pacifies, excludes or marginalises our attention to the independent existence of nonhuman forces, objects and materialities and the significant part they play in shaping and conditioning human life and reality. This continues right up to the present where the linguistic, semiotic and cultural turns are seen as a perpetuation of the traditional eclipse of matter in theory.

To New Materialism and speculative realist theories, the priority that has been granted to reality as a linguistic and sociocultural construction since the beginning of the twentieth century reiterates the omission in theory of material otherness and nonhuman realities and life forms. As Barad succinctly coins the critique, 'it seems that at every turn lately every "thing" – even materiality – is turned into a matter of language or some other form of cultural representation' (2003: 801). In a New Materialist critique of the linguistic turn, Vicky Kirby summarises how Saussure's theory of the sign locks us into an immaterial and anthropocentric 'prison-house of language' (1997: 53). Saussure cut off the sign from the material thing world, or non-linguistic reality, when he established that '[t]he linguistic sign unites, not a thing and a name, but a concept and a sound image' (Saussure quoted in Kirby 1997: 10). In other words, Saussurians view language as having no connection with anything extra-linguistic: a sign consists of a *signifier*, that is, an arbitrary sound image (like the sound image 'bird') and a *signified* which is not a physical being outside language but an abstract human *concept* (i.e. our *conceptual idea* of the material being that is a 'bird'). Consequently, Saussure gives expression to a linguistic version of Kant's a priori categories: like Kant's conceptual categories, language 'worlds the world', as Saussure puts it, or 'the word worlds' (Saussure quoted in Kirby 1997: 17, 19).

Similarly, we see in Quentin Meillassoux's attack on what he designates 'correlationism' – that is, the kind of philosophy that 'maintains the impossibility of acceding, through thought, to a being *independent* of thought' (Meillassoux 2016: 216, 118, emphasis in the original) – a critique of the Saussurian conception of the sign as a 'correlation' of a signifier and signified. Rather than the sign always referring to (or correlating with) something *for humans* – whether a meaning, an object or a reference – Meillassoux directs our attention to 'the signifier *before* its link to the signified' (2016: 169, emphasis in the original), and, with inspiration from mathematics, he searches for speculative ways of apprehending signs that are devoid of human meaning or signs that only (and meaninglessly) refer to themselves as signs, and that are thus capable of opening up or revealing a reality radically independent of human thought and existence (2016: 163–4).

Later in the twentieth century, when the cultural turn grows strong and overlaps with Saussurian linguistic idealism, language comes to be read as an ideological, sociocultural and political vehicle before anything else. By now, classic examples are structuralism and poststructuralism and (overlapping) critical analyses of the representation of class, race and gender in social and cultural texts and artefacts. Here the sign is mostly engaged as a vehicle for ideological and counter-ideological productions of meaning, or 'overmining' (Harman), ranging from authoritarian sociocultural discourses (e.g. capitalist, imperialist and fallocentric discourses) to counter-discursive interpretations of reality and interhuman relations (e.g. Marxist, postcolonial, feminist and queer studies).

Finally, Derrida and deconstruction are also frequently criticised, like Saussure, for rejecting the possibility of accessing a reality exterior to the sign or human perception. 'Writing supplements perception before perception even appears to itself', says Derrida; 'the absolute present, Nature, that which words like "real mother" name, have always already escaped, have never existed' (1976: 158–9). This prompts Harman to speak of Derrida's philosophy as a continuation of the 'anti-realism' that speculative and object-oriented philosophy locate in prominent Western theories of thought: 'the thing itself is a sign' (Derrida quoted in Harman 2012: 197). Another critic, Pheng Cheah, notes that if deconstruction allows anything to escape sociocultural signification, Derrida's philosophy (like Kant's) can only talk of it in terms of an *absolute Other*, that is, as something that is radically inaccessible by language and cut off from any kind of human apprehension altogether: 'unless this, then talk of matter is complicit with idealism' (Derrida quoted in Cheah 2010: 72).

Yet, as with Harman's rethinking of Kant, Derrida, and his (in) famous axiom '*Il n'y a pas d'hors-texte*' ('there is nothing outside the text'), is also reconsidered in post-anthropocentric theory. To Morton, deconstruction is absolutely central to OOO. He sees deconstruction as part of a series of revolutions in thought and science that humiliate and displace the human from the centre of meaning, like Copernicus' discovery that the Earth goes around the Sun, or Freud's discovery of the unconscious, or Darwin's discovery of evolution' (Morton 2014: 295; see also Morton 2010). Deconstruction shows how any human knowledge and production of meaning is subject to the infinite regress of meaning – 'the meaning of a word is always another word' (Morton 2014: 298). Human knowledge and meaning production are in this way, right at their core, revealed to be inconsistent, ambivalent, shifting and unsteady: any final knowledge and meaning infinitely escapes us.

Similarly, deconstruction reveals how meaning interchanges with the meaningless, in Morton's view. All signs are marks that are 'at some level . . . made of meaningless squiggles' (Morton 2014: 294): '[a]ny given system of signs' depends on 'another system that distinguishes meaning from non-meaning' or a 'mark' from a 'non-mark' or a 'sign' from a 'squiggle' (Morton 2014: 294). With the infinite regress of meaning and the collapse of signs into meaningless marks or squiggles, Morton uses Derrida to destabilise the binary distinction between human made (i.e. 'cultural') texts and non-textual non-human reality. The boundaries between text/non-text erode insofar as writing and reading are, like all life forms, 'ambiguous and incoherent' (Morton 2014: 294). Everything is subject to the endless differentiation and dispersal of meaning (*différance*). The other way around, all life forms, like all texts, are made of (fundamentally undecidable) codes and marks (including humans): 'DNA and RNA are molecules that read and translate and encode: squiggles and marks, at the same time' (Morton 2014: 294). Accordingly, reading texts, to Morton, or reading any life form deconstructively becomes a de-anthropocentricising activity: all texts and all life forms withdraw from finite human meaning just as they are fundamentally entangled in their shared inscrutability (Morton 2014: 301).

Kirby re-employs Derrida's 'there is nothing outside the text' in similar ways, not as a theory of language being a self-enclosed system separated from its other, but as a theory asserting the point 'that there can be no final limit to language' (Kirby 1997: 52). Everything is and works and acts as a form of semiotic expression or representation or 'articulating energy' (Kirby 1997: 52). In this perspective Derrida's axiom is inverted: human writing becomes a decentred part of nature's writing itself – 'there is no outside of Nature' (Kirby 1997: 52, 5, xi, 87; see also 2017a: ix). If all is text, or a form of signifying force (even if far from always understandable to humans), deconstruction becomes helpful to the study of how matter and language, nature and culture are not separate but entangled; how they 'are all emergent within a force field of differentiations that has no exteriority in any final sense' (Kirby 1997: 127; also quoted in Barad 2007: 431).

To sum up more broadly, it is important to note that post-anthropocentric theory does not turn away from the critical insights and practices of poststructuralism or deconstruction and the disclosure of representations of reality as linguistic and sociocultural constructions. Despite its criticism of 'the hegemony of cultural, discursive and textual methodologies' (Kirby 2017b: 9), the linguistic, semiotic and cultural turns are in a broad view recognised in post-anthropocentric theory as having moved us on from a naive positivism and naturalistic assumptions of objective and transparent representations of reality, which makes for a complex starting point for new studies of representations of matter and objects.

In order to rethink the nature and significance of matter and non-human ontologies, post-anthropocentric theory engages in dialogues with the heritage from Plato, Descartes, Kant, Saussure and Derrida (as in the examples above), but it also seeks to re-invoke other figures as an alternative and, it is understood, less anthropocentric philosophical tradition. Among others, these include Spinoza, Heidegger, Merleau-Ponty and Deleuze.

In *Vibrant Matter* (2010), for instance, Bennett re-engages a vitalist tradition from Spinoza, Kant (his notion of *Bildungstrieb*), Nietzsche, Bergson, Hans Driesch to Deleuze, which all propel her theory of the intrinsic life and agency of matter. She gathers and combines concepts like Spinoza's 'conatus' and 'affective bodies', Bergson's '*élan vital*', Driesch's 'entelechy' and Deleuze's ideas of 'impersonal vitality', 'intensities' and life as 'a pure a-subjective current' to counter the conception of matter as inert, deterministic or mechanistic, to remystify the notion of human agency and to describe the 'continuity between human and other beings' (Bennett 2010: 53, 2). With regard to the latter, Deleuze's concepts of 'assemblage' and 'immanence' (itself drawing on Spinoza) play a central role for Bennett. Immanence describes how all life (all matter and all bodies), including the human, is immersed in and interacts on the same (depersonalised) plane of existence, and assemblage becomes a working concept for Bennett in analyses of how the nonhuman is indeed an 'active principle' (Bennett 2010: 61) in complex systems of events that are commonly thought to be only cultural and controlled by human will and intention – like electrical power grids, gender, capitalism and globalisation (e.g. see Bennett 2010: 20–38).

Although contemporary, Bruno Latour's ANT is another alternative philosophy that greatly inspires nonhuman theory. Jane Bennett points to Latour's concept of 'actant' as a way of breaking free from received notions of agency attributed solely to the subject/human and thereby a classical Cartesian dualism:

> *Actant*, recall, is Bruno Latour's term for a source of action; an actant can be human or not, or most likely, a combination of both ... An actant is neither an object nor a subject but an 'intervener', akin to the Deleuzean 'quasi-causal operator'. (Bennett 2010: 9)

'Actant' and 'operator' become substitute words, for Bennett, for 'agentic capacity' which 'is now seen as differentially distributed across a wider range of ontological types' (Bennett 2010: 9). The tradition of Deleuzean and Latourean thought becomes important for Bennett's own development of a horizontal or flat ontology through the assemblage: what Latour's Actor Network Theory opens up to is a non-hierarchical conception of reality and therefore a possibility 'to *experience* the relationship between persons and other materialities more horizontally' (Bennett 2010: 10).

OOO's and specifically Harman's relationship to Latour is (perhaps more) complicated in that he, on the one hand, recognises the philosophical and ontological merits of Latour's thinking, but on the other hand also criticises its basic notion of objects as 'actants' (Harman 2016: 1–7). Harman recognises that ANT brings objects to the foreground of our reflection/experience in 'a flat ontology in which everything is real insofar as it *acts*' (2016: 2). Yet at the same time ANT also 'loses objects completely, by abolishing any hidden depth in things while reducing them to their actions' (Harman 2016: 2). As will be explained shortly, OOO differs from ANT and New Materialism precisely in viewing an object for what it *is* and not for what it *does* ('actant').

Merleau-Ponty is also re-engaged by New Materialists in particular for the de-anthropocentric implications of his body-phenomenology. Merleau-Ponty brings to thinking an 'intercorporeity' of the human and the flesh of the world, as Florence Chiew puts it (2017: 63), which causes a dissolution of clear distinctions between subject and object, body and mind and re-understands the human and human subjectivity as always co-produced by the material reality it is immersed in, not least through the human body itself. Bennett notes how the authority of human intentionality, will and reason is decentred by Merleau-Ponty's focus on the embodied nature of subject experience and a non-cognitive, pre-personal bodily being. This opens for theorisations of how subjectivity is co-produced by the non-subjective and nonhuman agencies that she re-accentuates through vitalist philosophy – how 'the us and the it slipslide into each other', as she puts it (Bennett 2010: 29–30, 4). Both Bennett and a feminist New Materialist like Diana Coole are attentive to the role of bodily perception in relations between the human and the nonhuman. Like Merleau-Ponty, they recognise that human perception already organises reality according to, for example, pre-established sociocultural categories, codes and values, but they follow him in showing how such categories and codes, along with the intention of the subject, do not determine all of human perception or explain all of embodied sensory experience and bodily being. In Coole's words, the New Materialist task of showing how consciousness 'emerges from [and] yet remains enmeshed in' the material world becomes a matter of suspending 'this culturally fashioned perception in order to uncover the "vertical" world of "brute" or "wild" perception' (Coole 2010: 101, 105).

Finally, Heidegger is another prominent philosopher who greatly inspires post-anthropocentric bids for a less human-centred philosophical tradition. Brown and Harman, in particular, set out to reinterpret Heidegger's thing-phenomenology in order to bracket the subject and in that way enable a thinking of thingness that goes beyond both existing practical and theoretical conceptions of objects. In Brown's reading of Heidegger a thing emerges as thing and not as object when it is misused. As he notes:

> For the life of things made manifest in the time of misuse is, should we look, a secret in plain sight – not a life behind or beneath the object but a life that is its fluctuating shape and substance and surface, a life that the subject must catalyse but cannot contain. (Brown 1999: 2)

Inscribing an instability in the human relation to things, Brown tries to 'liberate material objects' (1999: 1). As Maurizia Boscagli explains, 'Brown's approach counters the anthropological view. His is less a case of the social life of things than the secret life of things, which go on strike on the subject and enjoy an existence of their own' (2014: 20).

Harman pushes Heidegger further, connecting Heidegger's famous tool-analysis with his own rethinking of the Kantian things-in-themselves. He argues that 'both theory and praxis are distortions of the hammer in its subterranean reality. Object-oriented philosophy pushes this a step further by saying that objects distort one another even in sheer causal interaction' (2012: 186–7). For Harman (and Morton), objects are – as already noted in his critique of 'overmining' – more than their relations. They understand relations as *appearances*, and an object, for them, is precisely not exhausted by its relations or the ways in which it appears within the context of this or the other relation. Apart from appearing in numerous ways, an object also hides a deeply non-relational essence, that is, something withdrawn from all access both practical and theoretical.

One way of briefly summarising the overlaps between New Materialism and OOO as they have come to appear in this brief philosophical survey is to say that they both work to make visible how matter and objects are commonly reduced to sociocultural, ideological and anthropocentric meaning (or relations/appearances), and how sociocultural and anthropocentric meaning production come to organise the ways in which we perceive and relate to reality, thus obscuring the agency and independent realities of non-subjects or nonhuman objects. Yet, in spite of similarities and their common philosophical backdrop, there are great differences between New Materialism and OOO.

The Surplus of Thingness: Differences Between New Materialism and OOO

New Materialists are particularly interested in how nonhuman objects and matter (including the matter-being of humans themselves) are not inert but actively entangled with sociocultural and anthropocentric productions of meaning. OOO takes part in such de-anthropocentricising analyses while also seeing itself as moving a step further to philosophise (and negatively trace) the radical withdrawal of objects from their relations to the human, that is, their reality outside human perception, thought and meaning-production. There is an ongoing discussion on this between OOO and New Materialism, explicitly articulated by Harman and Morton on the one hand and Bennett on the other. While they agree on the need for a reformulation of our understanding of objects, they each develop a different ontology of objects. One way of approaching this difference is through their accounts of how things retain *a surplus of thingness*.

For OOO as represented by Harman and Morton, the central feature of objects is their essence. As Harman puts it: 'Everything has an autonomous essence, however transient it may be, and our practices grasp it no better than our theories do. What a thing *is* turns out to be more interesting than what it does' (2016: 16). For Morton this kind of 'essentialism' is confirmed in his idea of translation, through which objects are seen as constantly translating and affecting each other, but in order for this translation or change to happen something has to exist prior to this action. Morton thus makes the claim

> that objects are ontologically prior to their relations [which] logically [follows] from the fact that no one 'translation' of an object is that object. To hypostatize fluidity above the static is to apply a single translation to all objects. OOO is not saying that behind every flow there is a static object. OOO is saying that behind every flow, behind every stasis, there is an object that cannot be reduced to anything whatsoever. (2012: 208)

The most prominent feature of objects for OOO thus becomes their withdrawnness, which means that we can only 'gain access to [them] . . . by indirect allusive or vicarious means' (Harman 2016: 17), a strategy that both Morton and Harman deploy in their readings of literature (Harman 2011; Morton 2007). In *Immaterialism* Harman juxtaposes what he calls 'immaterialist essentialism' to New Materialism's 'relational metaphysics' (2016: 17), which reiterates OOO's critique of a thinking and a practice that explains objects by reducing them to their relations ('overmining').

New Materialism as represented by Jane Bennett, on the other hand, understands objects along the lines of Bruno Latour's actant; that is, as 'a source of action that can be either human or nonhuman; it is that which has efficacy, can *do* things, has sufficient coherence to make a difference, produce effects, alter the course of events' (Bennett 2010: viii).

In contrast to OOO, New Materialism is in this way interested in what a thing *does* more than what it *is*, and what a thing does it always does in relation to something else. As a way of understanding relations between things Bennett invokes the Deleuzian concept of assemblage, as we have seen in the above. For her,

> [t]he effects generated by an assemblage are, rather, emergent properties, emergent in that their ability to make something happen (a newly inflected materialism, a blackout, a hurricane, a war on terror) is distinct from the sum of the vital force of each materiality considered alone. Each member and proto-member of the assemblage has a certain vital force, but there is also an effectivity proper to the grouping as such: an agency *of* the assemblage. And precisely because each member-actant maintains an energetic pulse slightly 'off' from that of the assemblage, an assemblage is never a stolid block but an open-ended collective, a 'non-totalizable' sum. (2010: 24)

In the relational assemblage the thing maintains its own power, on the one hand, as an individual thing, but, on the other hand, it participates in a collective efficacy that generates something new and unexpected. Because the thing and the assemblage are not reducible to each other, they maintain a crucial difference: they always 'house an underdetermined surplus, and assemblage theories can offer an account of the emergence of novelty without also rendering the trajectory, impetus, drive, or energetic push of any existing body epiphenomenal to its relations' (Bennett 2012: 231).

Accordingly, for Bennett the question of understanding and explaining objects as relational or as an 'actant' does not imply a reduction of the object. On the contrary, the irreducibility of the object is the prerequisite for the object both as a thing in itself and as part of a larger network. The 'underdetermined surplus' is to be found in precisely this difference between the object's own 'vital force' and the effectivity of the assemblage. The overall endeavour of New Materialism is summarised by Diana Coole and Samantha Frost as one of facilitating a new mode of thinking where 'materiality' is always understood as

> something more than 'mere' matter: an excess, force, vitality, relationality, or difference that renders matter active, self-creative, productive, unpredictable. In sum, new materialists are discovering a materiality that materialises, evincing immanent modes of self-transformation that compel us to think of causation in far more complex terms; to recognise that phenomena are caught in a multitude of interlocking systems and forces and to consider anew the location and nature of capacities for agency. (2010: 9)

All the same, Morton criticises the New Materialist notion of matter for implying 'the existence of at least one other entity from which the matter in question differs': the New Materialist stress on Deleuzian relational systems, processes and flows amounts to a reductionism that 'maintains that some things are more real than others: flowing liquids become templates for everything else'. To Morton, it is 'an ontotheological claim that some things are more real than others', and, he stresses, 'OOO is saying that behind every flow, behind every stasis, there is an object that cannot be reduced to anything whatsoever' (2012: 208). All relations or appearances may be understood as 'interpretations' or 'translations' of objects (Morton 2012: 206–8). 'Flow' is such a translation of reality, and 'no one "translation" of an object is that object' (Morton 2012: 208). In comparison, OOO asserts that nothing is more real than anything else. It 'offers a reality without privileged categories: an anarchic plenitude of objects crowds around us and in us' (Morton 2012: 205).

The differences between OOO and New Materialism also become apparent in the ways in which they work with literature. While all three, Bennett, Harman and Morton, ascribe significance to literature as a particular space of reflection in which to access or contemplate new understandings of objects, their disagreements about access also set them apart when it come to the question of what literature presents. For Bennett, literature creates awareness and alerts her to the overlooked thingness of everyday reality and the 'thing-power' that is co-productive of human reality. For Harman and Morton, though, literature is an emblematic example of translation (human–object, object–human as well as object–object translations) but it is also a medium that discloses the limits of human translations: through various aesthetic strategies literature bears witness to the fact that in reality there is always something outside that we cannot access.

How Literature Comes to Matter in Post-Anthropocentric Perspectives

Although the renewed theoretical interest in material and nonhuman realities has been an emerging and growing field of study since the turn of the millennium, and although literature is often valued by post-anthropocentric theorists as a particular space of reflection, it is still only at the point of opening up to and being further opened up by the literary field of research. The following offers a broad (yet not exhaustive) overview of how literature has been engaged in the field so far.

The question that is commonly explored in the field is how literature may offer a unique space of reflection in which objects, matter and human–reality relations come into play in ways that are not entirely governed by anthropocentric knowledge and meaning constructions. Bill Brown inspires the field with a point of departure in literature and Thing Theory – and a link to new historicism – notably with the book *A Sense of Things: The Object Matter of American Literature* (2003) and essays like 'The Matter of Materialism: Literary Mediations' (2010) and 'The Secret Life of Things (Virginia Woolf and the Matter of Modernism)' (1999). Through a study of the appearance of matter in literature and philosophy, Brown tries to write an alternative to the common history of modernity and modernism by asking '*how*, in history (how, in one cultural formation), human subjects and material objects constitute one another, and *what* remains outside the regularities of that constitution that can disrupt the cultural memory of modernity and modernism' (1999: 5). On one hand, he traces how the invention, production and development of materialities, like glass or iron, affect the literary imagination, while on the other hand he studies the ways in which literature itself works to change common perceptions of matter, especially as an aesthetic medium that is capable of depicting the instability of things, when they are no longer objects defined by use. He traces broken or misused things – 'the discarded remains of modern objects' (Brown 1999: 5) – in the works of Virginia Woolf, for instance. Indeed, for Brown, literature's 'aesthetic practices work to compensate' for 'the loss of the thingness of things . . . that characterizes modernity' (1999: 5).

In her contribution to the *The Nonhuman Turn* (2015), Bennett briefly says about the significance of literature that '[p]oetry can help us feel more of the liveliness hidden in . . . things and reveal more of the threads of connection binding our fate to theirs' (2015: 235). In *Vibrant Matter*, she makes a very brief analysis of Franz Kafka's short story 'Cares of a Family Man' that illustrates her point. In Kafka's story the human narrator is confused and unsettled by a small wooden object, Odradek, that is animated by human characteristics like speech, self-naming and willfulness. The story plays right into the overall importance Bennett ascribes to an 'anthropomorphic interpretation' of things turned on its head. To Bennett, as in Kafka's story, anthropomorphisation may work not as a humanising interpretation of nonhuman objects (that suits them with human purposes and reasons for being), but as a form of interpretation that yields a flat human–nonhuman ontology where creative energies are no longer only human and the categories of subject and object are blurred. Anthropomorphisation reveals 'similarities across categorical divides . . . and structural parallels between material forms in "nature" and those in "culture"' (Bennett 2010: 99). Ultimately, anthropomorphisation is 'a gesture toward the inadequacy of understanding' and becomes a counter to 'the narcissism of humans in charge of the world': Odradek is animated with an inscrutable existence on its own, independent from the usual ways in which we make sense of things and the 'feelings they provoke in us' (Bennett 2010: 25, xiv, xvi).

From a literary point of view, Bennett may be criticised for using literature simply as exemplifications of her theoretical points – she refers to Kafka's story as a 'literary dramatization' of her idea of 'thing-power' and impersonal life of matter (2010: 7), but at least her inverted thinking of a common literary ploy like anthropomorphisation inspires one way of rereading subject–object relations and nonhuman agencies in literature (one of the following chapters expands significantly on this by revisiting Hans Christian Andersen's 'thing fairy tales' from a New Materialist perspective).

While literature and the arts are not Bennett's main concern, the role of the aesthetic takes centre stage in Maurizia Boscagli's *Stuff Theory: Everyday Objects, Radical Materialism* (2014). Here she introduces her concept of 'stuff' as a materiality 'whose plasticity, its transformative potential, comes into being, inextricably, with the human' (Boscagli 2014: 2). Differing from OOO's concern with the essence of thingness, Boscagli wants to reconnect the recent critical language on materiality with the spheres of everyday life and the aesthetic. For her, stuff is already-worked-upon matter, it is 'everyday matter with style' (2014: 4). Boscagli is not interested in things outside the human sphere, but in commodities that have turned into useless possessions and trash. Similar to Bennett's assemblage, stuff is 'protean, volatile, always on the verge of becoming valueless while never ceasing to be commodified' (Boscagli 2014: 2). Literature, and culture more broadly, plays a crucial role for her as spaces in which the volatility and unruliness of stuff can make a 'flash appearance' (Boscagli 2014: 2). Her historical approach places her alongside Bill Brown's Thing Theory, also sharing his concept of the misused thing, as she too is interested in the moment when the commodity turns into something else. Like Brown, Boscagli is interested in modernist aesthetics and, through the prisms of 'stuff' and unstably hybrid materialities, she reads writers like Virginia Woolf and George Perec in ways that highlight the impossibility of 'the conventional split between subject and object' (Boscagli 2014: 3).

As for the inclusion of literature in OOO, Harman, for his part, is generally interested in what he refers to as 'mind-independent' realism, that is, a reality that is not converted into thought and that is 'deeper than our understanding of it' (2012: 184–5, 186). He sees literature, in this respect, as capable of reflecting a more than human reality insofar as the literary text 'runs deeper than any coherent meaning, and outruns the intentions of author and reader alike' (Harman 2012: 200). Literary texts do not 'use up the reality of things' (Harman 2012: 186), he says, which owes to literature's relation to reality as 'one of "allusion"' (2012: 187). Literature only hints – 'allures to' – the reality of a thing 'without ever making it directly present to mind' (Harman 2012: 187). Sometimes he speaks of this as a '*weird* realism in which real individual objects resist all forms of causal or cognitive mastery' (Harman 2012: 188). In his book on Lovecraft, Harman most effectively demonstrates how readings that are sensitive to the allure of the text may show literature to create holes in human knowledge and understanding, for example by dramatising – even ubiquitising – the gap (and, hence, the state of *allusion*) 'between an ungraspable thing and the vaguely relevant descriptions the narrator is able to attempt' (Harman 2011: 24). Literature, he argues, is in this way capable of performing a 'deeply non-relational conception of the reality of things' (Harman 2012: 187). Continuing the discussion posed by Harman of the relationship between Speculative Realism and literature, Brian Willems in *Speculative Realism and Science Fiction* (2017) and Grant Hamilton in *The World of Failing Machines: Speculative Realism and Literature* (2015) offer close readings of nonhuman realities in literature and critical engagement with the field of literary criticism, but mostly predicated on the genre of science fiction.

In his 'ambient poetics', launched in the ecocritical *Ecology without Nature*, Morton offers what he terms 'a materialist way of reading texts' (2009: 3). His *ambient poetics* argues that a text can describe nonhuman reality while at the same time reflecting upon its own representational status (making use of the alluring strategies Harman notes). For Morton 'ambience tries to evoke the background *as* background [i.e. the nonhuman environment in eco-mimetic texts] – to drag it into the foreground would dissolve it', which is why the work 'must resort to oblique rhetorical [or 'ambient'] strategies' (2009: 45). The task for Morton is thus to trace that which is outside language in a literary language without turning it into something else. To achieve this he introduces a 'slow reading' (Morton 2009: 3) that reads for the rhetorical strategies used in the text to render the environment. His approach is two-sided: on the one hand, he shows how the goal of the eco-mimetic text is to simulate reality; that is, to render the environment as if we 'do not think there is an aesthetic framework here' (Morton 2009: 35), but on the other hand, he works to show how reality in the text is construed. Morton's ambient poetics proposes foregrounding the medium on which this rendering takes place. This means paying attention to the places in a text where 'the medium of communication thickens' (Morton 2009: 37); any places in which the text highlights itself as text, either through graphical signs (as in the instance of the italics in the passage from Woolf's novel) or through the paper upon which it is written. In a combination of deconstruction and ecocriticism Morton thus searches for the ways in which a text makes us aware of what it is not: marks in texts that both stress their textuality while also point to the environment beyond. Later, he takes up the question of literary representation again in 'An Object-Oriented Defense of Poetry', which he offers as an 'essay on how literary scholarship can think about OOO' (Morton 2012: 205). In this text Morton turns the inherent linguistic gap between nonhuman realities and the medium of language into an advantage. The gap 'forces us to confront an illusions-like reality' (2012: 212), which indeed is what literature portrays. In the same text, Morton also takes up the question of anthropomorphisation. Like Bennett, he chooses not to reject anthropomorphisation, which he sees as an impossibility. Instead he lets in the agency of the nonhuman through the backdoor of anthropomorphisms, so to speak, by dissolving anthropomorphisms into a ubiquitous 'itselfpomorphizing' activity that is central to all object interrelations:

> Just as I fail to avoid anthropomorphizing everything, so all entities whatsoever constantly translate other objects into their own terms. My back maps out a small backpomorphic slice of this tree that I'm leaning on. The strings of the wind harp stringpomorphize the wind. The wind windpomorphizes the temperature differentials between the mountains and the flat land ... A nail is an anthropomorphic piece of iron. An iron deposit is a bacteriapomorphic rendering of bacteria metabolism. (Morton 2012: 207)

Looked at in this way, anthropomorphisms as a literary ploy may be argued to give expression to the encounter between something 'subjective' and something 'non-subjective' as a mutually shaping event. Morton's anthropomorphism, or 'itselfpomorphization' offers an inclusion in perception, thought and literary analysis of the mute and unintelligible ways in which the human is caused to appear by nonhuman phenomena as well as the other way round.

Timothy Clark's work must also be mentioned here because his study of nonhuman realities, ecology and literature brings in the increasingly urgent perspective of the Anthropocene. In his book *Ecocriticism on the*

Edge – The Anthropocene as a Threshold Concept (2015), Clark tries to outline different ways for how we may (re)read literature in the age of the Anthropocene. In a reading of Raymond Carver's 'Elephant', for instance, Clark shows how it may be fruitful and necessary to operate with different 'scales' or spatio-temporal viewpoints in approaching a literary text, because '[t]he scale at which one reads a text, and the scale effects implicated, drastically alter the kinds of significance attached to elements of it' (2015: 99). Accordingly, Clark proposes reading Carver's short story through three different spatio-temporal scales: a 'personal scale' (the near family), a 'historical scale' (a 'traditional' historical context, like national and culture within a few decades) and a 'hypothetical scale' (e.g. a 600 years frame) (2015: 99–100). Depending on the scale on which we read a story like 'Elephant', our attention and judgement shift from those of narrow human relations to capitalist consumerism and a broader environmental history. On the first and second scales, a car may be viewed as a positive thing (a background for social relations, a practical vehicle that facilitates human connectivity); on the second level, the car may instantiate the possibility for individual freedom in a larger context of an alienating consumer society; and on the last scale the car may come to be read as the epitome of fossil capitalism and part of (unpredicted) environmental degradation and climate change (Clark 2015: 99–101). Obviously, the third scale of reading involves a challenge to the idea of humans as sole historical agents (2015: 104). In this spatio-temporal frame, 'a certain impersonal ecological dynamic starts to become visible and shade out more conventional considerations' in our reading, like 'issues of identity and cultural representation' (Clark 2015: 100, 104). Consequently, in Clark's approach to literature, the dichotomy between the human and nonhuman forces of change is increasingly blurred according to the broadness of the spatio-temporal scale through which we read a text – ultimately, we begin to read 'the human, so to speak, on the same level as nonhuman agency, that is, reading people as things' (Clark 2015: 103).[1]

Themes and Perspectives in the Book

Expanding on existing experiments and explorations of the crossroads between literature and the recent post-anthropocentric turn in theory, the following chapters state the collective claim, paradoxically, that it is in literature, presumably the most semiotic and subject-centric medium of all, that a rethinking of the relationship between the subject and the object and the human and the nonhuman may be brought to the fore. The chapters illustrate the applicability of post-anthropocentric theory and the significance and agency of more than human realities with close readings in such different areas as postcolonial, queer and feminist literature, romantic and modernist literature, science fiction and postmillennial crisis literature. Principally, they all aim to develop different ways of approaching, understanding and analysing literary texts through the perspectives of post-anthropocentric theory. Certain key concepts and analytical approaches follow from this overall endeavour.

Marlene Marcussen and Marco Caracciolo are in different ways interested in showing how material and nonhuman agencies are deliberately construed in literary depictions of reality. Through a rethinking and fusion of the narratological concept of 'description' and the post-anthropocentric concept of 'ecomimesis', Marcussen examines how certain modes of representation unveil and release the agency of material and nonhuman backgrounds in the literary work of Georges Perec. Continuing to question the way literature formally represents nonhuman vitality, Marco Caracciolo deploys a New Formalist method to explore what he terms 'slow narratives' in the works of Italo Calvino's *Mr Palomar* and Jon McNaught's *Kingdom*. By analysing formal techniques that require slow reading he shows how the artworks can deepen our perception and appreciation of nonhuman vitality.

Michael Karlsson Pedersen, Torsten Bøgh Thomsen and Sten Moslund all show how a post-anthropocentric and thing-oriented perspective on apparently highly subject-centred texts may, in crucial ways, alter the manner they are usually read: Sten Moslund explores the relations between post-anthropocentric theories and literary language and modes of representation. Illustrated through a postcolonial reading of Ayi Kwei Armah's *The Beautyful Ones Are Not Yet Born* (1968), he proposes a sensuous approach to language and representation as the basis of an 'aisthetic' (or sense-aesthetic) frame of reading that illuminates how the thoughts, emotions, sensations and perceptions of a political character like Armah's 'man' are produced by an entanglement of subjective, collective and (rarely noticed in postcolonial readings) depersonalised and de-anthropocentisised productions of reality. Rereading the lyrical subject in Sylvia Plath's poetry, Karlsson Pedersen shows the life of Plath's subject to be in various ways entwined with the life of things. Remarkably, his reading fuses key incongruities between New Materialism and OOO by showing, through Plath, how the self-receding nature of things is a prerequisite for its relational agency and material power. Thomsen revisits popular anthropomorphisms in Hans Christian Andersen's thing fairy tales to show how post-anthropocentric theory (mainly New Materialism) may open a surprising and previously unheeded object-centred and anti-anthropocentric side to romanticism.

Tobias Skiveren, Laura Oulanne and Karin Sellberg are, in different ways, engaged in showing the implications of and relationship between (represented) material realities, gendered bodies and readers or authors. From a feminist-material perspective, Skiveren revisits the history of feminist theory and literary criticism, from the first wave to recent New Materialist feminist criticism, in order to further explore and contribute to the embodied and affective readings offered by the latter. Centred on the unruliness of the body/flesh, and building on Stacy Alaimo's work, among others, he analyses contemporary Danish writer Maja Lucas's novel *Mor* as an illustrative case of a new, as he terms it, 'carnacritical' mode of reading. Through the use of post-anthropocentric theory Oulanne proposes an affective reading of Djuna Barnes's modernist fiction. Questioning gendered notions of domesticity and interiority, she outlines a queering of interiority by inviting readers to engage in descriptions of bodies and domestic spaces as phenomena devoid of gendered symbolic presumptions. Expanding on notions like 'queer time', Sellberg points to how a new mode of corporeal reading of the 'Shakespearean novels' *Wise Children* (1991) by Angela Carter and *The Gap of Time* (2015) by Jeanette Winterson must be predicated on a conceptual framework of (non-linear) relationality. Combining queer theory, New Materialist feminist philosophy and the corporal imaginations and performances in Carter and Winterson, she shows how corporeality is continually shaped by and made possible through a complicated relationship between temporal entanglements and material ontology, where bodies exist in and out of time, in a complex hub of relationality and connectivity.

Moving on to the three chapters that finish the book, Rune Graulund, Martin Karlsson Pedersen and Maurizia Boscagli deal with implications of and relations between literature and the crisis of capitalism. Working with science fiction and Paolo Bacigalupi's *The Windup Girl*, Graulund proposes a new concept for reading matter in literature, 'reading for resources', as a way of re-engaging literature in the age of the Anthropocene. Through a reading of Alex Preston's *This Bleeding City*, Karlsson Pedersen develops a material–affective approach to the realist novels of the financial crisis centred on the notion of 'dry ontology' that brings to the fore the non-referential agency of finance money-signs in co-shaping financial subjectivity and its affective reality. Finally, Boscagli affirms the role of literature in the current mood of capitalism's economic and ecological crisis through its ability to open up new possible futures. By revisiting Félix Guattari and Walter Benjamin, she analyses auratic experiences in Ben Lerner's novel *10:04* (2014), confronting the ontological stasis of 'Capitalist Realism' and the configuration of subjectivity as human exceptionalism.

We have divided the chapters into four parts according to their overall angles and thematic clusters: (1) 'Matter-oriented Perspectives on Literary Techniques, Language and Representation'; (2) 'Object Intrusions in Subject-Centric Texts'; (3) 'Carnal Realities: Lively Flesh in Feminist and Queer Readings'; and (4) 'Capitalism, Crisis and the Anthropocene'. However, central concerns and perspectives also cut across the chapters in different ways. For instance, corporeal and affective modes of reading that focus on bodily encounters *in* literary texts and on new kinds of reading experiences are explored in the chapters by Skiveren, Sellberg, Oulanne, Moslund and Martin Pedersen. The focus on the material reality in and of literary texts offers new possibilities for and challenges to narratological approaches to literature, and in the chapters by Caracciolo, Marcussen and Oulanne the concept of description is critically engaged and developed in order to bring forth nonhuman perspectives in literary texts. The nonhuman perspective is further developed and fleshed out in the chapters by Bøgh Thomsen, Oulanne, Michael Pedersen, Marcussen and Caracciolo by a specific attention to what Morton in his Afterword, echoing Heidegger, calls the 'thingliness of things' and their lively materialities, in order to show how reality in literature is essentially unruly and unpredictable. As Morton accentuates, literature is the site of ambiguity and surprise where matter comes alive, resisting any static and reductionist ontology. This is exactly what the chapters by Boscagli, Sellberg and Graulund express in their reconceptualisation of temporality and the strange entanglements of time and matter where the future is not automatically determined by the past.

As will be apparent to readers, the chapters do not comprise any close study of just one corner of literature (say, science fiction or problems of narration or contemporary literature). They offer shorter studies across a range of literary issues, genres and social, cultural and historical contexts. This is the paramount ambition of the collection: to exemplify and broaden the scope for how new post-anthropocentric theory may bring to the fore the significance of nonhuman relations in literature and, the other way round, how literature, in various forms and from across various contexts, may also contribute to current reflections on the complex relations between humans and material reality as a specific medium of representation. It is also an important decision for the book as a whole to be sympathetic to and curious about the projects and concerns of post-anthropocentric theory, which is why it does not offer – in any systematic sense – a critical assessment of these new and diverse perspectives. What ultimately ties the chapters together is not a mood of critical hostility but rather a common concern with and interest in expanding the dimensions of reality that are studied in literature, illustrated with concrete applications of post-anthropocentric theory in close readings of literary texts.

Note

1. Other promising new works include the anthology *Diffractive Reading: New Materialism, Theory and Critique* (2020), edited by Kai Mertens, which engages a critical intervention in the practice of reading. The anthology revisits poststructuralism and critical theory and highlights how world and reading are entangled both materially and discursively. In *New Directions in Philosophy and Literature* (2019), edited by David Rudrum, Ridvan Askin and Frida Beckman, the chapters map out how new developments in twenty-first-century philosophy like OOO, posthumanism and New Materialism are entering into a dialogue with the study of literature.

References

Barad, Karen (2003), 'Posthumanist performativity: toward an understanding of how matter comes to matter', *Signs: Journal of Women in Culture and Society*, 28: 1, pp. 801–31.

Barad, Karen (2007), *Meeting the Universe Halfway: Quantum Physics and the Entanglement of Matter and Meaning*, Durham, NC: Duke University Press.

Bennett, Jane (2010), *Vibrant Matter: A Political Ecology of Things*, Durham, NC: Duke University Press.

Bennett, Jane (2012), 'Systems and things: a response to Graham Harman and Timothy Morton', *New Literary History*, 43: 2, pp. 225–33.

Bennett, Jane (2015), 'Systems and things', in Richard Grusin (ed.), *The Nonhuman Turn*, Minneapolis: University of Minnesota Press.

Boscagli, Maurizia (2014), *Stuff Theory: Everyday Objects, Radical Materialism*, London: Bloomsbury.

Brown, Bill (1999), 'The secret life of things (Virginia Woolf and the matter of modernism)', *Modernism/Modernity*, 6: 2, pp. 1–28.

Brown, Bill (2003), *A Sense of Things: The Object Matter of American Literature*, Chicago: Chicago University Press.

Brown, Bill (2010), 'The matter of materialism: literary mediations', in Tony Bennett and Patrick Joyce (eds), *Material Powers: Cultural Studies, History and the Material Turn*, New York: Routledge, pp. 60–78.

Bryant, Levi, Nick Srnicek and Graham Harman (eds) (2011), *The Speculative Turn: Continental Materialism and Realism*, Victoria, Australia: re.press (Open Access).
Cheah, Pheng (2010), 'Non-dielectical materialism', in Diana Coole and Samantha Frost (eds), *New Materialisms: Ontology, Agency, and Politics*, Durham, NC: Duke University Press, pp. 70–91.
Chiew, Florence (2017), 'Sensory substitution: the plasticity of the eye/I', in Vicky Kirby (ed.), *What If Culture Was Nature All Along?* Edinburgh: Edinburgh University Press, pp. 48–69.
Clark, Timothy (2015), *Ecocriticism on the Edge: The Anthropocene as a Threshold Concept*, London: Bloomsbury.
Coole, Diana (2010), 'The inertia of matter and the generativity of flesh', in Diana Coole and Samantha Frost (eds), *New Materialisms: Ontology, Agency, and Politics*, Durham, NC: Duke University Press, pp. 92–115.
Coole, Diana and Samantha Frost (eds) (2010), *New Materialisms: Ontology, Agency, and Politics*, Durham, NC: Duke University Press.
Derrida, Jacques (1976 [1967]), *Of Grammatology*, Baltimore: Johns Hopkins University Press.
Hamilton, Grant (2015), *The World of Failing Machines: Speculative Realism and Literature*, Washington: Zer0 Books.
Harman, Graham (2011), *Weird Realism: Lovecraft and Philosophy*, Washington: Zer0 Books.
Harman, Graham (2012), 'The well-wrought broken hammer: object-oriented literary criticism', *New Literary History*, 43: 2, pp. 183–203.
Harman, Graham (2016), *Immaterialism*, Cambridge: Polity Press.
Kirby, Vicki (1997), *Telling Flesh: The Substance of the Corporeal*, New York: Routledge.
Kirby, Vicki (2017a), 'Foreword', in Vicky Kirby (ed.), *What If Culture Was Nature All Along?*, Edinburgh: Edinburgh University Press, pp. xiii–xii.
Kirby, Vicki (2017b), 'Matter out of place: "New Materialism" in review', in Vicky Kirby (ed.), *What If Culture Was Nature All Along?* Edinburgh: Edinburgh University Press, pp. 1–25.
Meillassoux, Quentin (2016), 'Iteration, reiteration, repetition: a speculative analysis of the sign devoid of meaning', in Armen Avanessian and Suhail Malik (eds), *Genealogies of Speculation: Materialism and Subjectivity since Structuralism*, London: Bloomsbury Academic.
Mertens, Kai (ed.) (2020), *Diffractive Reading: New Materialism, Theory and Critique*, Lanham, MD: Rowman & Littlefield.
Morton, Timothy (2007), *Ecology Without Nature – Rethinking Environmental Aesthetics*, Cambridge, MA: Harvard University Press.
Morton, Timothy (2009), *Ecology without Nature*, Cambridge, MA: Harvard University Press.
Morton, Timothy (2010), 'Ecology as text, text as ecology', *The Oxford Literary Review*, 32: 1, pp. 1–17.

Morton, Timothy (2012), 'An object-oriented defense of poetry', *New Literary History*, 43: 2, pp. 205–24.
Morton, Timothy (2014), 'Deconstruction and/as ecology', in Greg Garrad (ed.), *The Oxford Handbook of Ecocriticism*, Oxford: Oxford University Press, pp. 291–304.
Rudrum, David, Ridvan Askin and Frida Beckman (eds) (2019), *New Directions in Philosophy and Literature*, Edinburgh: Edinburgh University Press.
Willems, Brian (2017), *Speculative Realism and Science Fiction*, Edinburgh: Edinburgh University Press.

I

Matter-Oriented Perspectives on Literary Techniques, Language and Representation

CHAPTER 1

The Abundance of Things in the Midst of Writing: A Post-Anthropocentric View on Description and Georges Perec's 'Still Life/Style Leaf'

Marlene Karlsson Marcussen

> The solid wood desk, on which I am writing, formerly a jeweler's workbench, is equipped with four large drawers and a top whose surface, slightly sloping inwards from the edges (no doubt so that the pearls that were once sifted on it would run no risk of falling to the floor) is covered with black fabric of very tightly woven mesh.
>
> Georges Perec, 'Still Life/Style Leaf', 1981

So begins Georges Perec's 'Still Life/Style Leaf' (1981), which is a short *mise en abyme* description of a writing desk: The desk is described in detail, and, as the description comes to an end – as it reaches the paper on the desk, upon which the description has been written – a second description takes over, retelling what is written on the paper, thus repeating the first description with small variations. With its repeated description of the environment of a writing desk, the text places itself squarely between the recent post-anthropocentric discussion of the problem of representing the material background as exemplified by Timothy Morton and the ongoing narratological discussion of description's relation to reality, and further, to the broader claim of the role of description in narratology. It implicitly questions the relationship between foreground and background, text and space, word and thing, and it does so both formally and thematically. Perec's short text serves as a fitting ground for an encounter between post-anthropocentric theory and narratology. It is this encounter that this chapter will stage.

The aim is to provide a material reading inspired by narratology and Timothy Morton's ambient poetics of what could be termed a deconstructive text such as Perec's. I intend to put Morton's often quite diffuse literary devices to use by combining them with narratology, and sketching a possible mode of reading literary texts in light of the 'material turn'. The encounter has a twofold effect: on the one hand, it addresses the underdeveloped field of literary analysis within the material turn, by employing a narratological 'toolkit' whenever Morton's philosophical interests take over his literary readings. The aim is to examine how literature represents the more-than-human background for human action. On the other hand, by framing narratology in light of post-anthropocentric theory, it becomes possible to offer a non-anthropocentric re-evaluation and expansion of the otherwise limited approach to descriptions of the more-than-human reality in narratology.

Narratology's Subject-Centric and Representational Focus

The publication history of Perec's text shares a theoretical kinship with narratology and more specifically with its sub-branch, descriptive theory, as 'Still Life/Style Leaf' was written to form the end piece of the very edition of *Yale French Studies* (1981) that launched a re-evaluation of description in narratology. Before looking more closely at Perec's text and the way it indirectly reflects on narratology, it is necessary to make a brief sketch of the role that the more-than-human plays in narratology, and more specifically in descriptive theory.

There is in narratology a consensus stemming from classic narratology – as represented by Gérard Genette and Roland Barthes up until contemporary narratologists like Marie-Laure Ryan and James Phelan – that description is to be distinguished from narration as two different types of text that, as Ryan notes, are defined by 'a changing world for narrative, a static one for description' (Ryan 2007: 27). In the long history of narratology, description has played a minor role, and the more-than-human that is often part of description an even smaller part, as the experiencing human subject, its actions, and the way these are ordered temporally through discourse have instead been foregrounded in narratology. Narrative is typically defined as the representation of an event or of a sequence of events that is ordered according to change, causality and an experiencing subject (see Ryan 2007: 23 for a discussion of the problem of defining narrative). From a rhetorical perspective, Phelan defines narrative as a 'purposive act of communication about characters and events: somebody telling somebody else on some occasion and for some purpose(s) that something happened' (Phelan 2006: 9). Oppositely, description, when relaunched in the *Yale French Studies* (1981) by Philippe Hamon, is defined as:

$$C + F + IT (V + PEq/PEf) \text{ (Hamon 1982: 160)}$$

A description, according to Hamon, consists of a character (C), a form of action (F) and the setting with its introductory theme of the description (IT). The form of action can be either: looking at/speaking with/acting with the setting, which can be either a milieu/landscape/ collection of objects, which then triggers a series of sub-themes. The latter is described in the bracket through a vocabulary (V), which is in a metonymic relation to the setting. The sub-themes can be expanded by a predicative (PE) that can either be qualitative (q) or functional (f). According to Hamon, the bracket can be compared to a dictionary sequence of entry → definition → examples. Given such a formulaic definition, and with the comparison to a dictionary sequence, one may find ample reason why descriptions of settings have been overlooked in narratology.

Descriptions have a reputation for boring the reader with static presentation and accumulative information in direct opposition to what Peter Brooks (1992) has termed the desire for the plot in narrative.[1] Yet, apart from any reservations one may have about formulaic thinking, the formula still successfully raises the question of the more-than-human, since one of the formula's three components is an IT = setting, which necessarily implicates something more-than- human: air and light, the sky, or the wood a table is made of. The more-than-human is here regarded as a constitute part of description. Yet when assessed only in relation to an action carried out by a character, it (whether 'it' is space, objects or landscapes) remains one of the implicit problems when speaking of description in narratology, and one that is never addressed from its own material point of view, but is always transferred to a question of character. The problem with narratology from a post-anthropocentric perspective is its one-dimensional focus on the human subject, whether in the form of narration or description; focus is always on the experiencing human subject acting on or perceiving an object, allowing no room for the object to be the agent that affects and transforms the subject in a text.

It is not merely in this subject-centric focus that the narratological theory of description bypasses the more-than-human reality, but in its concept of language as a closed system of signs. In the 1981 issue of *Yale French Studies*, Hamon argues against the dominant notion of description that goes as far back as Boileau. In 'The Rhetorical Status of the Descriptive' (1981), Hamon writes that since Boileau's *Art Poétique* (1674), description has been regarded as 'pure' rhetorical ornament; something which must be as compressed and take up as little space as possible, so as not to bore the reader. Description, for Boileau, is considered a means by which the author can display his or her rhetorical skills, something not belonging to the sensuous world but conjured up in mind of the author. Hamon quotes Boileau for the following humorous passage:

> Sometimes an Author, fond of his own Thought,
> Pursues his object till it's over-wrought:
> If he describes a House he shews the Face,
> And after walks you round from place to place;
> Here is the vista, there the doors unfold,
> Balconies here are ballustered with Gold.
> Then counts the Rounds and Ovals in the Halls,
> 'The Festoons the Friezes and the Astragals.'
> Tir'd with his tedious Pomp, away I run,
> And skip over twenty Pages to be gone.
> Of such Descriptions the vain Folly flee,
> And shun their barren superfluity.
> All that is needless [*detail inutile*] carefully avoid.
>
> (Hamon 1981: 9)

In opposition to this view, Hamon tries to restore description by allowing it meaning in relation to the narrative. To him, description is not just a setting or a pause that the reader can skip, but something packed with meaning that can be an indicator for characters as well as the development of the plot. Yet, as mentioned, the issue I take with Hamon is that the meaning of the more-than-human reality remains subservient to human characters.

What is lacking in narratology is a new understanding of the relation between narrative and description; one that does not exclude objects from being narrated, that is, to be described as something happening on their own accord, actively co-shaping the setting and human reality, not simply as forming a setting for the characters' actions and perceptions. This is possible when description and narration are combined with post-anthropocentric theory. Then Hamon's formula might be revised, so that it is no longer only the subject that acts upon an object. An object may come to relate to the subject or even to another object without any human subject to initiate the action. Conversely, specific narratological attention to change and differences may prove itself useful in a post-anthropocentric reading of literature. Any 'static description' may be analysed as a narrative event, an event where change takes the form of one object transforming the materiality of another, or transforming a human character.

Perec's Repetitive Description of a Writing Desk

Through its history of publication in a literary journal, and with its English title, 'Still Life/Style Leaf' hovers at the periphery of Perec's work. Despite this peripheral role, 'Still Life/Style Leaf' is the one example that Sabine Buchholz and Manfred Jahn mention in their article 'Space in Narrative' in the *Routledge Encyclopedia of Narrative Theory*. Using Perec's text as an example of narrative's temporal preference, Buchholz and Jahn explain how 'a story cannot have too much of temporal sequentiality, but it does grind to a halt when overloaded with spatial description (cf. Georges Perec's short story "Still Life/Style Leaf")' (Buchholz and Jahn 2005: 551). They regard Perec's text as a spatial description that overwhelms the reader with its overload of materials and question the text's narrative readability. Mimicking Boileau's descriptive boredom, the two narratologists reproduce a specific claim on narrative where descriptions of space and things are secondary to temporal sequentiality. By doing so, they happen to miss what is really taking place in Perec's text, which, as I will explain later, can be understood as a search for materiality by means of its own spatial and descriptive sequentiality.

While Buchholz and Jahn reproduce the gap between temporal narration and descriptive space, another narratologist, Jeffrey Kittay, reproduces Hamon's focus on the subject and on description's representational status in his reading of the text. In his introduction to *Yale French Studies* (1981), he writes that

> [t]he volume closes with 'Still Life/Style Leaf', a description, or so it seems, written for this issue by Georges Perec. . . . Derrida is talking about writing, and Perec's piece is a description of a writing, or rather of a written. (Kittay 1981: iv)

In the context of the re-evaluation of description in narratology, where the textual relation to a material reality is downplayed in favour of meaningful narrative elements, it is significant that what Kittay takes away from Perec's description, as he compares it to Derrida's self-reflective understanding of language, is its only narrative element, that is, the narrative action of writing. The text is reduced to writing itself in a Derridean sense, that is, the text can be read as a description of language writing itself, even if the writing subject is mentioned but a single time in the entire story.

If Perec's text was to fit into Hamon's formula, the 'I' would be analysed as the character that writes at the table, but this only fits one sentence out of the story's six and a half pages. Indeed, the rest of the text (the entire description of the desk and the *mise en abyme*) would merely serve as sub-themes, according to Hamon, that is, as the bracket in his formula. But Perec has formed a text that acts as the exact opposite to Boileau's claim – it in fact turns Hamon's formula upside down, as in it the bracketed sub-themes take over the text. The story evolves from the table and the relation between the things on it, and, with the *mise en abyme*, a kind of dynamic description is created both formally and thematically. Hamon's formula does not seem to be able to catch what is really at work in Perec's text.

What we need instead is a new dynamic understanding of description as well as a new understanding of its representational status. As for Kittay, his reading pays no attention to the things that take up the whole of Perec's description, as he considers the description to be unrelated to any reality outside of itself (that is, outside writing/the language of the written text). Indirectly, Kittay continues Boileau's critique of description as nothing but a show of rhetorical skills by the author. In this same line of thought, the repetitive structure of the text only stresses its own representational status as a description of a writing that never comes to a halt, where one sign only mirrors another sign without any reference to any space or anything beyond the page – it is 'a description of a written' (Kittay 1981: iv).

This repetitive structure looks very different through the lens of Timothy Morton. Morton is one of the few theorists who has offered a reflection upon the role of literature in a post-anthropocentric perspective by addressing the problem of representing the more-than-human background in language. Morton writes in *Ecology without Nature: Rethinking Environmental Aesthetics* (2009: 1): 'when you mention the environment, you bring it into the foreground. In other words, it stops being the environment. It stops being That Thing Over There that surrounds and sustains us'. To deal with the ever-evasive background, he introduces

> a theory of *ambient poetics*, a materialist way of reading texts with a view to how they encode the literal space of their inscription – if there is such a thing – the spaces between words, the margins of the page, the physical and social environments of the reader. (2009: 3)

Ambient poetics tries to represent the more-than-human background by taking the physical conditions of creating and reading a text into account. By directing our attention to the material background of a text, we are, according to Morton, reminded of the fact that in reality there is always something beyond our human point of view. Combining the textual preference from deconstruction with ecocriticism, Morton depicts the irreducible problem of rendering. He writes: 'the more convincingly I render my surroundings, the more figurative language I end up with. The more I try to show you what lies beyond this page, the more of a page I have' (2009: 30). Instead of regarding this growing textuality as a hindrance, Morton proceeds instead to investigate the mediality of the text and to show the impossibility of ever presenting reality as it exists without mediation. To this effect, he employs the concept of ambient poetics to describe how there is in fact always a made-up framework at work in the text: 'ambient poetics describes the "material makeup" that is used to render the environment' (2009: 34). The question is thus how to find instances in the work of art that call our attention to the fact that there is always a material space beyond the page, and *on* the page, even in a self-reflective text such as Perec's. As Morton notes, 'Since ambience tries to evoke the background *as* background – to drag it into the foreground would dissolve it – it must resort to oblique rhetorical strategies' (2009: 45). I will soon return to these oblique rhetorical strategies and their makeup, but first let us return to the question of Perec's repetitive structure.

Instead of narratology's purely discursive focus, it is possible through a combination of ecocriticism and deconstruction to read the *mise en abyme* in Perec's text as a way in which the text throws the reader back into its space and creates a new material awareness both formally in text and thematically beyond the page. This means that instead of reading the *mise en abyme* as a prison-house of language, the repetition might be read as a way of disorienting the reader's sequential and temporal reading. Instead of boring the reader, it situates and engages her even more in the space of the text, as Morton notes in a later text, 'Deconstruction and/as Ecology': 'repetition disorients our sense of direction' (Morton 2014: 292) in a text. For Morton,

> Reading is *formally* ecological, since in order to read we must take account of the dark side of things, as intimately connected with the 'lighter' sides as the recto and verso of a piece of writing paper. Reading discovers a constantly flowing, shifting play of temporality and a constant process of differentiation ... You can't get rid of the dark side, but it keeps disappearing, just ahead and just behind. This dark side manifests between pages, sentences, and words. (2014: 292–3)

Perec's text is exemplary for such a 'formally ecological' reading. When reading Perec's text for the first time, you easily overlook the many things accumulated on the desk.² But with Morton's ecological reading and with his ambient poetics in mind, a new type of reading appears, which makes Perec's text surface as a text that through its textuality points to something beyond itself.

When the description repeats itself with the *mise en abyme*, you suddenly begin to notice small variations from the first, and so, instead of the reading coming to a halt, you begin to reread with a new curiosity in a process of differentiation. Take this description of a calculator: in the first part, it is described as 'a Casio pocket calculator on which the number 315308 read upside down spells the word BOESIE' (Perec 1981: 299), which in the second part is changed into 'a Casio pocket calculator on which the number 35079 read upside down spells the word GLOSE' (1981: 302). The effect of the repetition is casting you, the reader, back into the first description in a material way, making you aware of your own distracted first reading. This then results in a rereading of the entire first part; suddenly you search for the small variations and pay new attention to miniscule details.

This rereading is material on more than one level. First, the reader's attention is turned towards the letters as graphic markings in the way that the signs on the calculator are stylistically described on the page with capital letters; it makes these words stand out as larger and darker than the rest, thus making you aware of words as material marks on a page, as opposed to skimming them as accumulative descriptive and signifying nouns. Second, the difference described actually refers to signs on the calculators – two different types of calculators: BOESIE and GLOSE. This double sign (a sign on the page as well as a sign on the thing described) directs the reader's attention to the calculator as a thing, yet not as a thing of use for someone. The calculator is here mainly present as a difference between the two types of calculator, whereas the physical calculator hovers in the background, a material thing with different sides, sizes and details, never fully present. So, instead of narratological boredom over static descriptions, the reader is now set on a search for materialities, perhaps closer in nature to Brook's desire for plot – a desire close to the one you may experience when solving a crossword puzzle.

Style Leafs – An Invitation into the Environment of Writing

As 'Still Life/Style Leaf' demonstrates, Georges Perec was a writer who dealt directly with questions of things and words, language and space, yet in the reception of his work, the material aspect is often downplayed in favour of his linguistic experiments with words – similar to the narratological reading by Kittay.[3] This is partly due to the fact that Perec was a constituent member of the *Oulipo* group, founded in 1960 by writers and mathematicians whose aim it was to investigate 'the research, the discovery, and the invention of *constraints* for the composition of literary texts . . . An *Oulipian author* is one who *writes under constraints*' (Roubaud 2004: 100). The most famous Oulipian novel is Perec's *La Vie mode d'emploi* (1978), which used mathematical structures to construct and constrain its structure.

In Perec's case, the investigation into the formal structures of language and the intersection between mathematics and literature do not result in an obliteration of literature's relation to a material reality. Indeed, the opposite occurs: for Perec, it is through concrete experimental descriptions that the materiality of what he calls 'the infra-ordinary' appears (2008a: 210). The infra-ordinary resembles Morton's understanding of 'the environment', that is, the often invisible background setting that is overlooked in ordinary life, overshadowed by those extra-ordinary actions performed by humans. Perec asks: 'how should we take account of, question, describe what happens everyday day and recurs every day: the banal, the quotidian, the obvious, the common, the ordinary, the infra-ordinary, the background noise, the habitual?' (2008a: 210). His interest is material, as he continues: 'What we need to question is bricks, concrete, glass, our table manners, our utensils, our tools . . . describe your street. Describe another street compare. Make an inventory of your pockets, of your bag . . . Question your tea spoons' (2008a: 210). Language serves as a vehicle for Perec; it is the fracture that is needed in order to make the otherwise hidden infra-ordinary material background emerge.

This is also obvious in *Espèces d'espaces* (1974) and in *tentative d'epuisement d'un lieu parisien* (1975) where he investigates types of material spaces through experimental descriptions, as for instance when he tries to describe a square in Paris while experiencing it. These texts belong to a phase in his work that he himself has referred to as guided by an interest in 'the "sociological": how to look at the everyday' (2008b: 141) and it is within this interpretation of Perec's work that 'Still Life/Style Leaf' can be regarded as something more than a static description of a desk. Indeed, it might be seen as a prime example of the way that 'writing overwhelms what it is depicting' (Morton 2009: 19) and through this overwhelming gesture, Perec's words account for something beyond the very words on the page.

A post-anthropocentric reading of Perec's text offers a different understanding of the repetitive structure of Perec's text than Kittay's. To further exemplify this and propose a way of focusing on the more-than-human descriptions in narratology, while at the same time addressing the underdeveloped field of literary analysis within the material turn, I now turn to Morton's concept of ambient poetics, which will serve as the platform from which a new mode of reading may emerge.

However, Morton's own literary examples are often diffuse and lacking in concrete tools for literary analysis – owing to his philosophical inquiries and his use of various forms of art – so I propose a combination of his ambient poetics and revised close reading tools from narratology, making it possible to look at the way the story negotiates between narrative elements, such as change, sequentiality and a human acting character, and descriptive elements, such as stasis, setting and mimetic rendering. Combining these two strategies, the narratological identification of a narrator is substituted with a concept of situatedness, which invokes a new form of reader engagement through which the representational status of description is exchanged with a new idea of medial rendering. By outlining the six rhetorical strategies of ambient poetics through a reading of Perec's text with the help from these narratological devices, I hope to provide a concrete mode of reading in light of the material turn.

Ambient poetics consists of six elements: '*rendering*, the *medial*, the *timbral*, the *Aeolian*, the *tone*, and most fundamentally, the *re-mark*' (Morton 2009: 34). Morton explains rendering as 'the result of ambient poetics, its telos' (2009: 34). The goal of using rendering as a device is to simulate reality; to make the aesthetic framework invisible by inviting the reader to share the same space as the 'I' of the text. In a narratological framework this corresponds to the diegetic level of the narrator, but whereas narratology would focus on temporal relations in order to identify the person and distinguish the narrator from what is told, Morton's ambient poetics accentuates the way 'the reader glimpses the environment rather than the person' (2009: 33), though without mentioning the concept of narrator. By combining the narratological concept of narrator with Morton's concept of rendering, a concrete mode of reading that accentuates spatial situatedness rather than temporal sequentiality in the discursive statement becomes possible.

In relation to Perec's text, this would mean reading the statement 'on which I am writing' (Perec 1981: 299) not along the lines of Kittay's subject-centric reading as an action concerning self-reflective writing practice, but as an invitation for the reader to share the same space as the 'I' of the text. Central here is not the subject performing the action of writing, as Hamon's formula would have it, but the environment of writing.

While rendering is an authenticating device, the medial foregrounds the medium, alerting the reader's attention to the aesthetic framework. It expresses how the environment is rendered, that is, reminding us that what is rendered is rendered on a piece of paper: 'medial writing highlights the page upon which the words are written' (2009: 37). The medial is apparent in the places in a text where 'the medium of communication [is] thickened' (2009: 37), revealing the simulated reality, the illusion created by rendering. It foregrounds the material background of the written: the page, the graphic signs and the margin. In the case of Perec's text, self-awareness of its medial aspect is inherent in its English title 'Still Life/Style Leaf'.

The first part of Perec's title refers to the visual genre of 'still life', described in the same issue of *Yale French Studies* by Marc Eli Blanchard as 'the description of objects originally set apart from the course of daily life' (Blanchard 1981: 276). Blanchard continues to identify its 'static qualities', depicting 'nature morte' and how it 'lacks a subject' (1981: 277). By entitling the piece 'Still Life', Perec is directly commenting on this genre while also departing from it in important ways, especially seen in relation to the narratological difference between narration and description.

First, Perec describes objects in their daily environment, which relates to his concept of the infra-ordinary, thus making description a way of paying attention to that which is frequently – especially in narratology – overlooked in relation to writing, that is, the infra-ordinary background of writing: the paper, the desk, the pen, the eraser, and so on.

Second, the text does have a subject, but even so, the subject does not require the reader's full attention as narratology and Hamon would have it. Instead its title situates the text, inviting the reader into the space of writing, which then continues to grow and surround the reader.

Third, and in relation to the medial, the static qualities of this particular genre are also contested by that second part of the title, which switches the meaning of the words referring to the *mise en abyme* in the text, leading the reader to search for differences in the varied repetition of the things described. The second part of the title does not refer to language presenting objects as nature mortes, but to language itself, which in turn changes the static objects of the first description into something unstable in the second.

Description can be said to employ one of the trademarks of narrative: change. 'Style Leaf' is a play on words; a variation on 'Still Life', referring to the materiality of the letter, and it can be interpreted as a leaf that has been stylised, matter that has been given a style, and as a page in a style booklet. The latter refers to the sheet of paper on the desk that triggers repetition of the description within the text, referring in turn to the sheet of paper that the text itself is written upon. Hence the phrase 'Style Leaf' directs our attention to the surprising change within the text, provoked by the materiality of paper, while it also makes us aware of a textual materiality outside the words on the page, namely to that of the paper upon which the text is written, and, lastly, its wordplay emphasises the physicality of letters.

The timbral is one of the elements that Morton does not explore in relation to literature. He refers to musical metaphors and bodily references, such as Heidegger's reflections on sound, described as the way 'we never hear sound in the abstract. Instead, we hear the way *things sound*' (2009: 40) and Barthes' physical voice; 'the timbral voice is vivid with the resonance of the lungs, throat, salvia, teeth, and skull: the grain of the voice' (2009: 40); it is Yves Klein's pure blue canvases and the way 'a guitar note brings to mind the wood out of which it is made' (2009: 40). But the question remains how to read the timbral in literature.

I would suggest that one way of understanding the timbral in a literary analysis is through the rhetorical use of alliterations, onomatopoeia, and other examples of how words, in addition to their signifying, also attract attention to their phonetic and acoustic aspects. In this way, the act of reading words makes you, the reader, aware of your own mouth or tongue movements when pronouncing them, whether aloud or silently. Understood in this way, the timbral in Perec's text is exemplified by the alliteration in the title, in the shift from 'Still' to 'Style'; attention to sound is attracted here because of the repetition of a range of consonant sounds, but they all occur in combination with different vowel sounds; similar but with a difference. The vowel sound in the first word is the short [i], a sound that is pronounced by using the tip of the tongue and whose sound and tongue movement is shorter and more abrupt than the [ai] in the second part of the title, which prolongs the sound a bit and lies further back in the mouth. The pronunciation makes you aware of your own body while reading, turning the attention of reading from a signifying process to a bodily experience.

While the timbral is related to the sound of words and the reader's body, tone is 'the way in which matter is vibrating' (2009: 43) in the text. The definition of tone is only vaguely described, as Morton quickly moves on to allude to other similar elusive concepts such as 'Stimmung' or 'atmosphere' (2009: 43). Despite its elusive character, tone is a concept that is closely related to the narratological concept and history of description. Tone is created in a text when narrative time is suspended and a vivid sensuous description takes over the text. Continuing with musical examples (and not mentioning narratology at all), Morton describes it as 'the narrative aspect of ecomimesis that generates tone. Specifically, this is a strong form of ekphrasis (*description*, vivid description) . . . The effect on the reader is that the time of narration is held in stasis' (2009: 44).

The only literary example Morton gives is the most famous example of ekphrasis: the visual description of Achilles' shield in Homer's *Iliad*. Using Hamon's formula, tone can be found in Perec's text in the description of a picture on an ashtray. The ashtray with a picture on it suspends the description of things on the desk and shifts instead to a visual description of the picture that tells a story about the Martyrs of Beirut:

> a tiny round ashtray of white porcelain in which a painted scene where greens dominate depicts the Monument to the Martyrs of Beirut (that is to say, insofar as its precision allows interpretation: at the center of a square adorned with cedars and palms and surrounded by modern edifices, from a stone pedestal whose three visible sides are embellished with wreath of red flowers, three figures emerge – a wounded man who has fallen on his side and is stretching out one hand as he struggles to get back to his feet; above him a, atop a stone of block indeterminate shape, a woman . . . (1981: 300)

Whereas Hamon's formula puts the description of the object in a bracket and makes a central point of the perceiving subject at the beginning, Perec not only turns the bracket upside down (that is, the whole text makes up the bracket), he also changes the role of description and narration, as it is from the description of an object that narration emerges. Description is not subordinated plot and characters, instead narration is subordinate to description as the material description of the ashtray sets off the narrative of the story in the bracket. Or, in other words, the story containing three characters is bracketed and the described object sets the story in motion. Description as *tone* drives the text forward, giving it a sort of spatial sequentiality as one object appears along with the next, described in minute detail, whereas the story in the bracket is what stops it when description is brought to a halt by the bracketed narration of the event of the martyrs. Perec lets description drive the text forward and the narration of the martyrs disturbs it.

In continuation of the relationship between description and narration, a redefinition of the relationship between subject and object in the text is needed, which is possible through use of Morton's concept of the Aeolian. Morton describes the Aeolian as 'processes continuing without a subject or an author' (2009: 41). It occurs in literature when a human narrator cannot be identified, and language seems to act on its own without a direct source.

In narratological terms, this is what Ann Banfield has called 'unspeakable sentences' (Banfield 1982: 1): to describe perceptive sentences without any subject present in the sentence to perceive. She describes this feature as a 'uniquely novelistic style [which] seeks to capture, to arrest within the moment, the appearance of things independent of any observer and his or her desires, prejudices, intentions' (Banfield 1987: 278). Perec's text is Aeolian in the sense that the 'I' that is writing in the first sentence has disappeared in the rest of the text, leaving the rest of the description to be guided by verbs, or an 'it' that refers to the things and how they relate to one another in their concrete positions on the desk, as for instance the table being illuminated by a lamp: 'illuminating *it* is an architect's lamp made of blue metal' (1981: 299). This ensures that that which is described, though on a writer's work desk, does not bear witness to the identity of the writer, but to the materials surrounding him, to his situatedness. Hence Perec's text seems to raise the matter of hierarchical ownership between author and text – it is not the author that makes this text, but the concrete materials surrounding him: The desk, the pen and paper, and, indeed, even the material text itself are all co-creating the *mise en abyme*.

The *mise en abyme* in Perec's text is an excellent example of Morton's last feature; the re-mark. The re-mark is an echo in a text. It refers to a specific mark in a text making the reader aware that what she has been reading is indeed only a text; a mark that makes her aware of the illusion of rendering. The re-mark turns the backgrounded medial aspect of the text into the foreground: 'it is a special mark (or series of them) that makes us aware that we are in the presence of (significant) marks' (2009: 48). To identify the re-mark that Morton describes 'is to answer the question: how little does the text need to differentiate between foreground and background?' (2009: 49).

Perec's text directly reflects upon this relationship and even combines it with the act of writing. Instead of foregrounding the act of writing as mediation – as narratologists would – the text displays a nuanced relationship between foreground and background. The background, in this instance the desk, is foregrounded as background in the description as the material background for writing. The moment the background is no longer foregrounded as the background for writing but gets foregrounded as mediation, a loop begins that resembles Morton's re-mark. When the act of writing is thematised, as the text zooms in on the paper – thus becoming foregrounded as an object separated from the rest of the desk – the sheet of paper with the written words on it takes over the description, and the *mise en abyme* begins:

> In the foreground, standing out clearly against the black fabric of the table, lies a sheet of 8¼ x 11¾ ruled paper that is almost entirely covered with the overly compact handwriting, and on which can be read: The lacquered wood desk on which I am writing, formerly a jeweller's workbench (1981: 302)

Stressing the shift between foreground and background in the description by 'in the foreground', the text expressly makes its readers aware that something is happening. The style leaf from the title is repeated as 'a sheet of 8 ¼ x 11 ¾ ruled paper', an object that is not only foregrounded, but also draws attention to the background paper, upon which the foregrounded words are written. The foregrounded background in this way causes the background materiality of paper to come into focus. In doing so, Perec has created a still life of a writing desk not as a static description: the displacement occurring between the first and the second description instals a sort of puzzle within the description – copying a narrative strategy from the narration of plots that adds temporality to the still life. In this reading, the style leaf turns the reader's attention towards the often overlooked background of the written, while also proposing a new material search for materials on and beyond the page.

Conclusion

When combining descriptive devices from narratology with Morton's ambient poetics, a new material mode of reading appears; a mode that is useful not only in texts about nature, but in self-reflective texts such as Perec's. Indeed, with its descriptive point of departure, Perec's 'Still Life/Style Leaf' makes it possible to confront and introduce the more-than-human background as something important in itself in addition to narratology's subject-centric and purely signifying theory of language. This form of reading strives to revise the illusion of an autonomous human subject acting upon a passive objectified world: as my reading has illustrated, to write and read is co-creation.

Through Morton's vocabulary a new matter-oriented reading is made possible, one that narratology has not taken into account: that of the bodily aspect of reading, the background, and the physical space of the book. In this reading, the page and the letter as graphic marks present a background for reading and writing that is otherwise overlooked. This mode of reading allows attention to be paid to conventionally insignificant remarks such as brackets, margins and gaps between words. Reading becomes 'ecological', in Morton's sense of the term, and even in a text about writing, writing is revealed to be something more than just signs referring to other signs. The difference between the two descriptions separated by the *mise en abyme* makes the reader aware of the infra-ordinary elements of writing and reading. At the same time, this kind of reading is only possible when informed by a revised narratological toolkit, which have made the subtleties in the text apparent. Through this combination, I contend that a new understanding of narration and description has emerged along with a spatially situated narrator with environmental reader engagement, as well as a new understanding of discourse with the foregrounding of the material background of representation.

This kind of material reading requires that we read descriptive passages slowly to avoid skipping or skimming descriptions of space and things in literature, and that we instead pay attention to the ways in which objects appear in a text. It teaches us not to take for granted that an 'I' in the beginning of a text necessarily means that all of the text has to be read from the perspective of this 'I', or that everything is necessarily subjected by a human subject. Combining Morton and narratology, to read materially is to look at how a text renders its environment, to not dismiss descriptions as static, but with the help of narratological devices to see how things are described: whether they are described through verbs or adjectives and, indeed, if things can be said to not merely be subordinated a narrative plot, but instead actively order and structure narration. The result is a re-evaluation of the relationship between description and narration, between foreground and background. Along with it comes an imperative to pay close attention to presentations of the relationship between characters and settings, subjects and objects.

A material reading calls for a departure from the dominant mode of searching for hidden meanings. Instead of reading for things as symbols for the character or clues to the narrative plot, a material reading makes visible a reality that consists of more-than-human environments – a fact that is supported by the very mediality of the text itself. This means looking closely at the way literature presents, includes and involves the more-than-human reality, and it means to grasp literature itself as a material thing.

Notes

1. Perec's novels and essays explicitly toy with this dictionary form, which may explain why Perec's text 'Still Life/Style Leaf' is mentioned in the reference in *Routledge Encyclopedia of Narrative Theory* concerning unreadability in cases of an overload of space in texts (Buchholz and Jahn 2005: 551–5).
2. I experimented with different readings of this text in a class on New Materialism. Here all of the students in their first reading of Perec's text had the same experience as the two narratologists: that is, the overload of things described stopped their reading, as they ceased paying attention to what they read.
3. See, for instance, Warren Motte and Jean-Jacques Poucel's special issue on Perec in *Yale French Studies* (2004). It is not until recently that a whole issue of the annual *Cahier Georges Perec* was devoted to his spatial thinking; see *Cahier Georges Perec* (2015).

References

Banfield, Ann (1982), *Unspeakable Sentences*, Boston, MA: Routledge & Kegan Paul.
Banfield, Ann (1987), 'Describing the unobserved: event grouped around an empty centre', in Nigel Fabb, Colin MacCabe, Derek Attridge and Alan Durant (eds), *The Linguistics of Writing: Arguments Between Language and Literature*, Manchester: Manchester University Press, pp. 265–85.
Blanchard, Marc Eli (1981), 'On still life', *Yale French Studies*, no. 61: *Towards a Theory of Description*, New Haven, CT: Yale University Press, pp. 276–98.
Brooks, Peter (1992), *Reading for the Plot. Design and Intention in Narrative*, Cambridge, MA: Harvard University Press.
Buchholz, Sabine and Manfred Jahn (2005), 'Space in narrative', in David Herman, Manfred Jahn and Marie-Laure Ryan (eds), *Routledge Encyclopedia of Narrative Theory*, London and New York: Routledge, pp. 551–5.
Hamon, Philippe (1981), 'Rhetorical status of the descriptive', *Yale French Studies*, no. 61: *Towards a Theory of Description*, New Haven, CT: Yale University Press, pp. 1–26.
Hamon, Philippe (1982), 'What is a description', in Tzvetan Todorov (ed.), *French Literary Theory Today*, Cambridge: Cambridge University Press, pp. 147–78.
Kittay, Jeffrey (1981), 'Introduction', *Yale French Studies*, no. 61: *Towards a Theory of Description*, New Haven, CT: Yale University Press, pp. i–v.
Morton, Timothy (2009), *Ecology without Nature: Rethinking Environmental Aesthetics*, Cambridge, MA: Harvard University Press.
Morton, Timothy (2014), 'Deconstruction and/as ecology', in Greg Garrard (ed.), *The Oxford Handbook of Ecocriticism*, Oxford: Oxford University Press, pp. 291–304.

Motte, Warren and Jean-Jacques Poucel (2004), 'Editors' preface: on reading Georges Perec', *Yale French Studies*, no. 105: *Pereckonings: Reading Georges Perec*, New Haven, CT: Yale University Press, pp. 1–3.
Perec, Georges (1975), *tentative d'epuisement d'un lieu parisien*, Paris: Christian Bourgois éditeur.
Perec, Georges (1981), 'Still life/style leaf', *Yale French Studies*, no. 61: *Towards a Theory of Description*, trans. Harry Mathews, New Haven, CT: Yale University Press, pp. 299–305.
Perec Georges (2000 [1974]), *Espèces d'espaces*, Paris: Galilée.
Perec, Georges (2008a [1973]), 'Approaches to what', in *Species of Spaces and Other Pieces*, ed. and trans. John Sturruck, London: Penguin Classics, pp. 209–11.
Perec, Georges (2008b [1985]), 'Notes on what I'm looking for', in *Species of Spaces and Other Pieces*, ed. and trans. John Sturruck, London: Penguin Classics, pp. 141–3.
Phelan, James (2006), 'Narrative theory, 1966–2006: a narrative', in Robert Scholes, James Phelan and Robert Kellogg (eds), *The Nature of Narrative*, Oxford: Oxford University Press, pp. 283–336.
Roubaud, Jacques (2004), 'Perecquian OULIPO', *Yale French Studies*, no. 105: *Pereckonings: Reading Georges Perec*, New Haven, CT: Yale University Press, pp. 99–109.
Ryan, Marie-Laure (2007), 'Toward a definition of narrative', in David Herman (ed.), *The Cambridge Companion to Narrative*, Cambridge: Cambridge University Press, pp. 22–38.

CHAPTER 2

Slow Narrative and the Perception of Material Forms

Marco Caracciolo

Introduction

> On a sunny Tuesday morning on 4 June in the grate over the storm drain to the Chesapeake Bay in front of Sam's Bagels on Cold Spring Lane in Baltimore, there was:
> one large men's black plastic work glove
> one dense mat of oak pollen
> one unblemished dead rat
> one white plastic bottle cap
> one smooth stick of wood
> Glove, pollen, rat, cap, stick. As I encountered these items, they shimmied back and forth between debris and thing – between, on the one hand, stuff to ignore, except insofar as it betokened human activity . . . , and, on the other hand, stuff that commanded attention in its own right. (Bennett 2010)

Jane Bennett's *Vibrant Matter*, with its influential account of the efficacy of matter, or 'thing-power', takes its cue from this encounter with the debris clogging a sewer drain in Baltimore.[1] Bennett's epiphany of the nonhuman world takes the form of a list: by typographically isolating each item, the enumeration brings out the rich materiality of objects that everyday language would brush aside as mere 'garbage'. This anecdote is also, as Bennett acknowledges, a story, and more precisely a 'speculative onto-story'. Certainly, speculation is what the encounter with the glove-pollen-rat-cap-stick assemblage *triggers*, and it plays a central role in post-anthropocentric philosophies such as Bennett's. Before the speculative leap can happen, however, Bennett's encounter builds on *focused attention* to the forms of the sensory world. With its strategic use of a formal device (the list), the narrative seeks to channel – and elicit in readers – precisely this state of focused attention, which involves the attunement of perception to the rich vitality of the nonhuman world.

Bennett's anecdote thus slows down everyday perception and enables readers to appreciate and become absorbed in the forms of materiality.

Bennett's account suggests that narrative can create a sense of attunement to the nonhuman world through the protracted perception of forms that are, at the same time, material and textual. This stretching out of perception gives rise to the distinctive slowness of what I call in this chapter 'slow narrative'. As I will detail in a moment, slow narrative is marked by an uneventful plot, a sense of detachment from the world of human action, and an interest in the texture of material objects and landscapes. This narrative exercise ties in with, and can serve to advance, the philosophical agenda of New Materialism, with its extension of concepts of efficacy, vitality and even agency to the nonhuman world (for discussion, see Dolphijn and van der Tuin 2012). This New Materialist move is deeply counterintuitive, because it contradicts assumptions about the separation of (human) subjects and (nonhuman) objects – assumptions that are fundamentally ingrained in human psychology, at least in a Western context. A large body of research, from developmental psychology (Johnson 2000) to ecolinguistics (Goatly 1996) and ecological philosophy (Abram 1997), shows that subject–object binaries run deep in the Western world. New Materialist thinking needs to foster forms of attention to the nonhuman world that are capable of countering this cognitively entrenched dualism. My proposition is that artistic engagements have a key role to play in retraining our perception and focusing it on the efficacy of matter. After all, in introducing the concept of artistic defamiliarisation or 'ostraneniye' Viktor Shklovsky famously argued that 'art exists that one may recover the sensation of life; it exists to make one feel things, to make the stone *stony*. The purpose of art is to impart the sensation of things as they are perceived and not as they are known' (1965: 12, emphasis in the original). 'To make the stone stony' involves recovering the perceptual thickness of the thing, which is not interchangeable with conceptual knowledge ('as they are known'): as Shklovsky suggests, concepts *erase* the perceptual richness of the material world, leading to an understanding of matter as passive and inert. Through their defamiliarising strategies, the arts are in an excellent position to convey the sensory impact of nonhuman things and should thus be central to the New Materialist project.[2] As Shklovsky himself argued, the artistic means of pursuing that goal is the deceleration of perception: 'A work is created "artistically" so that its perception is impeded and the greatest possible effect is produced through the slowness of the perception' (1965: 22).

My specific focus in this chapter is on *narrative* art and what it can achieve by deploying techniques that encourage slow reading and viewing practices. The methodology I adopt is inspired by a renewed interest in literary and narrative form within the field of so-called New Formalism (Levinson 2007; Levine 2015). From the standpoint of New Formalism, form straddles the divide between literary texts and sociocultural contexts: there are forms in literary art but also in culture at large (for instance, social hierarchies and cultural systems for organising time). Slowness, as I conceptualise it, is a function of formal strategies responsible for slowing down audiences' imaginative engagement with artworks; but it also has repercussions for the broader form of human–nonhuman relations: the experience of slowness resonates with New Materialist ideas in that it brings into view the material texture of humans' encounters with the nonhuman world. I thus build on the inextricable link between form and its effects in order to explore the significance of slowness for narrative's engagement with the nonhuman.

The concept of slowness has been discussed in the context of 'slow cinema', which – in the words of Matthew Flanagan – refers to 'a unique type of reflective art where form and temporality are never less than emphatically present, and a diminution of pace serves to displace the dominant momentum of narrative causality' (2008; see also Jaffe 2014). For Lutz Koepnick, 'slow cinema stresses the thickness of time so as to cater to contemplative modes of viewing film' (2017: 56). These experimentations with cinematic time work at two levels: first, they adopt formal strategies that undercut medium-specific expectations of narrative pacing and teleology (for instance, in action film); and, second, they serve as a radical alternative to the frantic speed of our highly interconnected world, which favours 'hyper' attention over 'deep' attentional modes (Hayles 2007). Scholarship on slow film has concentrated on the genre's inherent critique of contemporary practices of media consumption. Extending this interest in slowness and the modes of readership or viewership it can foster, I aim to explore how certain narratives can deepen our perception and appreciation of nonhuman vitality. I also argue that slow storytelling is not specific to film but widely represented in a range of other narrative media. The examples I discuss in this chapter are drawn from prose fiction and comics: respectively, they are Italo Calvino's *Mr Palomar* (Calvino 1985; originally published in Italian in 1983) and *Kingdom*, a graphic novel by British artist Jon McNaught (2018).

Mr Palomar is centred on the titular character, a middle-aged man who seemingly devotes his days to the thoughtful observation of natural and social phenomena. Calling this work a 'novel' certainly stretches the definition of the genre, given that there is no overt progression or plot (although the book does display a degree of closure, in that it concludes with Mr Palomar's unexpected death). But the framing is unmistakably narrative, and the method episodic: the book is organised thematically, with every chapter exploring Mr Palomar's thought processes in a particular situation (on vacation, in his home, while shopping, etc.). Mr Palomar's method is highly analytical and scientific: whether his gaze is pointed at the starry sky, deliberately avoids a woman's naked breasts on a beach, or admires the display of cheeses in a Parisian store, Mr Palomar is looking for the 'single, absolute principle from which actions and forms are derived' (1985: 13). In other words, Mr Palomar seeks to impose order and rationality on the sheer variety of natural and social forms. But Mr Palomar doesn't stop there, because he is prone to examining the very logic of his search for order, with periodic shifts to introspection that bring into view his personality as well as broader epistemological questions. This tension between sensory investigation and reflection on the inherent limitations of human knowledge, which runs through the text, was captured by Seamus Heaney in an early review of Calvino's work:

> Mr. Calvino may divide and categorise in triplicate the visual, the cultural and the speculative aspects of Mr. Palomar's world, he may prompt and tag and analyse and juxtapose to his (and our) heart's content, but Mr. Palomar himself remains wonderfully spontaneous and receptive to the pell-mell of the senses. (Heaney 1985)

The constant back-and-forths between the sensuous world and the protagonist's ruminations create a markedly slow place, which invites readers to perceive reality through Mr Palomar's eyes and even compensate for the shortcomings of his attention.

Kingdom by Jon McNaught is a graphic novel focusing on a seaside vacation shared by a mother and her two children, a daughter and an older boy in his teenage years. The basic elements of the plot are rather unremarkable: the family drives to 'Kingdom Fields' (a fictional seaside resort in England) and gets settled in a cottage overlooking the sea. While mother and daughter go on a hike along the beach and later visit a great-aunt who lives nearby, the boy mostly stays inside, playing video games and sulking over the lack of phone signal. Later during the vacation, he meets another boy of roughly his age, with whom he starts exploring the surroundings. Against this quotidian backdrop McNaught explores the embedding of the characters' lives in a rich texture of natural forms – a theme that is grafted onto the plot via the family's visit to the local natural history museum. Stylistically,

McNaught's panels alternate two dominant colours (blue and red), which are juxtaposed on the page in ways that create deep resonances and rhythms: for instance, two pages where blue serves as the main colour are followed by two red-based pages, and then by pages where the two colours are deployed jointly. The effect of these rhythms, as we'll see, is to stretch out time in a way that works analogously to the descriptive and introspective passages in Calvino's narrative. McNaught's colour shifts have the function of focusing the reader's attention on subtle patterns and variations in the material world that surrounds the characters. This approach, I will argue, slows down the pace of the narrative (and, potentially, of the reading experience) while foregrounding nonhuman materiality, but it uses the resources of visual narrative instead of Calvino's verbal strategies.

Instead of examining each of these texts individually, I will place them side by side in order to highlight the stylistic and narratological features that define slow narrative and enable it to foster perceptual attunement to the nonhuman in both print fiction and comics. These features are: a low overall level of tellability; a narrative frame in which human characters display a sense of detachment from the social world, an emotional state that readers are invited to adopt and complement as they make up for the characters' lapses in attention; a slow rhythm (or pacing) of narrative sequence that underscores the characters' emotional detachment; the use of nonhuman viewpoints that complicate the inherent anthropocentrism of narrative practices; the evocation of multiple scalar levels; and, finally, the exploration of formal patterns, and especially patterns that trouble the human–nonhuman divide. In the following sections I will bring these features into focus one by one, with examples from both Calvino's and McNaught's work.

Low Tellability

Scholars of narrative define tellability as the interest of a story within a particular communicative context (see Baroni 2013). Tellability can be distinguished from narrativity (that is, the minimal conditions whereby a text qualifies as a narrative), because a text can have a narrative form without scoring high on tellability. As Marie-Laure Ryan writes, tellability 'is a quality that makes stories inherently worth telling, independently of their textualisation. It contrasts with narrativity, a property found in all texts interpretable as stories, whether they elicit a "so what" or a "wow" reaction' (2005: 589). Drawing on Jerome Bruner's (1991) seminal work, David Herman offers an account of tellability as a deviation from expectations concerning what normally happens in a given situation: narrative, Herman writes, 'is a cognitive and communicative strategy for navigating the gap, in everyday experience, between what was expected and what actually takes place' (2009: 20). The more salient this gap is, the higher the tellability of the resulting story; for instance (to riff on Bennett's anecdote), a story in which I find a magic necklace over a sewer grate is typically more tellable than a story in which I find there a dead rat and a discarded work glove. Slow narrative tends to display low tellability, shifting the emphasis from the inherent interest of what happens to a more static, descriptive imagination of a storyworld.[3]

Calvino's *Mr Palomar* captures the titular character in a variety of situations that fail to build much narrative momentum, either internally or across the book: in the opening section ('Reading a Wave'), we see Mr Palomar on the beach struggling to understand the intrinsic structure of waves as they advance and break on the shore. Three dense pages dissect the waves as well as Mr Palomar's state of mind without a single external happening interfering with the character's ruminations. Even when human interactions are involved (for instance, in 'The Naked Bosom' or 'The Cheese Museum'), they hardly depart from what can be expected in these situations. Likewise, the plot of *Kingdom*, as seen above, fits comfortably within the schema of a seaside vacation: there is no turning point in the story, no event that stands out because of its unexpected or dramatic nature. This effect is reinforced through intermedial references to high-tellability genres such as the science fiction film that the characters watch in their vacation home. The inherent eventfulness of this narrative throws into sharp relief the lack of overt action in the characters' own lives.

Thus, both narratives deliberately maintain tellability at a minimum level, creating a 'flat' emotional landscape in which no overall arc of suspense comes into view in the reading experience. This strategy evokes intimacy with the characters' everyday lives, but also disrupts a goal-oriented way of reading ('what is going to happen next?'), fostering instead a sense of meditative distance from the subject matter. Put otherwise, the low tellability frees up attentional resources that willing readers can invest elsewhere, particularly on the formal qualities of the narrative presentation.

Emotional Distance and Readers' Engagements with Characters

The low tellability of slow narratives is accompanied by the foregrounding of characters who appear disconnected from the world of everyday intersubjectivity. Prototypical instances of narrative, as scholars in both narrative theory and cognitive psychology have demonstrated, are fundamentally bound up with social interaction: 'stories model and abstract the human social world', write two psychologists, Raymond Mar and Keith Oatley (2008: 173). Just as they dispense with intrinsically tellable plot lines, both *Mr Palomar* and *Kingdom* put pressure on narrative's bias towards intricate social situations by focusing on characters who shy away from sociality. Their characters – more specifically, Mr Palomar and the boy in *Kingdom* – foreground modes of attention that are alternative to those of everyday interaction and call for a readjustment in readers' own engagement with the text.

In Calvino's work, intersubjective interactions are limited and mostly go awry (such as in Mr Palomar's encounters with a topless beachgoer in 'The Naked Bosom' or with a snappish store employee in 'The Cheese Museum'). Instead, the text turns inward, adopting an introspective method that follows closely Mr Palomar's emotional and cognitive states, so that all social exchanges appear distant and muffled by the protagonist's mental life. In 'The Blackbird's Whistle', for instance, we see Mr Palomar marvelling at the complexity of birdsong: 'he concentrates on distinguishing . . . one song from another, grouping them into categories of increasing complexity: punctiform chirps; two-note trills (one note long, one short); brief vibrato whistling; gurgles, little cascades of notes that pour down, spin out, then stop; overlapping twirls of modulation; and so on, to extended warbling' (1985: 20–1). Freed from social pressures, Mr Palomar can become absorbed in concentration – in this case, of the extravagant materiality of birdsong (rendered, in both Calvino's Italian and William Weaver's translation, through onomatopoeias such as 'chirps', 'trills', 'gurgles').[4] At the same time, Mr Palomar expresses frustration at his inability to recognise the calls of different bird species, with the blackbird as the only exception. This observation triggers a meditation on the uniquely human-like quality of the blackbirds' calls and interactions: 'but is human dialogue really any different?' (1985: 22), wonders Mr Palomar. A rare exchange between Mr and Mrs Palomar follows, but the protagonist's thoughts on blackbird social life still linger between the lines, offering an incongruous and humorous template through which to view human intersubjectivity (and, in this particular case, an instance of marital indifference and misunderstanding).

However, Palomar's contemplative efforts are not always successful. Throughout the book, the narrator keeps pointing out how his ego, impatience and perfectionism tend to get in the way of a truly detached attitude. Already on the first page, we read that Mr Palomar 'is not contemplating, because for contemplation you need the right temperament, the right mood, and the right combination of exterior circumstances; and though Mr. Palomar has nothing against contemplation in principle, none of these three conditions applies to him' (1985: 3). If *Mr Palomar* calls for a reading strategy that foregrounds perceptual attunement to the nonhuman, it is not via complete identification with the protagonist but rather by learning from his mistakes – by finding, in the act of reading and through the narrator's guidance, the emotional distance that Mr Palomar struggles to find in himself. The stylistic form of Calvino's work – such as the onomatopoeias or the parallelism between blackbirds and humans – is crucial in allowing readers to share the protagonist's focused attention while embracing emotional detachment more fully than he does.

Kingdom tells the story of three characters, with part of the narrative bifurcating into two storylines: one follows mother and daughter, the other focuses on the boy. A sense of emotional distance emerges in the latter plot strand via the boy's estrangement from his family; but teenage alienation is not the same as genuine detachment. Just as in *Mr Palomar*, but far more pronouncedly, readers are asked to make up for the character's shortcomings. Initially, the boy's self-imposed isolation is signalled by his addiction to video games. In an exchange early on in the graphic novel, the boy refuses his mother's invitation to leave the house, hardly looking away from the screen. The suggestion here, and throughout the first part of the graphic novel, is that the boy's seemingly exclusive interest in digital media obstructs his appreciation of the beauty of his material surroundings.

Yet the character's attentional skills change gradually in the course of the story, partly through a budding friendship with a local boy. Later on, as he explores the beach, we see him climbing up and down a sand dune in a sequence of eight small panels, with a larger interposed panel showing the boy standing in front of an expansive seascape, his gaze and body fully level with the horizon (see Figure 2.1). Encountered in this way, the natural scenery attenuates the character's alienation (as expressed through his addiction to digital technologies), allowing him to take a more balanced stance towards reality. The character's trajectory thus suggests the intrinsic value of the training of perception to align with the textural richness of the nonhuman world. This is the movement that readers themselves are asked to perform as they distance themselves from expectations of high tellability and become attuned to McNaught's formalised exploration of the natural world. The relationship between the readers and the character is thus fundamentally complex, partly diverging but also gradually overlapping as the boy overcomes his initial indifference to the natural world.

SLOW NARRATIVE AND THE PERCEPTION OF MATERIAL FORMS 57

Figure 2.1 The boy learns to appreciate the forms of the natural world in *Kingdom* (McNaught 2018). © 2019 Nobrow and Jon McNaught.

Narrative Rhythm and Slow Temporality

Narrative, like music, has an inherent rhythmicity deriving from strategies of formal segmentation that can modulate the perceived pace of the story. Structuralist narratology has tended to analyse rhythm as an ideal 'ratio' of story time (that is, the reconstructed events and actions that make up a narrative) to discourse time (the textual presentation of those events and actions; see Genette 1980: 93–5): for instance, discourse can suddenly accelerate in what Genette calls a 'summary' (where numerous events are recounted in a limited space) or come to a standstill in what Genette calls a descriptive 'pause'. More recent work in post-classical narratology has tended to conceptualise rhythm more broadly, to discuss the inscription of temporal patterns in the reader's embodied experience

(Caracciolo 2014) or to denote the formal qualities of narrative that disrupt 'the "classic" balance of fast and slow' (Baetens and Hume 2006: 354) – that is, the average pace at which narrative is culturally expected to operate. From the latter perspective, slow narrative performs an implicit critique of fast-paced, action-oriented narratives in mainstream film and television. Both my case studies exploit the deceleration or suspension of narrative time to bring out the textural qualities of matter – the sensory patterns that suggest the vitality of the nonhuman world but tend to fall through the cracks of everyday perception.

In *Mr Palomar*, perception is slowed down and defamiliarised by the character's introspective verbosity. In the first section, 'Reading a Wave', for instance, Mr Palomar is intent on the observation of a single wave. In itself, the advance and dissolution of a wave takes no more than a few seconds: 'Mr. Palomar sees a wave rise in the distance, grow, approach, change form and color, fold over itself, break, vanish, and flow again' (1985: 3). But as soon as the wave breaks, Mr Palomar is reminded of the difficulty of fixating on a *single* wave – how the abstract concept of wave does not capture the empirical reality in which waves are part of a system and can never be isolated from a chain of physical events. This consideration gives rise to a *second* description of a wave, which takes into account the material convolutions of the foam on top of the wave ('there is time for the foam to fold over upon itself and vanish again, as if swallowed, and at the same moment invade the whole'; 1985: 4) as well as the configuration of the wave's front. Here time *almost* approximates a descriptive pause but retains a minimum level of narrativity in that the formation of a wave is a temporally developing event, however cyclically repeated. The rhythm inherent in the wave's temporality is complicated, and further diluted, by the rhythmicity of Mr Palomar's own disjointed meditations: his frequent changes of descriptive tack (such as, in this section, the second account of the wave) create a cadence of their own, which feeds into the perceived slowness of the narrative. Thus, Mr Palomar's analytic mindset deautomatises the perception (as Shklovsky would put it) of the wave-form: what he sees – and what we, as readers, can imagine – is a slow-motion account of the wave that emphasises its textural (formal and material) complexity.[5]

Further, for Mr Palomar, the sensory patterns of the material world are not a mere human projection, but the physical trace of a perceptual encounter in which things take on an active role. In a later chapter ('The Meditations of Mr. Palomar'), the protagonist performs a series of experiments with the suspension of attention, exposing himself to what the text characterises as the gaze of things: 'now it is not he who is looking; it is the world of outside that is looking outside' (1985: 102). The act of waiting for a 'summons' originating in the 'mute distance of things' (1985: 102) finally brings narrative temporality to a halt, in that Mr Palomar's observations no longer have an empirical target – not even a visual pattern like the wave: instead, what comes to the fore in an unadulterated form is the abstract 'thing-power' that normally *underlies* sensory configurations in the material world. This is what the narrative suggests through rhythmic variations – decelerations and philosophical pauses – that draw attention to the perceptual entanglement (the intra-action, in Karen Barad's terminology; see Barad 2007) of human subjectivity and nonhuman entities.

Instead of Mr Palomar's introspective moves, *Kingdom* uses the rhythmic possibilities of panel layout and colour scheme (the already mentioned blue vs. red contrast) to slow down narrative time.[6] In Figure 2.2,

Figure 2.2 Rhythmic visual patterns in *Kingdom* (McNaught 2018). © 2019 Nobrow and Jon McNaught.

for example, the family is driving through heavy rain, and a series of disparate images (a footbridge, a horse grazing by an electricity pylon, and so on) convey the fragmentation of the perceptual world. Each panel has its own visual orientation, with the diagonal shape of the footbridge echoing the car seats in the first row, and the third row juxtaposing the circular motion of the windshield wiper with the diagonal motion of the rain drops. Visual shapes are broken down and stylised in a way that creates a number of descriptive pockets in the already slow-paced narrative of the family's seaside vacation. The result is a sense of continuously suspended progression: to make their way through the graphic novel, readers are asked to adjust the temporality of the reading experience to nonhuman rhythms uncoupled from human society. This slow rhythmicity contrasts sharply with the frantic temporality of the boy's video game, in which a few clicks are sufficient to kill an animal and harvest it for resources in the space of two panels.

The onomatopoeic attribution of sounds to the nonhuman world also contributes to slowing down the reading of the panels. McNaught's panels visualise a variety of sounds originating in the animal or material world: car engines, bird calls, a humming radio, a dog barking inside a car – all these acoustic prompts are given their own speech bubbles, as if animals and even objects spoke in their individual languages. These sounds reproduced on the page encourage the reader to 'perform' the panels instead of merely taking them in visually, thus causing a deceleration in the interlinked rhythms of the narrative and of the reading experience. Through these verbal and visual strategies, McNaught's narrative conveys the inherent rhythmicity of nonhuman things, and how that rhythm – embodied in visual patterns – can disrupt the anthropocentrism of narrative progression, sending the graphic novel in directions that are as tangential to the family's vacation as they are sensuously vibrant.

Nonhuman Viewpoints

We have already seen that both Calvino and McNaught foreground nonhuman entities in their narratives: Mr Palomar is intrigued by bird calls and reflects on the inherent 'summons' of things, while McNaught's onomatopoeic speech bubbles suggest that the sounds produced by cars and other objects are a form of language. These are not isolated examples, but strategies employed consistently by both authors to destabilise the human subject and question the metaphysical primacy of the human – the view, central to Western culture, that human societies are both intrinsically distinct from and superior to the nonhuman world. By presenting nonhuman entities as autonomous from human subjectivity, *Mr Palomar* and *Kingdom* pursue an imaginative project that is, fundamentally, anti-anthropocentric: the object of the reader's attention is the material world as it appears once it is uncoupled from human subjectivity.

In 'The Sword of the Sun', for instance, Mr Palomar is swimming in the sea when he sees on the surface of the water a sword-shaped reflection 'stretching from the shore to him' (1985: 11). The reflection, produced by the setting sun, prompts a meditation on how 'this is happening not on the sea, not in the sun ... but inside my head, in the circuits between eyes and brain' (1985: 12). But this position, which front-loads the human (perceived reality being merely the product of the human sensory apparatus), is quickly discarded by Mr Palomar. Through one of the changes of meditative tack that (as seen above) take on rhythmic qualities in Calvino's book, the protagonist points to the fuel slick left behind by a motorboat as evidence that external reality cannot be a mere human projection: 'material consistency can be doubted in the glint of the sun, but not in this trace of the physical presence of man, who scatters excess fuel in his wake, detritus of combustion, residues that cannot be assimilated, mixing and multiplying the life and death around him' (1985: 14). It is the materiality of humankind's impact on the environment that disrupts Mr Palomar's reverie and questions the anthropocentric assumptions that underlie it. The next step in Mr Palomar's meditation is the paradoxical thought of the reflection forming, on the surface of the water, before there were any eyes (human or nonhuman) to perceive it: 'for millions of centuries the sun's rays rested on the water' (1985: 16). Finally, the endpoint of this line of reasoning is the contemplation of the world without humans – a radically nonhuman viewpoint that Calvino's signature humour juxtaposes, in the chapter's last sentence, with an extremely quotidian gesture: 'He has become convinced that the sword will exist even without him: finally he dries himself with a soft towel and goes home' (1985: 16).[7] Noteworthy in this chapter is that Mr Palomar's engagement with a nonhuman viewpoint is mediated by a metaphor – the sun's reflection as a 'sword' – that builds on a physical artefact and thus offers further proof of what Mr Palomar elsewhere characterises as the 'summons' of nonhuman things.

A page from *Kingdom* (see Figure 2.3) serves as a striking companion piece to Mr Palomar's encounter with the setting sun. The four panels in the central column show the sun dipping into the horizon, with the colour scheme (blue–red–red–blue) rhythmically accompanying the

Figure 2.3 Stages of the sunset, with nonhuman observers, in *Kingdom* (McNaught 2018). © 2019 Nobrow and Jon McNaught.

sun's downward movement. Despite the sense of visual continuity created by the sun's gradual motion, we realise on a closer look that the seascape is subtly different in each panel (involving, respectively, cliffs, a field, a fence, houses). We are thus denied a unified perspective on the sunset. The spatial fragmentation created by this unobtrusive device undermines the assumption of a coherent viewpoint mediating the scene. This effect is greatly enhanced by the eight panels that flank the sunset on either side: nonhuman animals (gulls, a sheep, and so on) and objects (toys, a house) are tidily aligned and oriented towards the setting sun, as if they were observing it. Ironically, the only humans present in the panels are facing *away* from the spectacle of the sunset, obliviously watching TV in their house – a device that again highlights the limitations of human attention when coupled with modern technologies.[8] The effect of this sophisticated compositional strategy is to uncouple the sunset from human subjectivity: instead, animals and things are endowed with a viewpoint that suggests a form of *nonhuman* subjectivity. This challenge reaches the reader of the graphic novel, who will initially assume an overlap between his or her spatial position and that of an implied human observer on the scene – but then is encouraged to discard this assumption when faced with the multiplication of nonhuman perspectives. Like Calvino's sword, but in visual terms, the mental state that McNaught's narrative aims to foster is one of calm contemplation of a world in which humans are a minor, and largely irrelevant, detail.

Scalar Shifts

Scale has become a core concept in ecocritical discussions engaging with the Anthropocene and the impact of human activities on the planet (Woods 2014; Clark 2015). The scale of the nonhuman world either overwhelms us – in the experience of the sublime (Hitt 1999) – or completely eludes us when facing phenomena (such as climate change) whose magnitude and spatio-temporal ramifications far transcend everyday experience. As Woods highlights, scalar shifts are at their most valuable when they expose *discontinuities* between levels of reality, through what Woods calls 'scale variance': how a large number of individual actions, in themselves seemingly harmless (such as driving a car to work), can have dramatic implications on a large scale (such as climate change via the release of carbon dioxide). In Woods's own words, 'scale variance means that the observation and the operation of systems are subject to different constraints at different scales due to real discontinuities' (2014: 133). Both Calvino's and McNaught's narratives deploy scalar strategies that highlight scale variance in order to evoke a sense of contemplative distance from human society and individual subjectivity. In a section entitled 'The Sand Garden', Mr Palomar is visiting the famous Zen garden of the Ryoanji temple in Kyoto; surrounded by a throng of tourists, he transfigures the garden into an allegory of the relationship between the Earth and the human crowds inhabiting it:

> He sees the human race in the era of great numbers, which extends in a crowd, leveled but still made up of distinct individualities like the sea of grains of sand that submerges the surface of the world. . . . He sees that the world, nevertheless, continues to turn the boulder-backs of its nature indifferent to the fate of mankind, its hard substance that cannot be reduced to human assimilation. . . . He sees the forms in which the assembled human sand tends to arrange itself along lines of movement, patterns that combine regularity and fluidity like the rectilinear or circular tracks of a rake. . . . (Calvino 1985: 85, ellipses in the original)

The allegory works by scaling 'up' the physical space of the Zen garden (with its carefully arranged rocks and sand) to the level of the entire planet: the grains of sand are the planet's growing population, the rocks stand for the nonhuman environments that remain unassimilable to humankind (with echoes of Mr Palomar's interest in a world devoid of humans). From this allegorical distance – and herein lies the scale variance – the grains of sand lose agency and subjectivity, they are mere numerical units within a pattern that *downplays* human action. By contrast, the normally inert nonhuman world is both foregrounded in its obstinate materiality ('its hard substance') and seen as a quasi-agent turning its rugged back on humankind. At scale, humankind and the nonhuman world swap places: the former loses its signature free will, the latter appears to act deliberately (via its indifference to humans). Through this and similar shifts in spatial and temporal perspective, Calvino uses scale variance to defamiliarise a worldview that frontloads human subjectivity.

Kingdom uses the visual resources of the comics medium to a similar effect. Large-scale temporality is implicated, thematically, via the characters' visit to a natural history museum, while the zooming in and out of the spatial perspective presents a world in which human characters are either too large or too small to be fully visible. Perhaps the most striking instance of scale variance is offered by the last two pages of the graphic novel (see Figure 2.4). The family is driving home after their vacation on the coast, and in three large panels – much larger than most in the graphic novel – the perspective pulls back from the protagonist's

Figure 2.4 Scale and loss of human individuality on the last pages of *Kingdom* (McNaught 2018). © 2019 Nobrow and Jon McNaught.

car so that it becomes indistinguishable in the stream of near-identical vehicles traveling up and down the highway. No human figure is visible on the page, only the sinuous shape of the highway, darkening fields, and white and red dots from numerous light sources (the cars, the lamps along the road, a distant city). These dots of light, along with the cars' uniform procession, serve a function analogous to the grains of sand in the passage from *Mr Palomar*: they level human individuality, creating affective distance that is particularly salient in this final scene, after readers have had the chance to develop an emotional connection to the family. Each of these cars enfolded by the night, the ending suggests, contains identities and life stories comparable to those of the graphic novel's protagonists. The scale variance comes as an emotional wrench from the unit of the family that had given coherence to the narrative so far: at this scalar level their individuality ceases to matter, only the regular, material patterning of their collective behaviour remains perceptible.

Foregrounding of Formal Patterns

Experimenting with scale is only one of the techniques employed by Calvino and McNaught to bring out the material patterning of reality.

Patterns emerge, repeatedly, whenever the characters hone their attentional skills and learn to experience their surroundings in new ways. Imagining a city from the perspective of a bird in flight, Mr Palomar envisions a complex assemblage of forms: 'The true form of the city is in this rise and fall of roofs, old tiles and new, curved and flat, slender or squat chimneys, arbors of reed matting and sheds of corrugated iron' (1985: 49). The description continues for another page, rendering the thick material texture of the city seen from above, each object with its own implied shape: the curved ruggedness of the roof tiles, the straight lines of the chimneys, and so on. But the same formal imagination can be trained on the nonhuman world; observing a flock of birds, Mr Palomar describes 'a circular shape, like a sphere, a bubble, the balloon-speech of someone who is thinking of a sky full of birds' (1985: 58). As the 'balloon-speech' metaphor suggests, the formal imagination expands from human thinking and its representation in culture (speech bubbles in comics) to the animal kingdom (the bird) to the organisation of the social world (the city seen from above). Finally, form embraces the cosmos as well, for instance when the protagonist marvels at 'the exact geometry of the sidereal spaces' (1985: 41). This multiplicity of abstract forms allows Mr Palomar and, potentially, the book's readers to extricate themselves from the world of human emotions while at the same time reducing the divide between human subjectivity and nonhuman materiality. *Kingdom* similarly brims with forms, as the examples I've discussed so far have no doubt demonstrated: through the patterning of rain drops, the motion of windshield wipers, or the shape of a highway, form encompasses and bridges the scalar divides between human and nonhuman phenomena.

It is perhaps not too far-fetched to compare the superimposition of forms in both Calvino's and McNaught's works to the role of mandalas in certain Buddhist meditation practices. A mandala is a highly symmetrical, diagrammatic (and thus formalised) representation of the universe that serves as an aid to deep meditation (Brauen 1997). Likewise, but in secular terms, the formal imagination fostered by Calvino and McNaught brings out the interrelatedness of reality in a way that, if my reading is correct, promises to focus readers' attention, pushing back against anthropocentric assumptions and defusing the anxieties of the quotidian. Formalism and New Materialism are not opposed in this imaginative project, because the abstraction of form originates in the rich textures and patterns of the nonhuman world, which are skilfully evoked by Calvino and McNaught through verbal and visual strategies.

Conclusion

This chapter has explored the ways in which narrative can resonate with modes of attention focusing on the materiality of the nonhuman world. With the aid of narrative-theoretical concepts such as tellability, rhythm and focalisation, I have identified six features of slow narrative that encourage this kind of nonhuman-focused readership in literature and comics; similar features could be found in media such as film as well as video games: *Le quattro volte*, a 2010 film directed by Michelangelo Frammartino, and *Everything*, a 2017 game developed by David OReilly, come to mind (see, respectively, Caracciolo forthcoming and Caracciolo 2020). Slow narrative can, of course, be used for other purposes than attuning the audience's imagination to nonhuman materiality, but it seems particularly well positioned to advance a New Materialist agenda. By probing materiality, slow narrative also foregrounds formal patterns, as we've seen. In this way, New Materialism and the New Formalism advocated, among others, by Caroline Levine (2015), converge. The latter approach argues that form is conceptual structure at work in both literary texts and the social world (for instance, through hierarchical or network-like social organisations). In my reading of Calvino and McNaught, I have extended New Formalist models from social to human–nonhuman relations: whether verbally or visually realised, textual form becomes the locus of an inscription of nonhuman materiality that challenges traditional notions of anthropocentric agency. The abstraction inherent in the concept of form does not push away from materiality; on the contrary, it trains readers' sensitivities and enables willing audiences to reach a state of attention fully attuned to the nonhuman. Material form thus becomes a pathway for suspending – defamiliarising – anthropocentric modes of perception and confronting the efficacy and vitality of the nonhuman world. In this respect, it seems to me that the formal analysis of artworks (as made possible in this chapter by the tools of narrative theory) has a great deal to offer to the New Materialist project.

Notes

1. This chapter is based on research funded by the European Research Council (ERC) under the European Union's Horizon 2020 research and innovation programme (grant agreement no. 714166).
2. I build here on Ridvan Askin's astute reading of Shklovsky's essay: 'From a posthumanist perspective, what is interesting in this conception of literature is that Shklovsky presents literature as the very *human* means of going *beyond the human*' (2016: 172).

3. See also Dan Irving's (2017) insightful discussion of 'slow TV' where, however, Irving frames the analysis in terms of 'weak narrativity' instead of 'low tellability', as I do here.
4. Respectively, 'trilli', 'zirli' and 'chioccolii' in Italian (Calvino 2016: 22–3).
5. 'Texture' is, of course, a metaphor that foregrounds the domain of touch, and in fact in Calvino's book vision is frequently destabilised and slowed down by haptic patterns. See also Algirdas-Julien Greimas's reading of 'The Naked Bosom' in *De l'imperfection*: for Greimas, Calvino's narrative reveals that aesthetic 'appreciation is of a tactile, not cognitive, order' (Greimas 1987: 31, my translation). I would like to thank Marlene Marcussen for drawing my attention to Greimas's reading of *Mr Palomar*.
6. In his discussion of time in comics, Kai Mikkonen points out that 'in visual narratives, such as films and comics, the rhythmic formula of *stretch* seems to be one of the basic rhythmic variations. . . . cartoonists have various graphic and spatial techniques at their disposal to slow down discourse-time considerably' (2017: 54).
7. For more on the narrative imagination of the world without humans, see Garrard (2012).
8. This device is thus reminiscent of what Ann Banfield (1987) calls an 'empty deictic center' text – a scene captured in the absence of human observers, where the deictic centre, the spatio-temporal position from which the description originates, is left vacant. In McNaught's rendering of the sunset, the deictic centre is not empty but occupied by an assemblage of nonhuman entities.

References

Abram, David (1997), *The Spell of the Sensuous: Perception and Language in a More-Than-Human World*, New York: Vintage.
Askin, Ridvan (2016), 'Objects', in Bruce Clarke and Manuela Rossini (eds), *The Cambridge Companion to Literature and the Posthuman*, Cambridge: Cambridge University Press, pp. 170–81.
Baetens, Jan and Kathryn Hume (2006), 'Speed, rhythm, movement: a dialogue on K. Hume's article "Narrative speed"', *Narrative*, 14: 3, pp. 349–55.
Banfield, Ann (1987), 'Describing the unobserved: events grouped around an empty centre', in Nigel Fabb, Colin MacCabe, Derek Attridge and Alan Durant (eds), *The Linguistics of Writing: Arguments Between Language and Literature*, Manchester: Manchester University Press, pp. 265–85.
Barad, Karen (2007), *Meeting the Universe Halfway: Quantum Physics and the Entanglement of Matter and Meaning*, Durham, NC: Duke University Press.
Baroni, Raphaël (2013), 'Tellability', in *The Living Handbook of Narratology*, Hamburg: Hamburg University Press. www.lhn.uni-hamburg.de/article/tellability (last accessed 19 March 2019).

Bennett, Jane (2010), *Vibrant Matter: A Political Ecology of Things*, Durham, NC: Duke University Press.
Brauen, Martin (1997), *The Mandala: Sacred Circle in Tibetan Buddhism*, Boston, MA: Shambala.
Bruner, Jerome (1991), 'The narrative construction of reality', *Critical Inquiry*, 18, pp. 1–21.
Calvino, Italo (1985 [1983]), *Mr. Palomar*, trans. William Weaver, Orlando, FL: Harcourt.
Calvino, Italo (2016), *Il signor Palomar*, Milan: Mondadori.
Caracciolo, Marco (2014), 'Tell-tale rhythms: embodiment and narrative discourse', *Storyworlds*, 6: 2, pp. 49–73.
Caracciolo, Marco (2020), 'Immersion for entangled audiences: the nonhuman world and affective patterning in narrative experiences', *Kinephanos*, March. https://www.kinephanos.ca/2020/entangled-audiences/ (last accessed 23 June 2020).
Caracciolo, Marco (forthcoming), 'Everything dances: the Gesamtkunstwerk and the nonhuman in digital media', in Massimo Fusillo and Marina Grishakova (eds), *The Gesamtkunstwerk: A Synthesis of Arts*, New York: Peter Lang.
Clark, Timothy (2015), *Ecocriticism on the Edge: The Anthropocene as a Threshold Concept*, London: Bloomsbury.
Dolphijn, Rick and Iris van der Tuin (eds) (2012), *New Materialism: Interviews & Cartographies*, Ann Arbor: Open Humanities Press. http://hdl.handle.net/2027/spo.11515701.0001.001 (last accessed 19 March 2019).
Flanagan, Matthew (2008), 'Towards an aesthetic of slow in contemporary cinema', *16:9: Danmarks Klogeste Filmtidsskrift*, 6: 29. www.16-9.dk/2008-11/side11_inenglish.htm (last accessed 19 March 2019).
Garrard, Greg (2012), 'Worlds without us: some types of disanthropy', *SubStance*, 41: 1, pp. 40–60.
Genette, Gérard (1980), *Narrative Discourse: An Essay in Method*, trans. J. E. Lewin, Ithaca, NY: Cornell University Press.
Goatly, Andrew (1996), 'Green grammar and grammatical metaphor, or language and the myth of power, or metaphors we die by', *Journal of Pragmatics*, 25: 4, pp. 537–60.
Greimas, Algirdas-Julien (1987), *De l'imperfection*, Périgeux: Pierre Fanlac.
Hayles, N. Katherine (2007), 'Hyper and deep attention: the generational divide in cognitive modes', *Profession*, pp. 187–99.
Heaney, Seamus (1985), 'The sensual philosopher', *New York Times*, 29 September 1985. www.nytimes.com/1985/09/29/books/the-sensual-philosopher.html (last accessed 19 March 2019).
Herman, David (2009), *Basic Elements of Narrative*, Chichester: Wiley Blackwell.
Hitt, Christopher (1999), 'Toward an ecological sublime', *New Literary History*, 30: 3, pp. 603–23.

Irving, Dan (2017), 'Eighteen hours of salmon: on the narrativity of slow TV', *Frontiers of Narrative Studies*, 3: 2, pp. 238–55.

Jaffe, Ira (2014), *Slow Movies: Countering the Cinema of Action*, London: Wallflower Press.

Johnson, Susan C. (2000), 'The recognition of mentalistic agents in infancy', *Trends in Cognitive Sciences*, 4: 1, pp. 22–8.

Koepnick, Lutz (2017), *The Long Take: Art Cinema and the Wondrous*, Minneapolis: University of Minnesota Press.

Levine, Caroline (2015), *Forms: Whole, Rhythm, Hierarchy, Network*, Princeton, NJ: Princeton University Press.

Levinson, Marjorie (2007), 'What is new formalism?', *PMLA*, 122: 2, pp. 558–69.

Mar, Raymond A. and Keith Oatley (2008), 'The function of fiction is the abstraction and simulation of social experience', *Perspectives on Psychological Science*, 3: 3, pp. 173–92.

McNaught, Jon (2018), *Kingdom*, London: Nobrow.

Mikkonen, Kai (2017), *The Narratology of Comic Art*, New York: Routledge.

Ryan, Marie-Laure (2005), 'Tellability', in David Herman, Manfred Jahn and Marie-Laure Ryan (eds), *Routledge Encyclopedia of Narrative Theory*, London: Routledge, pp. 589–91.

Shklovsky, Viktor (1965), 'Art as technique', in Lee T. Lemon and Marion J. Reis (eds), *Russian Formalist Criticism: Four Essays*, Lincoln: University of Nebraska Press, pp. 3–24.

Woods, Derek (2014), 'Scale critique for the Anthropocene', *Minnesota Review*, 83, pp. 133–42.

II

Object Intrusions in Subject-Centric Texts

CHAPTER 3

Aisthetic Realities in Ayi Kwei Armah's *The Beautyful Ones Are Not Yet Born*: A Matter-Oriented Reading of Postcolonial Literature

Sten Pultz Moslund

Ayi Kwei Armah's *The Beautyful Ones Are Not Yet Born* (1968) is a classic in African literature. The novel describes a newly independent Ghana in the 1960s as a society challenged by tremendous power inequities, corruption and poverty. A story of massive decay – socially, culturally, morally, politically, environmentally – the novel grimly depicts a precarious reality of squalor, shit and rot, heaps of waste, and a desperate self-destructive race for scraps as the consequence of a global capitalist world order (all of it dishearteningly familiar today, fifty years on). Following the colonial regime, the newly liberated country appears powerless against the brutal conditions that rule the fag end of world inequality. Not only are the forces of global capitalism strong and faceless, they also inscribe themselves locally as an unquestioned obsession with modern commodities – even among the poor, the greatest victims of the economic reality they have been caused to share: 'expensive things.... all that white man's food, the beautiful long rice in the packet with the Afro-American Uncle Ben smiling on it, the tinned cake which had traveled thousands of miles from rich people's countries', 'nothing else mattered', the governing aim in life is 'the getting of these comfortable things' (Armah [1968] 1988: 114–15, 151). Everything is experienced from the perspective of a government official – anonymously referred to as 'the man' – who struggles to create a decent and respectable life without participating in the bribery and the political, moral and cultural corruption that surrounds him, even if this choice gains him nothing but social isolation.

The Beautyful Ones Are Not Yet Born is obviously a highly political novel, critically depicting individual and collective experiences of the new nation, imperial legacy and new capitalist consumer values. Historically, it falls in line with novels of disillusionment like Chinua Achebe's *A Man of the People* (1966) and Ngũgĩ wa Thiong'o's *Petals of Blood* (1977) as a generation of African literature that responded to the rise of new corrupt regimes that would soon hollow out the social and democratic promise of national independence. In light of the momentum in the novel of such historical concerns, the radical realisms offered by the current theorisations of matter and more-than-human ontologies may seem a bad fit at a first glance.[1] The latter theorise not the empowerment but the dissolution of the subject and subjective agency; not the primacy of national politics and interhuman relations, but a decentralisation of the human and human-led history – and, when it comes to art, they often appear to be concerned with the deeper philosophical implications of form and aesthetics, more than overtly political or discursive signification. Graham Harman, for instance, is interested in 'mind independent' realism and a reality that is not 'converted into thought' and he sees the literary text as something that 'runs deeper than any coherent meaning' and does not 'use up the reality of things' (2012: 186), and Jane Bennett speaks of 'thing-power' and giving expression to something in language that is 'radically free from representation' (2010: 4). Yet, in each their separate ways, theories like Object-Oriented Ontology and New Materialism are already deeply involved in the political. Directly and indirectly, they uncover political implications embedded in anthropocentricism, in human interactions with the nonhuman world and, in that regard, the politics of subjective and collective ascriptions of meaning to things and phenomena.[2]

One way in which political concerns in Armah's novel and the concerns of new matter and object-oriented theories may be said to cross, accordingly, is in the analysis of how the matter world is turned into socially powerful abstractions – in Armah's case, how capitalist abstractions in particular come to dominate and shape human reality. Armah's novel quite evidently dramatises reality as governed by anonymous capitalist forces of commodification. In terms of Bill Brown's Marx-inspired Thing Theory, it dramatises a 'socialisation of the psyche' through the 'fetishisation of the sign-value of things' (2003: 48); specifically, how human perception of collective reality is colonised by consumer value ascriptions and how, in fact, such value ascriptions superimpose themselves on the individual subject's bodily senses – or the 'corporeal imagination' (Brown 2001: 9), by which things and matter are apprehended.[3] The corporeal imagination observed by Armah's man allows no object any reality of its own. Everything that is sought after by the characters around him is sought after for its attraction as an object of consumption or possession, an object of profitable value and social power. The human – and political – consequence, as depicted by Armah, is a radical impoverishment of the imagination and an equally impoverished human relation with reality and fellow humans – an impoverishment that, at its worst, thrives on crude, yet powerful, emotions of greed and selfishness while excluding or eclipsing any genuine concern for (human and nonhuman) others, let alone any concern for future generations or deeper questions of life and existence.

Unsurprisingly, Armah's novel is frequently read as a Marxist novel and the man as a Marxist hero (see for instance Lazarus 1987). Yet it is also now and then pointed out that Marxist readings do not exhaust all of the novel's potential. Some readers see the story as delving deeply into existential explorations of the human condition and the open futurority of the novel's poetic title as reaching further than any programmatic reading would allow – often dismally so, as when Kofi Anyidoho relates the novel to Frantz Fanon's 'zone of nonbeing' (1992: 34) and Neil Lazarus reads it as calling up 'the bleakness of the material universe' (1987: 138). More recently (and less cynically), Hugh O'Connell notes a 'weak-utopian' impulse in the novel in a reading that draws on Adorno's notion of 'non-identity' and Derrida's 'messianicity' to show how Armah uses the possibility of 'difference itself' to disrupt hegemonies of 'what is' and their 'strictures of teleology and history' (O'Connell 2011: 371–80). Adding such paths of enquiry to the ontological mutability that the novel already implicates with its critique of capitalist abstractions of the matter world, an analysis that reads for more-than-human modes of reality may offer surprising insights into what a literary work like Armah's can do as a deep reflection of human social, existential and material conditions.

As for the exploration of human relations with more-than-human realities in post-anthropocentric theory, my own emphasis is on the sensuous – or *aisthetic* – dimensions of literature; that is, the sense-aesthetic appearances of reality in the work.[4] Inspired by Jacques Rancière (among others), I look at the novel's 'distributions of the sensible', ranging from its reiterations of sociopolitical distributions of sensible reality to creative redistributions. Whenever the sensuous is distributed by governing sociopolitical ideas of the real (ideas that orchestrate our very perception of things), things appear in the story's world as perceived through specific meaning investments (for example, trees may appear or be perceived by characters as objects of economic value). Yet, literature often works to cause phenomena and events to appear in multiple ways, for instance as perceived by different psychological/subjective perspectives or through diverse cultural or political ways of cutting up the real, but also, it will be argued, in ways in which the sensible is no longer entirely governed by specific meaning-invested pretexts (subjective, cultural, political). In the latter mode, objects or the matter world come to appear in ways that do not lend themselves readily to semantic interpretation or allow themselves to be rationally or discursively explained. Rancière speaks of a mode of appearance like that as a de-organisation of the usual regimes that parcel out the visible, the audible, the touchable by 'the heterogeneous powers of the sensible' (see 2000: 28, 82, 39).

The analysis of Armah will propose 'heterogeneous' disruptions of usual distributions of the sensible as one way of tracing the nonhuman agency of matter in the story's depiction of reality. In order to do so, however, we need to supplement our analytical sensitivity to the semantic performance of language (typically pursued by examining what a particular word or image means or symbolises) with a sensitivity to the sense-aesthetic (aisthetic) performance of language: a reading that notes how the matter world appears in the work as events of bodily sensation. The proposed reading will look at how the novel's sensible, or aesthetic, dimension is charged by meaning-invested pretexts, but also by other distributions of the sensible: by sensuous heterogeneities or de-semanticising intensities of sensation that are not laid to rest by a specific human meaning-ascription (whether psychologically, politically, economically or culturally).[5]

Armah's novel is striking in its attentiveness to the sensuous experience of reality. Events and phenomena come to appear in the novel through the entire synaesthetic register of the sensuous apparatus – the touch of things by fingers and bodies, sensations of warmth, light, colour, taste, sounds and smells of matter. A matter-oriented reading that tunes in to such sensuous qualities – reading the novel as an *aisthetic* work of art – may show the novel's instantiations of reality to appear not only historico-politically, but also in ways less controlled by human intention and agency. My notion of an aisthetic reading in this way connects with New Materialist endeavours to think in terms of an 'intercorporeity' (Chiew) between pre-personal bodily experience and the flesh of the world as well as their interest in an autonomous complexity in human perception that reaches deeper than the body's translation of reality as governed by subjective and sociocultural categories (see Chiew, Coole and Bennett in Introduction). As I intend to show, the minds and the bodies of characters – their entire being-in-the-world – may come to appear as shaped not only by forces of sociopolitical design, but also by nonhuman forces, such as the impersonal agency of biological micro-organisms in smelled matter, the feel of sunlight on the body and the wordless noise of waves hitting sand on the beach. Or, to put it differently, suprasensuous ideas and discourses (nation, imperial ideology, consumer values) shape and form concrete reality in the novel, including the characters' sensuous perception and experience of reality, but they do not use up all of the novel's reality (to paraphrase Harman). A surplus of reality emerges in the novel's aisthetic dimensions in light of which its dramatisation of sociopolitical and economic forces come to form only one appearance of the sensuous which is ultimately shown to be embedded within a more-than-human making of the real. The surplus reality exhibits the bleak indifference of a 'material universe' (Lazarus), a universe of bacterial rot and decomposition, but it also clears a space for a 'weak utopia' (O'Connell) in the novel – although, as we shall see, a matter-oriented reading will differ somewhat from O'Connell's conclusions.

Simultaneous Modes of Reality in *The Beautyful Ones Are Not Yet Born*

In the established postcolonial frame of reading, Armah's novel is primarily understood from within a very specific politico-historical horizon of interpretation: as a disillusioned response to the failed promise of a new independent national government. This is one side to Armah's novel, a hugely important side, and, obviously, quite central to the novel's immediate historical motivation. Yet, the novel's general reception is also excessively moulded by allegorical readings – somewhat confirming Fredric Jameson's provocative essay that 'third world' literature only reads as allegories of the nation (Jameson 1986: 69). This goes for the notable role of sensuous perceptions of matter in the novel, too. Characteristically, Kolawole Ogungbesan writes that '[t]he deliberate sensuosity of [Armah's] style has no aesthetic value in itself; its values lie in the subtle means by which sensuous details become symbols' (quoted in Lazarus 1987: 159). Likewise, Derek Wright reads the novel as a narrative 'absorbed into and engulfed by metaphor' (1989: 210). It strives to perform an 'absorption of incident into image' or a 'passing of fact into figure' with the result of a total 'dominance of metaphoric reality' – all the many 'rotten things' in the novel, all of its descriptions of waste, piss and excrement, are but 'totalising' metaphors for a political condition (Wright 1989: 211). To be sure, allegorisations and metaphorisations remain effective frames for interpreting Armah's novel. As will be shown, the novel's narrative habitually invites allegorising readings of the world it describes and all the phenomena in it. Yet, from a matter-oriented perspective, readings of the novel as macro-historical allegory, when on their own, are lacking in explanatory power when it comes to the material and bodily complexity and thickness of the reality produced by the novel's sensuous language. The novel's production of reality as perceived matter – the taste of salty air, the feel of sun and heat waves, smells of shit and sweat – is simply too marked, too remarkable, for us to restrict our reading of the novel's language to that of a disembodied sociopolitical commentary or isolate its importance as a work of art exclusively to the history and metaphysics of the postcolonial nation. Far from having 'no aesthetic value in itself', the 'sensuosity' of Armah's novel actuates a rich and complex aisthesis that beckons readings of the economic and the political as both interlaced with and exceeded by a material fullness of life and nonhuman reality.

If we shift from an exclusively allegorical and metaphorical analysis to an *aisthetic* reading of Armah's language, something happens. The novel's characters and its setting and all of the things that appear in it become at least as phenomenally, or sensuously, performative in their creation of the novel's realism as they are symbolically performative in relation to specific sociopolitical and historical intentions. The language in Armah's novel regains a sensuous intensity that, along with its metaphorical quality, activates several simultaneous modes of reality, or ontologies, which ultimately clears the way for the important point in the novel that the sociopolitical present (whatever it may look like) is but one part of the real, with only a limited range of existence and only a limited share in the possible.

To illustrate these various performances of language and the reality modes they produce, I would like to revisit a powerful description of a particular object in the novel, a banister, that has always caught the attention of Armah's critics. At the beginning of the story Armah's man is on his way to work, mounting a flight of stairs inside 'the Block', a massive, murky, yellow-brown colonial building that hosts the Railway & Harbour Administration:

> The touch of the banister on the balls of his fingertips had something uncomfortably organic about it. A weak bulb hung over the whole staircase suspended on some thin, invisible thread. By its light it was barely possible to see the banister, and the sight was like that of a very long piece of diseased skin. The banister had originally been a wooden one, and to this time it was still possible to see, in the deepest of the cracks between the swellings of other matter. . . . And there were many cracks, though most of them did not reach all the way down to the wood

underneath. They were no longer sharp . . . but all rounded out and smoothed, consumed by some soft, gentle process of decay. In places the wood seemed to have been painted over, but that must have been long ago indeed. . . . It would be impossible to calculate how much polish on how many rags the wood on the stair banister had seen. . . . The wood underneath would win and win till the end of time. . . . [I]t was in the nature of the wood to rot with age. The polish . . . would catch the rot. . . . in the end it was the rot which imprisoned everything in its effortless embrace. It did not really have to fight. Being was enough. In the natural course of things it would always take the newness of the different kinds of polish and the vaunted cleansing power of the chemicals in them, and it would convert all to victorious filth, awaiting yet more polish again and again and again. And the wood was not alone. Apart from the wood itself there were, of course, people themselves . . . so many hands and fingers bringing help to the wood in its course toward putrefaction. Left-hand fingers in their careless journey from a hasty anus sliding all the way up the banister as their owners made the return trip from the lavatory . . . Right-hand fingers still dripping with the after-piss and the stale sweat from fat crotches. The calloused palms of messengers after they had blown their clogged noses reaching for a convenient place to leave the well-rubbed moisture. Afternoon hands not entirely licked clean of palm soup and remnants of *kenkey*. The wood would always win. (1988 [1968]: 11–13)

The common allegorical interpretations of this particular scene read the banister's paint and polish as a symbolic representation of how the continuation of colonial structures of power and the corruption and ineptitude of the country's new leaders show through cracks in surface images of independence. The man's frequent reflections on the national leadership's betrayal of the promises of liberation support such readings: 'No difference at all between the white men and their apes', all 'new men' being greedy, selfish and oppressive 'like the old' (Armah 1988: 89).

However, if we insist that the appearance of things and phenomena in the novel are to be read allegorically only, as semantic signs with a very specific sociopolitical frame of reference, we will fail to appreciate how the novel, as a complex work of art, strives to exercise a wider range of intention than the forthright communication of a particular politico-historical point.[6] Distributed within an aesthetic form, the novel's representation of reality is capable of more than dramatising a certain discourse through metaphorisations and allegorisations of things and events. It is capable of situating its historical context and political discourse in a fullness of reality that is made of sociopolitical organisations of reality *and more* – a fullness of reality that, in the end, both harbours and exceeds any particular sociopolitical or economic organisation of reality. Discursive organisations of the real are part of the man's world of thought and they mostly determine his sensuous and bodily interaction with the world, but not all of it: even if the dominant part, sociocultural organisations of the body's interpretation of reality are only part of the man's being-in-the-world and only part of how the novel causes reality to appear. Consider a brief passage like this one:

> Out ahead . . . the tracks drove straight in clean shiny lines and the air above the steel shook with the power of the sun until all the afternoon things seen through the air seemed fluid. . . . (Armah 1988: 22)

Clearly, this is not a 'metaphoric' passage where all fact and incident are absorbed into image or symbolic figure. A metaphorically oriented reading typically skips over such descriptive details, not really noting them in the first place or else banalising them as background 'fillers' that serve merely to give a sense of realism. Yet in an aisthetic reading, a non-semantic *excess* of reality is at work here that shows how human activity (the man) is immersed in and emerges from within a reality produced by an intermixture of a human shaping of matter (tracks, straight, steel) with nonhuman agencies (sun, light, dust, heat), all of it sensuously bending and waving in the watery shimmer of bodily registered heat waves. More than metaphor, the passage appears to rely on the sensuous dimensions of words. Such dimensions are translatable to semantic meaning (that is, subjective and sociocultural categories through which the sensible is sensed), but they are also capable of pushing the effects of words further than that; into the non-semantic signification where words escape their reduction by sociocultural translation. Deleuze calls them the 'sense-effects' of words, which work in other ways than the 'meaning-effects' of words. When words metamorphose into their sense-effects, he says, they cease to 'speak "of" things' and enter into a mode of performance 'on the same level as states of things', where 'signs and concepts vanish, and things begin to write by themselves and for themselves' (Deleuze 1997 [1993]: 159, 150). Brought forth by the sense-effects of words, objects in the passage no longer appear as passive objects entirely determined by human purpose. They appear as de-semanticised sensuous intensities that exceed (or exist side by side with) specific sociocultural intentions and meaning-investments. Or to put it in another way, nonhuman phenomena (sun, light, heat, steel) are shown to be co-productive of the novel's reality in ways that ultimately withdraw from finite human intentions and meaning investments – what, ultimately, is the semantic meaning of bodily sensations of heat waves and shimmering sharp light?

Returning to the example of the banister with a reading that does not begin and end in allegory but taps into the aisthetic emergence of reality in the novel, the man's bodily sensations of matter still produce a series of (seemingly half-conscious) associative connections between physical decay and a corrupt government: the tangibly drab, decaying interior of the government building and the filth from hands trigger loose associations – and flesh out a lived experience – of the new regime's attempts to conceal its corrupt continuation of colonial structures under new and burnished surfaces. But at the same time the man's sensations of matter are also very much exactly that: sensations of *matter* – bodily sensations of impersonal physical phenomena independent of the signification of their socioeconomic and historical context. On this level of the text, fingertips on the banister, the dim light, colours and smells, the tactile sensations of minute swellings and smoothed cracks emerge as mute sensations of a bodily being-in-the world that ultimately resists metaphorisation beyond the appearance of the sensations themselves ('mute' in the sense that the body–matter relation ultimately withdraws from being translated into a semantically explicable articulation). Language in the passage comes to perform a series of pre-semantic sense-effects, or non-semantic bodily sensations; words pass into sensuous intensities: sensations of the smoothness of 'smooth' or the faintly damp sensations of moisture (from bodily fluids) and the soft, slightly sticky and rubbery sensation of layers of greasy matter. Rather than a semantic or conceptual *wording* of the world, the sensuous fullness of the room fills up the language, as if a sensuous *worlding* of words. As in the previous examples, language in this way reproduces the body's sensation of immersion in a material human and more-than-human reality. Yet, the excess of uninterpreted (unmetaphorised) sense-effects do not replace the other performance of language in the man's consciousness. The man's half-expressed, half-conscious political associations happen along with and through the bodily sensations of matter. It is only that the latter also have a muted *other* existence in excess to the former.

In addition to the subjective and sociopolitical organisation of the sensible that an allegorical reading may help along, a matter-oriented reading will see a description like that of the banister as important for the way in which it simultaneously intimates an impersonal mode of reality that does not necessarily work to confirm any particular social organisation of the real. As the passage already expresses itself, this deeper mode of reality is not mastered by human subjectivity or a rational, free, intentional and self-moving consciousness. Rather, the appearance of matter at a certain level ceases to translate as metaphor for a human–human reality; it emerges instead as so many 'existents in excess of their association with human meanings, habits and projects' (Bennett 2010: 4). Swellings of matter, cracks, well-rubbed moisture, wood and rot, stale sweat, after-piss, sharpnesses, roundnesses and smoothnesses come to appear (within the sensuous) as self-moving 'non-subjects' (Bennett) in their own right, whose agencies relocate the human ontologically and epistemologically. The scene – and the diverse semantic and sensuous performances of language in the scene – embeds the history of human agency in a much larger history of nonhuman forces, which the man – like humanity – is integrated with and affected by through his own bodily matter-being (ultimately 'imprisoned' in the 'effortless embrace' of its 'being'). This is not a history that conforms to human reality constructions, or human distributions and redistributions of the sensible. Regardless of human intention, the matter of 'victorious filth', wood and rot continue their effortless 'course toward putrefaction'; on and on, the nonhuman distribution of matter will 'win and win' – which altogether rings in tune with Lazarus's reading of the novel as exposing 'the bleakness of the material universe'.

To make a brief summing-up, we may now speak of at least two simultaneous ontologies, or modes of interaction between consciousness, body and the thing world – brought about in and by the language in the banister scene when read aisthetically: one, a viscous, sensuous and affective appearance of a physical reality conditioned by an interhuman and macro-historical state of affairs (such as the lived and sensed experience of reality as shaped by (neo)imperial structures of power, corruption and neglect); and two, the sensuous appearance of a deeper and silently working nonhuman conditioning of human reality (a biological matter-reality with a life and force of its own that operates quite independently from human-centred histories and sociopolitical constructions and shapings of the real). Both levels run along each other throughout the novel.

As indicated, the second mode seems to constitute a persistent challenge to human reality constructions which are revealed to depend on constant maintenance to prevent them from being changed or eroded by the self-moving forces of nonhuman matter (natural matter and the forces of rot will 'win and win till the end of time'). Yet, as the story unfolds, the most immediate destructive force in the novel turns out not to be the nonhuman life of matter as it exists in absolute indifference to the human, but the indifference to life effected by sociopolitical organisations of reality and economic abstractions that translate all of material reality into resources for capital accumulation and overconsumption. In this respect most readings rightly ascribe the novel's pessimism to its depiction of unrestrained capitalism as a rapacious and hegemonic mechanism that results in destructive mounds of waste and life-negating interhuman relations.

Hegemonic Organisations and Creative Redistributions of the Sensible

For good reason, *The Beautyful Ones Are Not Yet Born* is mostly read as a deeply 'misanthropic vision', a 'novel of disillusion' and 'hopeless despair' (Onwueme 1990: 71). At its core it dramatises the consequences of a raw capitalist organisation of the real as they are actualised most strongly in the non-Western world where the contrasts between the few who profit from inequality and the masses who do not are most extreme, most immediate and most apparent. The novel's sensuous thickness fleshes out how, materially and violently, the health and security enjoyed and maintained by one social group thrive on the deepening precarity of others. While the beneficiaries of the system, like the cabinet minister Koomson and his wife, enjoy a 'clean life' and avoid stepping into the street from their cars, 'as if contact was a well-known calamity', the distribution of bodies and matter among the masses materialises (among other things) as a nauseating sensation of putrid and bacteria-infested air. Literally living in the waste of the consumer economy, the bodies of the poor become part of the decomposition process. Rotting smells hit the senses 'like a strong wall' and 'the stench claws inward to the throat', which explains why people spit so much: 'all around decaying things push inward and mix all the body's juices with the taste of rot' (Armah 1988: 40). Armah's narrative in this way causes impersonal capitalist distributions of power to emerge viscously within an unbroken continuum of matter and humans as a force that alternately creates, shapes, shelters and destroys human bodies and minds and the environment they inhabit.

Describing how filth begins to 'cake together' among the 'many walking dead' with '[s]o many desperate needs' (1988: 22, 35, 36), the novel dramatises how, in Henri Lefebvre's bitter formulation, the power of capital 'constructs and erects itself on a contempt for life. . . . Which does not cease to amaze: that a society, a *civilisation*, a culture is able to construct itself from such disdain' (Lefebvre 2004 [1992]: 51–2). The material consequences of unrestrained capitalism emerge in the novel not only as an immediate social, bodily and environmental disaster, but as an imaginative and existential disaster too. Despite the fact that it is so obviously destroying humans, interhumans and the environing world, all but a few of Armah's characters have come to relate to life and reality entirely in terms of economic gain. 'Money was life' (1988: 77), sounds the triumphant and definitive abstraction of existence and reality (a sentence that becomes ever more outrageous and terrifying the deeper you contemplate it). Visiting Koomson, the man is overwhelmed by the extravagance of a home filled with the intricate and shiny light that 'glinted off every object in the room' – objects 'that must have come from foreign lands' (1988: 146). He reflects on the general social effect the glitter has; specifically, the power of such shiny things to direct the sociopsychological response of the appellated beholder: 'There were things here to attract the beholding eye and make it accept the power of their owner. Things of intricate and obviously expensive design. . . . that forced the admiration of even the unwilling' (1988: 144).

'[T]he object's unquestioned importance stabilises the structure of meaning', says Bill Brown (2003: 41). Accordingly, if everyone relates to the same thing in the same way – the same objectification of the matter world – the thing-turned-object becomes a silently working apparatus that sustains a hegemonic sociocultural reality, defining what the nature of the world is, the hierarchies of beings and how life is to be lived. As a work of art, however, Armah's novel has in its nature a capacity to interrupt and destabilise hegemonic ideas and organisations of the real. The man's observations and perceptions of physical decay, sick bodies and his exhibition of unseen and unquestioned structures of meaning work in themselves as such interruptions. Through the man's critical gaze, inequality and extreme limitations of agency and life possibilities are exposed in the novel as caused not by a cultural or individual failure to fulfil the capitalist promise (as a capitalist logic would have it), but as the very *causes* of the capitalist organisation of the real. Less than misanthropic, then, the gap between the man's (re)perception of things and the socially habitualised 'corporeal imagination' around him in itself draws the contour of residual potentialities. Correspondingly, the common reception of Armah's novel as a novel of misanthropic hopelessness is interrupted now and again by readings that note other energies in the work – especially with reference to the future promise in the title's 'not yet'. Lazarus reads the work as a dialectic between 'degraded reality' and 'affirmative vision' and while it postulates 'the bleakness of the material universe', the man's 'denial of gleam' is also 'creative' (1987: 157). Similarly, O'Connell locates an 'ephemeral quality of hope' emanating from what he refers to as the novel's 'weak-utopian' impulse (2011: 375).

Inspired by Derrida, O'Connell defines 'weak utopia' as 'a desire for difference that is not immediately calculable, definitive nor eschatological in the fullest sense, as are the traditional ideals of Utopianism' (2011: 375). Stripped of the proposition of any ideological alternative to the present, 'weak utopianism' works as a 'placeholder for that which is the not here and not now' (O'Connell 2011: 378). The 'not yet' is then an obvious manifestation of 'weak utopianism' in Armah's novel, pointing to 'that which is other to the present' and, in its openness, 'unknowable to the teleological, western developmental discourse of history wrapped in the promise of the bourgeois nationalists' (O'Connell 2011: 379). The novel's title projects 'a Being-for-others' directed away from the present to the 'not yet born' (O'Connell 2011: 380).

The dislodgment of identity by difference is crucial in O'Connell's notion of the 'weak-utopian': 'it is neither a fidelity to what is, nor what is assuredly to come through an operation of identity, but instead . . . a faith in and solidarity with the possibility of difference itself' (2011: 380). The challenge to identity and the 'strictures of teleology and history' (2011: 380) by the release of a greater power of difference, or otherness, rings in tune with some of the core concerns in New Materialist and object-oriented theories. Yet, in demonstrating how a 'weak utopianism' is actualised in the novel's narrative, O'Connell still points to the 'not yet' as an alternative vision for the nation and the nation's future: the novel privileges 'the anonymity of the national collectivity and the openness and incompletability of the nation' (2011: 381). O'Connell, and other critics, are not wrong to say that national visions are incorporated into the novel. Armah's man is concerned with current problems and the future in light of the nation. Yet, it may also be argued that there is hardly anything non-ideological or non-teleological about the idea of the nation, just as a nation-thinking is hardly possible that surrenders identity-thinking. In correspondence with the several simultaneous modes of reality that the novel may be shown to enact in an aisthetic reading, the 'weak utopianism' of the 'not yet born' – and O'Connell's powerful phrase that the novel refuses 'to withdraw entirely from life and possibility' (2011: 375) – may come to matter in another way, with far deeper than national repercussions. It is not in its attention to the nation but, paradoxically, in its attention to a nonhuman matter-reality that the novel invites 'weakly utopian' and radically different ways of thinking the surrender of identity and teleology to forces of difference.

The Novel's 'Weak Utopia' as a Radical De-organisation of the Sensible

In several passages in the novel, forces of radical difference, or otherness, are expressly and lavishly released to flood the man's consciousness and the narrative perspective, which causes reality to emerge as a profoundly heterogeneous and de-organised event of matter and sensation. One example is a (recurrent) situation that depicts the man, alone on the beach, as bodily immersed in a world moved by the impersonal powers of sea, sun and sand:

> I looked at the sea flowing toward and over the sand, and I no longer saw dead water hitting in senseless waves of noise. The water and the sand were alive for me then; the water coming in long, slow movements stretching back into ages so very long ago . . . , though in our dead moments we do not have eyes to see any of this. Sounds, the mild thunder of the night waves hitting calmer water and the sigh of retreating afterwaves. (1988: 72)

> The man felt something get out from him, from the endings of the nerves and the fingertips, from every part of his body, sinking into the sand. He closed his eyes again and lost himself in the dark pink shadows within. . . . Waves, furling at the edges, came all the way and broke into little pieces each right on top of the last. (1988: 181)

As in the banister scene, the power of the nonhuman and its indifference to human existence is strong in these passages. The man's sensations stimulate a de-anthropocentricising imagination of how phenomena 'stretch back' into an amorphous and depersonalised temporality outside human time (the ocean), like the prevailing wood and rot on the handrail. The stretch of the imagination into the nonhuman shifts in the last sentence in both passages to a disappearing of references to the human altogether ('night waves hitting calmer water and the sigh of retreating afterwaves' and waves breaking 'into little pieces each right on top of the last'). Reading the passages aisthetically, they both set out from the man's perception and imaginative mediation of the matter world (sun, water, sand) only to finally trail off into a submergence of individual consciousness (the man 'lost himself') below a sensuous surfacing in the text of nonhuman matter-agencies: the sounds and movements of waves in the last sentences (zooming out from the narrative focalisation on the man) are organised by no clear human-centred intention, reason or purpose. To borrow Ranicère's succinct way of putting it, the passages give expression to 'a greater, heterogeneous form of the sensible, or the idea that there is a zone of the sensible that distinguishes itself from the ordinary laws of the sensible universe, and testifies to the presence of another power' (2004: 10). Or in Brian Massumi's formulation, reality this way (the impersonal perspective in the final sentences) comes to emerge as a de-semanticised event emptied of 'all content other than its own occurrence' (2011: 151) – emptied of specific subjective, social or symbolic ascriptions of meaning and human purpose.

Owing to the loose and increasingly depersonalised quality of the perceived phenomena (emerging in the space left by the vanishing subject), a more-than-human matter world comes into view quite strongly. It comes into view not as passive background or setting, but as a phenomenal world of matter that is fundamentally co-productive of the novel's sensate realities, of human realities, and the man's deeper being-in-the-world. The novel in this way exploits its literary form to the fullest, if we follow a speculative realist like Steven Shaviro. It calls forth the existence of things (like sand and waves) as primarily *aesthetic*: in the sense that they cannot be finally 'cognized, or subordinated to concepts . . . they cannot be utilized, or normatively regulated or defined according to rules' (Shaviro 2014: 53). Generating no other content than an open, impersonal and heterogeneous assemblage of sensations, the aesthetic (I would say *aisthetic*) occurrence of body, sun, sand, sound, light, colours and waves causes a matter-reality to appear as an event 'deeper than any coherent meaning' (Harman 2012: 200): a human–reality relation in the process of withdrawing from human-centred intention, reason and purpose (at least as the latter manifest themselves in the novel as ideological organisations of reality).

All of this connects very powerfully with the 'weak utopian' impulse in the novel's future address. To Shaviro, the appearance of reality as a fundamentally 'aesthetic event' is an appearance of reality as something that 'does not belong to the already-said' or any 'previously-agreed-upon horizon'; to Massumi, the event that is emptied of all content other than its own occurrence constitutes 'a perpetual state of nascency'; and in terms of Rosi Braidotti's 'politics of "life itself"', a disappearance of the anthropocentric subject 'encourages a renewed sense of the human not as the ground from which a narratable life proceeds, but as a temporary production of the material flow of life itself' (Shaviro 2011: n.p.; Massumi 2011: 145; Braidotti 2010: 41). We are back at O'Connell's notion that the novel refuses 'to withdraw entirely from life and possibility', but now with an epistemological and ontological sweep that redirects the ethical address from a principal concern with the nation to include the human condition as such and its planetary future.

When its character's mind and body are read as entering into an assemblage with a more-than-human matter-reality (through the impersonal aisthesis emerging in the narrative shift to zero focalisation), Armah's novel may be said to collapse the false divide between the human and the more-than-human forces of life. Life emerges as that 'other power' Rancière refers to. Such forces of life may work against human sustenance, and the imagination of human sustenance as in the banister scene. Yet, in passages like the above (as in the novel's title) the imagination of the human as entwined with nonhuman forces of life emerges as a contradiction not to human life as such but to ego-centred subjectivity. Here the novel comes to affirm life itself as a force 'without a me at the centre', without the sovereign of a human 'I' or ego (Braidotti 2010: 212). What the novel allows to be perpetually born in causing the appearance of reality as an aisthetic event is the prospect not of a different national future, but of life as *difference itself* (a non-identity, a not-me, not-mine, not-ours, not-now). Reality in this mode appears as an 'other power' of possibility that outdoes 'the already said'; that is, the distribution of the sensible by identitarian politics and self-justifications whether they manifest themselves as (neo)imperialism, nationalism, or late capitalist paradigms of perpetual economic growth and consumption. The novel does not offer any redeeming or unifying vision, however. All its instantiations of diverse reality modes will never come together in a harmonious problem-solving and non-contradicting totality. Yet, when divested of identitarian possessiveness, life – or the condition of possibility – comes to belong not to the present but to the future. The reason for living comes to be defined not by self-seeking commands and demands in the present, but by an imagination shaped by a concern for those who are not yet born – which is 'a perfectly gratuitous gesture', in Braidotti's expression, insofar as 'posterity per definition cannot pay us back' (2010: 217).

Conclusion

What conclusions may be drawn from a fusion of Armah's novel with recent post-anthropocentric theorisations of matter and more-than-human realities? The suggestion in this chapter is that the latter expand the aesthetic, or aisthetic, potentiality of the work and deepen the operation of its historical, political, epistemological and ontological dimensions. *The Beautyful Ones* addresses the history of the postcolonial state, legacies of imperialist ideology, capitalism, waste and inequality on a local and global scale, and combines it all with a more than that. In an aisthetic frame of reading, the novel significantly, and quite stunningly, immerses human history in the forces of life itself – in a fullness of life constituted by human and more-than-human realities – with the consequence that political and socioeconomic questions and problems emerge along with (and on the same level as) existential, epistemological and ontological complexities. The world in Armah's novel comes to appear as sensuous experiences of matter and events through which the consciousness of a character like the man (thoughts, emotions, sensations and perceptions) gets to shift between subjective, collective, depersonalised and even de-anthropocentisised productions of reality. From within the aisthetic depths of the work and its language, life emerges as an impersonal force of otherness. It unconceals and enacts the presence of a power in shaping human reality (and futuority) other than (yet simultaneous and partially entwined with) the power of sociocultural, political and economic value-investments.

Notes

1. Post-anthropocentric theory has been received with a great deal of scepticism in postcolonial studies by, for example, Paul Gilroy – among other things for how an intellectual relativisation of the human may obscure or even desensitise the (continued) history of colonial dehumanisations (see Gilroy 2018: 3–5, 7, 10–11) – but post-anthropocentric theory is also already moving into the field. Mark Jackson's edited volume, *Coloniality, Ontology and the Question of the Posthuman* (2018), is one of the first book-length attempts to explore the common ground of the two theoretical strands and how they may enrich each other, notably in decentring the 'Eurocentric model of human exceptionalism' that has also limited 'the rational human . . . to a northern European character', not by reclaiming this powerful human figure for all humans, but by disclaiming the entire 'nature–culture distinction' it builds on (2018: 25, 27–8). For other reflections on the significance of postcolonial studies to post-anthropocentric theory, see Stacy Alaimo's *Exposed* (2016: 23–6 and 72–3) and Sten Moslund's 'Postcolonialism, the Anthropocene, and New Nonhuman Theory: A Postanthropocentric Reading of *Robinson Crusoe*' (forthcoming).
2. It is not the intention of this chapter to account for the similarities and differences between various strands of post-anthropocentric theory. Rather, from a very general point, I want to try out the various ways in which new theorisations of matter and nonhuman agencies may open a text in new ways, especially (and to be explained) as they may combine with an exploration of the sense-aesthetic, or *aisthetic*, potentialities of the story's representation of reality. For similarities and differences between New Materialism and OOO see Introduction.
3. New Materialists like Diana Coole, Samantha Frost and Jane Bennett view Marxist historical materialism as a forerunner to New Materialism. Marx studied the social and historical abstraction of matter and how the unassailably natural was in fact social and historical constructions (Coole and Frost 2010: 26), but historical materialism fell short of turning its

focus on matter as such, or the 'thingly power' of matter. It would concentrate only on 'human power-laden socioeconomic structures' (Bennett 2010: xiii, 129n). Somewhere in between historical materialism and New Materialism, Bill Brown's Thing Theory adds to the study of historical, cultural, aesthetic and political objectifications of things by also considering how things may prove unwilling to abandon the unruly (and secret) thingness of their physicality (Brown 2003: 29). In Harman's OOO perspective, Marxist materialism sorts under the various forms of 'social constructionisms' (or 'overmining', as he terms it) that are, in fact, and paradoxically, anti-materialist insofar as their explanations of everything as a sociopolitical construction deny the independent existence of individual objects (Harman 2016: 199).
4. Like other kinds of art, literature produces and invites experiences of *beauty* in the conventional sense of 'aesthetic', but, as I explore in more depth elsewhere, literature (like all art) is also *aisthetic*. *Aisthēsis*, the Greek root of the word 'aesthetic', refers not to categories of beauty but to that which is produced by *bodily feeling* or *sensory* experience. Accordingly, when exploring *aisthetic* dimensions in literature, I am (in my use of the term) exploring the ways in which the work causes reality to appear as it is experienced by the body; that is, reality as it emerges as sensations of smell, taste, touch, sight, sound and bodily movement (see Moslund 2015).
5. According to Morton, 'all kinds of nonhumans are already involved in the existence of a poem' (2014: 271). Morton means this quite literally, referring to the paper the text is written on, the wood the paper is made of, and so on. I expand on the observation, however, to include representations of nonhumans at the intratextual level, such as the ultimately more-than-human reality of the setting and bodies of characters: eventually, sunlight, dirt and water are all nonhuman phenomena that fill up settings, perceptions and consciousnesses in the work – even if the characters and the narrative perspective are aware of perceived objects only in the form of subjective or sociocultural interpretations.
6. On the other hand, a reading that does not pay attention to the novel's allegorical strategies and its overt address to a political and historical context would equally detract from the novel's complexity.

References

Achebe, Chinua (1966), *A Man of the People*, London: Heinemann.
Alaimo, Stacy (2016), *Exposed. Environmental Politics and Pleasures in Posthuman Times*, Minneapolis: University of Minnesota Press.
Anyidoho, Kofi (1992), 'Literature and African identity: the example of Ayi Kwei Armah', in Derek Wright (ed.), *Critical Perspectives on Ayi Kwei Armah*, Washington, DC: Three Continental Press, pp. 34–47.

Armah, Ayi Kwei (1988 [1968]), *The Beautyful Ones Are Not Yet Born*, London: Heinemann.
Bennett, Jane (2010), *Vibrant Matter: A Political Ecology of Things*, Durham, NC: Duke University Press.
Braidotti, Rosi (2010), 'The politics of "life itself" and new ways of dying', in Diana Coole and Samantha Frost (eds), *New Materialisms: Ontology, Agency, and Politics*, Durham, NC: Duke University Press, pp. 201–17.
Brown, Bill (2001), 'Thing theory', *Critical Inquiry*, 28: 1, pp. 1–22.
Brown, Bill (2003), *A Sense of Things: The Object Matter of American Literature*, Chicago: University of Chicago Press.
Coole, Diana and Samantha Frost (eds) (2010), *New Materialisms: Ontology, Agency, and Politics*, Durham, NC: Duke University Press.
Deleuze, Gilles (1997 [1993]), *Essays Critical and Clinical*, Minneapolis: University of Minnesota Press.
Gilroy, Paul (2018), '"Where every breeze speaks of courage and liberty": offshore humanism and marine xenology, or, racism and the problem of critique at sea level', *Antipode*, 50: 1, pp. 3–22.
Harman, Graham (2012), 'The well-wrought broken hammer: object-oriented literary criticism', *New Literary History*, 43: 2, pp. 183–203.
Harman, Graham (2016), *Immaterialism: Objects and Social Theory*, Cambridge, MA: Polity Press.
Jackson, Mark (ed.) (2018), *Coloniality, Ontology, and the Question of the Posthuman*, New York: Routledge.
Jameson, Fredric (1986), 'Third-world literature in the era of multinational capitalism', *Social Text*, 15, pp. 65–88.
Lazarus, Neil (1987), 'Pessimism of the intellect, optimism of the will: a reading of Ayi Kwei Armah's *The Beautyful Ones Are Not Yet Born*', *Research in African Literatures*, 18: 2, pp. 137–75.
Lefebvre, Henri (2004 [1992]), *Rhythmanalysis: Space, Time and Everyday Life*, London: Continuum.
Massumi, Brian (2011), *Semblance and Event: Activist Philosophy and the Occurrent Arts*, Cambridge, MA: MIT Press.
Morton, Timothy (2014), *Material Ecocriticism*, Bloomington: Indiana University Press.
Moslund, Sten Pultz (2015), *Literature's Sensuous Geographies: Postcolonial Matters of Place*, New York: Palgrave Macmillan.
Moslund, Sten Pultz (forthcoming), 'Postcolonialism, the Anthropocene, and new nonhuman theory: a postanthropocentric reading of *Robinson Crusoe*'.
O'Connell, Hugh Charles (2011), 'A weak utopianism of postcolonial nationalist bildung: re-reading Ayi Kwei Armah's *The Beautyful Ones Are Not Yet Born*', *Journal of Postcolonial Writing*, 48: 4, pp. 371–83.
Onwueme, Tess Akaeke (1990), 'Speaking without tongue: silence and self-search in Armah's *The Beautyful Ones Are Not Yet Born*', *Ufahamu: A Journal of African Studies*, 18: 1, pp. 71–81.

Rancière, Jacques (2000), *The Politics of Aesthetics: The Distribution of the Sensible*, London: Continuum.

Rancière, Jacques (2004), 'Is there a Deleuzian aesthetics?', *Qui Parle*, 14: 2, pp. 1–14.

Shaviro, Steven (2014), 'The universe of things', in Steven Shaviro (ed.), *The Universe of Things: On Speculative Realism*, Minneapolis: University of Minnesota Press, pp. 45–64.

Thiong'o, Ngũgĩ wa (1977), *Petals of Blood*, London: Heinemann.

Wright, Derek (1989), 'Totalitarian rhetoric: some aspects of metaphor in *The Beautyful Are Not Yet Born*', *Critique*, 30: 3, pp. 210–20.

CHAPTER 4

Sylvia Plath's 'Tulips': On the Hostile Nature of Things

Michael Karlsson Pedersen

Introduction

The closeness between life and writing in Sylvia Plath's poetry placed her, early on, within a broader movement of American poetry which was termed confessional. The critic M. L. Rosenthal was one of the first to come up with this label, which stuck to Plath for many years (see Brennan 1999: 27). He effectively states in regard to Plath's poem 'Lady Lazarus' and Robert Lowell's poem 'Skunk Hour', both 'true examples' of confessional poetry, that 'they put the speaker himself at the centre of the poem in such a way as to make his psychological vulnerability and shame an embodiment of his civilization' (Rosenthal 1970: 69). Rosenthal consequently launched a dominant mode of reading, which understands Plath's poetry as the expression of an intense subjectivity (see Brennan 1999: 27). In his study *The Confessional Poets* (1973), Robert Phillips makes this subject-centric mode of reading even clearer: 'Thus, the writing of each such poem is an ego-centered, though not an egocentric, act' (1973: 8). These early biographical and psychological readings consequently suggest that Plath's late poetry (above all the poems published in the posthumous collection *Ariel* from 1965) cast her as either a 'skilled suicide-artist' (Rosenthal 1970: 69) or a 'modern Electra' (Phillips 1973: 131). In any case, a confessional reading roots poetry in an urgent wish to express a private self and its agonies and terrors: 'The confessional poets chiefly employ the Self as sole poetic symbol' (Phillips 1973: 7–8).

If the early reception of Plath was governed by this subject-centric way of reading, there was at the same time an attempt at negating this label of confessional poetry by stressing its more thing-oriented qualities. In her brilliant article, '*Angst* and Animism in the Poetry of Sylvia Plath' (1970), Majorie Perloff definitively concludes: 'Despite its intensely personal quality, its stress on selfhood, Sylvia Plath's poetry is emphatically not, as is often argued, similar to that of Robert Lowell' (1984: 121). Instead Perloff argues that Plath's poems belong to a tradition of a 'poetry of process', whose ecstatic subject wholly identifies with the objects so that an act of 'imaginative animism' is performed (see Perloff 1984: 110). Consequently, there is no isolated subject who can observe and describe an outside object-world, but the subject itself is directly involved with objects, it becomes the objects themselves. The closest relative to Plath is then not the autobiographical mode of Lowell, but that of D. H. Lawrence, whose poems about birds and flowers are not symbolic representations, but identificatory attempts at showing 'what it is like to *be* a bat or a swan' (Perloff 1984: 111). In the end, Lawrence's ecstatic poems bear witness to 'the divine otherness of non-human life' (Perloff 1984: 111). Perloff opens up a new way of interpreting Plath's late poetry, which on the one hand breaks with the confessional-subjective mode of reading and on the other hand recognises the central status of things, animate or inanimate.

The way things come to matter for Plath is, however, of a paradoxical nature. If Perloff establishes an animistic pole in Plath's mature poetry, one where the subject identifies with the object, she also detects another pole of anxiety or *angst*, of being left alone and separated from the things of the world. It is precisely between these poles of worldly communion and solipsism that Plath's poetry can be understood and which builds its central paradox. As Perloff writes, 'at the heart of Sylvia Plath's poetry is thus that human beings are dead, inanimate, frozen, unreal, while everything that is non-human is intensely alive, vital, potent' (1984: 110). Perloff suggests that Plath sees human beings as inanimate things, a state that can only be transcended through the identification with nonhuman, but evidently vital things. I find that although Perloff indeed points out an important paradox in Plath's depiction of things, the inevitable problem with her mode of reading is the basic, but never challenged, assumption that Plath's poetry is based on a strict ontological division between thing and subject, nonhuman and human entities. Her idea of an 'imaginative animism' can also be said to repeat this subject–object schema. A new reading of things in Plath's poems must face this age-old binary head on.

I would like in this chapter to tap into this discussion of the status of things in Sylvia Plath's late poetry, which I do not read symbolically either (as if they stood for something else), but rather as things with their own ontology, a specific and autonomous state of being not governed only by human presence and mastery. Perloff makes a strong case for Plath's sensibility to nonhuman life and objects,[1] but her method of reading never transcends the metaphysical divide between subject and object, which to my mind does not do justice to Plath's poetry. Instead I would like to qualify the discussion of things by developing a more informed and therefore consequent thing-oriented reading of her poetry based on post-anthropocentric theory, whose basic interest is to challenge and ultimately get rid of the dominant view in Western philosophy that the human subject enjoys ontological supremacy in regard to other things and beings. As such, my reading of Plath is also an attempt at showing how recent ontological theories of things and matter can be a fruitful platform for analysing and understanding literature. I find here that the Heideggerian tradition of emphasising the non-relational aspects of things, which is continued and further developed in Graham Harman's Object-Oriented Ontology, is an especially productive way of opening Plath's poems. I will elaborate on this ontological theory of the thing in the next section.

One poem especially comes to mind when the role of things in Plath's poems is to be debated, and it is a poem that also Perloff has dealt with at great length (see Perloff 1975; 1984: 118–19): 'Tulips' (see Plath 2008: 160–3) was written on 18 March 1961 and posthumously published in *Ariel* (1965). The first line of the poem states its central conflict: 'The tulips are too excitable, it is winter here' (2008 [1961]: 1, 1).[2] The poem roughly divides between depictions of the winter state of the hospital room as well as of the patient (the lyrical I of the poem) and the intrusion of the tulips. Initially, the patient is recovering from an operation. This opening situation is rooted in an actual biographical experience, as Ted Hughes has explained: 'TULIPS belongs to March 1961, and records some tulips she had in the hospital where she was recovering from an appendectomy' (1970: 193). The poem's initial interest is oriented towards this postoperative state, which is dealt with through various depictions of sedate peacefulness, 'it is winter here' (2008: 1, 1). The patient virtually floats away from any commitments forced upon her from the outside world, be it husband and children or the weight of life as such. In the middle of the poem the tulips are introduced, however, which forcefully disturbs the calmness of the hospital scene and the winter state of the patient: 'The tulips are too red in the first place, they hurt me' (2008: 6, 1). Now, the patient is forced back to life, out of her death-like state. The tulips perform an intervention, which reconnects the subject with the aggressive and pulsating vitality of life.

With the mixing of the scene of the hospital and the domesticised nature of cut flowers, the poem activates different genres within Plath's late oeuvre. According to Susan Bassnett, 'Tulips' is part of Plath's hospital poems (see for instance 'In Plaster' (Plath 2008: 158–60), written on the same day as 'Tulips'), a kind of poetry that tends to belong 'more to women writers than to men, partly because the experience of childbirth is often in a hospital context but partly also because the doctor–patient relationship is a very powerful one in female mythology' (Bassnett 2005: 121). 'Tulips' also belongs to what Steven Gould Axelrod has called 'the domestic poem' (2006: 81), which Plath unfolds and explores between 1960 and 1962 – the 'third stage' of her poetry (see Axelrod 2006: 80) – and which 'have the power to shake up one's world, . . . and even enhance awareness of alterity within as well as outside the self' (Axelrod 2006: 81). The centre of the Tulips-poem is indeed built around not only a certain private subjectivity bent on confessing his or her self, but a fierce alienness inherent in the tulips. As such, although Axelrod does not connect the two, the domestic hospital-world in 'Tulips' is closely related to Plath's discovery of 'the nature poem' in the same third stage of her production, where nature appears tellingly as 'an inimical force' (Axelrod 2006: 80). Thus, the poem is a kind of splice between a domestic poem and a nature poem, where a private self is challenged by the alterity of a thing.

What Plath shows in her Tulips-poem is how a thing violently intrudes on the medicated and sedate state of the subject, a condition the subject paradoxically wishes to obtain and prolong. In other words, Plath establishes a genuine post-anthropocentric position (the tulips) within the poem, which in the form of aggression and hostility faces the subject (the patient) with full agential autonomy. It is from this position independent of the subject that Plath can deal with the central problem of a post-surgery depression: not as a psychological theme based on a solely mentalistic and non-material understanding of what it means to be human (which in effect also governs the confessional mode of reading), but rather as a relation between a material thing-world and the surely precarious state of the subject, which initiates an expansion of agency to things and finally casts a new thing-oriented definition of what human life is. Plath is in fact a poet of life, as I will argue at the end of this chapter.

The Self-Receding Nature of Things

The importance of developing an adequate concept of the thing was raised by Martin Heidegger in his seminal work *Being and Time* (1927) and later expanded upon in his lecture 'The Origin of the Work of Art' (1935–6).³ Both texts have different philosophical motivations: the first tries to develop a fundamental ontology of *Dasein*, the other an ontology of the artwork. The shift between the two texts is crucial as it marks the turn from an ontology still directed at a new concept of the human (opposing the worldlessness of the Cartesian subject, the basic mode of being for *Dasein* is *In-der-Welt-Sein* or Being-in-the-world) to an attempt at placing the thing at the centre of a new post-anthropocentric philosophy, which decentres the human and posits it as part of a wider relationality of things.⁴ I want to stress the continuity between the two texts, however, and point out how they both form the basis for the explication of three concepts of the thing in Heidegger's philosophy: the thing as practical and useable equipment (*Zeug*), as a theoretical object for scientific study or contemplation (*Objekt*) and as work or a work of art (*Werk* or *Kunstwerk*). From the perspective of *Dasein*, this trichotomy also names three modes of disclosing the world around us, which could be labelled 'everydayness', 'science' and 'aesthetics'. The first two concepts are developed in the famous tool-analysis in *Being and Time* (see §15–17), the last concept in the artwork-speech.

Through this conceptual differentiation Heidegger makes it clear that Western philosophy at large has been governed by a concept of the thing, which either reduces it to its use, thus making it transparent, or abstracts it to a passive object to be examined, measured and possibly controlled. In opposition to this anthropocentric ontology, where the thing is given importance only if it is set in relation to human activity and use, Heidegger introduces a new concept of the thing as work, which is founded on a striving (*Streit*) between earth (*Erde*) and world (*Welt*), or between a non-relational, obscure and closed materiality and an open, relational area of understanding and interpretation (see Heidegger 2001: 47). What is crucial for the work is that it can actually make the otherwise transparent materiality of the thing visible and sensible without reducing (tool) or abstracting (object) it: '*The work lets the earth be an earth*' (Heidegger 2001: 45, emphasis in the original).

The nature of the earthy aspect of the work – which really gives it its ontological radicalism and material power – is, according to Heidegger, 'selfsecluding' (Heidegger 2001: 46; 'das Sichverschließende'), that is, an evading and retreating movement away from any human action, inclusion or intervention. The worldliness of the work accordingly marks the opposite movement: its nature is 'self-opening' (Heidegger 2001: 47; 'das Sichöffnende'). The work establishes the clash between these two opposite movements: world is the prerequisite for the showing of the earth, which would otherwise reside in darkness and invisibility, just as earth is a prerequisite for making the human world material, placial and sensible. It is, however, the earthiness of the work that demonstrates an anti-anthropocentric power, which forcefully resists the possible reduction of a world bent on human understanding and instead sweeps off any attempts at human control – or, as Heidegger puts it, '[human] mastery nevertheless remains an impotence of will' (2001: 46). The Heideggerian model of earth and work discloses the thing as a material process of radical negativity, which not only is beyond human understanding and reach, but in fact shows hostility towards it.

At this point I find it instructive to explore and clarify Heidegger's ontology of the thing within the framework of contemporary post-anthropocentric theory. Although all of what is now termed either Thing Theory (Bill Brown), vital materialism (Jane Bennett) or Object-Oriented Ontology (OOO; Graham Harman and Timothy Morton) is influenced by Heidegger's early insight that the nature of a thing far exceeds any trite subject-centrism, I will focus here on the inherent inaccessibility or receding nature of the thing. As it happens, this is an important if not decisive aspect of OOO, which sets it apart from, for instance, Bennett's more relational-oriented concept of the agentic assemblage of things (see Bennett 2010: 5, 20–4).[5]

Harman – highly influenced by Heidegger's tool-analysis, to which he dedicated his first study, *Tool-Being: Heidegger and the Metaphysics of Objects* (2002) – writes most unequivocally: 'This deeply *non-relational* conception of the reality of things is the heart of object-oriented philosophy' (2012: 187). Although Harman does not use Heidegger's concept of earth (he does not put as much emphasis on the artwork-speech as he does on the tool-analysis of *Being and Time*), he could however be said to allude to it, when he refers to the non-relationality of the thing as 'its subterranean reality' (Harman 2012: 186). Heidegger's description of the 'selfsecluding' earth does effectively resonate in the following passage from Harman's Lovecraft study, *Weird Realism: Lovecraft and Philosophy* (2011), which also recounts the two other thing-concepts in Heidegger's philosophy:

> To sit in a chair does not exhaust its reality any more than visual observation of the chair ever does. Human theory and human praxis are both prone to surprises from sudden eruptions of unknown properties from the chair-being of the chair, which recedes into the darkness beyond all human access. Pushing things another step further, it must be seen that the same holds for inanimate entities, since the chair and floor distort one another no less than humans distort the chair. (Harman 2011: 15–16)

Neither the tool of practical everydayness nor the object of theoretical study can fully explain the nature of a thing. Instead a theory of the earthy-aesthetic thing (or work) must highlight how an area of obscurity and inaccessibility is always retained. Harman goes a step further than Heidegger, however, when he considers the interaction not only between humans and things, but also between things and things.

If the initial opposition between New Materialism and OOO could be founded on the highlighting of the agentic relationality of things (Bennett's assemblage) and the non-relational withdrawnness of things (Harman's subterranean reality), I find that both tend to reduce what is quite clearly balanced in Heidegger's trichotomy of work, world and earth. Rather, relationality and non-relationality, world and earth, productively determine each other in the thing, which can never be exhausted by its relations; it always retains the possibility for something else, but it also keeps making relations, binding itself to other things, human beings and spaces. Already Harman's description of the chair hints to the fact that the non-relationality of a thing is not just something that is oriented towards a passive retreat into obscurity, as if it only longed for a solitary life in a secluded cabin in the woods away from the world, but it effectively 'surprises from sudden eruptions of unknown properties'. The earthiness of the thing is its potential for surprise, for making relations that were not thought of before. Because a thing retains something outside of human control it can act so much more freely and independently, making surprising relations, as is the case with Plath's tulips. An adequate ontology of things must therefore maintain both sides: the self-receding nature of a thing is indeed already a description of its agential, material power; it is the obscure even inimical force of things, which charges its relations.

Eventually, Harman refers to a world-description as founded on his new ontology of the non-relational or receding thing as a *'weird* realism in which real individual objects resist all forms of causal or cognitive mastery' (2012: 188). This is evident, for instance, in the world of H. P. Lovecraft's horror tales which is governed by the noumenal and pre-human force of the Cthulhu-Myth (see Harman 2011: 27). Although obviously written in a completely different poetic vocabulary and tradition, Plath's late poetry – here especially the Tulips-poem – does, however, show the same sense of a thing-world that is really not human-friendly, but attests to a clash between human intentions and the will of an alien, even hostile materiality. The lure of Plath's poems is in this regard that she imports this alien thing-ontology, as depicted by Heidegger and Harman, into a private environment – her poems are 'confessional' (Rosenthal) or 'domestic' (Axelrod) in this specific thing-oriented way. Plath's tulips are an example of how a fairly well-known thing suddenly appears as something completely different, even alien, and begins to make relations that wholly overtake the human subject. The tulips disclose themselves as an aesthetic thing in the Heideggerian sense; that is, they achieve the ontological status of a work, because they make their own earthiness appear as a red, hostile materiality, which aggressively erupts and disturbs the patient from her medicated, almost deadly slumber. The agency of Plath's tulips is founded on their hostility.

The Red Mouth of the Tulips

Plath uses the first four stanzas of 'Tulips' to establish the state of the patient and the hospital room. The room is identified with the colour white: 'Look how white everything is, how quiet, how snowed-in' (2008: 1, 2). This wintery image-compound of whiteness, coldness and snow is at a first glance quite dominant as it depicts the lifeless stasis of the room and the dormant state of the subject, but its main function is to set up a visual contrast to the emphatic red of the tulips. Already in the first stanza – 'The tulips are too excitable, it is winter here' (2008: 1, 1) – a powerful clash is underway. I would argue, however, that the winter-compound is really subsumed under a more dominant interest in the poem. That is, it is connected to an act of purification, forgetting and dematerialisation, which is evoked by maritime images of sea, beach and boat:[6] the nurses 'pass the way gulls pass inland in their white caps' (2008: 2, 5) and 'My body is a pebble to them, they tend it as water / Tends to the pebbles it must run over, smoothing them gently' (2008: 3, 1–2). The image of being 'run over' by water is concluded upon at the end of the fourth stanza. Here the subject is compared to 'a thirty-year-old cargo boat' (2008: 4, 1), that is, a being full of baggage and weight, which is then sunk and relieved by medication: 'the water went over my head. / I am a nun now, I have never been so pure' (2008: 4, 6–7). The watery purification is a simultaneous unloading of identity, body, history and family: 'I am nobody; I have nothing to do with explosions. / I have given my name and my day-clothes up to the nurses / And my history to the anesthetist and my body to surgeons' (2008: 1, 5–7). This state is obviously something the subject longs for: 'Now I have lost myself I am sick of baggage' (2008: 3, 4). When the image-compounds of the winter landscape and the maritime topos are considered, the state of the subject can be described as a striving towards immaterial relief governed by freedom, oblivion, lightness and even happiness, a fact that becomes painfully clear when the tulips arrive: 'They [the tulips] concentrate my attention, that was happy / Playing and resting without committing itself' (2008: 8, 6–7). Happiness is to be relieved from everything that binds and weights down. This striving is also endowed with religious and spiritual meanings ('I am a nun now'), which further highlight the anti-material longing of the subject. The consequence of this frozen and purified condition is lethal, however, as it entails a longing for death.

Throughout the first four stanzas, I would argue, things are disclosed at such a great distance that they border on being no-things, that is, things without earthy resistance, endurance and sustainability; it is the fragile and ungraspable thingness of frosty air and of running water. The beginning of the poem thus depicts a state of the subject hovering in a detached mode, where the surrounding thing-world in a similar vein loses its substantiality. Within the Heideggerian terminology, the things are almost without earth and are therefore bordering on being solely worldly if not mental constructs. To be pure, to Plath, means to achieve such distance to the thing-world; interestingly enough, this negation of the world is identified with water – in Plath, cold water seems to constitute a direct material opposition to things and, of course, to earth.[7] To be purified, therefore, discloses a state where the subject is most abstracted from the world; it is a state where the subject is most clearly shown as subject – or rather, as *Dasein*. It could be compared – as Perloff also does (1984: 119) – to a state of *angst*, as Heidegger describes it in his lecture 'What is Metaphysics?' (1929). Here, being human is depicted as something that is always outside itself: 'Da-sein means: being held out into the nothing. Holding itself out into the nothing, Dasein is in each case already beyond beings as a whole' (Heidegger 1993 [1929]: 103). The fact that human beings can never be at one with their surroundings or with things means that human beings are always beyond themselves, and it is exactly this beyondness of being that constitutes what it means to be human. But this also means that a state of *angst* hovers at the centre of the human condition: as Heidegger puts it, a state of hovering and floating in no-thing – 'we "hover" in anxiety' (1993: 101) – where the apparent steady ground of things falls away and shows itself as an abyss.

In the perspective of a thing-oriented reading, Plath's description of this state of hovering *angst* is conceptually difficult as it evidently assumes that things can fall away from a particular mode or mood of human existence. Actually, *angst* and uncanniness (*Unheimlichkeit*) could be seen as the existential equivalent to the earth as it also describes a non-relationality or abyss within everyday human existence. As such, it is a privileged (if terrifying) mode of being, wherefrom human beings can recognise their own particularity and finitude – or their own dissolution in earthiness, as it were (see the analysis of *angst* in *Being and Time*, §40). In any case, Plath operates within a more human-centric framework at the beginning of her poem as she focuses on this specific uncanny state, that is, the sense of not being and not wanting to be at home in the world. However, she also tries to render this state as concrete and perhaps as material as possible, when she uses a winter landscape and the movements of water to elucidate the condition not only of the subject, but also of the room. Even *angst*, it seems, has a material correlate, although it is directed at making everything materially lighter and less binding, undoing all relations to the world. One could argue, however, that the following turn of the poem towards the tulips mimics Heidegger's turn from an ontology of *Dasein* (based on *angst*) to a thing-oriented ontology (based on earth). In that case, Plath's interest in the poem is quite consistent, as she seems to depict how both human beings and things have non-relational areas, that is, they are at their core being governed by an alien and abysmal essence.

There are early indications in the poem that the state of uncanniness and abstraction from the world is about to terminate: the mentioning of the tulips in the first stanza – their excitability (2008: 1, 1) and explosiveness (2008: 1, 5) – infuses uneasiness in the description of the rest of the winter-landscape of anxiety, which culminates in the fifth stanza: 'I didn't want any flowers, I only wanted / To lie with my hands turned up and be utterly empty' (2008: 5, 1–2). The rest of the poem shows how this intention of the subject of losing itself is abruptly annulled by the introduction of the tulips, which marks the return of the earthy thing-world. As mentioned before, it is the color, the redness, which is given primacy in the description of the material force of the tulips: 'The tulips are too red in the first place, they hurt me' (2008: 6, 1). Instead of being gently tended to by 'water', that is, being purified, abstracted and immaterialised, the subject is now actually being hurt, that is, the subject is rematerialising, re-entering life. It is the violence and disturbing force of the red tulips which determines their earthy and anti-anthropocentric character – red is the colour of earth, so to speak – as it directly negates the will and mastery of the human subject (the desire for purity or death). The encounter between patient and tulips makes evident a conflict of interest: the autonomy of the subject wishing to lose itself in a sedated sleep is overridden by the thing and its own independent power to influence not only the subject, but the hospital room: 'The walls, also, seem to be warming themselves' (2008: 9, 1). The red tulips cast themselves as the agentic though hostile centre of the poem as they effectively destroy the subject's desired level or mode of abstraction as well as they change the environment of the room. As such, the tulips as things not only retain a powerful (and alien) aggressiveness (earth), but it is precisely this material power which acts upon and thus implicates the surrounding subject and space. A thing-oriented reading delivers a productive frame for an understanding of Plath's tulips, because it regards the twin movement of establishing relations and retaining their alien force. Plath's tulips never get wholly domesticated or emptied out; their fierceness flows from sources beyond human reach and command.

The last four stanzas of 'Tulips' then attempt to fathom this hurting or hostile nature of the tulips. Here I would like to emphasise how Plath apparently fuses the colour of red with the image of the mouth as a guiding vehicle to show the dangerous nature of the tulips. The tulips have a red mouth. As is evident in the sixth stanza, the tulips 'breathe' (2008: 6, 2), 'Their redness talks' (2008: 6, 4), they have 'sudden tongues' (2008: 6, 6). The image of a breathing mouth is then continued in the next stanza: 'The vivid tulips eat my oxygen' (2008: 7, 7). The aliveness of the tulips is in this way manifested through a rather violent activity of an opening, red mouth, which corresponds to 'my wound' (2008: 6, 4) – that is, the open mouth of the tulips is mirrored in the wound of the patient: both are red, bloody and hurting.

The red mouth-image of the tulips obtains its most surprising and conclusive expression at the end of the poem: 'The tulips should be behind bars like dangerous animals; / They are opening like the mouth of some great African cat' (2008: 9, 2–3). The mouth is not even human; it is animal, wild and undomesticated, alien and dangerous. The violence of the tulips stems from their opening onto a red presence of animal terror, which reactivates the bodily thingness of the patient-subject herself. Again, the earthiness of the thing generates new, productive relations and actions. This act is confirmed through yet another correspondence between the tulips and the heart: 'And I am aware of my heart: 'it opens and closes / Its bowl of red blooms out of sheer love of me' (2008: 9, 4–5). As the tulips open their redness and (arguably) their intrusiveness peaks through the wildness of the African cat-image, the patient is finally made aware of the fact that her heart is beating and pulsating with blood and life; the tulips-mouth has in fact performed an act of resuscitation on the patient. The moment the violence of things makes the subject aware of its heart, an affirmative turn takes place: the redness is now not only the colour of hostility and intrusion (tulips), but also of the subject's own life (bloody heart). The earthy negativity of the tulips forces a basic will to live on the patient, although this very will conflicts with her own intentions and is outside her control.

The poem then comes full circle at the end, when the patient fully returns to life and reacts by shedding tears: 'The water I taste is warm and salt, like the sea, / And comes from a country far away as health' (2008: 9, 6–7). Water, which was cold and purified, is now disclosed as warm and salty, that is, it is no longer the water of death or oblivion, but of life and health. If water represented an opposition to things at the beginning of the poem, it appears here as a kind of earthy water endowed with the warmth of life. In the end, the impact of the tulips makes clear that the state of the subject shown in the poem is really a matter of water, that is, of the material condition of liquids: from the death-like abstraction of pure, cold water and of water crystalised as snow (depicting an abstract state of *angst*) to the life-giving earthiness of warm water, of tears and of blood (depicting a state of physical and emotional recovery)

A Poet of Life

Based on a thing-oriented reading of 'Tulips', the paradox at the heart of Plath's poetry as recognised by Perloff (see Perloff 1984: 110) can be elaborated and ultimately reformulated. Arguably, there is a tendency in Plath's 'Tulips' to make a division between human and nonhuman, death and vitality, as is quite clear in the turn from the human-centric part of the poem (state of *angst*) to the thing-oriented part (the material impact of the tulips). I have tried to avoid this division, however, and would instead propose understanding the patient-subject and the tulips as two different material movements within the poem: the first seeks out abstraction and lightness and the second performs an oppressive and intrusive act. It is the clash between these two dynamisms that constitutes the drama of the poem, which means that the subject enjoys no primacy whatsoever; its intentions and actions are part of those performed by things. As such, 'Tulips' has a genuine intention of casting aside any notion of human exceptionalism with regard to things, which simply cannot truly be recognised if Perloff's subject–object schema is maintained.

In a Heideggerian vocabulary, the first movement resembles the opening dynamics of the world, the other the closing dynamics of the earth. That is, the subject seeks to leave its material foundations behind by abstracting itself into the pure immateriality of an open, resistance-free world. This is visualised by the use of winter and water imagery. When the tulips arrive, however, the earth arrives; the world of the subject is brought back to the ground manifested in the alien and unavoidable material power of a thing. This reintroduction of the earth marks not a pleasant disturbance, but is rather of a fundamentally negative and aggressive nature. The paradox of Plath's poems is then basically that an affirmation of human life is based on this material negativity: it is the hostile nature of the thing that performs the saving act of bringing the subject back to its material- and bodily-being as the patient becomes aware of its beating heart. The earthy withdrawnness of the tulips, their ontological hostility towards human abstractions, simultaneously establishes a relation which commits and binds human beings to their own finite, bodily existence. Thus, Plath seems to suggest that the retaining of an alien animality of things, a post-anthropocentric dimension as it were, subverts a human existence otherwise bent on a solipsistic retreat into an earthless world of pure mentalism.

It is therefore not a question of the subject's identification with an object, as Perloff interprets it, whereby the correspondence between tulips and patient is understood as a way for the subject of becoming the tulips thus retrieving vitality. This claim certainly would eliminate the negativity of the thing and Plath's animism would simply be a showcase of how a subject endows an object with its own qualities: 'In "Tulips", for example, the anguish of the "I" is inextricably bound up with the personality with which she endows a bunch of flowers' (Perloff 1984: 118). Rather, I would argue, it is precisely because the patient cannot perform an act of identification – the tulips are not at all willingly inert objects, but exercise an aggressive resistance – that it can come truly and vitally alive again. If at all, it is the tulips that overtake the subject, forcing it to recognise its pulsating heart, its inherent will to live. Plath's animism is therefore based on a core of material negativity, of earth, which means that the aliveness of things is fed by their sustained indifference to human life. The subject becomes aware of the heart and of life, not because 'the "I" finally *becomes* the hated tulips' (Perloff 1984: 119), but because something other than itself forces it to.

The explosion of material redness is an aggressive assault, which is finally disclosed as an act of worldly and bodily affirmation. Paradoxically, life in the subject as a will to live seems to be a consequence of this assault on the subject, something that happens against its own will. The more the tulips harass and torment the subject, the more it is brought back into its material- and bodily-being, the more its heart beats, the more its tears float. I therefore agree with Bassnett, when she tries to emphasise how Plath is not a poet of death, but of life: 'Far from foregrounding death there is a conscious effort to foreground life, even when the poems speak of the greatest pain, and it is this characteristic of her poetry which marks Sylvia Plath as a survivor poet, a writer with a message of hope' (2005: 129). Surviving, however, is an act that is sometimes beyond human mastery; it happens – as Plath shows – even against will and intention; it happens because of things beyond human command. When the earth opens its red lion-mouth, not even the most 'skilled suicide-artist' (Rosenthal) can look away.

In the end, Plath offers an emphatically – with Harman – weird definition of life as something that is kept outside of us, in things, in an earthy obscurity, whose permanent refusal and demarcation only reminds us of our inevitable bond with the physical world of things, with ourselves as finite beings and eventually with our family. Plath's Tulips-poem is a contribution to an ongoing post-anthropocentric ambition of picturing what human existence looks like when things are not just thought of as dead, inanimate objects, but as material forces and agents; also, even when they do not please human endeavours and intentions. To my mind, Plath fosters a concrete, relatable and therefore clear awareness of how the alien hostility inherent in things is in fact living right in our midst, in our own everyday worlds – standing right there on a table just beside you.

Notes

1. For possible ecological aspects of Plath's work, see Tracy Brain's study *The Other Sylvia Plath* (2001) (especially Brain 2001: 84–140). Brain argues that Plath's work shows 'an attentiveness to environmental pollution', that is, 'there is a recurrent exploration of the ways that substances are exchanged between human beings and the environment' (2001: 84). Brain gives weight to this argument by tracing an interest of Plath's – shared by her husband Ted Hughes – in the books of one of the mothers of modern environmentalism, Rachel Carson (see Brain 2001: 85–8).
2. When I quote from the poem (see Plath 2008: 160–3), I note the number of the stanza and then of the line.
3. Heidegger was not the only philosopher dealing with an ontology of the thing in the interwar years, as has recently been expanded upon by Christian Benne in his study *Die Erfindung des Manuskripts: Zur Theorie und Geschichte literarischer Gegenständlichkeit* (2015). Here Benne highlights a theory of objecthood (*Gegenständlichkeit*) by drawing forth such (now relatively unknown) philosophers as Nicolai Hartmann and above all Richard Hönigswald (see Benne 2015: 108–33). Benne's study indicates an ontological turn in philosophy at the beginning of the twentieth century,

which to my knowledge prefigures much of the interest in things, objects and matter in various recent post-anthropocentric theories. I take my cue from Heidegger, however; it is his concepts of thing and matter that enjoy a sustained influence on current philosophies.
4. This specific ambition is further developed by Heidegger in his postwar writings, such as 'The Thing' (1950) and 'Building Dwelling Thinking' (1951).
5. To be fair, Bennett does in fact mention this aspect of the thing at the beginning of her study *Vibrant Matter: A Political Ecology of Things* (2010): 'I, too, will feature the negative power or recalcitrance of things. But I will also seek to highlight a positive, productive power of their own' (2010: 1). As her interest lies in 'the active role of *nonhuman* material in public life' (2010: 2), that is, how political agency is also governed by things, the non-relational nature of things is simply not her main concern.
6. In her autobiographical BBC radio speech 'Ocean 1212-W' (1962), Plath attests to the importance of the ocean as it was formed during her childhood: 'My childhood landscape was not land but the end of the land – the cold, salt, running hills of the Atlantic. I sometimes think my vision of the sea is the clearest thing I own' (Plath 1979: 117). The fact that water is connected with a state of forgetting, in Plath's Tulips-poem, is founded on the old Greek myth of one of the five rivers in the underworld of Hades, the river Lethe (Greek for forgetting, oblivion). The mythic bond between water and death has accordingly had an influential presence in much literature up until the present; see for instance Gaston Bachelard's treatment of an 'Ophelia Complex' and 'Charon Complex' in his informative, material study on water and literature, *Water and Dreams: An Essay on the Imagination of Matter*, published in 1942 (see Bachelard 1999: 71–92).
7. On the existential-material conflict between the sea as erasure and the earth as retainment, that is, between forgetting and memory, see Robert Pogue Harrison's article 'The Earth and Its Dead' (2003). In contrast to Plath, Harrison does not sympathise at all with the possibilities of water for obtaining a state of oblivion and release from history. To Harrison, the sea is 'inhuman', because it rejects any inscription and therefore any way of marking history and memory (see Harrison 2003: 12). Instead, the sea is part of humankind's apocalyptic imagination (see Harrison 2003: 16) – a claim that is perhaps not that incompatible with Plath's striving towards a sedated deathlike state (although the private apocalypse is averted by the earthiness of the tulips in the end).

References

Axelrod, Steven Gould (2006), 'The poetry of Sylvia Plath', in Jo Gill (ed.), *The Cambridge Companion to Sylvia Plath*, New York: Cambridge University Press, pp. 73–89.

Bachelard, Gaston (1999 [1942]), *Water and Dreams: An Essay On the Imagination of Matter*, The Dallas Institute of Humanities and Culture.

Bassnett, Susan (2005), *Sylvia Plath: An Introduction to the Poetry*, 2nd edn, New York: Palgrave Macmillan.

Benne, Christian (2015), *Die Erfindung des Manuskripts: Zur Theorie und Geschichte literarischer Gegenständlichkeit*, Berlin: Suhrkamp.

Bennett, Jane (2010), *Vibrant Matter: A Political Ecology of Things*, Durham, NC: Duke University Press.

Brain, Tracy (2001), *The Other Sylvia Plath*, Harlow: Pearson Education.

Brennan, Claire (ed.) (1999), *The Poetry of Sylvia Plath*, New York: Columbia University Press.

Harman, Graham (2002), *Tool-Being: Heidegger and the Metaphysics of Objects*, Peru, IL: Open Court Publishing.

Harman, Graham (2011), *Weird Realism: Lovecraft and Philosophy*, London: Zer0 Books.

Harman, Graham (2012), 'The well-wrought broken hammer: object-oriented literary criticism', *New Literary History*, 43: 2, pp. 183–203.

Harrison, Robert Pogue (2003), 'The earth and its dead', in Robert Pogue Harrison, *The Dominion of the Dead*, Chicago: University of Chicago Press, pp. 1–16.

Heidegger, Martin (1993 [1929]), 'What is metaphysics?', in Martin Heidegger, *Basic Writings*, 2nd revised and expanded edition, ed. David Farrell Krell, New York: HarperCollins, pp. 89–110.

Heidegger, Martin (2001 [1935–6]), 'The origin of the work of art', in Martin Heidegger, *Poetry, Language, Thought*, ed. Albert Hofstadter, New York: Harper Perennial Classics, pp. 15–86.

Hughes, Ted (1970), 'Notes on the chronological order of Sylvia Plath's poems', in Charles Newman (ed.), *The Art of Sylvia Plath: A Symposium*, London: Faber & Faber, pp. 187–95.

Perloff, Marjorie (1975), 'On Sylvia Plath's Tulips', in *Paunch 42–43* (December 1975), Buffalo, NY, pp. 105–10.

Perloff, Marjorie (1984 [1970]), '*Angst* and animism in the poetry of Sylvia Plath', in Linda W. Wagner (ed.), *Critical Essays on Sylvia Plath*, Boston, MA: G. K. Hall & Company, pp. 109–24.

Phillips, Robert (1973), *The Confessional Poets*, Carbondale: Southern Illinois University Press.

Plath, Sylvia (1979 [1962]), 'Ocean 1212-W', in Sylvia Plath, *Johnny Panic and the Bible of Dreams and Other Prose Writings*, London and Boston, MA: Faber & Faber, pp. 117–24.

Plath, Sylvia (2008 [1961]), 'Tulips', in Sylvia Plath, *The Collected Poems*, ed. Ted Hughes, New York: Harper Perennial Modern Classics.

Rosenthal, M. L. (1970), 'Sylvia Plath and confessional poetry', in Charles Newman (ed.), *The Art of Sylvia Plath: A Symposium*, London: Faber & Faber, pp. 69–88.

CHAPTER 5

'We have nothing to be arrogant about' – Hans Christian Andersen and Anti-Anthropocentrism

Torsten Bøgh Thomsen

> There goes a newspaper. Everybody has forgotten what was written on it, but still it spreads itself out . . .
> Hans Christian Andersen, 'The Darning Needle', 1846

When Hans Christian Andersen wrote 'The Darning Needle' in 1846, universal Romanticism had dominated literature in Denmark for decades. Writers mostly concerned themselves with the relationship between the ideal and the world and the ability of art to mend the divide between matter and thinking that René Descartes had identified a few hundred years earlier. Ideals were paramount. The physical world was interesting merely as a means of achieving true insight into the underlying, absolute subject. But Andersen wrote with an understanding of materiality that differed from the traditional Romantic. In the quote above, we see how the newspaper's content fades into the background while its materiality is brought to the fore. Knowledge perishes, whilst materiality remains, and the point of a newspaper being spread propagates from its content to its materiality, as if not only the words in the texts but also every fibre of the paper is driven by an inner impulse to spread out.

Andersen wrote with a sensibility to the material world that seems remarkably topical. Considering global warming, the material world has asserted itself in the past decades in ways that have re-actualised basic questions for both humanists and natural scientists about humanity and the material world and the relationship between the two. Artists and thinkers may always have been preoccupied by these questions, but in an artistic and literary-historical perspective, one can argue that questions of the relationship between the human and nonhuman found their clearest artistic manifestations in Romanticism and have been crucial for the Western human's understanding of itself and its (dis)connection with the material world throughout modernity.[1] Therefore, it may be fruitful to consider these Romantic discussions in a historical perspective and allow them to inform the current cultural and scientific debates on environmentalism, materiality, humanity and art.

The theories used in this chapter stem from the complex of theories that has scantily been called 'the material turn' within the humanities. I will primarily be drawing upon perspectives from New Materialism and posthumanism. These theories have their different centres of gravity and mutual discrepancies, but share a common ground in the form of an interest in rethinking humanity's position in the world in ways that go beyond the traditional dualisms of subject/object, human/non-human, immaterial/material and the hierarchies they entail, in order to let more egalitarian views of the world emerge.

In the following, I will trace what could be termed a growing anti-anthropocentric tendency in Andersen's work linked to the historical tensions between Romanticism, modernity, Christianity, science and aesthetics, which took place during his lifetime and which are addressed in his texts. Initially, I will explain Andersen's position within Danish cultural history and the late Romantic period of the nineteenth century, which is considered an artistic golden age in Denmark. Then I will discuss the so-called fairytales of things in Andersen's oeuvre, taking my point of departure in the lesser known 'Pen and Inkstand'. This fairytale, like the fairytales of things in general, is interesting in relation to current New Materialist and posthumanist theories insofar as it shows a displacement of the human from the centre of existence. Then, I will pan out to a consideration of some of Andersen's more explicitly philosophical texts about science. I will discuss the relationship between religion and materialism, hierarchies and flat ontologies in relation to Romantic philosophy and New Materialist theory. Finally, I consider Andersen's deliberations on the relationship between art and science that come across in his more poetological texts.

Andersen and Romanticism(s)

It may seem anachronistic to read canonical texts through current theoretical perspectives, but it is actually a common, if not in fact the traditionally preferred practice of ecocriticism. Since the consolidation of this theoretical field in the 1990s, ecocritics have discussed literary representations of the relationship between the human and the natural world based on the conviction that the literature of earlier times can tell us something about how changing understandings of the natural world have replaced each other. The period in which Andersen lived and worked (1805–75) is specifically relevant when it comes to supplying the current ecocritical debates about nature and nonhuman realities with historical perspectives. At the beginning of his career, he undertakes a series of discussions of Romantic dogma about art, and towards the latter part of his authorship he tries to formulate a poetics that can accommodate the natural sciences. In his early works (such as *Journey on Foot* [1829] and *The Improvisatore* [1835]) he tries to meet the ideals of universal Romanticism but continually exceeds and discusses them metapoetically in ways in which the Romantic ideals come to reveal their own limitations. Placed as he is in the midst of events, Andersen has a nuanced understanding of the different kinds of Romanticism that were in vogue at the time, and one could, to be more precise, say that Andersen problematises the variety of Romantic idealism derived from the philosophy of Friedrich von Schelling, which was carried forward in Denmark by the dominating arbiter of taste Johan Ludvig Heiberg, who also had a particular fascination with G. W. F. Hegel's absolute idealism. Heiberg promoted a view of art that focused on synthesis and harmonisation, which quickly came to dominate art in Denmark to such an extent that it became synonymous with Romanticism, and eventually turned into the overripe bourgeois variety of late Romanticism called Biedermeier. Against this, Andersen cultivated an interest in the grotesque, arabesque and darker avant-garde versions of Romanticism closer to the type of Romanticism we know from Friedrich Schlegel.[2]

Fairytales of 'Thing-Power'

When hearing the word 'Romanticism', one might think of an artistic movement that represents a strong focus on the subject rather than the object and the immaterial rather than the material. However true this may be when we are talking about Danish universal Romanticism, I believe that Andersen's authorship displays an interest in the empirical world and its materialities in ways that nuance this and which can be brought to the fore when his texts are read with perspectives from the contemporary theoretical fields of posthumanism and New Materialism. Especially in connection with the fairytales of things, I am interested in how Andersen's preoccupation with materiality can make things and objects in the texts dominant to a degree that they challenge the autonomy of the human subject in ways that might make sense in relation to Jane Bennett's thoughts about the vibrancy and semiotic inexhaustibility of matter. More specifically, I believe that the things we encounter in Andersen's fairytales of things can be rewardingly analysed with Bennett's notion of 'thing-power' as she develops it in her book *Vibrant Matter* (2010). Bennett distinguishes between objects understood as dead and malleable materiality and things as 'vivid entities not entirely reducible to the contexts in which (human) subjects set them, never entirely exhausted by their semiotics' (2010: 5). In addition, she writes about the power of things:

> The notion of thing-power aims . . . to attend to the it as actant; I will try, impossibly, to name the moment of independence (from subjectivity) possessed by things, a moment that must be there, since things do in fact affect other bodies, enhancing or weakening their power. . . . I will try to give voice to a vitality intrinsic to materiality, in the process absolving matter from its long history of attachment to automatism or mechanism. (2010: 3)

It is productive to keep this in mind when reading Andersen's fairytales of things and their negotiations of the relation between subject and object. I am not suggesting that Andersen succeeds in representing things uninfluenced by subjective projection or anthropomorphisation. Indeed, there is a long tradition of interpreting Andersen's use of objects as projections and anthropomorphisations dating back to the Danish critic Georg Brandes' mention of the fairytales in the portrait 'Andersen as a Fairytale Writer' ('Andersen som Eventyrdigter'; Brandes 1964 [1870]: 192–236). Similarly, Karin Sanders writes in the article 'Let's be Human – On the Politics of the Inanimate':

> Kleist used marionettes to examine consciousness through unconsciousness; Hoffmann used automatons as a way to articulate the uncanny; and Shelley used a golem-like monster in order to ponder the ethics of man's quest for creative powers. Andersen, in contrast, used dolls, marionettes and automatons in order to speak about *social* beings. (2012: 32)

While I believe this to be a reasonable way of reading the texts, I would like to supplement the allegorical reading strategy with an awareness of how Andersen is aesthetically utilising the material composition of things in his fairytales. This is an awareness that has been increasing over the last decades (Mylius 2003: 73) and which Sanders also points out:

> That is to say, when Andersen parses specific properties of given material objects and assigns human attributes to them, he rarely violates their unique form or functionality (the pen-ness of a pen, the ink-ness of an inkwell, the bottle-ness of a bottle, the steadfastness of a toy soldier and so on). (2012: 30)

I would like to stress the importance of this 'sensitivity to the specificity of physical objects' (Sanders 2012: 30). However, rather than isolating either the social or the material aspects of the fairytales, what I argue is that the relationship, the correlations, between thinking and thing and thing and object is negotiated metapoetically in ways that often come across as an emphasis on the agency of things and a critique of human notions of mastery.

'Pen and Inkstand'

This can be seen in Andersen's fairytale 'Pen and Inkstand' from 1859. It is about a poet's office supplies on a desk discussing who is to be credited for the works of art that they are contributory in creating. The pen says to the inkstand:

> If you did take the trouble to think, you would understand that nothing comes out of you except a liquid. You just supply me with the means of putting down on paper what I have in me; that's what I write with. It's the pen that does the writing. (Andersen 1949)

To which the inkstand replies:

> You've hardly been in service a week, and already you're half worn out. Do you imagine you're the poet? Why, you're only a servant; I have had a great many like you before you came, some from the goose family and some of English make. I'm familiar with both quill pens and steel pens. (Andersen 1949)

The discussion stops because the human of the house, the poet, returns. He has been to a concert where the musicians have played so skilfully that they have made it seem as if the instruments were playing on their own. He reflects on this in his notes:

> How foolish it would be for the violin and bow to boast of their achievements! And yet we human beings often do so. Poets, artists, scientists, generals – we are all proud of ourselves, and yet we're only instruments in the hands of our Lord! To Him alone be the glory! We have nothing to be arrogant about. (Andersen 1949)

Pitted against the highest authority, God, traditional hierarchies start to dissolve. We see the contours of a posthumanist argument in a Christian setting. New Materialism alongside posthumanism[3] represents a critique of the idea that the human is qualitatively different from the rest of the world and is vested with powers to transcend materiality.[4] This anthropocentric notion, which is central to Renaissance humanism, rests on a presumed boundary between the human and the nonhuman.

The human is assumed to be at the centre of creation and in possession of spirit, the ultimate immateriality that rules the material world.

Posthumanists recognise that anthropocentrism has been a significant structure in Western culture, but also believe that the idea that the human is qualitatively different from its surroundings is an ideological creation and epistemological consequence rather than an ontological fact. Accordingly, posthumanists want to nuance the human-centred perspective. They want to examine how anthropocentrism is constructed and if there might be other, more egalitarian ways of approaching the world.

In this context, 'Pen and Inkstand' seems relevant. As Klaus Müller-Wille argues in the article 'Hans Christian Andersen's Things', the discussion of the subject–object dualism is prominent in this fairytale. Müller-Wille does not think that the animation of things in Andersen's fairytales can be seen purely as allegory – a projection of human qualities onto toys in order to discuss social issues more freely. These are not just humans disguised as things in order to avoid censorship. According to Müller-Wille, what goes on is not merely subjective projection but also 'attempts to give an outline of the limits of this projection by constantly referring to the world of things and thereby also to the limits of the understanding of the subject and the text' (2014: 50–1, my translation).

The Conditionality of Things

The things in Andersen's fairytales are things as defined by Bennett. They are not objects but they never quite become full subjects either. They always retain some of their thingness and are bound by the qualities of their material configurations. Furthermore, the thingness of the things does not only function as a humorous element in the stories but is essential from a narratological point of view. Andersen's universe of things is a universe in which materials such as mahogany, porcelain, tin and paper have as much influence on the development of the plot as the intentions of the protagonists – sometimes even more so as things are at the mercy of the possibilities and limitations offered by their material compositions which often come in the way of their personal wishes.

If there had not been too little tin, 'The Steadfast Tin Soldier' (1838) would not have felt compelled to compensate for the missing leg, and the story might never have begun. To begin with, this manufacturing glitch is the very reason why 'he'll be the remarkable one' (Andersen 1949). Similarly, his adored dancer would not be able to be moved by a gust of wind and swept into the stove to the soldier at the end of the story had she not been made out of paper. If porcelain is present in an Andersen fairytale, you can rest assured that – in accordance with the character of the material – it represents something brittle, refined and fragile. This is the case with the Chinese emperor's palace in 'The Nightingale' (1843), which is 'made entirely of fine porcelain, extremely expensive but so delicate that you could touch it only with the greatest of care' (Andersen 1949). Overall this is a story about the fragility of extreme civilisational sophistication which is supported by the recurring use of porcelain. Another example is 'The Shepherdess and the Chimney Sweep' (1852) in which the timid Biedermeier couple consists of porcelain. Hence 'neither could stand a shock' and they come to represent a bourgeoisie that is unreasonably delicate and unwordly (Andersen 1949).

This fairytale is also an example of how a material condition can have importance for the development of the plot and the ending of the story. The fairytale ends when the two figurines return to the table under the mirror from where they set out – terrified by the outside world. In the meantime, the grandfather statuette, who is also made of porcelain, has fallen to the floor and broken into pieces but he is afterwards riveted in a way that prevents him from nodding, which he could before, and, accordingly, from granting his consent to marry off the shepherdess to the carved goat on the old cupboard. If these characters are pure allegories of human situations, how then are we to understand the use of the term 'riveting'? This is a way of mending that works within the logic of the material world but does not work as an allegory of social situations. The narrative possibilities of the materials exceed what makes sense on an allegorical social level. Andersen might be transporting human relations into the world of things, but some things are possible in the nonhuman sphere that are not possible in the human one. Things are overtaken by the agency of the materials they consist of in such a way that they cannot be translated directly back to the human when the story is over. You might be able to rivet porcelain but you cannot unbreak a human neck. Things in the fairytales thus occupy an intermediate position between the human and the nonhuman – a position that might also discreetly point out that the human may not be as autonomous as it likes to think. Maybe it is also subjected to conditions both cultural and material and just as thinglike and conditioned as a porcelain figurine.

I am aware that my readings retain a focus on human relationships and that I read things as anthropomorphisations. However, I am not interested in reading strategies that disregard social conditions in order to focus on the semantic inexhaustibility of materiality. Rather, I am interested in situations where synergies or discrepancies occur between the materiality of things and their allegoric functions. Like Karen Barad, I think that the discursive and the material are mutually constituent (Barad 2007: 152), but I do not share her reservations regarding representation as such, provided that we do not equate representation with understanding or other such terms that would suggest a hierarchy between the human and the nonhuman. To a greater extent, I am in agreement with Jane Bennett who notes:

> A touch of anthropomorphism, then, can catalyze a sensibility that finds a world filled not with ontologically distinct categories of beings (subjects and objects) but with variously composed materialities that form confederations. In revealing similarities across categorical divides and lighting up structural parallels between material forms in 'nature' and those in 'culture,' anthropomorphism can reveal isomorphisms. (2010: 99)

Or Timothy Morton who writes that, 'I *anthropomorphise*. It's not that I anthropomorphise in some situations but not in others. It's that, because of the fact of phenomenological *sincerity*, I can't help anthropomorphizing everything I handle' (2012: 207). I share the belief of both thinkers that anthropomorphisation is inevitable. But I also share the optimistic notion that this way of approaching materiality is not necessarily hierarchical. I want to explore how correlationism works in works of art and literature rather than champion a particular interpretation of correlationism. Consequently, I once again stress that it is the relationship *between* matter and mind that interests me, not matter taken on its own.

The Autonomy of Things

Returning to 'Pen and Inkstand', the fairytale seems to achieve a flat ontology in which the human exists on the same level as everything else. But only by employing a divine perspective. Instead of anthropocentrism we seem to have theocentrism.

In this context it should be emphasised that there are some clear differences between the Christian-religious and New Materialist understanding of the world, the main one being that New Materialism (also as it is expressed by Bennett in the concept of 'vital materialism') does not believe in dichotomies between the tangible and intangible. Everything is immanence; there is no transcendence. Bennett argues that the agency of things emerges from the materials themselves and not as a result of the material world being animated by immaterialities. She is inspired by philosophical notions of organising principles such as *Bildungstrieb* (Kant), *entelechy* (Aristotle/Driesch) or *élan vital* (Bergson) (Bennett 2010: 61–89), but only to the extent that they are understood as material properties and not immaterial animators. Consequently, Bennett's anti-hierarchical ontology would also be in conflict with both the Romantic and the Christian ideals of material reality as permeated by an underlying immaterial entity – be this an underlying subjectivity or the Holy Spirit or both rolled into one. Thus, it may seem counter-intuitive that I trace an anti-anthropocentric theme in a text in which Andersen lets his character invoke a Christian God and thus an ontological hierarchy in the world. However, I think we can push this pious reading further. It is important to notice how the story is continued.

A commentary follows the self-confident note of the poet: 'Yes, that is what the Poet wrote down, and he titled his essay, "The Master and the Instruments"' (Andersen 1949). The poet expresses his thoughts in a genre that is different from the fairytale we are reading. The fairytale as it unfolds in Andersen's modern styling takes the form of explorations of ethical, ontological and artistic dilemmas. The parable, however (Hersholt inaccurately translates the Danish word 'parabel' as 'essay'), is the opposite: a pre-modern (and biblical) genre of didactic stories that are supposed to convey prescriptive truths about the world. And I think we would be wrong to confuse the parable written by the poet with the overall meaning of the text – because we are not reading the parable, we are reading the fairytale of 'Pen and Inkstand'.

This displacement of narration and play upon genres destabilises the poet's Christian message and begs the question whether there really is any such universalism that guarantees such a stable worldview. At the end, the belief that everything owes its existence to God is repeated but only after a detour in which both pen and inkstand have also repeated how they continue to believe that they are to be credited as responsible for the texts:

> They were both satisfied with their answers, and it is a great comfort to feel that one has made a witty reply – one sleeps better afterward. So they both went to sleep. But the poet didn't sleep. His thoughts rushed forth like the violin's tones, falling like pearls, sweeping on like a storm through the forest. He understood the sentiments of his own heart; he caught a ray of the light from the everlasting Master. To him alone be the glory! (Andersen 1949)

Who makes the final outburst? Is it the narrator or the poet's thoughts communicated by the narrator? In any case, all of the characters stick to their own convictions throughout the story. No one succeeds in convincing the other, so why should we the readers be convinced by the concluding outburst regardless of whose it is? The Christian self-confidence seems even less convincing when one considers that the issue has kept the poet awake all night. His insomnia could be a sign to us that this hierarchical Christian worldview may not stand as unchallenged as it is presented.

Therefore, when I argue that it makes sense to read Andersen's text using New Materialist theory, although his texts teem with dualisms and hierarchies in ways that seem to clash with the flat ontology of New Materialism, it is primarily due to the fact that I do not think that Andersen ever presents a sufficiently assertive worldview for it to be proselytising. His writings are polyphonic, hesitant, ironic and contain too many narrative shifts, too much uncertainty and ambivalence to be denominational. I concede that he operates with a dualism between the intangible and the tangible, in which the intangible appears to be awarded primacy: the abstraction of God is staged as an almost Olympic perspective which confuses all of material reality, and as such we do have a hierarchy which puts God on one side and all the rest of existence on the other. However, we are presented with so much doubt about the existence of this postulated God that we, after having had the entire material reality levelled by his immaterial majesty, are brought to question the existence of this selfsame majesty – so much so that we are, in effect, left with a potentially flattened reality in which things quarrel and strive to assert themselves, and this is the only thing we can be sure of.

Assemblages

Returning to the question of the production of art and applying Bennett's notion of assemblages, which she borrows from Deleuze and Guattari, you could say that the poet struggles to assert his own dominant position in the assemblage that is the artistic production process. Bennett writes:

> Assemblages are ad hoc groupings of diverse elements, of vibrant materials of all sorts. Assemblages are living, throbbing confederations that are able to function despite the persistent presence of energies that confound them from within. . . . Assemblages are not governed by any central head: no one materiality or type of material has sufficient competence to determine consistently the trajectory or impact of the group. The effects generated by an assemblage are, rather, emergent properties, . . . Each member and proto member of the assemblage has a certain vital force, but there is also an effectivity proper to the grouping as such: an agency *of* the assemblage. (2010: 23–4)

Seen in relation to the quarrelling office supplies, this individual vitality of the things becomes comically evident. Concerning the concept of assemblage more generally, you could say that the poet is trying to invoke a traditional hierarchy between the immaterial and the material by placing God and divine inspiration as the wellspring of art even though we have already been told that poetic production involves the collaboration of several material actants (Latour): paper, ink, metal, feathers in addition to imagination and inspiration. What the different things as well as the poet do not seem to understand, even though it is suggested by the poet's philharmonic experience, is that art can never be made from just one single actant, one source. Whether you are producing a symphony or a poem you need a lot of actants other than the human mind (and the human intention of orchestrating things and naming them 'art') to work together in an assemblage – in concert, so to speak.

It is thus shown how everyone is stuck in their own self-induced convictions. We are witnessing a mocking display of the limitations of human consciousness that emerges when the office supplies are endowed with the same kind of conceited faith in their own beliefs and capabilities as the human subject. Delusions of grandeur are democratically distributed amongst all the actants in the story. This point is in line with Müller-Wille, who also notes:

> Thus the text is in no way making fun of the instruments . . . On the contrary, the poet is criticized because he, by use of his office supplies, tries to become the master of the very autonomy of things that threaten his subjectivity. (2014: 56, my translation)

So, the relationship between subject and object is challenged in the fairytale – partly because the subject is removed from its position of mastery and becomes thing-like, and partly because the object, in turn, is set free from its traditional role as an inert item. The stable dualisms are set in motion through shifts in narration. But they are only set in motion – not fixed in a new context.

Inner and Outer

Andersen's interest in how materials can be used to create narratological displacements and examine the relationship between the human and material reality goes back to some of the earliest fairytales of things. I am going to illustrate this through two passages from 'The Steadfast Tin Soldier' and 'The Sweethearts'. At a first glance these quotes may seem insignificant, but I cannot help but notice them because they have almost identical wording, and because they – like 'Pen and Inkstand' – present a narrator whose omniscience is limited by the opacity of the things. In 'The Sweethearts' (1843) we meet a top courting a ball who thinks very highly of herself. She believes herself to be engaged to a swallow and every time someone plays with her in the courtyard, she believes that he pops his head out to greet her. Her impressive bounciness is described like this:

> The next day the ball was taken out, and the top saw her flying high up into the air, just like a bird; so high that you could hardly see her. And every time she came back, she bounced up again, as soon as she touched the ground. That was either because she was longing for the swallow or because she had cork in her body. (Andersen 1949)

The narrator wavers between two explanations for the ball's high jump. It is either the result of an inner longing for something higher or it is a causal consequence of the ball's material composition. The fairytale is playing with a dialectics between the material and the social, and not just in this quote. Like the fairytales of things in general, this one is preoccupied with deliberations on what it means to be made out of Moroccan leather, mahogany, becoming gilded, having a cork in one's body, getting a copper nail hammered into one and being left in the drain for years. All of these speculations about materials and their associated social consequences might look like some sort of essentialism or determinism – a sort of logic that signifies how your existence must necessarily take a predefined course in accordance with the particular material you are made from. However, against this, I would argue that through the top and ball's many material alterations the story actually achieves the opposite. These materials are not fixed but highly transformative, and rather than presenting existence as something firm and static, it is presented as fluid through a masquerade of material conditions and discursive expectations.

It would be easy to dismiss the narrator's rhetorical ambivalence as an arbitrary one-time occurrence instead of reading so much into it, as I do. But we find the same rhetorical ambiguity expressed in 'The Steadfast Tin Soldier'. As might be known, it is the story of a tin soldier that is sent on quite a journey. He falls out the window, down the gutter, into the ocean where he gets eaten by a fish only to eventually find himself back in the kitchen of the house where he first started out. He ends up in the stove alongside the paper dancer that he fell in love with in the beginning of the tale, and as he melts the narrator observes: 'The tin soldier stood there dressed in flames. He felt a terrible heat, but whether it came from the flames or from his love he didn't know' (Andersen 1949). Again the narrator wavers between the different explanations for the condition of the toy, and repeats this rhetorical figure in the following line that reads: 'He'd lost his splendid colors, maybe from his hard journey, maybe from grief, nobody can say' (Andersen 1949). It is not only the tin soldier who is unable to decide whether his condition is due to outer or inner circumstances; the narrator does not have access to the answer either.

By choosing these examples, I do not mean to go against my own and Müller-Wille's advice not to transfer the experiences of things directly onto human life or read them as pure anthropomorphisations, because the top, ball and tin soldier are indeed things, but I do think that on a more abstract level they express a fundamental uncertainty concerning the relationship between the material and immaterial in Andersen's universe of things. The narrator's doubt and lack of access to the ultimate meaning of things can be said to exemplify what Bennett calls the vibrancy and semiotic inexhaustibility of things. Seen in a contemporary context, you could even call this a discussion of the relationship between constructivist and material understandings of the self: To what extent are we the subjects of an outer material reality that plays upon our senses and bodies? And to what extent are we governed by an inner mental life conditioned by traditions and culture? Who is the master and what is the instrument?

This Hobby-Horse of Ørsted's

'The Sweethearts' and 'The Steadfast Tin Soldier' are both fairly early texts in Andersen's oeuvre, but already we detect a play upon the concrete and abstract which is intensified in the following decades. During the 1850s and 1860s, Andersen becomes preoccupied with the question of the relationship between science and religion in his writings and he supplements this discussion with a metapoetical debate about what kind of aesthetic is most suited to facilitate a new way of writing about the world as informed by the natural sciences. The decisive shift in the way natural science appears in the oeuvre occurs in 1851 with the publication of the travelogue *In Sweden*. In this text, science and religion join forces in a shared ambition to decentralise the human from the centre of reality. The two chapters 'Faith and Science (Sermon in Nature)' and 'The California of Poetry' in particular express this unification of the two paradigms and are both inspired by the Danish physicist Hans Christian Ørsted's (the discoverer of electromagnetism) publication

The Spirit in Nature that was published the year before in *In Sweden*. In this work, Ørsted formulated a universalist understanding of the world which was very close to the Romantic, with the important exception that it was rooted in science rather than philosophy. Thus it was less teleological and anthropocentric. Accordingly, Andersen's chapter 'Faith and Science (Sermon in Nature)' shows a belief in a fundamental harmony in the world: 'There is harmonious beauty from the smallest leaf and flower to the grand voluminous bouquet, from our Earth to the infinite amount of orbs in space' (Andersen 1944 [1851]: 90, my translation[5]). But at the same time, he says in 'The California of Poetry' that this is a harmony that does not elevate but rather humiliates humanity:

> What world of fairytales cannot unfold under the microscope, when we transpose our human world therein; Electromagnetism can become the life spark of new comedies and novels, and how much humorous poetry will not grow forth, as we from our speck of dust, our little Earth with its small, arrogant people, gaze into the infinity of existence from Milky Way to Milky Way. (Andersen 1944: 121, my translation)

Andersen's incorporation of Ørsted's thoughts can easily be seen as a continuation of a Romantic anthropocentric project. This could be further supported by the fact that 'The California of Poetry' ends with a call for a new Romantic hero-poet, a new Aladdin to venture singlehandedly into the cave of science and bring back the poetry of the age to come. But if we look more closely, we might also detect a decentralisation of the human. Characterisations like 'small' and 'arrogant' do not go unnoticed. Andersen's friend through many years, the poet and priest Bernhard Severin Ingemann, does not agree that the natural sciences, what he calls 'this hobby-horse of Ørsted's', can inspire poetry. He writes to his friend:

> No, believe me, my dear friend! The divine and forever true in the human nature, in the human spirit – in its life and history – that is the eternal, fresh and inexhaustible wellspring of poetry. All the rest of nature in all its beauty and glory is but trappings and frame for the human and the God-human and God – such as we would see him here. (Andersen 1944: 144, XXII, my translation)

What Ingemann attacks is precisely the anti-anthropocentric undercurrents that are finding their way into Andersen's writings. Nature and the material world have come to occupy a far too important role in his works and Ingemann is warning Andersen not to make the mistake he believes it to be to bestow as much importance on creation as on the Creator. Simultaneously, he also finds that the human has been too drastically dethroned in the texts and therefore also sees it fit to remind

Andersen that an insult to humanity is an insult to the likeness of God and therefore also Jesus Christ – God as human.

'The New Century's Goddess'

Thoughts like these are developed in the oeuvre during the 1850s and I would like to conclude by showing how Andersen's thoughts about faith and knowledge, Romanticism and natural science can be said to culminate in a colourful medley in his perhaps most programmatic text about art, 'The New Century's Goddess' from 1861. Here the narrator expounds his visions for the poetry of the future – a dawning age of scientific modernisation – and begins by explaining what poetry actually is:

> These resonant outpourings of feeling and thought, they are only the offspring of nervous vibrations. Enthusiasm, joy, pain, all the movements of the organism, the wise men tell us, are but nerve vibrations. Each of us is but a string instrument. But who touches the strings? Who causes them to vibrate into sound? The Spirit, the unseen Heavenly Spirit, who echoes in them His emotion, His feelings; and these are understood by other string instruments, which respond in melting harmonies or clashing dissonances. So it was, and so it will be, in mankind's mighty onward march in the consciousness of freedom. (Andersen 1949)

Here we find a coupling of the Romantic spirit with the Christian God in a context where a contemporary artistic expression is sought after. Various worldviews and poetics collide. The mentioning of the spirit can create associations to Romanticism as well as Christianity while at the same time the striving towards harmony they both convey can be connected to Ørsted's post-Romantic, scientifically informed notion of the (electromagnetic) connection between everything. This harmony is complemented, however, by clashing dissonances, which can both be read as Romantic irony such as Schlegel understood it – that is, as the formal situation in which no statement in the text goes unchallenged (Schlegel 1967 [1799]: 312–20). At the same time, these dissonances might refer to a modernity characterised by secularisation, industrialisation and urbanisation, which makes the overall ambition of the texts one of finding a poetic form that is capable of expressing a modern experience of fragmentation. It is crucial to mention that Hersholt's translation in this case dramatically alters the meaning of the text. Hersholt translates the ending as 'melting harmonies or clashing dissonances'. The direct translation would be 'coalescing tones and strong dissonances of opposition'.[6] The substitution of 'and' by 'or' suggests a mutual exclusivity between harmony and dissonance that is not present in the original text. In the Danish original they exist in dialectic entanglement.

The artist in the text is one who on the one hand can be seen as the ultimate artistic subject of the new age, and on the other hand a blurred, almost erased subject – a collection of nerve fibres, a plaything in the hands of unconscious nature or an instrument through which the great master can express His intentions and make Himself known – not unlike the poet's understanding of art in 'Pen and Inkstand'.

Similarly, the conceptualisation of the human as a string instrument can make sense in both a Romantic and a scientific context. In 1795 Coleridge wrote the poem 'The Aeolian Harp', supporting a trend to regard the artist as a wind harp. Just as the invisible wind affected the harp strings, the artist was supposed to be moved by the Spirit that was believed to underlie everything but be particularly present in nature.[7] It became a favoured allegory – bordering on cliché – of the divinely inspired artist, which I believe that Andersen draws deliberately upon in his 'Goddess'. But he blurs the cliché and creates uncertainty about its meaning. One of the reasons why the wind harp was a fitting allegory for the Romantic artist was that its strings are struck by the wind in a smooth motion. Consequently, it plays harmonies and not the clashing dissonances which the narrator in the text also calls for. In addition, the text seems just as inspired by natural science as by Romantic idealism. When the narrator states that people are played upon like instruments, the comparison refers to biology as much as it works as an allegory for the artist as a harp. What the 'wise men' had begun to deal with were actual physical nerves. In the 1800s, researchers of neurology were interested in how we as humans are neurally affected and as such 'played upon' like instruments by our surroundings. In light of Andersen's general interest in science and technology, it makes sense that this human stringed instrument is eventually metaphorically linked to telegraph wires at the end of the text. The harp, an emblem of art since antiquity, gets entangled with biological nerves and telegraph wires and art, biology and science come together in productive confusion.

As for the Christian theme, I would argue that the introduction of the divine serves the same function as in 'Pen and Inkstand'. It is used as a perspective that aligns things and people. As such it is similar to how the natural sciences work in the texts. When Andersen writes about arrogant humans looking out from the speck of dust they call Earth, it is a similar anti-anthropocentric move. The divine can create a shift in scale that can be used to keep human megalomania in check – just as the scientific advances, as they are presented in Andersen's work, serve to shed light on the world in a way that humbles the human. This is where I find a connection between Christianity and science in Andersen's oeuvre.

They can both keep arrogance at bay by reminding humans that they are only a small part of something much bigger. Although both Christianity and science can be seen as humanity's primary instruments for hierarchy and self-aggrandisement, I maintain that in Andersen's literary universe they do not serve to support anthropocentrism, but rather to decentre humankind from the centre of the world.

Concerning the question of poetry, it is art which can accommodate the paradigms of religion and science in a whole that may suggest fragmentation and unity at the same time without letting the one exclude the other. Art can present a view on the world that contains Romantic as well as modern aspects in a composite form that brings various poetics and views of art into play and allows them to exist side by side. By doing that, Andersen's texts make room for statements and beliefs to co-exist in a tension, an undecidedness, instead of reifying them into unambiguous understandings of the world.

In conclusion, I want to emphasise that it is not my claim that we find an ontology or aesthetic that is directly comparable to New Materialist ontologies in Andersen's works. My point is rather that aesthetic representations take place that deal with many of the same questions regarding the human and the nonhuman that prevail in current theory and which therefore can be explained through them. There is no 'message', however, if by that we mean some kind of moralising point. Andersen is a master formalist and his writings can be used to show how something so seemingly anthropocentric as artistic form can become a crucial element in New Materialist dealings with literature. Through his attention to style, he uses literary form to liberate oppositions that seem philosophically and stylistically locked. The fairytales of things negotiate the relationship between the discursive and the material, as well as between the human and the nonhuman in ways that free both from their traditional oppositions. This artistic liberation can furthermore be used to suggest that art and representation can do a lot more than glorify the human. It can serve the opposite agenda, questioning hierarchies, deconstructing patterns of thought and making room for the emergence of more egalitarian ways of looking at the world.

Author's Note

This is a translated and reworked edition of the article 'Vi har intet at hovmode os over' which was first published in the Danish literary journal *Passage*, in 2017.

Notes

1. As Timothy Morton notes, 'The "thing" we call nature becomes, in the Romantic period and afterward, a way of healing what modern society has damaged. Nature is like that other Romantic-period invention, the aesthetic. The damage done, goes the argument, has sundered subjects from objects, so that human beings are forlornly alienated from their world. Contact with nature, and with the aesthetic, will mend the bridge between subject and object' (2007: 22–3).
2. Andersen often makes critical references to Hegel, whose thoughts are presented as nearly incomprehensible (*Journey on Foot*, ch. 13, *Shadow Pictures* [1831], ch. 3, *A Poet's Bazar* [1842], ch. 4). Schelling is also mentioned, but only in passing, as 'the philosopher' in *A Poet's Bazar*, ch. 10. In general, Andersen was most likely not very well read within philosophy but was more inspired by literature. His literary preferences did, however, involve a particular taste for Romantic writers with a leaning towards the humorous, ironic and grotesque. *A Poet's Bazar* is dedicated to Ludwig Tieck, and during the entire *Journey on Foot* the narrator carries a copy of E. T. A Hoffmann's *Elixiere des Teufels* in his inner pocket.
3. In affiliating these two theoretical disciplines so closely with each other, I am inspired by Karen Barad. In *Meeting the Universe Halfway* (2007) she draws upon social constructivism and quantum physics in order to formulate a 'material-discursive agential realism' that is also described as 'a posthumanist performative approach to understanding technoscientific and other naturalcultural practices that specifically acknowledges and takes account of matter's dynamism' (Barad 2007: 135).
4. Cary Wolfe describes humanism in his book *What is Posthumanism?*: '"the human" is achieved by escaping or repressing not just its animal origins in nature, the biological, and the evolutionary, but more generally by transcending the bonds of materiality and embodiment altogether' (2010: xv). For a more detailed discussion of different understandings of posthumanism in relation to humanism, see Wolfe's introduction to the book (2010: xi–xxxiv).
5. As no official translation of the travelogue exists, I have taken the liberty of translating it myself.
6. The original Danish reads: 'sammensmeltende Toner og . . . Modsætningens stærke Dissonantser' (Andersen 1861).
7. Likewise, Morton links 'the Aeolian' to his concept of an ambient poetics and to a Romantic ideal of immediacy between the human and nonhuman in art: 'the narrator becomes an Aeolian harp, a conduit. The narrator is plugged directly into the world, receiving its reality like paper receiving ink: ecorhapsody. . . . the worker receives an unfinished, fragmentary product and does what he or she can to complete it' (2007: 134).

References

Andersen, Hans Christian (1944 [1851]), *I Sverrig*, in H. Topsøe-Jensen (ed.), *H.C. Andersens Romaner og Rejseskildringer*, Det Danske Sprog- og Litteraturselskab, Copenhagen: Gyldendal.

Andersen, Hans Christian (1949), *The Complete Andersen*, trans. Jean Hersholt, Limited Editions Club. Available at www.andersen.sdu.dk/vaerk/hersholt/index_e.html#I (last accessed 12 April 2019).

Andersen, Hans Christian (1861), 'Det nye Aarhundredes Musa', The Royal Danish Library. www2.kb.dk/elib/lit/dan/andersen/eventyr.dsl/hcaev107.htm (last accessed 12 April 2019).

Barad, Karen (2007), *Meeting the Universe Halfway: Quantum Physics and the Entanglement of Matter and Meaning*, Durham, NC: Duke University Press.

Bennett, Jane (2010), *Vibrant Matter: A Political Ecology of Things*, Durham, NC: Duke University Press.

Brandes, Georg (1964 [1870]), 'H.C. Andersen som Eventyrdigter', in S. Møller Kristensen (ed.), *Udvalgte skrifter 1–9*, vol. 2, Copenhagen: Tiderne Skifter, pp. 203–47.

Morton, Timothy (2007), *Ecology Without Nature*, Cambridge, MA and London: Harvard University Press.

Morton, Timothy (2012), 'An object-oriented defense of poetry', *New Literary History*, 43: 2, pp. 205–24.

Müller-Wille, Klaus (2014), 'H.C. Andersens ting', in A. K. Bom, J. Bøggild and J. Nørregaard Frandsen (eds), *H.C. Andersen i det moderne samfund*, Odense: University Press of Southern Denmark, pp. 49–74.

Mylius, Johan de (2003), *Forvandlingens pris: H.C. Andersen og hans eventyr*, Copenhagen: Høst & Søn.

Sanders, Karin (2012): 'Let's be human – on the politics of the inanimate', *Romantik: Journal for the Study of Romanticisms*, 1: 1, pp. 29–50.

Schlegel, Friedrich (1967 [1799]), 'Gespräch über die Poesie', in H. Eichner (ed.), *Kritische Friedrich Schlegel-Ausgabe seiner Werke*, vol. 2: *Charakteristiken und Kritiken I (1796–1801)*, Vienna: Verlag Ferdinand Schöningh, pp. 284–90.

Wolfe, Cary (2010), *What is Posthumanism?*, Minneapolis: University of Minnesota Press.

III

Carnal Realities: Lively Flesh in Feminist and Queer Readings

CHAPTER 6

Feminist New Materialism and Literary Studies: Methodological Meditations on the Tradition of Feminist Literary Criticism and (Post)Critique

Tobias Skiveren

In recent years feminist theory has witnessed the emergence of a new trend frequently dubbed 'feminist new materialism'. Framing its thinking as a corrective to prevailing constructionist currents within feminist theory, feminist new materialism entered the stage with a good deal of palaver. Its advocates immediately positioned notions like 'sign', 'culture' and 'discourse' as trivial and anachronistic, allegedly even emblematic of a widespread 'somatophobia' (Kirby 1991: 10) – a fear of grappling with the material and fleshy dimensions of corporality – and naturally, such accusations in turn provoked fierce responses from established feminists claiming engagement with matter to be an integral and already well-established part of feminist thinking (Ahmed 2008). In any case, the language of semiotics had shifted to the language of materiality. No longer simply a matter of defending the omnipresence of signs, the feminist tradition was recast as already materialist. The heydays of constructionism, it seems, had come to an end.

However, despite this significant impact on feminist thinking, feminist literary criticism seems almost untouched by these latest developments, not least when compared to how literary critics have been particularly receptive to earlier theoretical transformations in the field. While the ideas of second wave feminism of the 1970s, French feminist theory of the 1980s, and queer theory of the 1990s left clear marks on feminist literary criticism, reconfiguring its approaches to and conceptions of literature, feminist New Materialism has simply not had the same sway. Despite several sporadic readings, here and there informed by its thinkers, no new distinct method for a feminist New Materialist study of literature has yet emerged.

The main aim of this chapter is to examine the potential embedded in feminist New Materialism for transforming established methods, conceptualisations and attitudes within feminist literary criticism. In short, what is literature, and how do we study it, if we adopt the framework of feminist New Materialism? Inasmuch as this trend has been criticised for ignoring earlier perspectives and arguments from the tradition of feminist theory, such an endeavour calls for a methodological approach sensitive to the complex history of changing theories and methods. Accordingly, the chapter starts out by sketching a chronological outline of feminist theory and feminist literary criticism in order to situate feminist New Materialism as the latest cross-disciplinary transfer in an ongoing history of dialogues and appropriations from (1) second wave feminism, (2) French feminist theory and (3) queer theory. Doing so enables the chapter to show how most earlier responses to feminist thinking have often resulted in not only changing conceptions of literature, but also the proliferation of what Rita Felski has named a 'critical mood' (Felski 2015). At play here is a set of conventional styles of thought and modes of argument which guide the feminist literary critic to scrutinise the work in case with the primary aim of evaluating whether or not it engages in *critique*. Taking a literary testimony of embodying care work in the welfare state as my main example, the chapter in constrast argues that the methodological potential of feminist New Materialism lies in its capacity to expand such critical modes of inquiry with postcritical readings by instead revitalising the emphasis on affect and experience also characteristic of the gynocritical approaches of the 1970s. By drawing on ideas from Mayra Rivera, Donna Haraway, Karen Barad and others, the chapter thus suggests that the lines of thought promoted by these figures are best adopted to literary criticism by engaging literature as an affective and imaginative site for witnessing what it *feels* like to live as a specific carnal configuration, subjected not only to the powers of discourse, but also to the recalcitrant materiality of the flesh.

Sticking It to the Man: Second Wave Feminism, Feminist Critique and Gynocriticism

'One is not born, but rather becomes, a woman' (Beauvoir 1979 [1949]: 295). Thus reads Simone de Beauvoir's oft-cited credo from *Le Deuxième Sexe* (1949). Following Beauvoir's logic, one might be born with a specific anatomy (sex), but insofar as our social identity (gender) grows from encounters with the social world, this anatomic facticity in no way entails an anatomic destiny. Rather, from childhood onwards, we are constantly socialised into specific gender roles, rendering the personality traits we usually perceive as private and solid a product of social life. Femininity – however we define it – stems not from the uterus, but from the ideological myths that permeate our societies, shaping our ways of perceiving and treating each other.

Consequently, Beauvoir's phrase provides a suggestive emancipatory promise: the anatomy of our bodies does not define us. Things could be different. Women need not be the second sex, the inferior sidekick to the male hero also known as Man. 'Yes,' Beauvoir writes, 'women on the whole *are* today inferior to men; that is, their situation affords them fewer possibilities. The question is: should that state of affairs continue?' (1979: 24). What is needed is a critical exposure of and activist battle against the ideologies, narratives and practices that reproduce patriarchy. Accordingly, the progressive potential of feminism must run through women's recognition of and resistance to the gender identities so far defined by patriarchy.

Obviously, this line of thinking is not exclusive to Beauvoir. But the influence of *Le Deuxième Sexe* should not be underestimated. Pinpointing the now well-known split between sex and gender,[1] her famous phrase became emblematic of the theoretical impetus driving feminist movements for many years to come. This might especially be the case for the so-called second wave feminism of the 1960s and 1970s as well as feminist literary criticism written in this period, most obviously Kate Millett's canonical dissertation *Sexual Politics* (1970). Although Beauvoir is only credited a couple of times in this highly influential book, Millett's dependence on *Le Deuxième Sexe* is today widely acknowledged (Moi 1985: 25; Fallaize 2007: 85), as her many suspicious readings of male writers clearly echo Beauvoir's exposure of patriarchal ideologies. Launching from an analysis of the power structures regulating sexual relations, Millett delivers a fierce attack on a string of celebrated male authors, exposing how their works are saturated by patriarchal ideas that tie women to restricted roles and inferior identities, objects for the male subject to govern. Accordingly, Millett's reading strategy is in essence *critical*, insofar as she claims her right to disagree with the author, regardless of his status or appraisal. In fact, one might even pose it as one of the early instances of the 'critical mood', recently claimed by Rita Felski to be a dominating trend in contemporary literary studies (Felski 2015).[2] Highlighting some facets as more important than others, this mood, Felski claims, has for long seduced literary critics to engage with texts with the primary purpose of *critically* evaluating the normativity of its ideas, ideologies and discourses, most frequently resulting in either celebrations of subversion or accusations of naivety; and although Felski does not engage specifically with the tradition of feminist literary criticism, this description indeed holds true for Millett as well: no longer simply an awe-inspiring work of art, literature, in her writings, becomes a site for debunking sexist ideas and dynamics otherwise left unnoticed. Like Beauvoir's essay, Millett's readings are supposed to make her readers critically aware of the misogynist structures that permeate even our most intimate situations and relationships.

Moving forward, this critical mode of analysis later inspired hosts of feminist literary criticism in the 1970s, not least the many studies of stereotypical 'images of Women' which allegedly permeated writings by male authors; and yet, the influence of Millett's attitude was not uncontested. Characterising such iconoclastic methods as 'feminist critique', Elaine Showalter, another influential critic at the time, stressed the significance of *not* ascribing this reading strategy methodological monopoly. Feminist critique, she claimed, should not crowd out all other modes of inquiry, as its focus on male writers, critical or not, risks overlooking the experiences and voices of females themselves, thereby repeating the founding gesture of the very same patriarchal ideologies it is criticising. As a corrective to feminist critique, Showalter advocates what she names 'gynocritics'. '[T]he program of gynocritics,' Showalter declares, 'is to construct a female framework for the analysis of women's literature, to develop new models based on the study of female experience' (1979: 28). As a case in point, she takes her own study *A Literature of Their Own* (1977), which charts the experiences and aesthetics of British women novelists from 1840 and onwards, through a three-step historical development. Rather than demystifying sexist ideologies in works by male authors, gynocriticism was to dig up and explore literary works written by women in order to recover female experiences and feelings otherwise neglected. Returning to Beauvoir's vocabulary, gynocriticism set out to explore aesthetic testimonies of what it feels like to become a woman, whereas feminist critique probed literature for misogynist myths on gender roles.

Accordingly, Millett's and Showalter's respective approaches demonstrate how feminist literary criticism from around the 1970s had generally only two methods available. By adopting lines of thought originating in Beauvoir,[3] literature became either a site for exposing sexist ideologies or a medium through which the true voices of oppressed women could be heard. Feminist literary criticism oscillated between a hermeneutics of suspicion and a hermeneutics of trust; and as we will soon see, the mood of critique, suspicion and scepticism embedded in the former approach left a comparatively more conspicuous legacy for feminist literary criticism than the latter.

Writing the Body: French Feminism and *Écriture Féminine*

'Woman must write her self' (Cixous 2009 [1975]: 417), Hélène Cixous declares in her famous essay *Le rire de la Méduse* (1975). Echoing poststructuralist philosophies expanding rapidly in French theory at the time, the phrase is indicative of the renewed understanding of language, which was later to influence both feminist theory and feminist literary criticism. If we ordinarily believe that selves write, Cixous contrarily claims that selves are written. Rather than being a simple tool for the subject to use, language becomes the condition of possibility for subjects to emerge. Womanhood, in other words, is not simply within the individual, but comes into being in and through structures of meaning or signifying processes.

Furthermore, Cixous claims, women are written by men. This does not simply mean that male authors have written about women, casting them in stereotypical roles, as the 'images of women' criticism would suggest; rather, the language through which women come to be is intrinsically marked by the patriarchal patterns of Western thought. The semantic equation between 'man' and 'human' is of course the most obvious proof of this circumstance, but more generally, Cixous maintains, language is imbued with phallogocentric dichotomies (reason/chaos, identity/other, and man/nature), which allegedly represses women's corporeal experiences on a systematic basis. Accordingly, in order to change their position and gain control of their identities, a reconfiguring of the dominant language is needed: women must (re-)write their selves, as Cixous urged, by digging into the immanent intensities and rhythmic flows of their bodies. 'By writing her self, woman will return to the body which has been more than confiscated from her' (2009: 419), Cixous writes. And so, the task becomes one of inventing a corrective to the discourse of Man, an alternative way of writing capable of accommodating female experiences, a women's writing beyond masculine patterns of thought: *écriture féminine*.

Along with the thinking of Luce Irigaray and Julia Kristeva, Cixous's idea of *écriture féminine* set a fashion for feminist literary criticism around 1980, inciting alternative readings of the aesthetic forms of, amongst others, George Eliot (Jacobus 1981) and Marguerite Duras (Marini 1977), as well as renewed discussions on the peculiarity of women's writing (Abel 1982; Marks and Courtivron 1980). Moreover, established approaches within feminist literary criticism suddenly seemed somewhat naive in the light of the highly advanced theories of language promoted by French feminism. Millett, for instance, was criticised for underestimating the scope of patriarchal ideologies, which were now recast as subliminal signifying processes residing *everywhere*, even within the obstinate unconscious of the individual woman. In her highly influential evaluation of Anglo-American feminist criticism and French feminist theory in *Sexual/Textual Politics* (1985), Toril Moi asserts with evident scepticism: 'For Millett, woman is an oppressed being without a recalcitrant unconscious to reckon with; she merely has to see through the false ideology of ruling male patriarchy in order to cast it off and be free' (1985: 29). Realising the presence of discriminatory ideologies is simply not enough, Moi maintains. One needs to reconfigure the very (linguistic) structures operating in our most inner regions. And just as Millett's feminist critique seems to misjudge the powers of language, the gynocriticism of Showalter, Moi continues, literally sees through the very signifying matter texts are made of. The gynocritic, Moi writes, is encouraged to attend 'to historical, anthropological, psychological and sociological aspects of the "female" text; in short, it would seem, to everything but the text as a signifying process' (1985: 76). Investigating female novelists as some sort of witnesses of truth unproblematically conveying 'real' experiences of 'real' women, the text in Showalter's studies 'has disappeared', Moi writes, 'or become the transparent medium through which "experience" can be seized' (1985: 76). Accordingly, for Moi, the future of feminist literary criticism lies in neither feminist critique nor traditional gynocriticism, but in a thorough reworking of analytical strategies on the basis of the lessons learned by French feminism, locating the *critical* potential of literature in its textual, linguistic and semiotic processes, rather than its ideological or experiential reflections.

Switching from the thinking typical of second wave feminism to the Theory (with a capital T) of French feminism, methods and conceptions within feminist literary criticism were thus partly transformed. Despite somewhat intense debates (see e.g. Jones 1981: 253–61), language, at least, would never be the same again, and accordingly, neither would literature. No longer a propagator of false consciousness or an authentic source of experiential truth, literary works were conceptualised as signifying processes with a hidden potential for transforming the language of Man. Yet, the attitude of critique remained. What now needed scrutiny were the forms of writing resisting the categories and logic of established phallogocentric thinking. Rather than *critiquing* male writings for misogynist ideas, feminist literary criticism became interested in studying the ways in which selected (female) aesthetics might themselves be perceived as a *critique* of patriarchal discourse.

Beyond 'Women': Gender Trouble and Queer Critique

In a retrospective reflection on her participation in feminist activism, Ann Snitow voices her frustration with constantly being categorised as female. '"Woman" is my slave name' (2015 [1990]: 21), she declares, implicating a clear-cut analogy: just as slave owners gave their human property names with no regard for personal histories or wishes, so too patriarchy captures and controls its inferior subjects by naming them 'women' with or without their consent. Certainly, one might find the comparison between the literal slavery of colonialism and the linguistic slavery of patriarchy overstated, but the phrase nonetheless delivers an incisive mantra for postfeminism's founding attitude: feeling captivated, imprisoned, tied down, and manipulated by linguistic and semantic categorisations, the problem of feminism is not simply the various patriarchal myths of the other sex, but the concept of 'women' altogether.

Indisputably, the most influential theoretical catalyser for this line of thought is Judith Butler's (in)famous book *Gender Trouble* (1990). As a contribution to the so-called 'identity crisis in feminist theory' (Alcoff 1988) unfolding in the late 1980s, Butler's text was a fierce argument for abandoning 'Woman' as the subject of feminism. Responding to testimonies like Snitow's, Butler relinquished the demand for locating a unified foundation from which feminists could speak on behalf of each other, arguing that such common ground would subjugate rather than emancipate. Along with a host of other ideas from the established feminist tradition, *écriture féminine* was consequently criticised as a 'transcultural structure' underpinning the assertion of 'universalistic claims' that unintentionally excluded individuals not able to identify with the description (Butler 2014 [1990]: 19). 'The internal paradox of this foundationalism', Butler writes, 'is that it presumes, fixes, and constrains the very "subjects" that it hopes to represent and liberate' (2014: 203). Thus, Butler's feminism is a postfeminism: its main aim is neither to upgrade the status of females nor defend women's rights, but to transcend the binary logic that divides individuals into one of two sexes.

In order to do this, however, one of feminism's key distinctions stands in the way. If we do like Beauvoir, Butler maintains,[4] and insist on a split between sex and gender, we risk presenting the biology of the female body as some sort of natural, maybe even metaphysical foundation, positioned beyond the reach of the dynamic forces of culture; and along with fixing individuals like Snitow to a specific identity, this does not fit the many insights Butler has appropriated from poststructuralist thought. Since language, discourse and culture in this framework are construed as all-pervading structures from which there can be no escape, 'sex could not qualify as a prediscursive anatomical facticity', Butler writes. 'Indeed, sex, by definition, will be shown to have been gender all along' (2014: 11).

By construing even the male–female dichotomy – and not simply the masculine–feminine dichotomy – as a product of the mutable structures of discourse, the possibility for altering one of the most sedimented ways of categorising individuals transpires. The next step, Butler claims, is to uncover ways of subverting the prevailing cultural mechanisms that continue to uphold this dichotomy and order individuals to be identified as either one of two mutually exclusive sexes, preferably united in compulsory heterosexuality. 'The critical task for feminism is not to establish a point of view outside of constructed identities,' Butler writes. "The critical task is, rather, to locate strategies of subversive repetition enabled by those constructions' (2014: 201).

This call may be one of *Gender Trouble*'s greatest legacies. Moving beyond the disciplinary boundaries of feminist theory, the search for strategies capable of subverting established constructions of identity has influenced hosts of scholarly work within the humanities, not least literary studies. This transfer of theoretical ideas, however, also transforms the ways in which literary works are perceived and approached. Even though, as Gill Plain and Susan Sellers have noted, defining the key texts of feminist literary criticism has become harder in the wake of poststructuralism (Plain and Sellers 2007: 210), there seems to be a recurrent methodological assumption at play in the many studies of literature inspired by Butler's thinking. Echoing the critical mood of earlier appropriations of feminist theory, queer literary critics inspired by *Gender Trouble* most often engage literature as a discursive site for uncovering subversive strategies able to undo oppressive gender and sexual identities – regardless of whether the text at hand itself aims at participating in this project or not. In *Queer Theories* (2002), Donald E. Hall, for instance, claims that 'all texts have certain queer internal aspects, traces, and resonances and, of course, all texts can be used "queerly" by any reader or set of readers who wish to do so' (2002: 148). To Hall, queer theory undeniably seems to qualify as a 'strong theory',[5] insofar as its applicability is practically universal; but as his phrasing suggests, queer readings simultaneously reduce engagements with texts to two principal strategies. First, the literary critic can seek to bring out the queer identities presented by the work itself. This is the case when texts depicting unorthodox gender and sexual identities are praised for their 'carnialesque', 'camp' or 'destabilising' qualities (see e.g. Piggford 1999; Chess 2016: 39–102). If the text, however, operates in a more orthodox manner, queer literary critics conveniently pull out a second analytical strategy, now reading the work against the grain. Instead of highlighting the text's queer qualities, the orthodox work is *queered*, that is, deconstructed and criticised for circulating 'heteronormative', 'essentialist' or simply 'discriminatory' ideas, which in the end, of course, undermine themselves under the scrutinising eye of the queer critic (see e.g. Sedgwick 1990: 213–51). In any case, the point of departure remains the same: both strategies assume that every identity category – 'man', 'woman', 'heterosexual', 'homosexual' etc. – is an arbitrary construct open for transformation, and the task simply becomes one of uncovering how the literary work might embrace or try to deny this assumption.

With the appropriation of Butlerian ideas, feminist literary criticism thus loses its foundation in the female subject, but instead gains an elusive mode of critique, whose main identity lies in the struggle for undermining identity itself. Accordingly, the project is no longer to recover a specific female way of writing, but to proliferate the amount of intelligible sexual and gender identities by either queering discourses or enhancing discourses with queer qualities. In this double-edged queer procedure, literature is still thought of in terms of structures of meaning or signifying processes, but the anchoring in (female) corporality typical of French feminism is abandoned in favour of the arbitrary play of more or less heteronormative signs.

Recalcitrant Flesh: Feminist New Materialism, Modest Witnesses and Carnacriticism

'Flesh twists and turns', Mayra Rivera writes in *Poetics of the Flesh* (2015: 84). As a pre-individual and pre-phenomenological force, flesh has the ability to take us by surprise, overrule our decisions and drive our actions. Its creative will can emerge from nowhere exactly because it resides everywhere. Rather than a dead lump of meat ready for the human subject to carve and consume, flesh, for Rivera, is the vivacious nonhuman material out of which distinct human bodies arrive.

This in turn also means that flesh and bodies are not the same. Drawing on, amongst others, the late Maurice Merleau-Ponty, Rivera claims that 'the body' as a theoretical category 'fosters an illusion of completeness and wholeness easily naturalised, normalised, and deployed as part of cultural systems of representation' (2015: 7), whereas 'flesh is an ambivalent term that names as rather slippery materiality[,] formless and impermanent, crossing boundaries between the individual body and the world' (2015: 2). Flesh, in other words, is not contained beneath the skin of the body, but runs straight through it. What we usually perceive and comprehend as finite bodies in fact turn out to be provisional coagulations of the infinite flows and rhythms of flesh. Insofar as we want a nuanced picture of the dynamics and processes of corporeal becoming, Rivera holds, we consequently need to expand our investigations of discursive fixations of the individual body with explorations digging into the trans-subjective and recalcitrant activities of the flesh.

Rivera, however, is not alone in such endeavours. In fact, her work is but the latest budding of a much larger theoretical enterprise. In recent years, the slogan of materialism has resonated across the humanities, incited by the promise of New Materialism, Actor Network Theory, Object Oriented Ontology, Speculative Realism and others. Although this shift has certainly gained momentum lately, it obviously did not happen overnight. One might get this impression, though, witnessing the celebration of, for instance, Jane Bennett's influential *Vibrant Matter* (2010) or Graham Harman's various works on Object-Oriented Ontology (OOO), which have gained significant popularity after the (in)famous launch of Speculative Realism in 2007 along with the advancement of Harman's ecocritical partner in crime, Timothy Morton. As much as the (male) protagonists of Speculative Realism might be the new boys in town, they are, however, *not* the first to claim the territory. As Rebekah Sheldon has implied recently, feminist theory can be said to have paved the way for the emergence of this trend, insofar as the role of materiality, the limits of discourse and the impotence of (the hu)man have been the subject of debate in these circles since the 1990s at the very least (Sheldon 2015: 203).

Especially in the wake of the poststructuralist feminism of Butler and others from this period, a series of feminist theorists emerged, including Elizabeth Grosz, Karen Barad, Vicky Kirby, Donna Haraway, Claire Colebrook and Rosi Braidotti, who would claim – with various degrees of intensity – that a return to more material modes of investigation was needed. Although the theoretical backgrounds of these scholars are diverse, ranging from Gilles Deleuze's philosophy of becoming to Maurice Merleau-Ponty's corporeal phenomenology, they seem to share a common goal of renegotiating the role of matter and materiality as a corrective to the thinking of both second wave feminism, French feminism and poststructuralist (post)feminism in particular. Unsurprisingly, the ideas presented in *Gender Trouble*, along with Butler's sequel, *Bodies That Matter* (1993), are often used as symptomatic of the type of thinking that feminist New Materialists seek to distance themselves from. In short, these thinkers claim that Butler's theories indirectly overstate the agency of discourse and thereby construe matter as more passive and malleable than is actually the case. 'Language has been granted too much power', Barad writes: 'The space of agency is much larger than that postulated by Butler's or Louis Althusser's theories. There is more to agency than the possibilities of linguistic resignification' (2003: 801, 826). Such objections to Butler's framework, though, do not entail repositioning biological sex beyond the intrusive forces of culture. Indeed, feminist New Materialists generally agree with Butler's claim that biological sex is always-already social, as our perceptions of and practices as specific bodies can never escape the historically contingent values, norms and concepts in which they are situated. What feminist New Materialists stress, though, is that the body does not always smoothly obey these social, cultural and discursive commands; and by underestimating this ability of recalcitrance, of 'kicking back' (French: *ré-* 'back' and *calcitrare* 'to kick'), Butler, the argument runs, implicitly reproduces a misguiding conception of materiality. 'Unfortunately,' Barad writes, 'Butler's theory ultimately reinscribes matter as a passive product of discursive practices rather than as an active agent participating in the very process of materialization' (2003: 821).

Although Barad's phrasings are directed specifically at Butler's theories, her general argument runs through most of what qualifies as feminist New Materialism: matter is not unmarked by discourse; still, it bears its own agential capacities. 'Representations and cultural inscriptions quite literally constitute bodies and help to produce them as such', Elizabeth Grosz contends in *Volatile Bodies* (1994). Yet, 'bodies are not inert; they function interactively and productively. They act and react. They generate what is new, surprising, unpredictable' (Grosz 1994: x–xi). Contesting the dictation of discourse, corporal materiality is a 'trickster', to use Haraway's figuration, always capable of getting in the way (Haraway 1988: 593). And even though Rivera reserves the term 'flesh' for this type of phenomenon, the point in principle remains the same. 'Associating flesh with material life', she reiterates, 'does not imply claiming that it is prior to or unaffected by the conceits of power-knowledge.

Flesh is shaped by cultures, languages, and representation, but it is not determined by them' (Rivera 2015: 94). Following this line of thought, subjects are subjected not only to the normative interpellations of discourse and culture, but also to fleshy material forces within and around its particular embodiments. Losing the omnipotent status ascribed by humanism, the subject is now perceived as nothing but a specifically situated active corporality deeply enmeshed in material-discursive forces co-producing its lines of becoming and affective experiences.

Accordingly, investigations informed by feminist New Materialism represent an expanded field of interest. Instead of only focusing on the ways in which bodies are constructed in more or less appropriate ways, the interest here is broadened to include how bodies arise from flesh, to use Rivera's distinction; that is, how corporeal forces transcending the individual subject can suddenly reveal themselves as agentic and recalcitrant tricksters, not easily manipulated by either the consciousness of Man or the constructions of culture. Yet, the question in this context remains how this expanded field of interest translates to the study of literature. What does feminist literary criticism gain from appropriating this latest development within feminist theory? Which alternative modes of analysis, attitudes and conceptions of literature might such a move generate? If many earlier studies within feminist literary criticism have examined texts by means of critique, then how and why should we read for the powers of the flesh?

Thus far, only a few attempts at formulating answers to such questions have been made; and despite the fact that these attempts do not form fully fleshed methodologies, it is actually possible to track down two general trends. Both relate the idea of agential materiality to the notion of literature; yet, the conclusions are wide apart. The first trend conceptualises the literary text as a specific instance of *active* materiality, highlighting its immanent ability – as recalcitrant matter – to *resist* the epistemological inspections and knowledge claims of the reader. To perceive 'seemingly and obviously immaterial events such as a reading of a text' as in fact deeply entangled with complex material forces, writes Claire Colebrook, seems to return 'us to what Derrida referred to as undecidability. There is *no* way of knowing the proper sense of a text' (Colebrook 2011: 12, 19). However, considering the current 'poststructuralist fatigue' (Puar 2012: 49) towards the deconstructionist readings for aporias that dominated literary criticism in the 1990s, this line of thought – which has been particularly popular in literary theory informed by Speculative Realism (Harman 2012; Joy 2013) – might not seem as promising as the second trend. Rather than reinterpreting the deconstructionist notion of the materiality of the signifier as the materiality of the object – both hindering epistemological insights beyond the text – a number of New Materialist thinkers hint at literature as a privileged site for affectively and imaginatively exploring the world of material forces. 'Poetry', Bennett writes, 'can help us feel more of the liveliness hidden in such things and reveal more of the threads of connection binding our fate to theirs' (2015: 235). Likewise, Stacy Alaimo notes that 'producers of various works of literature, art, and activism may themselves grapple with ways to render murky material forces palpable' (2010: 9). Examining the fleshy embodiment in postcolonial writings, Rivera too holds that 'literary language, such as [Frantz] Fanon's, engages our imaginations at a visceral level, to help us feel what cannot be seen' (2015: 141).[6] For Bennett, Alaimo and Rivera – all key figures in recent New Materialist thinking – literature is a means of rendering their somewhat abstract notions of materiality palpable, sensible and tangible. Instead of noting that literary works can never be fully known, this trend insists on literature's ability to 'help us feel', to engage us 'at a visceral level', and to 'rende[r] murky material forces palpable'. Without drawing explicitly on affect theory – whose emphasis on affect as a pre-individual and pre-cognitive corporeal force at times comes close to a New Materialism (see especially Massumi 2002) – these three figures seem to emphasise literature's *affective* and *sensory* potential for transforming the perceptual sensibility of the reader.

Admittedly, there is quite a distance from such sporadic comments to a distinct reading strategy. Yet, these observations nonetheless point out a methodological trajectory that might propel us to expand the current modus operandi of queer critique with readings engaging the carnal affects of literature, a 'carnacriticism' of sorts. As an addition to studying literature as a means for undoing sexual and gendered identities, this type of criticism would engage literature as an affective and imaginative site for witnessing what it *feels* like to live as a specific corporal configuration, subjected not only to the powers of discourse, but also to the recalcitrant materiality of the flesh. Rather than examining the text for the underlying discourses regulating its ideas and norms, we could explore the affective experiences of the corporealities it presents by diving into the various material-discursive forces producing them. In such a mode of inquiry, characters would not simply be manifestations of (gendered) identity constructs, but corporeal figures that move us at a visceral level just as much as they themselves are moved by the material forces within and around them. Likewise, metaphors would not just be the manifestations of the linguistic play of writing itself, much less of metaphysical epiphanies, but paradoxical attempts at accounting for the extra-discursive affects of the flesh by employing the sensual and imaginative capacities of the language at hand. And in general, compositions would not only entail maps of subject positions, let alone plot dynamics between *fabula* and *sjuzet*, but would also involve multiple planes of corporeal movements and transformations, patterns of ways of affecting and being affected, rhythmic trajectories of material-discursive becomings.

The possibilities, here, are numerous. What, for instance, can literature reveal about the embodied experiences of a sick body in fast disintegration; an aging body in slow decline; a body that suddenly aborts; a pregnant body growing spontaneously on its own; an inherited corporal morphology vulnerable to current racialising discourses? Turning to the genre of maternity leave novels, I would like, however, to end with a brief elaboration on a rather specific way in which a methodological recalibration would enable feminist literary criticism to analyse literary works with the aim of highlighting what life as a specific configuration of unruly flesh might feel like in certain environments. As much as this type of writing might conjure up imaginaries differing significantly from idealised ideas on motherhood, and thus in principle could be read as a sort of critical counter-discourse, they also pose an opportunity for examining the affective becomings of a particular kind of enfleshment doing particular kinds of things in a particular kind of milieu. The end goal of such an analysis, though, would not be to uncover a transcultural common ground for all mothers, but, remembering Haraway's famous call (1988), to reflect on the specifically *situated* experiences of particular bodies that, in this case, care for their offspring. For that reason, let us be more specific and focus for a moment on experiences of maternity leave in one of the most socialist environments of the Western world: the Nordic welfare state. Compared to many other women around the globe, mothers in the Scandinavian countries are typically provided with accessible institutional care for their children. And yet, local literary works suggest that the care work carried out by mothers themselves is still framed by Western ideas of the nuclear family which individualise parenting practices in ways that risk triggering unruly carnal powers not intended. The novel *Mor* (2016) (*Mother* in English) by the Danish writer Maja Lucas is a case in point. By blocking out most references to a world outside the home, it demonstrates some of the embodied experiences that might arise when care work plays out within a domestic space of isolation, exhibiting an otherwise closed-off arena in which two bodies – mother and child – intermingle in what turns out to be a destructive dance of flesh touching flesh.

The novel opens with the child's delivery and ends with a car accident a couple of years later. In between these events we are presented with a string of specific situations in which the mother and the child interact, followed by the mother's reflection on her own actions. While many things can be said about these situations, a reading focusing on the protagonist's lived enfleshment would be struck by a specific corporeal pattern that centres around the cultivation of a certain sensibility. At first, the autonomous sphere of the home seems to help the mother develop an increased perceptual openness that makes her body react to even the subtlest movements of the child. It is as if simply being with the infant augments her sensory apparatus, allowing her to pick up otherwise imperceptible activities. In phenomenological terms, this means that everything about the baby intensifies. Physical contact feels like electricity, and the noises of tranquil sleep sound as noises of despair. She cannot *not* check up on the sleeping baby. 'The girl is like a force that should be obeyed unconditionally', Lucas writes (Lucas 2016: 20, all translations are mine), and continues:

> [W]hen the girl touches her, it feels like a flow of electricity is running through her. Never before has she enjoyed touching this much, never has she longed that much for physical contact with another human being, not even during her biggest crushes. When the girl cuddles up to her, the mother often begins to chuckle, as if the happiness is too much, a joy that is too intense. She is not used to such unconditional love. She has never been touched this much, not even by the father. The girl sits on her lap when they are done eating and holds her hand when they read. She is like a cat wanting to be petted, she flatters the mother with her needs. It is as if she seeks the whirlwind of hormones that is shared between them, the rush of attachment. (2016: 67)

The attachment between mother and child is not perceived, here, as a spiritual connection between two interrelated personalities; rather, it emerges as flesh touches flesh in a circuit of automatic affective stimuli. Emotional bonds, in other words, are folded into carnal ones. In that way, the cultivation of a corporeal sensibility in Lucas's book seems to be intimately tied up with the cultivation of what María Puig de la Bellacasa has recently described as 'practices of care in more than human worlds', insofar as the mother's impulse to uphold the well-being of their common world is contingent on the augmentation of a sensory apparatus whose workings play out beyond the full control of individual humans as well as human cultures (Bellacasa 2017). By locating the practice of care at the level of corporeality, in other words, Lucas also locates the forces regulating such practices in the flesh as well as in the body, to use Rivera's distinction.

Unsurprisingly, then, as the life of isolation and constant exposure to the clumsy and noisy infant unfolds, her mode of response also starts to develop in unexpected and unfortunate ways. Gradually, the sensitivity that initially helped secure the comfort and security of the child morphs into a *hyper*sensitivity that turns attunement to irritability. The presence of the child's body, Lucas writes, is no longer simply perceived as overwhelming, but an outright menace: 'It is as if she is constantly threatened by the girl, her presence is a source of stress' (2016: 48). Consequently, the noises and movements of the child begin to trigger aggressive scolding and uncontrollable rage rather than careful attention. What initially protected the well-being of a vulnerable offspring now becomes a source of danger. Again and again the protagonist loses control; the affective charge building up in her limbs simply boils over. A symptomatic interaction now goes like this:

> The girl crawls up on her lap, puts her arms around her, presses her face tight against hers. The mother tries to tell her that it is too much, but unwillingly laughs along with the girl's laughter. In the end, she has to push the girl away in order to breathe. Then the girl grabs a ringlet and pulls. The mother's mood shifts immediately, she gets angry. The girl registers the change and lashes at her. The mother puts her firmly on the floor and says that she will not have it. She kicks a plastic hammer as she leaves for the bathroom. She slams the door shut. (2016: 68)

In such scenes, the body of the mother stops being a simple tool for the human subject to wield. Riffing on Grosz's and Haraway's phrasings quoted above, the body instead reveals itself as an obstructive trickster that acts and reacts in a process of autopoiesis, creating surprising and unpredictable effects. First, the laughter transmits from child to mother, easing her scepticism; a moment later, the clumsy hair pull triggers an aggressive repulse. Like before, the interaction between the two first and foremost builds on affective fluctuations that oscillate all by themselves, and the mother and child cannot help being caught up in the intensities of that trans-corporeal dynamic. Yet, the outcome this time around is not attachment and care, but physical and psychical distanciation. Sure, the mother in Lucas's book might try to break this destructive tendency by isolating herself in the bathroom to reflect on her own reactions as well as the reasons why they are not 'appropriate'; and yet, as soon as she re-enters the corporeal circuit of care work she feels out of control once again. 'The situation repeats, again and again' (2016: 85), Lucas writes: 'It is as if the rage constantly looms within her when she is with the girl' (2016: 81). In fact, they seems to grow for each encounter, which ultimately results in scenes of almost outright physical violence, but also ultimately causes a – perhaps lethal – car accident, as the mother drives off in a moment of intense rage and exhaustion. While the mother might be following the individualised practices of maternity characteristic of the Western world, these practices simultaneously trigger recalcitrant forces of materiality that in turn violate other people's norms of correct motherhood. Flesh, as Rivera puts it, is not prior to or unaffected by the powers of culture; but it is not determined by them either.

Obviously, there is a lot more to be said about this book; yet, what this brief sketch of Lucas's maternity leave novel has attempted to lay out is that reading literature as affective testimonies might help grasp the specific embodied experiences in a particular environment. In *Mor* the dominant affective mode is a pervasive sense of being submerged in carnal processes that inflict her disposition towards her own offspring. Though the institutions of the Nordic welfare states might in principle counterwork such affective overloading, care work is still a lonely business; and in this case, the dyadic isolation not only leads to an augmented embodied attunement between parent and child, it also sparks undesirable corporeal transformations and modes of affecting and being affected that are hard to contain.

While the sensibility for the recalcitrance of flesh is novel, such analysis has both continuities and discontinuities with the various feminist approaches to literature so far presented. Most obviously, the emphasis on the stubborn and unruly activities, rhythms and textures of various forms of embodiment aligns with the focus in French feminism, while leaving out the idea of a particular rebellious way of writing tied to the female sex. Likewise, the insistence on literature's ability to convey experiences and feelings converges with the project of gynocriticism, although the main aim is not only to form a forum for women to identify with other women, but also to put forward an affective and imaginative site where experiences of different enfleshments can meet and, sometimes, touch each other. And finally, while this analysis focuses on female embodiment, it would share with queer literary criticism an openness towards intersectional analysis of all types of bodies and subject positions, without, however, primarily engaging literature by means of a critical evaluation of its various constructions of male and female identities.

Although returning to literature's experiential and affective dimensions might at first sight seem somewhat naive, this revitalisation nonetheless could help invigorate more empathetic and sensitive modes of inquiry, moving beyond the 'critical mood' that has dominated the tradition of feminist literary criticism for decades. While Millett's *Sexual Politics* might have incited this attitude, its traits permeate all of the reading strategies above, with the exception of gynocriticism, insofar as the main aim of both feminist critique, *écriture féminine* and queer critique is to evaluate whether the work at hand contests or reinforces 'patriarchal myths', 'phallogocentric discourse' or 'essentialist notions of identity'. While the various critical strategies of feminist criticism have done a fine job revealing discriminating structures and practices, such strategies are currently in need of supplementation – not replacement(!) – as their dependence on mistrust, scepticism and negativity has come at the expense of more affirmative, edifying and affective encounters with texts (Sedgwick 2003; Braidotti 2002). Some contemporary feminist thinkers have even construed 'fellow-feeling' as a 'fantasy' (Ahmed 2014: 41) and 'compassionate emotions' as 'instruments of suffering' (Berlant 2004: 5), while, in turn, implicitly hypostasising critique as the only legitimate mode of inquiry. Such dismissals, however, are sympotomatic of an either/or line of thought that fails to invision feminist literary criticism as a methodological multitude with several complementary analytical approaches complementing each other. Re-emphasising literature's capacity for transmitting corporeal feelings and sensations might incite feminist literary criticism to expand its critical repertoire with studies that explore the affective dynamics presented by literary works with the primary purpose of accessing hitherto inaccessible experiences. Doing so, affects might become just as important as discourses, and careful registration just as important as condemnation.

Adopting one of Haraway's famous figurations, we might even pose the notion of the 'modest witness' as carnacriticism's complement to the critical literary critic (Haraway 1996).[7] When reading for the experiences of others, we need to be humble, not supercilious, and aim 'at witnessing, not at judging', to use Braidotti's explication of Haraway's idea (2006: 206). Carnacriticism's prioritisation of the hermeneutics of trust over the hermeneutics of suspicion thus clearly echoes the founding attitude of gynocriticism, where 'the role of the feminist critic', as Moi writes, 'is . . . to sit quietly and listen to her mistress's voice as it expresses authentic female experience' (1985: 78). Moi's phrasing is clearly sarcastic,[8] and indeed, uncritical credulousness is never recommended; but one might ask if attentive listening is always to be posed as such a dubious ideal? The fact that knowledge is always situated, generalisations impossible and literature's transfer of experience never pure should indeed make us humble and sensitive in our approach, but not prompt us to altogether abandon practices of reading for the experiences of others. Being modest must simply not exclude us from witnessing. For even though we can never completely understand the situated and entangled realities of the Other, as feminist philosopher Lorraine Code writes, we at times are able to 'listen well enough' for our ways of feeling, perceiving and acting to change (2006: 231). Engaging literature as a site for witnessing the affects of the flesh might, in other words, be perceived as a significant technique for producing alternative patterns of response, changing our perceptual modes and ability to be affected by the corporal materialities around us. While critique is important, so is our general response-ability – that is, the ability to respond to, be sensitive towards, and com-passionate with the range of different bodies we meet throughout our lives. And in a world, as Code notes, where the increasing mediatisation may generate 'more and more talk', but simultaneously appear to provoke 'less and less listening' (2006: 236), cultivating practices of reading as practices of attentive listening or modest witnessing, as it were, might prompt a helpful responsiveness that – in combination with critical exposés – might open new ways of moving forward.

Notes

1. Whether the phrase actually supports the sex/gender division has been the subject of debate (see e.g. Moi 1999: 72–3).
2. Felski's account is obviously inspired by Eve K. Sedgwick's idea of paranoid reading (Sedgwick 2003).
3. Although (Anglo-American) feminist literary criticism in this period had a declared distaste for theory, worrying about neglecting the practical business of political activism (Showalter 1979: 24), its studies nonetheless, as we have seen, build on assumptions which can be traced back to Beauvoir's theoretical reflections (see also Gallop 1992: 43).
4. For Butler's take on Beauvoir specifically, see Butler (1986).
5. The term 'strong theory' is borrowed from Eve Kosofsky Sedgwick's *Touching Feeling* (2003).
6. Similar points can be found in the different ecocritical studies inspired by New Materialism (Trumpeter 2015; Johnson 2014; Iovino and Oppermann 2014).
7. This notion of the modest witness is in line with the general shift from critical or paranoid methods to more redemptive or affirmative procedures currently emerging in (new) materialist and affect-oriented circles in recent years (Grosz 2005: 3; Massumi 2002: 12–13; van der Tuin 2011: 23–9; Sedgwick 2003: 123–51). Adopting Rita Felski's term, we might name this trend 'postcritical' (as opposed to 'uncritical') (Felski 2015: 172–82).
8. In her recent work on Wittgenstein, Moi has clearly revised her scepticism (Moi 2017: 196–221).

References

Abel, Elizabeth (ed.) (1982), *Writing and Sexual Difference*, Chicago: University of Chicago Press.
Ahmed, Sara (2008), 'Open forum imaginary prohibitions', *European Journal of Women's Studies*, 15: 1, pp. 23–39.
Ahmed, Sara (2014 [2004]), *The Cultural Politics of Emotion*, Edinburgh: Edinburgh University Press.
Alaimo, Stacy (2010), *Bodily Natures*, Bloomington and Indianapolis: Indiana University Press.
Alcoff, Linda (1988), 'Cultural feminism versus post-structuralism: the identity crisis in feminist theory', *Signs*, 13: 3, pp. 405–36.
Barad, Karen (2003), 'Posthumanist performativity', *Signs*, 28: 3, pp. 801–31.
Beauvoir, Simone de (1979 [1949]), *The Second Sex*, Harmondsworth: Penguin.
Bellacasa, María Puig de la (2017), *Matters of Care*, Minneapolis: University of Minnesota Press.
Bennett, Jane (2010), *Vibrant Matter*, Durham, NC: Duke University Press.
Bennett, Jane (2015), 'Systems and things', in Richard Grusin (ed.), *The Nonhuman Turn*, Minneapolis: University of Minnesota Press.
Berlant, Lauren (ed.) (2004), *Compassion*, New York: Routledge.
Braidotti, Rosi (2002), *Metamorphosis*, Cambridge: Polity Press.
Braidotti, Rosi (2006), 'Human, all too human', *Theory, Culture, and Society*, 23: 6–7, pp. 197–208.
Butler, Judith (1986), 'Sex and gender in Simone de Beauvoir's *Second Sex*', *Yale French Studies*, no. 72, pp. 35–49.
Butler, Judith (2011 [1993]), *Bodies That Matter*, New York: Routledge.
Butler, Judith (2014 [1990]), *Gender Trouble*, New York: Routledge.
Chess, Simone (2016), *Male-to-Female Crossdressing in Early Modern English Literature*, New York: Routledge.
Cixous, Hélène (2009 [1975]), 'The laugh of the Medusa', in Robyn Warhol-Down and Diane Herndl (eds), *Feminisms Redux*, New Brunswick, NJ: Rutgers University Press.
Code, Lorraine (2006), *Ecological Thinking*, New York: Oxford University Press.
Colebrook, Claire (2011), 'Matter without bodies', *Derrida Today*, 4: 1, pp. 1–20.
Fallaize, Elizabeth (2007), 'Simone de Beauvoir and the demystification of woman', in Gill Plain and Susan Sellers (eds), *A History of Feminist Literary Criticism*, New York: Cambridge University Press.
Felski, Rita (2015), *The Limits of Critique*, Chicago: University of Chicago Press.
Gallop, Jane (1992), *Around 1981*, New York: Routledge.
Grosz, Elizabeth (1994), *Volatile Bodies*, Bloomington: Indiana University Press.
Grosz, Elizabeth (2005), *Time Travels*, Durham, NC: Duke University Press.

Hall, Donald E. (2002), *Queer Theories*, Basingstoke: Palgrave Macmillan.
Haraway, Donna (1988), 'Situated knowledges', *Feminist Studies*, 14: 3.
Haraway, Donna (1996), 'Modest witness', in Peter Galison and David Stump (eds), *The Disunity of Sciences*, Stanford: Stanford University Press.
Harman, Graham (2012), 'The well-wrought broken hammer', *New Literary Criticism*, 43: 2, pp. 183–203.
Iovino, Serenella and Serpil Oppermann (eds) (2014), *Material Ecocriticism*, Bloomington: Indiana University Press.
Jacobus, Mary (1981), 'The question of language: men of maxims and *The Mill on the Floss*', *Critical Inquiry*, 8: 2, pp. 207–22.
Johnson, Rochelle L. (2014), '"This enchantment is no delusion": Henry David Thoreau, the new materialisms, and ineffable materiality', *Isle*, 21: 3, pp. 606–35.
Jones, Ann Rosalind (1981), 'Writing the body', *Feminist Studies*, 7: 2, pp. 247–63.
Joy, Eleen A. (2013), 'Weird reading', *Speculations*, 4, pp. 28–34.
Kirby, Vicky (1991), 'Corporeal habits', *Hypatha*, 6: 3, pp. 4–24.
Lucas, Maja (2016) *Mor*, Copenhagen: Forlaget C&K.
Marini, Marcelle (1977), *Territoires du féminin*, Paris: Minuit.
Marks, Elaine and Isabelle de Courtivron (1980), *New French Feminisms*, Amherst: University of Massachusetts Press.
Massumi, Brian (2002), *Parables for the Virtual*, Durham, NC: Duke University Press.
Millett, Kate (1989 [1970]), *Sexual Politics*, London: Virago.
Moi, Toril (1985), *Sexual/Textual Politics*, London and New York: Routledge.
Moi, Toril (1999), *What is a Woman?*, Oxford: Oxford University Press.
Moi, Toril (2017), *Revolution of the Ordinary*, Chicago: University of Chicago Press.
Piggford, George (1999), '"Who's that girl?" Annie Lennox, Woolf's *Orlando*, and female camp androgyny', in Fabio Cleto (ed.), *Camp*, Edinburgh: Edinburgh University Press.
Plain, Gill and Susan Sellers (eds) (2007), *A History of Feminist Literary Criticism*, New York: Cambridge University Press.
Puar, Jasbir (2012), '"I would rather be a cyborg than a goddess"', *philoSOPHIA*, 2: 1, pp. 49–66.
Rivera, Mayra (2015), *Poetics of the Flesh*, Durham, NC: Duke University Press.
Sedgwick, Eve Kosofsky (1990), *Epistemology of the Closet*, Berkeley: University of California Press.
Sedgwick, Eve Kosofsky (2003), *Touching Feeling*, Durham, NC: Duke University Press.
Sheldon, Rebekah (2015), 'Form/matter/chora', in Richard Grusin (ed.), *The Nonhuman Turn*, Minneapolis: University of Minnesota Press.
Showalter, Elaine (1978 [1977]), *A Literature of Their Own*, London: Virago.

Showalter, Elaine (1979), 'Towards a feminist poetics', in Mary Jacobus (ed.), *Women Writing and Writing about Women*, London: Croom Helm.

Snitow, Ann (2015), 'A gender diary' in *The Feminism of Uncertainty*, Durham, NC: Duke University Press.

Trumpeter, Kevin (2015), 'The language of the stones', *American Literature*, 87: 2, pp. 225–52.

van der Tuin, Iris (2011), '"A different starting point, a different metaphysics": reading Bergson and Barad Diffractivel', *Hypatia*, 26: 1, pp. 22–42.

CHAPTER 7

Djuna Barnes and Queer Interiorities

Laura Oulanne

Djuna Barnes's modernist works are populated by characters whose essence seems to be in their bodily being rather than in their fictional heads. She invites readers to feel for and with characters who do not open up for internalist psychology. The characters inhabit houses and apartments, yet these spaces seem to lack the stability, safety and continuity commonly associated with dwelling places.[1] The spaces are often decaying and liminal, with windows and doors that are open to the world outside and allow characters to move through.[2] Barnes's domestic spaces host all-female salons, performances and collections of objects, disrupting the tacit expectations of a house filled by a heterosexual family. In the 'stunt' journalism of Barnes's early career, in which she reports about her experience as a test subject in various extreme situations, she pushes the boundaries of both house interiors and the interior of the body, while transgressing gendered norms of behaviour: she dangles by the side of a building while being rescued, spends time in cage with a gorilla, goes to a boxing match – and undergoes force-feeding.

In this chapter, I study interiority both as a psychological condition for the subject and as a structural condition for domestic values, and investigate how it is reimagined in two of Barnes's short stories and one piece of journalism. By 'queer interiorities' I mean Barnes's rewritings of the metaphorical connotations and ideologies attached to the human subject and to house interiors: the normative conception of the subject as a spiritual essence contained within the body and detached from the material reality, and the house interior as the locus of heterosexual relations. I hope to show how paying attention to the materiality and affectivity of both the human body and its spaces of dwelling, as they appear in Barnes's writing, will illuminate the way metaphors and norms rest on lived bodies and spaces and the way they can be challenged in both literary and journalistic means of expression.

I approach the materiality of spaces and bodies in Barnes's work by reading them through the New Materialist idea of networks of permeable material bodies 'intra-acting' in assemblages. Stacy Alaimo's account of 'trans-corporeality' underlines 'the extent to which the substance of the human is ultimately inseparable from "the environment"': how 'the human is always the very stuff of the messy, contingent, emergent mix of the material world' (Alaimo 2010: 2, 11). Karen Barad has coined the therm 'intra-action' to grasp the way human and nonhuman agents not only interact in different constellations but are also constituted in and through them (Barad 2007: 33). To bring the ideas of bodily permeability, interconnectedness and emergence closer to the domains of the affective and the experiential, I turn to Jane Bennett's discussion of agency in affective assemblages. Bennett uses the Deleuzean notion of assemblages to describe a similar emergent agency and foreground its affectivity: human and nonhuman bodies that simultaneously affect and are affected produce a force 'distinct from the sum of the vital force of each materiality considered alone' (Bennett 2010: 24). Furthermore, I draw on the way Bennett's work challenges the notion of 'life' as something tied to an individual (human) subject.

I propose a 'reading of affective materialities' that is akin to the version of 'surface reading'[3] drafted by Rita Felski: an 'embodied mode of attentiveness that involves us in acts of sensing, perceiving, feeling, registering and engaging' (Felski 2015: 176), with focus on the affective and performative potential of the text and the materialities it depicts rather than their possible hidden meaning. Accordingly, I use of the notion of the reader to refer to a being implied by the text, but one whose reading requires the basic cognitive processes defined by our situatedness as material bodies in a material world.[4] While this conception of a reader is rather universal, we also need to remember that sociocultural norms affect the meanings of materialities for different bodies, which is why I will draw on feminist and queer phenomenology to pay attention to the normativity of domestic and subjective interior spaces.

Feminist phenomenologist Iris Marion Young notes that for women and feminists, the house and the home can be conflicted spaces that offer both confinement and security:

> If house and home mean the confinement of women for the sake of nourishing male projects, then feminists have good reason to reject home as a value. But it is difficult even for feminists to exorcise a positive valence to the idea of home. (Young 2005: 123)

According to Sara Ahmed, who takes a queer approach to phenomenology, homes tend to be more welcoming to certain bodies, and to be furnished with heteronormative ideas of life. A queer orientation can manifest as a disturbance in the stability of the domestic space: 'Homes too can be "giddy" places where things are not always held in place' (Ahmed 2006: 9). These accounts are helpful in studying how the cultural meanings of interior domestic spaces intermingle with the concrete and lived material spaces depicted by the texts.

Together, the New Materialist and phenomenological approaches address the multiple intra-actions between the material and cultural spheres and the human and nonhuman bodies that populate Barnes's texts. The aim of my readings is to investigate not only how select theoretical approaches can shed light on unnoticed characteristics of a singular literary text, but how literary, creative language use can contribute to addressing theoretical issues. I ask how descriptions of material house interiors and bodies and the metaphorical expressions drawing on them interact in the process of reading Barnes's texts, and how the descriptions and metaphors contribute to rethinking tacit understandings attached to interiority in general. My reading of metaphors revisits the basic argument of cognitive metaphor theory: that the tacit everyday metaphors we use have their roots in our mixture of embodied and cultural being in the world (Lakoff and Johnson 2003), and that poetic, 'new' metaphors result from the creative use of the same resources (Lakoff and Johnson 2003: 139; Lakoff and Turner 1989). Combining this understanding with the insight from New Materialist and feminist approaches, I suggest that metaphors that rely on house and body interiors in literary, journalistic and theoretical texts alike can enforce but also challenge 'hardened' norms and ideologies – sometimes within one and the same text. My reading shows that Barnes's use of concrete and metaphorical materialities to distribute agency and affectivity and dethrone the human subject also affords a queer vision of life and relations and surpasses the restrictive bounds of heteronormativity. What I call the 'indifference' of the text to anthropocentrism invites a shift of perspective that also shows the impermanence and malleability of sociocultural norms.

'Dusie' (1927), a story depicting a drama of love and deception between four women in an all-female salon, with abundant spatial description and thing-like characters, is the first example of how the queering of domesticity relies on an embodied and material reimagining of subjective interiority. In my reading, I will focus on how the unconventional use of spatial and bodily metaphors in the story challenges patriarchal and heteronormative values. 'Finale' (1918), a descriptive account of a family gathered around the coffin of the dead father, invites the study of how metaphors of subjective interiority interact with the description and narration of material bodies intra-acting in material spaces, and how they are used to rethink what constitutes human subjectivity and life. Finally, I will read 'How It Feels to be Forcibly Fed' (1914), a journalistic text that uses a mixture of conventional metaphors and affective evocations of materiality to describe the experience of being bound to a hospital bed and force-fed with a rubber tube. I suggest that this text, like Barnes's fiction, 'queers' metaphors of subjective and spatial interiorities, but that it also provides meta-reflection on the political and ethical potential of telling a story of affective, embodied experience with their help.

Undomesticated Space and Affective Bodies

Mary Wilson has called Barnes's writing 'unhoused fictions', in which, according to her,

> Homes and sentences appear as collections of objects that accumulate meaning through the very fact of the collection. No character ever feels at home in these spaces, which alternately display the collection like a museum or invite performance like a vaudeville stage. (Wilson 2011: 431)

Wilson suggests that Barnes's destabilisation of domestic space entails a questioning of the validity of stable (gender) identity as an objective. The disrupted domesticity aligns with a queer politics of space. According to Ahmed, the arrangements of the home and its furnishings reveal presumptions of how life should be organised. Paying attention to furniture can lead to seeing what is normative or 'queer' about it, as it ceases to remain in the background of habitual human action (2006: 168). Barnes's fictional furnishings, when read not only with their object functions and symbolic meanings but also and especially with their materiality in mind, certainly demand a position in the foreground. The destabilisation of spatial interiors affects the anthropocentric categorisations of subjectivity as well as the norms of gender identity and sexuality.

'Dusie' is part of a cycle of stories situated in Paris, narrated by a young cosmopolitan woman called Katya to someone she refers to as 'madame'. In 'Dusie', Katya's story features Madame K–, who hosts an all-female salon in her home. Among its frequent visitors are Dusie, a young woman who has a love affair with Madame K–, and Clarissa, whom Madame K– regards with indifference. The story moves from the description of the house and the central characters to the narration of events occurring on a rainy night, when Madame K– is away, and Dusie asks Katya to stay the night because she is afraid. As they lie in bed talking, Clarissa enters, and Dusie shoos Katya away; from another room, through sleep, Katya overhears a discussion that she does not repeat in the story. In the morning she hears Dusie crying, and enters her room simultaneously with Madame K– to see Dusie lying mute and helpless on the bed with a 'crushed', bleeding foot – it remains unclear what has happened. The story ends with Katya's enigmatic comment about how she is already forgetting the story: 'it is so in Paris; France eats her own history, *n'est-ce-pas* [sic], madame?' (Barnes 1996: 410)

The story moves from a brief characterisation of Dusie[5] to the house and to Madame K–. The lengthy description of the house interior creates the effect of a flood of nonhuman bodies:

> There were many chrysanthemums, and a long white harp in the embrasure of the window, and in the dust lying upon it many women had written 'Dusie.' And above all, in an enamelled cage, two canaries, the one who sang, and the one who listened. But in the boudoirs there was much pink, and everything was brittle and glazed and intricate. Ribbons dangled from everything and bon-bons were everywhere, and statuettes of little boys in satin breeches, offering tiny ladies in bouffant skirts, fans and finches and flowers, and all about in the grass were stuck shiny slinking foxes. A thin powder was over everything upon the dressing table, mauve and sweet smelling, and a great litter of *La Vie Parisienne* and *Le Rire*, and when you picked up the most solemn looking volume, engravings of Watteau fell out and Greuze, and in the hall a tall clock tinkled and rang. (1996: 404–5)

The description evokes a rococo aesthetic, with a dose of baroque abundance, emphasised by repeating denominators like 'very', 'many', 'much', 'everything', 'everywhere' and 'tall'. The method of listing foregrounds individual things, from ribbons to chrysanthemums to harps to statuettes to engravings, while the description binds them together as a mass by the signs of decay and the all-encompassing dust and powder, which suggests a collection of things in a museum-like space. As the house becomes a scene of action, Wilson's comparison of a theatre seems equally apt: the things are staged, 'pretending' to be in everyday use. They are also 'misused': the women write on the harp, and potentially valuable art objects appear alongside cheap magazines or fall on the floor. The female space of the house substitutes a patriarchal version of domesticity, and the space is queered in this way by the way the women use it. Following Ahmed:

> Queer furnishings support proximity between those who are supposed to live on parallel lines, *as points that should not meet*. A queer object hence makes contact possible. . . . The contact is bodily, and it unsettles that line that divides spaces as worlds, thereby creating other kinds of connections where unexpected things can happen. (2006: 69, emphasis in the original)

By explicitly describing an all-female quasi-domestic space and as well as implying sexual relationships between the women housed by it, 'Dusie' rewrites the heterosexual connotations of a home and makes its objects queer.

In an affective, New Materialist reading, another kind of spatial destabilisation can be observed. Even though the nonhuman stuff described acquires meaning from human activities of art, journalism, collection and entertainment, the length of the catalogue dwarfs the preceding and subsequent descriptions of human subjects. The flood of things is posed as an assemblage with an affective vitality of its own, produced by its up-front positioning and length, the rapid succession of things in its list form, and the choice of verbs and adjectives with repeating phonetic patterns that evoke glow and a quivering movement: 'brittle', 'glazed', 'dangled', 'slinking', 'tinkled'. Although there are living creatures, like the canaries, and signs of human actions, like the 'you' picking up the books or magazines and the writing in the dust, the sense of liveliness rests on the material richness of the uneven whole. The difference between dead and lively matter is further blurred by the evocation of sounds, produced both by the living canary and by the clock. The space is not observed from any one human point of view even though the description relies on Katya's experience: the positioning of the things 'everywhere' rather than in specific locations and the aesthetic of listing create the sense of an aperspectival interior that exists for its own sake (Stanica 2014), or for the sake of a variety of bodies coming together. The fictional space thus allows for unexpected forms of contact not only between human bodies, but also between nonhuman ones, putting the normative subjectivity and domestic space in a shaky position.

If the list and the aperspectival description above imply the displacement of human interiority, the following description of the main inhabitant of the house makes this explicit:

> Madame K– was large, very full and blond. She went with the furniture as only a childless Frenchwoman can. She had been a surgeon, a physician, but nothing remained of it, only the tone of her voice when she was angry; then she removed the argument within the exact bounds of its sickness. When there was talk of spiritual matters, and there is always such talk, madame, when women, many women, are closed up together in a room, she listened, but she let you know definitely that she was mortal. (1996: 405–6)

Madame K– is first described as to her physiognomy, and her human status is destabilised by the expression 'went with the furniture': instead of the furniture reflecting the character, she follows its style, form and location. We learn about her past profession and some of her characteristics, but Katya's observations remain on a behavioural and externalised level. They are rendered in artful phrases accompanied by a gnomic present ('as only a childless Frenchwoman can'; 'there is always such talk'), all of which (as well as the presence of 'madame' as the narratee) keeps the reader emotionally and psychologically at a distance from the character described. Katya does not speculate about personal psychology but describes a general state of affairs matching the state of material things just before. Madame K–'s declaration of mortality as an antidote to spirituality suggests the illusoriness of the idea of a spirit detached from the body. Thus, the text extends the impersonality and undomesticity of the container-like interior space to the woman who denies her spiritual interiority. Nevertheless, the character retains agency and affective potential in what she does and how she relates to the space and the things and bodies surrounding her. While the passage highlights her unconventionality (a childless, educated, intellectual woman gathering other women around her), it also tempts a re-evaluation of conventional ways of reading any human character.

The same applies to Katya's description of Dusie, which likens the character not only to things but to space:

> For that is the way it was with Dusie always. All people gave her their attention, stroking her, and calling her pet or beast, according to their feelings. They touched her as if she were an idol, and she stood tall, or sat to drink, unheeding, absent. You felt that you must talk to Dusie, tell her everything, because all her beauty was there, but uninhabited, like a church, *n'est-ce-pas* [sic], madame? Only she was not holy, she was very mortal, and sometimes vulgar, a ferocious and oblivious vulgarity. (1996: 406, emphasis in the original)

If Dusie is like a container, there is nothing inside her. Katya also reports that 'when I asked her what she was thinking, she would say "nothing"' (1996: 407). Yet she remains capable of expression and of affecting other bodies. She emerges in physical contact with others, who touch her and talk to her and write her name on the surfaces of the space. Using the similes of the church and the idol creatively, the text lays bare the 'conceptual metaphors' (Lakoff and Johnson 2003: 3) for a human subject: a body 'filled' with the stuff of the spiritual or the material, as when liquid or air fills a container. The 'new metaphors' Barnes uses to describe Dusie deviate not only from the norm of a heterosexual body, but also from the normative depiction of the human body as filled with spiritual being. Barnes's presentation of a queer body as a dehumanised one is not unproblematic, but her descriptions of the embodied humans and the lively material space invite the realisation of the arbitrariness of norms inscribed on spaces, and replace them with affectivity that does not discriminate between bodies. In this way, a reading of affective materialities in a story like 'Dusie' can contribute to both queer and post-anthropocentric aims, even though the two may not automatically be aligned.[6]

Ideologies of domesticity, human relations and the mind–body relation rely on conceptual, spatial metaphors (home as the protection and continuity of the heterosexual family; space and things as background and support for human subjects and their normative relations; the human body as the container of the mind). Barnes's text invites its reader to engage with these metaphors in an affective textual assemblage of imaginable materialities, and offers the possibility to use this material to reimagine them. Barnes's descriptions play with but are ultimately indifferent to the restrictive cultural norms that regulate human relations. Instead they offer a basis of affectivity that enables a variety of encounters, including ones ignored by both anthropocentric and heteronormative ideologies.

Description, Action and Life

If the predominant mode of 'Dusie' is descriptive, this is even more true of 'Finale', a considerably shorter story also set in a domestic space. Its extradiegetic, third-person narrator describes a room with the body of a man lying at its centre in an open casket, surrounded by candles and a mourning, kneeling family, which consists of the man's wife, mother, a daughter and a son – a patriarchal and heteronormative assemblage of human bodies. From the start the description foregrounds the interplay of stagnancy and change:

> The body had been duly attended to. The undertaker had pared the nails, put the tongue back in the mouth, shut the eyes, and with a cloth dusted with bismuth had touched the edges of the nostrils. It had been washed and dressed and made to assume the conventional death pose – the hands crossed palm over knuckles. Everything else in the room seemed willing to go on changing – being. He alone remained cold and unwilling, like a stoppage in the atmosphere. (1996: 232)

The human body described is the one part of the assemblage that has, according to the description, stopped 'changing' and 'being', and has become the passive locus of conventions and other people's symbolic actions, frozen in the 'death pose'. Yet a corpse is certainly still 'changing', namely decomposing, and thus continues a material life of its own, in trans-corporeal intra-actions with its environment. Indeed, the rest of the story contradicts the idea of a 'lifeless' body as removed from the relational change and being of the world.

Although the narrator ascribes emotions to the human characters, their presentation foregrounds visible expression and bodily postures whereby readers are invited to see them primarily as affective bodies in an assemblage, rather than as examples of psychological interiority. The wife cries heavily, 'resting the middle of her breasts on the hard side of the coffin boards', the mother cries with some more 'comfort' that the narrator attributes to her having 'seen both the beginning and the end', while the children's attention wanders: the girl wants to look at her damp palms and the boy indulges in a pleasurable memory of rubbing his head against a nurse's arm (1996: 232–3). The narrator keeps returning the attention to the body, or to an impersonal gnomic statement, casting the family as expressive statues or mute actors in a *tableau vivant*, which also makes them comparable to the conventional pose of the dead man. Furthermore, the narrator attributes the 'mental' phenomenon of will to 'things' (the 'everything' also repeated in 'Dusie') and a dead body: '*everything* else in the room seemed *willing* to go on changing . . . he alone remained cold and *unwilling*'.

The assemblage also includes a scarf, the man's 'dearest possession', a memento of a possible romantic encounter received from a woman in Italy: 'It was a lovely thing, but much treasuring had lined it; and the marks of his thumbs as they passed over it in pleasant satisfaction had left their tarnish on the little spots of gold' (1996: 233). The scarf carries traces of memory and pleasure, which could be read as pointing towards human life – yet in my reading, 'life' is not commensurate with interior psychology or even the journey from birth to death pictured as an arch or a trajectory. The scarf is the carrier of traces of the man's actions and feelings, but it is its materiality that has invited the gestures of treasuring, which in turn have become part of the man's bodily and affective life. This imaginable materiality is also capable of affecting readers of the story. The liveliness of the scarf and 'everything' else in the room suggests not only that the material and the human are interconnected, but that we reconsider the notion of 'life'.

Following Bennett's interpretation of Deleuze, this could be read as an example of '*a* life' in the indefinite singular. This life is not personal or individual: it is a 'restless activeness, a destructive-creative force-presence that does not coincide fully with any specific body' (2010: 54, 57; Deleuze 2001). A life is not dependent on human consciousness or a human lifespan, with its (hetero)normative ideals of significant signposts (see Ahmed 2006: 90–2). A sense of an 'immanent life carrying with it the events or singularities that are merely actualized in subjects and objects' (Deleuze 2001: 29) sneaks into 'Finale' in its descriptions of the nonhuman or 'lifeless' elements of the space. Further, I suggest that life thus considered does not actually need the categories of subjects and objects to actualise. This becomes apparent in Bennett's vital materialist interpretation that points out immanent 'life' equally in the flashes of action in human bodies as in the persistent agency of things beyond the human conception of matter and time, such as grains of metal. Besides carrying traces of a human life story and a love affair, we may suggest that the scarf has a life of its own as a body with the affective power to contribute to emerging events. As a fictional thing, it carries the potential to affect readers' embodied experience of the story and their subsequent interpretation of it. Barnes uses the device of omniscient narration to introduce this nonhuman life to readers, passing by the consciousness of human characters. Like the flood of things in 'Dusie', the thing-life of the scarf asks to be recognised as independent of the conventional story of love and infidelity with its reserved roles for male and female subjects, and thereby it may evoke a potential reality not governed by those norms.

At its very end the story introduces another nonhuman agent, as it moves briefly from the descriptive mode that renders the elements of the scene into a narrative one that reports action:

> A large rat put his head out of a hole, long dusty, and peered into the room. The children were going to rise and go to bed soon. The bodies of the mourners had that half-sorrowful, half-bored look of people who do something that hurts too long. Presently the rat took hold of the scarf and trotted away with it into the darkness of the beyond. One thing only had the undertaker forgotten to do; he had failed to remove the cotton from the ears of the dead man, who had suffered from earache. (1996: 233)

The first and third sentences narrate present events and have the rat as their subject, while the sentences reserved for the mourning human bodies state the way things are, anticipate or recall future or past action. As in 'Dusie', this action appears as a gnomic 'matter of course' rather than the result of interior psychological developments: the children will rise because they are told to, because it is customary, or because their bodies hurt. The random occurrence of the undertaker's forgetting only gives rise to more description, and the rat's actions in stealing the scarf do not have any more psychological motivation than the actions of the human characters. The rat as an agent is indifferent to the love story (or life story) attached to the thing. The presence of the scarf continues in the material 'beyond' into which the rat drags it, beyond the death of the 'subject' of a story in which the scarf never quite played the part of a passive 'object'. The actions thus appear as emergent effects of a process, in which subjective interiority supported by the domestic space is of little consequence; what is contained by the space is an impersonal event in which human bodies are intermeshed with thing-bodies, one as lively as the other.

The story asks its reader to dwell on the 'surface' of material appearances, to register both the rat's swift movements and the postures and physical feelings of human and nonhuman bodies. It attributes a mind-dimension either to none of them or to 'everything' in a way that may cause confusion in readers, especially if the story is read within a psychologising framework. The central subject of the narrative action is actually the rat; yet its signifying and affective potential rests on the whole assemblage and the minor, intra-active events of being and changing that take place within it. The story presents trans-corporeal relations as crucially affective and experientially relevant to readers, binding human-centred phenomenology with an interest in agential and affective distribution. It portrays a *tableau* curiously *vivant* of a deceptively 'normal' family gathering, where things and bodies are in fact askew: the 'head' of the family has become a passive thing, and the women and children are joined by a rat and a scarf, whose participation in the scene shows more 'life' than any of the human bodies, living or dead – it could also be likened to a still-life that will not keep still. The dear possession of the man is shown as having possessed him, and the shape of the situation in the material space is presented as a force acting on human bodies living and dead. However, the sociocultural norms that partly regulate the human bodies do not govern the life of the nonhuman ones. The extension of the sense of 'life' beyond the human story suggests the arbitrary makings of any normative life story.

The final detail of the cotton in the corpse's ear evokes a sense of the interior of the body, but, again, a physical rather than a spiritual interior. The cotton is incorporated in the body as a vehicle of trans-corporeal interactions. According to Alaimo (2010: 11, 28), the physical permeability of the human body and the presence of nonhuman elements in its interior is rarely experienced directly, but can be revealed to startling effect with the help of scientific enhancements of perception, which in turn can be elaborated on in literary expression. However, I suggest that literary language itself, as an arena for the creative use of metaphors and modes of narration and description, may challenge readers to rethink their tacit understanding of enclosed and insular humanity, even without the aid of scientific instruments. The efficacy of this kind of language for challenging anthropocentric or heteronormative ideologies is subject to debate. In the fictional texts read above, both aims are by-products of other, aesthetic objectives that ask readers to imagine a reality indifferent to conventional norms and thereby to see arrangements of things and people in a new light. Barnes's journalism shares some of these aesthetic qualities, as it prefers the affective presentation of experience to direct arguments. It also explicitly reflects on the effects of affective reading as a means of producing insight. Thus her journalistic texts can be read as a commentary on the way her fiction produces affective responses and critical insights relying on bodies, spaces and normativity.

How Does it Feel?

Barnes's most famous journalistic experiment, 'How It Feels to Be Forcibly Fed', is part of a series of stunt journalism that she wrote for the *New York World Magazine*. Barnes enacts the contemporary ordeal of British suffragettes, many of whom were imprisoned and protested against not being recognised as political prisoners by going on hunger strike. Prisons responded to their efforts by force-feeding them, a practice that resulted in suffering and permanent damage to their health. For the article, Barnes has a doctor and assistants bind her to a table and repeat a similar procedure.

Kate Ridinger Smorul (2015) and Rebecca Loncraine (2008) note that in the early 1900s stunt journalism was a means for women to gain space for journalistic expression beyond the women's pages. According to Loncraine, stunt journalists used their bodies, performances and experiences to get a story: 'In her stunt journalism, Barnes' body is the subject of the news. Her body is put on display as protagonist, subject and illustration' (2008: 158).[7] Indeed, Barnes does not undertake a thorough explanation of what is happening to suffragettes in Britain, but foregrounds the sensory experience of 'how it feels'. Neither does she underline the political or ethical aims of her investigation. However, one aim seems to be to evoke embodied empathy, an understanding of 'what-it-is-like' that can only be achieved experientially, following philosopher Daniel Hutto:

> The only way to understand 'what-it-is-like' to have an experience is to actually undergo it or re-imagine undergoing it. Gaining insight into the phenomenal character of particular kinds of experience requires *practical* engagements, not theoretical insights. This kind of understanding 'what-it-is-like' to have such and such an experience requires responding in a way that is enactive, on-line and embodied or, alternatively, in a way that is re-enactive, off-line and imaginative – and still embodied. (Hutto 2006: 52)

At the very start of the piece, Barnes purports a form of understanding that relies on embodied experience: 'For me it was an experiment. It was only tragic in my imagination. But it offered sensations sufficiently poignant to compel comprehension of certain of the day's phenomena' (1989: 174–5). Barnes clearly understands the performative nature of her stunt, a fictional tragedy that is more like the crushed foot in 'Dusie' or the death of the nameless man in 'Finale' than an actual occurrence of violent injustice; yet she expects that the experiment will 'compel comprehension' of the contemporary issue, implying that what is needed for this comprehension is a bodily re-enactment of the experience of her 'English sisters' (1989: 175). The comprehension may also extend to readers through their capacity to re-enact the ordeal through the text. The text is an experiment in aesthetics and politics as well as in empathy: the question is not only 'how it feels' but also 'how to tell about how it feels', and what the consequences of this telling are.

By calling the ordeal 'familiar to my sex at this time' (1989: 175), Barnes creates a community of 'sisters' with an implied readiness for understanding her experience, imagining a space for contact between women affected by the issue, or perhaps by other forms of patriarchal power. She queers the event in a joking aside to this implied audience: as she lies on the table 'in as long and unbroken lines as any corpse', she notes that 'this, at least, is one picture that will never go into the family album' (1989: 176). As in 'Finale', the materiality and interconnectedness of the human body and the presence of death disrupt the normativity represented by the family and the album as a symbol of genealogy and continuity (see Ahmed 2006: 89–90).

The description of the actual force-feeding merges technical and physical details with acute experiences of pain:

> He had inserted the red tubing, with the funnel at the end, through my nose into the passages of the throat. It is utterly impossible to describe the anguish of it. . . . Unbidden visions of remote horrors danced madly through my mind. There arose the hideous thought of being gripped in the tentacles of some monster devil fish in the depths of a tropic sea, as the liquid slowly sensed its way along innumerable endless passages that seemed to traverse my nose, my ears, the inner interstices of my throbbing head. Unsuspected nerves thrilled pain tidings that racked the area of my face and bosom. They seared along my spine. They set my heart at catapultic plunging. (Barnes 1989: 177)

Barnes notes the 'impossibility' of describing the experience of pain, yet attempts it with the help of imaginary visions and affective body parts. Partly, the description portrays the body as passive in its physicality: 'I had lapsed into a physical mechanism without power to oppose or resent the outrage to my will' (1989: 178). However, the whole experience leads to the act of telling about how it feels to suffer and to resist and attributes pain and activity to parts of Barnes's body. The autobiographical body she describes, like the bodies in her stories, retains its agency as potential to express and affect, even when faced with the impossibility of describing the experience 'as it is'.

The text uses conventional metaphors, yet most turn out to be repetition with a difference, as in her fiction. Before lying down on the table, Barnes describes her dread: 'my soul stood terrified before a little yard of red rubber tubing' (1989: 175). She locates the feeling of fear in her 'soul', yet attributes to the soul the bodily posture of standing and evokes the 'thing-power' of the rubber tube; in the excerpt the 'soul' is separate from the tube, but the piece as a whole thrusts them together, as the tube invades the residence of the soul. She writes, following a customary dualist metaphor, that 'the spirit was betrayed by the body's weakness' (1989: 178), but picks up a more poetic and trans-corporeal one when she describes the operating table as 'pregnant with the pains of the future' (1989: 175). Similarly, when Barnes deliberates on the possibility of affective and bodily empathy, the metaphors become mixed:

> If I, playacting, felt my being burning with revolt at this brutal usurpation of my own functions, how they who actually suffered the ordeal in its acutest horror must have flamed at the violation of the sanctuaries of their spirits. (1989: 178)

I suggest that this polyphony of metaphors is partly due to the rhetorical genre of the piece. An article in a popular magazine may call for conservative expressions such as the spirit betrayed by the body's weakness, and the interior of the body as the 'sanctuary' of spirit. The more ambiguous metaphors of the piece recall the ways Barnes's stories highlight the materiality of bodies: her soul trembling before a rubber tube, her 'being' burning with revolt while her 'functions' are usurped, a table 'pregnant' with fear. Barnes is clearly not actively seeking expression for a precociously post-anthropocentric vision of the human mind and body, but the complexity of the experience the piece is trying to convey seems to require a blend of familiar and creative expressions. Even the traditionally dualistic metaphors become slightly askew in the context of the violent phenomenon described. In an affective reading of material surfaces, it is necessary to see the metaphors of the body as a (weak) temple of the soul as parallel with the concrete, material images of rubber tubing entering the cavities of that same body. Similarly, the image of the body as a corpse pairs with the descriptions of lived pain and struggle.

The metaphorical images have the potential to shift tacit meanings attached to the body and the mind. They present a material reality indifferent to oppressive norms, yet also directly and painfully affected by them. Thus the text has at least partly succeeded in conveying the 'what-it-is-like' of the body as a material, affective entity permeated by and intra-acting with the material world around it. This imagery likens Barnes's narrated body not only to the corpse in 'Finale' but also to the fictional body of Dusie as an empty, mortal and vulgar church.

It is debatable whether Barnes's 'playacting' helps the cause of suffragettes. Its intention seems to be more aesthetic and ethical than political, content with raising consciousness and presenting effective images:

> I saw in my hysteria a hundred women in grim prison hospitals – while white-robed doctors thrust rubber tubing into the delicate interstices of their nostrils and forced into their helpless bodies the crude fuel to sustain the life they longed to sacrifice. (1989: 178)

This vision posits bodily experience as not only a form of empathy but also a form of knowledge. Loncraine notes the 'bodily reality' of the 'gruesome details' of the descriptions, which blurs the line between pretence and experience (2008: 166). I read the performative piece as an attempt to show the lived pain induced by an 'objective' procedure of medical and correctional biopower. It displays the body undergoing the experience as an active agent rather than a passive object, complicating the attribution of victimhood to bound and force-fed female bodies. This happens in part via the deconstruction of internalist, psychological or spiritual notions of subjectivity observed in all the texts analysed.

The blend of material and metaphorical expressions in the piece grasps the lived experience of bodily pain and relationality in a way that a medical report could not, thereby actually surpassing the potential of scientific instruments that Alaimo sees as necessary for perceiving trans-corporeality. An appropriately phrased metaphorical passage from Audre Lorde meditates on the bodily practices of resistance and silencing:

> What are the words you do not yet have? What do you need to say? What are the tyrannies that you swallow day by day and attempt to make your own, until you will sicken and die of them, still in silence? (Lorde 1980 quoted in Alaimo 2010: 21)

Alaimo notes that this should not only be read as a generalised call to refuse to be silenced but also in the context of 'personal and psychological' experiences of illness: 'personal experience cannot be directly reckoned with, not only because discourse shapes experience, but also because an understanding of the self as material, trans-corporeal, and emergent entity often demands the specialized knowledge of science' (2010: 86). I hope to have shown that Barnes's experiment and the story she tells of it may offer a further mode of 'understanding' and 'knowledge' that can be phenomenological without being 'personal' or 'psychological', as conceptions of agency and life are extended beyond these denominators.

At the end of the piece, Barnes foregrounds the fictionality of the experience by assuming that the doctor 'had forgotten all but the play' and by describing the assistants leaving, 'having finished their minor roles in one minor tragedy' (1989: 179). Yet the text implies a belief in a possibility to share with her readers something of the experience that the medical professionals, here acting more as wielders of biopower than providers of an enhanced means of seeing the body, have missed. The actual political efficacy of the act may be slight, but it does succeed in creating a form of knowledge perhaps inaccessible to other means of expression. The material permanence and affective potential of the medium of writing is likely to enable readers to carry with them more than the doctor in the piece does: fresh words for the experiences of 'swallowing tyrannies' and resisting them in the physical space of the lived body.

Conclusion

In a letter to Emily Coleman recently quoted by Elizabeth Pender and Cathryn Setz, Barnes comments on a review of her novel *Nightwood* (1936) that complained about its lack of 'cheer': 'Split the most beautiful woman in half and is it cheering in his sense? No. In mine yes, to see the guts and gall and heart embroiled in that pit out of which beauty boiled' (Pender and Setz 2019: 1).[8] The comment exemplifies both her interest in the grotesque physicality of the body and her propensity for the creative use of metaphors. These characteristics make her writing engage in conversation with a reading that shows how her metaphorical language uses the experience of the material world to challenge tacit understandings of human life and subjectivity. Barnes reimagines fictional characters as material bodies whose interiority is physical rather than symbolic, attributes 'lives' to nonhuman things and rewrites interior spaces as unhomely yet active players in the unfolding of a story. Her texts invite readers to engage with lively material things, emergent occurrences and bodily sensations that push aside grand narratives centred around exclusively human relations and especially heteronormative ones. They use the creative power of language to reorganise the imagination of the world by rewriting metaphors rooted in the material world.

I propose an affective reading of materialities as a potential space where the queer and feminist phenomenological study of bodies, spaces and normativity can meet post-anthropocentric efforts to rethink mind/life/matter divisions. These approaches converge around questions of how to define subjects and objects, what is encompassed by a life, and what kind of communities and empathic relations can be constructed in and by different spaces. A queer phenomenological reading can point out the exclusive or oppressive qualities of a fictional space or the possibility for queer forms of contact it affords; a New Materialist one can turn away from anthropocentric interpretations and point out the agency of nonhuman fictional bodies and their intra-action with and permeation of human bodies. Both heteronormative and anthropocentric ideologies reside in tacit expressions, and slight alterations to these expressions may open up new ways of experiential understanding that reveal a plural, vibrant world of connections. While challenging the hegemony of the human subject, a reading of affective materialities also supports the aim of queer phenomenology by surpassing the restrictions carved in lived space by sociocultural norms and helping us imagine beyond them, while recognising the affective load carried by material spaces and things.

I suggest that Barnes's texts solicit comprehension of a variety of phenomena addressed by both theoretical approaches. This comprehension is of a material and affective kind and does not necessarily create or invite propositional knowledge. The form of experience the stories evoke is impersonal and non-psychological, which is why a reading focused on materiality and affectivity is needed to grasp them. Barnes's celebration of cutting a beautiful woman in half should perhaps not be read as an invitation to a probing reading that seeks to reveal the symbolic and symptomatic meanings below the surfaces of bodies, including the body of the text. It supports the reading of interiority as a physical yet affective space removed from the psychological and the spiritual: what is contained by human as well as by domestic interiorities is more materiality, more surfaces. In the margin of the same letter, Barnes writes: 'there is always more surface to a shattered object than a whole object' (Pender and Setz 2019: 1). I read this as an invitation to a peculiar kind of reading of the surface, in which 'objects' need not be differentiated from, but are intra-active with subjects of experience.

Notes

1. See Young (2005: 151–3).
2. For a more thorough discussion of these means, see Oulanne (2018).
3. The concept was first used by Stephen Best and Sharon Marcus (2009).
4. On the difference between 'embodied reader' and 'implied reader', see Kukkonen (2014).
5. She is young, tall, big and beautiful, absent and pale; 'She wore big shoes, and her ankles and wrists were large, and her legs beyond belief long. She used to sit in the corner of the café, day after day, drinking, and she had a bitter careless sort of ferocity with women. Not in anything she said, for she spoke seldom, but she handled them roughly, yet gladly. She was *dégagé*, but you could not know her well' (404).
6. In this case, the dehumanising metaphors used for Dusie can be seen as a productive non-anthropocentric gesture, while their contribution to a queer or feminist aim is less direct.
7. The piece was accompanied by five photographs of the action, with captions explaining each part of the procedure.
8. Djuna Barnes to Emily Holmes Coleman, 8 November 1935.

References

Ahmed, Sara (2006), *Queer Phenomenology: Orientations, Objects, Others*, Durham, NC: Duke University Press.
Alaimo, Stacy (2010), *Bodily Natures: Science, Environment, and the Material Self*, Bloomington: Indiana University Press.
Barad, Karen (2007), *Meeting the Universe Halfway: Quantum Physics and the Entanglement of Matter and Meaning*, Durham, NC: Duke University Press.
Barnes, Djuna (1989), *New York*. Los Angeles: Sun & Moon Press.
Barnes, Djuna (1996), *Collected Stories*, Los Angeles: Sun & Moon Press.
Bennett, Jane (2010), *Vibrant Matter: A Political Ecology of Things*, Durham, NC: Duke University Press.
Best, Stephen and Sharon Marcus (2009), 'Surface reading: an introduction', *Representations*, 108: 1, pp. 1–21.
Deleuze, Gilles (2001), 'Immanence: a life', in Gilles Deleuze, *Pure Immanence: Essays on A Life*, trans. Anne Boyman, New York: Zone Books, pp. 25–33.
Felski, Rita (2015), *The Limits of Critique*, Chicago: University of Chicago Press.
Hutto, Daniel D (2006), 'Impossible problems and careful expositions: reply to Myin and De Nul', in *Radical Enactivism: Focus on the Philosophy of Daniel D. Hutto*, ed. Richard Menary, Philadelphia and Amsterdam: John Benjamins, pp. 45–64.
Kukkonen, Karin (2014), 'Presence and prediction: the embodied reader's cascades of cognition', *Style*, 48: 3, pp. 367–84.

Lakoff, George and Mark Johnson (2003), *Metaphors We Live By*, Chicago: University of Chicago Press.

Lakoff, George and Mark Turner (1989), *More than Cool Reason: A Field Guide to Poetic Metaphor*, Chicago: University of Chicago Press.

Loncraine, Rebecca (2008), 'Voix-de-ville: Djuna Barnes' stunt journalism, Harry Houdini and the birth of cinema', *Women: A Cultural Review*, 19: 2, pp. 156–71.

Lorde, Audre (1980), *The Cancer Journals*, San Francisco: Aunt Lute.

Oulanne, Laura (2018), 'Lived things: materialities of agency, affect, and meaning in the short fiction of Djuna Barnes and Jean Rhys', dissertation, University of Helsinki. http://urn.fi/URN:ISBN:978-951-51-4143-9.

Pender, Elizabeth and Cathryn Setz (2019), 'Introduction', in Elizabeth Pender and Cathryn Setz (eds), *Shattered Objects: Djuna Barnes' Modernism*, University Park: Pennsylvania State University Press, pp. 1–24.

Ridinger Smorul, Kate (2015), 'Djuna Barnes' performative journalism', *Journal of Modern Literature*, 39: 1, pp. 55–71.

Stanica, Miruna (2014), 'Bundles, trunks, magazines: storage, aperspectival description, and the generation of narrative', *Style*, 48: 4, pp. 513–28.

Wilson, Mary (2011), 'No place like home: *Nightwood*'s unhoused fictions', *Studies in the Novel*, 43: 4, pp. 428–48.

Young, Iris Marion (2005), 'House and home: feminist variations on a theme', in Iris Marion Young, *On Female Body Experience: Throwing Like a Girl and Other Essays*, Oxford: Oxford University Press, pp. 123–54.

CHAPTER 8

Corporeal Creativity and Queer Gaps in Time

Karin Sellberg

Why do discussions of Western identity politics and psychology always return to William Shakespeare, Marjorie Garber asks in her seminal article 'Shakespeare as Fetish' (Garber 1990: 242). She argues that Shakespeare has become a symbol, catalyst and imaginative object in English, postcolonial and anglophone cultures, and although her article is now rather dated, its message holds true on many levels, especially with regard to national, cultural and gender identity, and ideas of what it means to be a modern individual. This chapter investigates the relationship formed with Shakespeare and the past in this cultural imaginary, conceptualised through New Materialist and queer philosophies of time. I will discuss two 'Shakespearean novels', published more than twenty years apart: *Wise Children* (1991) by Angela Carter and *The Gap of Time* (2015) by Jeanette Winterson, where individual identity never resides in one time and space alone. Indeed, the concepts of time and space are reconstructed as relational rather than linear or four-dimensional concepts, and corporeality and physical reality are matters of continual and creative reformation. This chapter examines the entanglement of time that sustains the realities of the two novels, and anatomises the material ontology that makes the authors' new corporealities possible.

These two specific novels are underrepresented in the vast literature on Carter's and Winterson's works, and open up a new reading of the ways in which bodies exist in and out of time, in a complex hub of relationality and connectivity. Carter's and Winterson's works have often been read in relation to feminist or queer theory, partly because they both identify as feminist, and, mostly in Winterson's case, queer writers. As I have argued elsewhere, their narrative tropes of performative embodiment and non-linear or queering of time have furthermore made them ideal representations of queer and feminist theoretical concepts (Sellberg 2015a, 2018). Bodies and flesh are made strange in their work, and queer readings of them, by critics such as Paulina Palmer (1987), Aidan Day (1998), Susan S. Lanser (1996) and Antje Lindenmeyer (1999), have brought an important understanding of how bodies and selves are shaped to theories of gender and embodiment. This chapter is doing something slightly different, however. Few queer critics have acknowledged the role of relationships and relationality inherent in the authors' treatment of corporeality and time, and this crucial dimension can be usefully teased out through a New Materialist analysis of the texts. The protagonists in both novels are aging, but simultaneously are eternally youthful. Their bodies are stiffening and deteriorating, but their corporeal imagination and expression remain agile. Carter and Winterson perform continual revivifications of voice and flesh – the voice and flesh of their characters, and the voice and flesh of themselves as authors and narrators – through the imaginative power of Shakespeare.

As a continuation of the novels' aesthetic breakdown between the binaries of self and other, past and present, author and reader, theory and practice, this chapter is written in the style of an entanglement between critical theory and literary exposition. Eve Kosofsky Sedgwick simply describes this type of engagement between critic and fiction as 'responsive' or 'close' reading (Sedgwick 2002: 45), whereas Lanser refers to this style of non-binary writing as 'queer narratology' (Lanser 1996: 116). Through this methodological lens, where theory and literary analysis emerge out of one another, I explore four types of material connections in and out of time in *Wise Children* and *The Gap of Time*: first, ideas of history, heredity and familial bonds between different generations of characters and philosophical traditions; second, the authors' attempts to connect with other voices across time in the process of writing; third, affective connections across time; and finally, material connections across time in the process of identity formation and becoming. Elizabeth Freeman suggests in *Time Binds* (2010) that there is an important affective value to relationships being forged across time, and similarly to Rosi Braidotti's philosophy of corporeality and relational being in *Metamorphoses* (2002) and *Transpositions* (2006), she argues that such bonds are necessary in each subject's formation of self and identity. I will suggest that each of Carter's and Winterson's characters are similarly incomplete when considered in historical isolation, outside of their Shakespearean connection. This fact points to a form of New Materialist historical connection articulated in the works of Karen Barad, Iris van der Tuin and Rick Dolphijn; their Shakespearean origin story is affectively inevitable, but always reinvented and fraught. As the characters are shaped and given life in the relationship between time periods and encounters, the authors in the two novels also move beyond their objective and temporal boundaries, continually problematising their perspectives and positions in the narratives and reformulating what it is to be a writer *of* a story, *in* a story, in history and time.

New Pasts and Paternities

Lanser's 'queer narratology' is based on non-binary thinking and approaches to time developed in feminist and queer theory (1996: 116). As Virginia Woolf establishes in 'Modern Fiction' (Woolf 2012 [1921]), the progress narratives of capitalist and patriarchal culture have simplified time in the interest of maintaining its social structures. According to Woolf, we have been taught to think of time as a steady and linear movement, but this is not how we actually experience time: in every moment,

> the mind receives a myriad impressions – trivial, fantastic, evanescent or engraved with the sharpness of steel. From all sides they come, an incessant shower of innumerable atoms, and as they fall, as they shape themselves into the life of Monday or Tuesday, the accent falls differently from of old. (2012 [1921]: 2152)

Various impressions and memories from different points in time congregate and contribute to each moment of human experience and, according to Woolf, fiction should abandon the traditional narrative conventions of linear storytelling in order to faithfully portray this process (2012: 2152). To illustrate her point, Woolf describes the difference between photographs and the then-recent boom of motion pictures. Whereas photographs capture one moment in time and thus become oddly static, films capture life as it happens and thus create a more realistic experience (2012: 2152).

Queer theory has continued to emphasise Woolf's concerns about the unreal constraints of normative conceptions of time, and a new type of temporality, queer time, has developed in response to this. Jack (Judith) Halberstam describes queer time as a rejection of heteronormative progress narratives, and binary relationships between past and present, or present and future, and a celebration of the diversity of temporal experiences. Most simply construed, a queer conception of time is an attempt to capture layers of temporality (past, present and future) within a multidimensional, yet distinct narrative framework. Halberstam argues that queer time is non-teleological and non-reproductive: like Woolf's dictate in 'Modern Fiction', it disrupts the linearity of time, the stable movement from cause to effect, and displaces the procreative principle of a 'biological clock' that measures the progressive movement of the body in time (Halberstam 2005: 5). Queer time is thus a more authentic portrayal of the experience of time. It emphasises future potentialities as well as the past of a body's movement through time and space. As Woolf establishes, bodies are never merely positioned in the present. In every moment, considerations of the past and future become part of how we experience our present. Bodies are moving towards spaces and away from spaces. Queer time reconfigures the 'regulatory fiction' of linear time in favour of reality as a type of temporal hybridity, in which the present resides in the past and the past is an integral part of the present (2005: 6).

We are yet to formulate a similarly specific and structured New Materialist conception of time, partly because New Materialist philosophy has not engaged extensively with histories and history writing. However, I have argued that there is a New Materialist position with regard to time formulated in a number of canonical texts, that has only just started to be conceptualised into a theoretical framework or directive (Sellberg 2019). New Materialist conceptions of time share a number of foundational premises with queer time. New Materialist philosophy rejects the teleological progress narratives of traditional engagements with the past and tends to be more focused on sustainable futures. As Iris van der Tuin and Rick Dolphijn argue, however, the past is always present in New Materialist thinking: it 'traverses and thereby rewrites thinking *as a whole*, leaving nothing untouched, redirecting every possible idea according to its new sense of orientation' (Dophjin and van der Tuin 2012: 12). New Materialist philosophy does not relate to time sequentially, or in a hierarchical and nostalgic manner. It embraces past events, finds connections across time, and makes these points of correlation always-already present: 'New materialism says "yes, *and*" to all of these intellectual traditions, traversing them, creating strings of thought that, in turn, create a remarkably powerful and fresh "rhythm" of academia today' (2012: 89). As Winterson puts it: 'Isn't there always a history to the story? You think you're living in the present, but the past is right behind you, like a shadow' (Winterson 2015: 6).

Dolphijn and van der Tuin acknowledge that New Materialism 'is not necessarily different from any other materialist, pragmatic or monist tradition' (2012: 89), and shares possible connections to earlier materialisms in New Materialist conceptions of time. Late twentieth-century cultural materialism (or 'new historicism', as is its North American moniker) aimed to find similar means of closing the divide between present and past. This school of thought professes to grasp history more acutely and conscientiously than previous historical methodologies, by rejecting the binary relationship between past and present dominant in previous historiography or historical methodologies, presenting historical narrative as universal and subject to objective facts. In the interest of considering the 'material' conditions of the past, they also abandon the more conventional methods and established social documentation of the discipline, and like the New Materialists they turn to multi-perspectival narratives, non-normative bodies and unconventional peripheries of society (Sellberg 2015b: 245). Cultural materialism, queer historicism and theories of queer time often operate in conjunction in late twentieth-century attempts to 'queer' time, or actively disrupt the 'regulatory fiction' of linear, three-dimensional and heteronormative temporality (Halberstam 2005: 6); and the role of the queer writer, historian or literary critic is pivotal in this effort.

Stephen Greenblatt, who is often hailed as the founder of new historicism, states in the introduction to his *Shakespearean Negotiations* (1988) that his engagement with history started with a desire to 'speak with the dead . . . If I never believed that the dead could hear me, and if I knew that the dead could not speak, I was nonetheless certain that I could re-create a conversation with them' (Greenblatt 1988: 1–2). He adds that, 'Conventional in my tastes, I found the most satisfying intensity of all in Shakespeare' (1988: 2). Similarly to Marjorie Garber, Greenblatt argues that William Shakespeare has become not only *a* father figure, but *the* father figure in contemporary Western culture (1988: 2). Because of the evocative nature or 'wantonness' of his language (1988: 1), and the (according to Greenblatt) universally recognisable dilemmas of his protagonists, Shakespeare provides a space for a past *within* the present, and this past is not merely a passive trace of previous actions, but a past that interacts with the present (1988: 3–4). Garber takes a more cynical approach to Western notions of Shakespeare. Using a Lacanian psychoanalytic framework, she analyses the popularity of Shakespeare in terms of something primary, nostalgic and always-already lost; a past we can never escape, but simultaneously can never capture (1990: 243). Shakespeare is the 'cradle' of our culture, our literary father, and we continue to seek assurance from his narratives. At the same time, we also strive to move beyond his original frameworks, making him into something perpetually exciting and new (1990: 245).

This type of thinking is also evident in Winterson's and Carter's queer and feminist fiction. Similarly to the queer theorists and historians, Winterson's *Gap of Time* and Carter's *Wise Children* strive to come to terms with their relationship to Shakespeare, and both make this process more personal than conventionally expected in a novel. In the final chapter of Winterson's *Gap of Time*, the semi-linear narration is suspended, and the author's voice becomes autobiographical and reflective: 'So I leave them now, in the theatre, with the music. I was sitting at the back, waiting to see what would happen' (2015: 284). The novel is a paraphrase of Shakespeare's *The Winter's Tale*, originally performed in 1606, where jealous husband Leontes, king of Sicilia, shuns his infant daughter Perdita, who grows up a foundling in Bohemia, exiles his best friend Polyxenes, shames and seemingly kills his wife Hermione, and instead worships her statue. In the imposed hiatus at the end of the *Gap of Time*, Winterson takes the opportunity to extrapolate on her personal relationship to the story:

> I wrote this cover version because the play has been a private text for me for more than thirty years. By that I mean part of the written wor(l)d I can't live without; without, not in the sense of lack, but in the sense of living outside of something. (2015: 284)

Winterson is known for breaking the fourth wall and introducing her own eponymous characters, voices and perspectives (see, for example, Sellberg 2015a, 2018). It is part of her queer feminist methodology of decentring and fracturing the grand narratives of identity formation, complicating individual characters and problematising narrative functions (Lanser 1996; Lindenmeyer 1999).

In this instance, the insertion of her own perspective is potentially more complex, however. The fact that the author appears as a form of classical *deus ex machina* at the very conclusion of the story is interesting on several levels. On the one hand, it emphasises the dramatic origins of the plot, and the type of stage craft imbued in any form of narration. This is further strengthened by an initial dramatis personae and map of the narrative's 'place', 'time' and 'story' in line with the rules of tragedy articulated by Aristotle. On the other hand, this autobiographical cameo also creates a personal origin myth, in which Winterson, alongside Shakespeare, comes to share in the responsibility of building a sustainable identity. They enter into a dialogue that moves beyond the limits of time and space.

Most critics argue that Carter also had a personal stake in her turn to Shakespeare in her final novel, *Wise Children*. Focusing on the life story of the aging, illegitimate and neglected twin daughters of the Shakespearean actor Melchior Hazard, Dora and Nora Chance, it is structurally more conventional than Carter's previous novels, and although it challenges the conventions of the stage (the twins take to the music hall, cabaret and the burlesque rather than the respectable stage of their father), it does not as overtly challenge set gender norms. As Sarah Gamble, Kate Webb and Aidan Day point out, this is because *Wise Children* loosely adheres to the generic form of classical comedy (Gamble 1997; Webb 2000; Day 1998). Beth A. Boehm suggests in '*Wise Children*: Angela Carter's Swan Song' that the novel should be read as a form of 'memento mori', considering that the author died of cancer only months after it was published: 'by choosing an aging song-and-dance girl who wonders if it is "high time for the final curtain" as the memoir-writing narrator of *Wise Children*, Carter self-consciously explores the powers of theatre and storytelling to hold the forces of the night at bay' (Boehm 1994: 85; Carter 1991: 230). It is problematic to connect this theme to Carter's personal or political reasons for writing the book, however, since Lorna Sage convincingly claims, in her biography of Carter, that the author was unaware of her cancer diagnosis when *Wise Children* was published (Sage 1994: 76).

Regardless of whether *Wise Children* signals a mounting awareness of death and finality, like Winterson's *Gap of Time* it stages an opportunity for the author to come to terms with her literary heritage: 'like the narrator of *Wise Children* who seeks reconciliation and acknowledgement from her father, a famous Shakespearean actor, Carter seeks and finds reconciliation with that most mythic of literary fathers in *Wise Children*' (Boehm 1994: 84). As Garber establishes, William Shakespeare is a ghostly father figure whose influence may only be exorcised through continual reiteration in Carter's and Winterson's works – and even so, the exorcism is never complete. The fathers become 'two-dimensional' (Carter 1991: 230); 'like statues ... the past was too strong' (Winterson 2015: 259), and in the end, Carter's and Winterson's characters merely find partial resolutions in the novels' classically Shakespearean moments of reunion, where the fathers reluctantly embrace the past, and the full cast moves on to an uncertain future.

Speaking with the Dead

Cultural materialism posits that the past always continues to reside in the present, and in adherence to this view, cultural materialism and queer theories of time arguably live on in New Materialism. Cultural and material heredity, and awareness of the tradition that has come before, is central to New Materialist conceptions of corporeality, narratives and thinking through time, but as van der Tuin has shown in *Generational Feminism* (2015), heredity is never a linear or one-directional process, nor relationships between generations simple (van der Tuin 2015: 3). Heredity is a process of recognition, sometimes paired with rejection, and response. Partial resolutions and uncertain heredity are, however, as typical in queer and New Materialist theory as they are in feminist and queer fiction. The ghost of the past is always-already present within these texts and theories, and its spectral presence carries possibilities as well as responsibilities (Derrida 1994: 22).

Indeed, both Carter and Winterson come to the conclusion that full exorcisms of the past are both impossible and undesirable: 'although history repeats itself, and we always fall, and I am a carrier of history whose brief excursion into time leaves no mark, I have known something worth knowing, wild and unlikely, and against every rote' (Winterson 2015: 289). Jonathan Goldberg and Medhavi Menon come to similar conclusions in their *PMLA* article 'Queering History', suggesting that we should not abandon the past, but in order to form a more useful relationship between the present and the past we should abandon the type of historicism 'which proposes to know the definitive *difference* between the past and the present' (Goldberg and Menon 2005: 1609, my emphasis). In other words, the past's position in relation to the present should be less rigidly *past*. It is the type of relationship that Greenblatt attempts to formulate in *Shakespearean Negotiations*. As he describes his struggle to 'speak with the dead', he emphasises that although the dead cannot directly speak back, and all he could hear were continual echoes of his own voice, the voices of the past did nonetheless respond in some way: 'It was true that I could only hear my own voice, but my voice was the voice of the dead' (1988: 1). Greenblatt recognises that his own voice carries the traces of the past, and in attempting to commune with the dead, the past thus appears within his present. This type of dialogue prepares space for a past *within* the present, and this past is not merely a passive trace of previous actions, but a past that directly interacts with the present.

Through their novels, Carter and Winterson directly engage this critical turn. Shakespeare, the father, the cradle and the universal bard, comes and goes throughout the texts, holding conversations with protagonists as well as readers. He is both present and absent in the contemporary moment, simultaneously building a stable traditional past, and inspiring new possible futures. Dora Chance is writing the twin sisters' combined memoir, and, like Greenblatt, she acknowledges that part of the purpose of memory is to conjure up the past:

> Sometimes I think, if I look hard enough, I can see back into the past. There, goes the wind, again. Crash. Over goes the dustbin, all the trash spills out . . . What a wind! Whooping and banging all along the street, the kind of wind that blows everything topsy-turvy. (Carter 1991: 3)

However, again similarly to Greenblatt, although the past comes alive in the Chance sisters' narrative, Dora recognises that it is a very specific version of the past, and one entirely taking shape through their very particular perspective. However hard they try to communicate with their father figure (their very own Shakespearean giant), they only hear their own story:

> I sometimes wonder if we haven't been making him up all along . . . if he isn't just a collection of our hopes and dreams and wishful thinking in the afternoons. Something to set our lives by, like the old clock in the hall, which is real enough, in itself, but which we've got to wind up to make it go. (1991: 230)

Voices from times past do not re-emerge on their own. They require the voices of the present to 'wind them up', draw them into further existence and ventriloquise their concerns.

Memory is more complex in *The Gap of Time*. As one of the characters puts it, 'What is memory anyway but a painful dispute with the past?' (2015: 11). Memories are painful, and produce continual abrasions in the protagonists' narratives, but these narratives are also what keeps them connected, and makes them who they are. As Rosi Braidotti establishes in *Metamorphoses* and *Transpositions*, these are the type of shared experiences that form identity (Braidotti 2002: 12). Her Deleuzean nomadic subjectivity functions somewhat like a tracer of consciousness or an inconsistent and inconclusive subjective narrative. Each moment of shared experience or recognition is a location of intersecting and interrelating forces and 'spatio-temporal variables' (Braidotti 2002: 21). Also in *The Gap of Time*, identity is conceptualised in terms of locations, directions and lines on the characters' skin, 'a map made of skin' (2015: 172). These locations are constantly altered. The subject-position is in continual flux. Each subject's identity forms in differently patterned 'revisitations and retakes' of shared encounters (Braidotti 2002: 12). As Carter's Dora Chance puts it, 'we painted the faces we always used to have on to the faces we have now' (1991: 192), and through the 'deceptions of memory' (1991: 192), embodiment and identity emerge out of a continual reconditioning of connective events and experiences.

Braidotti points out that the idea of nomadic subjectivity is not a matter of choice: 'A "location", in fact, is not a self-appointed and self-designed subject-position' (2002: 12). It is rather a tracer of consciousness or an inconsistent and inconclusive subjective narrative-in-becoming. Unlike in *Wise Children*, where identity can be traced within the scraps, rubbish piles, old stockings and crusted remnants of time, in *The Gap of Time*, identity is formed backwards. This is because most of Winterson's protagonists are stuck in the past, while time simultaneously continues to move outside of their control. The fuel of the novel's time is love (expressed in the form of parental care as well as obsessive desire) and connection, and time moves according to its ebbs and flows. However, time goes 'out of joint' the moment Leo (Shakespeare's Leontes) fails to recognise his wife Mimi's (Shakespeare's Hermione) love and fidelity, and rejects his newborn child, Perdita (the little lost one). Mimi and Perdita disappear (in Shakespeare's version Hermione dies of grief) and in this instance, and from this event onwards, time slips in and out of line, making some moments imperceptible, and others weighty with signification: 'There was a second, the kind that holds the whole world – and then the second hand moved on and she was gone' (2015: 6).

The protagonists in the novel are only able to reconnect through a complicated video game, developed by Leo's exiled best friend Xeno (Shakespeare's Polixenes) called 'The Gap of Time'. The narrative of the game is set in one of nine cities – London, Paris, Rome, Berlin, Barcelona, New York, Hong Kong, Sydney, Shanghai, and these cities are occupied by 'Dark Angels'. Players can choose to be angels, creatures with 'two, four or six wings' and 'two dicks' (2015: 38), armed with feather diamonds, and as fearsome and gravid as Walter Benjamin's 'Angel of History', bringing about a continual historical cycle of destruction and despair (Benjamin 1968: 260). Players can also choose to be members of 'the Resistance', protectors sweeping up and detonating these feathers before they cause irreparable destruction, and building strength in the process: 'If you fight with an angel and win, you get stronger, the Angel weakens' (2015: 38). In short, 'The story is this: the most important thing in the world has been lost. The Dark Angels don't want you to find it' (2015: 38). Xeno indicates that this 'most important thing' must be a baby: 'Think about all those fairy tales about babies that get swapped or stolen. Think about The Omen or Alien. The imposter child, the devil child and the true child who is the saviour. It's like King Arthur or Siegfried – new life. The shining centre' (2015: 38).

Xeno's video game remains elusively described throughout the novel, but in its simplest terms it is an abstract refection, or allegory of the novel's central narrative: it is about finding 'that which has been lost' (2015: 288), a baby and a set of characters that want to save her or destroy her. The various dimensions and levels of this game grow out of the characters' connections and relationships, and its rules change throughout the novel as Xeno changes his perception of life and time. The further the narrative unfolds, the longer Leo waits to correct his wrongs, the more overtly the different timelines of the story misalign with the fates and narratives of its players:

> And the world goes on regardless of joy or despair or one woman's future or one man's loss. And we can't know the lives of others. And we can't know our own lives beyond the details we can manage. And the things that change us forever happen without us knowing they would happen. And the moment that looks like the rest is one where hearts are broken or healed. And time that runs so steady and sure runs wild outside of the clocks. It takes so little time to change a lifetime and it takes a lifetime to understand the change. (2015: 270)

The only character in the novel with the power to bring time back into sequence is Perdita. She is the carrier of all other characters' lost opportunities: 'Traced inside her, faded now, were parents she would never know and a life that had vanished. Alternative routes she would never take. People she would never meet. The would-be-that-wouldn't be' (2015: 164). Winterson does not suggest that Perdita's destiny can be rewritten, or that she can rewrite the stories of the characters around her, but she can fill in the narrative gap in time. mending the temporal anomaly at the centre of the Shakespearean myth that, until now, has determined her life. She reconnects herself to the past she has lost, rekindles the connection to her biological parents, and makes sense of the disruptive event that should never have happened: 'Time can't unhappen but it can be unlost' (2015: 259).

Affective Time Binds

Time, according to queer theory, cultural materialism and New Materialism is an affective process. As Woolf would put it, the reality of time – the way we experience time – is connected to the relationships we form, the desires that propel us, and our sensual inputs. Time, both in Carter's and Winterson's novels, follows the affective flows of the protagonists, and, in both cases, there are painful slippages between past and present. Elizabeth Freeman argues that this is a truly queer conception of temporality, partly because of its non-binary construction of present and past, but also because of the 'strange' non-normative relationships that emerge in its embrace (Freeman 2010: 3). Referring to Jacques Derrida's formulation of a hauntological responsibility towards the other across time, Freeman argues in *Time Binds* that the present is 'always split': 'split by prior violence and future possibilities' (2010: 9–10). There will always be slippages between the present and significant markers in the past and future. Similarly to Winterson's and Carter's narratives, these slippages are propelled by desire. There is a simultaneous draw and pull away from the past; a type of formative friction, or temporal energy, fuelling the construction of the subject. Elizabeth Freeman refers to these types of relationships between past, present and future as affective 'time binds', borrowing her term from Freudian discourse on the management of desire. According to Freud, all human experience of desire must to some extent be 'bound' or related to previous experience or thought patterns, so we can contain and make sense of it (otherwise, the experience becomes boundless and unmanageable). However, a new 'bond' within a network of bonds does not merely tie two spatio-temporal modes, experience A to experience B. Instead, the network grows, and each new addition becomes connected to countless previous connections. Every time one experience of desire is connected to another, the emotional energy from additional experiences and memories, already connected to the initial experience, automatically follow: 'This very binding . . . produces a kind of rebound effect, in which whatever it takes to organise energy also triggers a release of energy that surpasses the original stimulus' (2010: xvi).

Rosi Braidotti makes a similar argument about the relationship between desire and becoming in *Transpositions*: 'Desire is the propelling and compelling force that is attracted to self-affirmation or the transformation of negative into positive passions . . . To enact different steps of this process of becoming, one has to work on the conceptual coordinates' (2006: 169). The arterial framework residing at the very core of the subject is always transforming and always in motion 'through processes of careful revisitations and retakes, or patterns of repetition . . . It is a transformative force that propels multiple, heterogeneous "becomings" of the subject' (2006: 169–70).

The body, for Braidotti, is a marker of subjectivity-in-becoming. It continually moves through essentialised and corporealised subjective 'locations'. These are not to be considered separate from each other, but rather as planes intermeshed by chains of memory (2002). Braidotti describes it in terms of speed perception: 'Just like travellers can capture the "essential lines" of landscape or of a place in the speed of crossing it, this is not superficiality, but a way of framing the longitudinal and latitudinal forces that structure a certain spatio-temporal "moment"' (2006: 172). This momentary subject-positioning is continually transposed. It is a recurrent conditioning of connective events that lead to new becomings.

Freeman's affective 'time binds' have the capacity of capturing these moments of becoming, the points in time that make us who we are, and momentarily making them unreal. When the moments of becoming, experienced in the 'real' present, are connected to the partially reconstructed and uncannily fractional moments of the past, the reality of the 'real' becomes somewhat displaced. Freeman particularly refers to 'visceral' moments, when the experience of our bodies and environment fall out of pace with the linear timeline, spinning us out of chrono-normative motion, and opening up dyssynchronous wounds and gashes in time (2010: 8). In the cataclysmic Shakespearean comedy finale of *Wise Children*, the twins Dora and Nora gain the ability to see the essential lines of their lives, and the world around them, including their father figures and their hopeless desire for his love and recognition, seems unreal and two-dimensional: 'tonight, he had an imitation look, even when he was crying, especially when he was crying, like one of those great big papier mache they have in the Notting Hill parade, larger than life, but not life like' (1991: 230). The unreality of the carnivalesque moment is what makes their lives and life stories real, however. It shows the seams and patches of the present, and finally disentangles the knots in the past. For the first time in their lives, Melchior Hazard publicly acknowledges his illegitimate twin daughters, and all the characters that had stayed apart out of fear and past trauma come together in the shared flow of tears and connection of blood, 'the precious, unique Hazard blood that binds parents to their children and turns daughter against mother!' (1991: 214). Also in *The Gap of Time*, the family blood lines reconnect when Leo recognises Perdita as his legitimate daughter. In this moment, Perdita ceases to just be her own person, and becomes part of a familial collective, returning from their various homes throughout the world, travelling through 'lines of arterial red, like a body-map of the world' (2015: 19), to the Shakespearean comic finale. Each personal narrative, and the wound inflicted by Leo's jealousy and distrust, had driven them further and further apart, but the dramatic structure allows them another chance at forgiveness and redemption. It allows them to return to the moment of loss and pain, 'smash the moment into pieces' and 'let it open into time' (2015: 262).

The pivotal concept in both Carter's and Winterson's novels is the comedic element of 'return', a possibility for redemption and renewal.

This is what differentiates it from a tragedy, where trauma, fate and loss are irreversible. Dora and Nora seize such a chance of return as they prepare themselves for the finale, dressing in the glad rags of their youth, despite it being their seventy-fifth birthday: 'Lovely shiny stockings and a couple of little short tight skirts in shiny silver stuff to match . . . everything you can think of, cheap and cheerful, we haven't laughed so much in years . . . we slipped on our toweling robes, we creamed off our morning faces, we started off from scratch' (1991: 191). Comedy thus offers an opportunity for individual and collective growth. As one of the characters in *The Gap of Time* puts it: 'if roundabouts had been invented sooner, the whole of Western civilization would be different' (2015: 141).

The possibility of revisitation and return is indeed also the basis of Freeman's and Braidotti's conceptions of temporality, and the formation of identity, affect and desire across time. Desire, for Braidotti as well as for Freeman, propels affective connections and bonds throughout time and space. The concept of 'becoming' that Braidotti develops in *Transpositions* relies on the revisitation and reiteration of shared conceptive constructions and spaces. She argues that '[t]hese multi-layered levels of affectivity are the building blocks for creative transpositions, which compose a plane of actualization of relations, that is to say points of contact between self and surroundings' (2006: 172). Such affect is the means by which the subjective becomes general and the general becomes subjective. The final act of recognition in Carter's and Winterson's novels, the overt signification of a 'rupture' in the flow of being, also leads to 'asignification' (Deleuze and Guattari 2007: 10). The very act of disrupting time allows it to be repaired. At the same time as the temporal disruption dislodges the subject from its linear path, the affective bonds across space and time it reveals allow a new subject-in-space to come into being, As Winterson puts it, 'time, that sets all limits, offers our one chance at freedom from limits. We were not trapped after all. Time can be redeemed. That which was lost can be found . . ."' (2015: 288). The holes and gashes in time always-already close the moment they are opened, to form a space of recognition and identification. As Braidotti expresses it, it is the becoming of 'the affective being of the middle, the interconnection, the Relation' (2006: 129).

Queer Temporal Entanglements

Time, considered through New Materialist and queer theory, leaves marks. Braidotti's concept of becoming is physical as well as psychological; memory is stored in our bodies as well as our minds, and the process of becoming is an entangled corporeal and temporal process. Although, as Winterson acknowledges, 'the body remakes itself every seven years. Every cell. Even the bones rebuild themselves like coral' (2015: 11), memory goes beyond material embodiment and the scars remain. Winterson and Carter's protagonists remain frozen in time, in what Freeman refers to as a 'Chronic Yesterday' (2010: 5). In Shakespeare's original narrative, Hermione dies of grief, but is replaced in the final act by a statue that comes to life, whereas Winterson's Mimi, Leo's faithful but forlorn wife, becomes encased in the home city to which she returns after her husband's rejection, Paris: 'she was held in time as they all were, the statues, friezes, reliefs, that watched and watched over the changing city' (2015: 228). She is not able to command time, because she is stuck in its embrace: 'it's always there, right in front of her, the past is right in front of her and every day she walks slam into it like a door that locks the future on the other side' (2015: 229). Dora and Nora, too, are unable to move freely in time. Until the final scene, they continuously live under the shadow of their father's nonchalance and rejection, burdened by the weight of his name and reputation, but unable to remove themselves from its allure. Their own stage careers parody the gravity of the 'great Shakespearean of our time' (1991: 14), and they seem doomed to playing comical and burlesque side characters in their father's productions, or to occupy the small stages in the wrong part of town. Perdita is similarly weighed down by her unrecognised patronage. She is found in a 'baby hatch', accompanied by a case full of money, a musical score with a note of her name, and a treasure from her mother: 'Underneath the notes there is a soft velvet bag. Diamonds. A necklace. Not little snips of diamonds – big-cut and generous like the heart of a woman. Time so deep and clear in the facets that it's like looking into a crystal ball' (2015: 16). Dora, Nora and Perdita literally carry time, wear time on their faces and chests, but they are unable to *become* part of their own timelines.

Diamonds come to simultaneously represent change and petrification, significance and irrelevance in *The Gap of Time*. It mirrors the continual juxtaposition of parenthood and disconnection between Perdita and her parents (both biological and adopted) – she is clear about the fact that her adoptive father will remain her operative father figure, but she also recognises her new genetic bonds (238) – alongside the oscillation between newness and recognition in the narrative's relationship to its Shakespearean parent narrative. Neither Winterson's nor Carter's novels stay 'true' or 'bound' to Shakespeare. They enact a close encounter with

Shakespeare, but they do not attempt to bring him back to life. Freeman describes this as

> a kind of visceral encounter between past and present figured as a tactile meeting, as a finger that in stitching, both touches and is touched, and that in reading, pokes and caresses the holes in the archival text even as it sutures them. (2010: 110)

Freeman refers to this historicising process as a queer historical encounter, but it could also be interpreted as a New Materialist 'yes-and' approach (Dolphijn and van der Tuin 2012: 89). Freeman considers it a type of 'erotohistoriography': 'Erotohistoriography is distinct from the desire for a fully present past, a restoration of bygone times. Erotohistoriography does not write the lost object into the present, so much as encounter it already in the present, by treating the present as hybrid' (2010: 95).

Considered from another perspective, such a temporality could also be interpreted in terms of what Karen Barad calls a 'quantum dis/continuity' (Barad 2007: 181). Spacetimematter in Carter's and Winterson's work is neither continuous, nor separable into non-relational elements. There are multiple entanglements – between characters, times, spaces – cutting through and re-splicing. The past, present and future of Dora's and Nora's lives literally emerge through the wrinkles and marks on their skin, and on top of this – as an additional entangled layer in the finale – they wear a cacophonous temporal collage, as they mix the clothes and makeup from the various stages of their lives. Perdita, on the other hand, is herself a temporal juxtaposition; a 'carrier of history', the embodiment of her parents' love, betrayal and loss, and the reincarnation of Shakespeare's mythical narrative: 'I am witness and evidence of what I know: this love. The atom and jot of my span' (2015: 289).

Throughout both novels, the narrative voice jumps from one scene to another, and in the case of *The Gap of Time*, from one character to another, but nonetheless there is a continual sense of connectivity through the traces of variously entangled threads and unending iterative reconfigurations. Perdita asks herself, 'Is life just a series of chance encounters that from a distance look like patterns?', but the novel concludes that this is irrelevant (2015: 245): patterns and connections emerge, regardless of intentionality. What comes across in this dis/jointed movement of chance encounters is an intra-activity, of agential separability – differentiations that cut together/apart – in *The Gap of Time*, the life vein of these quantum entanglements is desire, mutual affection or love: 'The size of it. The scale of it. Unimaginable. Vast. Your love for me. My love for you. Our love for each other' (2015: 289). In *Wise Children*, love is conceptualised in more material terms, and the connections are formed, on the one hand, through sexual intercourse – 'While we were doing it everything seemed possible, I must say. This is the illusion of the act' (1991: 222) – and on the other hand, the bonds of genetics, blood or seed: 'We're both of us mothers, and both of us fathers . . . They'll be wise children, all right' (1991: 230). This connective element, relationality, genetic or tactile 'encounter' in Freeman's terms, becomes the most notable agent in both texts – and in both novels the magnetic draw of love, blood and connection has to compete against time.

Xeno's video game becomes the means through which the various characters in *The Gap of Time* can connect across space. It is an allegorical layer to the story, bringing the characters out of the contexts of their everyday lives, into a space of pure connectivity, and a battle between destruction and preservation. The game continually opens up gateways throughout time and space, but it also becomes the keeper of these gates. Whether players choose to become angels or protectors, they become part of Benjamin's idea of history as a continual vicious cycle that only time itself can break (1968: 260). Winterson thus introduces time itself as an agent, or character in the game-narrative: 'at level 4 Time becomes a player. Time can stand still, move faster, slow down. But you are playing against Time too' (2015: 39). The Time character does not take the shape of an actual being, but rather acts as a form of allegorical *deus ex machina*, controlling the gameplay and the progression of the narrative. Once the players reach this level, the bonds and connections between characters are thus made real, and manifest as characters or agents in themselves. Indeed, the central character, around which the whole video game reality circulates, is a statue of Mimi, shut up in a room in Paris. All players, angels and protectors alike, continually return to this room, but nobody is able to penetrate it. She is the manifestation and embodiment of betrayed love – the cut in time and space, which Leo's jealousy has inflicted.

In conclusion, New Materialist conceptions of time are not singular – they are materialisations of earlier events, memories, affective connections and theoretical traditions, and they carry their scars and complexities. New Materialism says 'yes and' to its parental traditions, cultural materialism and queer theory (Dolphijn and van der Tuin 2012: 89), but it also moves beyond their scopes. New Materialism welcomes all previous conceptions of time. Like Woolf's attempt to portray the chaotic and multidimensional experience of lived time, New Materialist time is not linear or binary, and the material reality of heredity, embodiment and becoming are rhizomatic and continuously expanding entanglements of bodies in time. New Materialist temporality comes to life within the gaps and slippages of conventional and linear progress narratives. In recognition of this, I have used a queer or close reading methodology to dis- and re-entangle theoretical and fictional conceptions of time and embodiments in Carter's *Wise Children* and Winterson's *The Gap of Time*. Arguably, these novels are, in themselves, works of New Materialist philosophy, as well as fiction. Temporality and corporeality, philosophy and narrative appear inseparable throughout the texts; fractional, dis/continuous, viscous and fraught with abrasion and pain. Yet, this friction is what maintains the relationality between characters, spaces, times, authors and literary traditions. As Freeman establishes, 'history is not only what hurts, but what arouses, kindles, whets or itches' (2010: 117). It is the 'discharge' (Freeman 2010: 123) or 'trace' (Winterson 2015: 164) of the novels' simultaneously fated and chance encounters; their juxtaposed complementarity and uncertainty principles. As in Xeno's game, time, in these novels, is a player – sometimes an adversary and sometimes a friend – but the propellant is love.

References

Barad, Karen (2007), *Meeting the Universe Halfway: Quantum Physics and the Entanglement of Matter and Meaning*, Durham, NC: Duke University Press.

Benjamin, Walter (1968), 'Theses on the philosophy of history', in Hannah Arendt (ed.), *Illuminations: Essays and Reflections*, trans. Harry Zohn, New York: Schocken Books, pp. 253–64.

Boehm, Beth A. (1994), '*Wise Children*: Angela Carter's swan song', *A Review of Contemporary Fiction*, 14: 3, pp. 84–9.

Braidotti, Rosi (2002), *Metamorphoses: Towards a Materialist Theory of Becoming*, Cambridge: Polity Press.

Braidotti, Rosi (2006), *Transpositions: On Nomadic Ethics*, Cambridge: Polity Press.

Carter, Angela (1991), *Wise Children*, London: Quality Paperbacks Direct.

Day, Aidan (1998), *Angela Carter: The Rational Glass*, Manchester: Manchester University Press.

Deleuze, Gilles and Félix Guattari (2007), *A Thousand Plateaus*, trans. Brian Massumi, London: Continuum.

Derrida, Jacques (1994), *Spectres of Marx: The State of the Debt, the Work of Mourning and the New International*, trans. Peggy Kamuf, London: Routledge.

Dolphijn, Rick and Iris van der Tuin (2012), *New Materialism: Interviews and Cartographies*, Ann Arbor: Open Humanities Press.

Freeman, Elizabeth (2010), *Time Binds: Queer Temporalities, Queer Histories*, Durham, NC: Duke University Press.
Gamble, Sarah (1997), *Angela Carter: Writing from the Front Line*, Edinburgh: Edinburgh University Press.
Garber, Marjorie (1990), 'Shakespeare as fetish', *Shakespeare Quarterly*, 41: 2, pp. 242–50.
Goldberg, Jonathan and Medhavi Menon (2005), 'Queering history', *PMLA*, 120: 5, pp. 1608–17.
Greenblatt, Stephen (1988), *Shakespearean Negotiations*, Los Angeles: University of California Press.
Halberstam, Jack Judith (2005), *In a Queer Time and Place: Transgender Bodies, Subcultural Lives*, New York: New York University Press.
Lanser, Susan S. (1996), 'Queering narratology', in Kathy Mezei (ed.), *Ambiguous Discourse: Feminist Narratology and British Women Writers*, London: University of North Carolina Press.
Lindenmeyer, Antje (1999), 'Postmodern concepts of the body in Jeanette Winterson's *Written on the Body*', *Feminist Review*, 63, pp. 48–63.
Palmer, Paulina (1987), 'From "coded mannequin" to bird woman', in Sue Roe (ed.), *Women Reading Women's Writing*, Brighton: Harvester.
Sage, Lorna (1994), *Angela Carter*, Plymouth: Northcote House.
Sedgwick, Eve Kosofsky (2002), *Touching Feeling: Affect, Pedagogy, Performativity*, Durham, NC: Duke University Press.
Sellberg, Karin (2015a), 'Beyond queer time after 9/11: the work of Jeannette Winterson', in Sebastian Groes, Peter Childs and Claire Colebrook (eds), *Women's Fiction and Post-9/11 Contexts*, London and New York: Lexington Books, pp. 65–79.
Sellberg, Karin (2015b), 'Queer (mis)representations of early modern sexual monsters', in Kate Fisher and Rebecca Langlands (eds), *Sex, Knowledge and Receptions of the Past*, Oxford: Oxford University Press, pp. 243–64.
Sellberg, Karin (2018), 'Queer/feminist literary temporalities', in K. Sellberg (ed.), *Gender: Time*, New York: Cengage Macmillan, pp. 301–16.
Sellberg, Karin (2019), 'The "turns" of feminist time: evolutionary logic, life and renewal in "New Materialist" feminist philosophy', *Australian Feminist Studies*, 34: 99, pp. 9–106.
van der Tuin, Iris (2015), *Generational Feminism: New Materialist Introduction to a Generative Approach*, Lanham, MD: Lexington Books.
Webb, Kate (2000), 'Seriously funny: *Wise Children*', in Alison Easton (ed.), *Angela Carter*, London: Macmillan.
Winterson, Jeanette (2015), *The Gap of Time*, London: Hogarth Press.
Woolf, Virginia (2012 [1921]), 'Modern fiction', *The Norton Anthology of English Literature: The Twentieth Century and After*, New York: W. W. Norton, pp. 2150–5.

IV

Capitalism, Crisis and the Anthropocene

CHAPTER 9

Putting the Earth to Use: Reading Resources in the End Times (Through Science Fiction)

Rune Graulund

With increasing strain on all sorts of matter, from oil over wood, fish and bees, even on 'matters' as seemingly inexhaustible as water and air, the question of 'what things and what relations are valuable' is as important as ever (Moore 2015: 51). Through species loss, rising temperatures, the loss of topsoil, the end of oil and a global population that has more than tripled over the last century, it is becoming increasingly evident that we are caught in a spiral that may lead to the collapse of civilisation as we currently know it.[1] As Jason W. Moore argues in *Capitalism in the Web of Life: Ecology and the Accumulation of Capital* (2015), we therefore need to live up to the fact that we are witnessing the spasms of a system that must soon grind to a halt. For while it is possible to argue that humanity has damaged the environment through wasteful practices through thousands, if not tens of thousands, of years (White Jr. 1996; Flannery 2000), surely capitalism is the system most at odds with a world (or to be specific, *a planet*, singular) that is finite. Hence, as Moore makes clear, 'there are limits to how much new work capitalism can squeeze out of new working classes, forests, aquifers, oilfields, coal seams, and everything else. Nature is finite. Capital is premised on the infinite' (2015: 87).

In the Anthropocene, or as Moore and a range of other thinkers prefer to term it, the Capitalocene,[2] such limits are becoming increasingly difficult to deny but, paradoxically, also increasingly difficult to act on. As Slavoj Žižek suggested a decade ago in his evocatively titled *Living in the End Times* (2010), 'the global capitalist system is approaching an apocalyptic zero-point' (2010: x). While the apocalyptic zero-point has (perhaps) not yet been reached, Fredric Jameson's famous statement that 'it is easier to imagine the end of the world than to imagine the end of capitalism' nevertheless seems as true as ever (Jameson 2003: 76). For if 'capitalism has become coextensive with the Earth', it follows that to imagine the end of capitalism is indeed also to imagine the end of the world (Bonneuil and Fressoz 2016: 222). It is in the light of such a 'capitalist realist apocalypse' relying on 'a presupposition that resources are infinite' that I will pose three questions in this chapter, all of them framed in the fading light of 'an end' (Fisher 2009: 18). First, the chapter queries the problem of 'reading' the Anthropocene as text and narrative: why do we find it so hard to comprehend and act on both present and future anthropogenic change even while we have plenty of evidence available that makes it glaringly clear that not to act may in fact doom us? Science has provided us with the script, but we do not seem able to shape this into a narrative we fully accept. The chapter asks how literature and literary studies can help us make better sense of the Anthropocene. Second, it asks how a specific genre of literature, namely science fiction – and in particular the science fiction subgenres of apocalyptic and dystopian fiction – can be employed in order to problematise questions of consumption, collapse and depletion in a world of increasingly finite resources. Third, the chapter shows how contemporary examples of science fiction like Paolo Bacigalupi's *The Windup Girl* (2009) can help reframe the question of resources through the lens not just of the human in all its many manifold guises, privileged as well as poor, but possibly also beyond. Is it possible to reorient the distinctly human perspective of 'use' in order to expand it to involve the nonhuman in all its forms, including not just nonhuman species and plants, but matter of any kind, organic as well as inorganic? Can we, through an actual or imagined end of the human as we now know it, expand our horizons of use for less destructive and more inclusive purposes?

Reading the Anthropocene (Through Resources)

As Benjamin J. Robertson points out in *None of This is Normal: The Fiction of Jeff VanderMeer* (2018), we are living in a 'postnormal world' (2018: 4). The Anthropocene has undermined a wide range of assumptions about the world as we thought we knew it, hence the need to acknowledge that we now live, as Robertson phrases it, on 'a weird planet whose materiality defies human attempts to understand it' (2018: 5). Manifold, complex and perhaps ultimately impossible to fully comprehend, the Anthropocene can at least be summed up by our very inability to grasp the scale of the problem: 'If nothing else, the Anthropocene forces the human subject to confront finitude' (Robertson 2018: 15).

Taking the question of finitude and the human as an entry to discuss the material and the Anthropocene, a range of pertinent questions present themselves. First of all, in what manner do the notions of 'use' and 'resources' influence our view of matter and materiality once a given mode of engagement with matter ends and a new one begins? For instance, to what extent is our perspective on matter dependent on the invention of new technologies or on novel habits of production and capitalist consumption? Following from this, what do notions of use and resource tell us about 'us' once we move away from Anthropocentric/capitalist views of 'our' needs and desires and on to the point of view of other species and other (forms of) being(s)? What is and is not useful, valuable and desirable must change drastically if we could somehow view the world from the point of view of an ant or a whale. Even more so, if we are to 'think like a mountain', as ecologist Aldo Leopold once provocatively put it, the very concept of relating to the world through 'use' surely becomes moot (Leopold 1968: 129–33). While we can never hope 'to literally feel, or entirely understand, "what it is like" to be a bat or a dog', reading through 'resources' envisioned from the perspective of the nonhuman may at least take us part of the way (Shaviro 2015: 25). Similarly, reconsidering the notion of 'resources' in lieu of its anthropocentric origin allows us to probe the fault lines not only of a former worldview in which 'the environment' was seen simply as 'the place where humans went to extract resources', but also of the very (human) act of perceiving, evaluating and engaging with matter and environment through questions of use and value (Bonneuil and Fressoz 2016: 20). If the act of '[t]reating land as a commodity implicitly says that human beings stand outside of nature', we might usefully ask how imaginaries of other kinds of uses (by nonhuman beings) might change the human perspective as well (Emmett and Nye 2017: 23).

More specifically, but following directly from the above, this chapter examines what role literature in general and speculative fiction in particular can play in a debate on dwindling resources in an ever more populous yet also impoverished world. As a range of critics have recently pointed out, literature seems for a long time to have been at an impasse as to how to deal with anthropogenic change like global warming, shifting weather patterns, peak oil, depleting aquifers, microplastics and so on. Adam Trexler's *Anthropocene Fictions: The Novel in a Time of Climate Change* (2015), Timothy Clark's *Ecocriticism on the Edge: The Anthropocene as a Threshold Concept* (2015) and Amitav Ghosh's *The Great Derangement: Climate Change and the Unthinkable* (2016), for instance, all suggest that contemporary literature has been slow to react to the massive yet paradoxically also imperceptible global changes instigated by the Anthropocene. 'What tropes are necessary to comprehend climate change or to articulate the possible futures faced by humanity?', Trexler asks, a question reiterated by Clark's claim that 'the Anthropocene names a newly recognized context that entails a chastening recognition of the limits of cultural representation' (Trexler 2015: 5; Clark 2015: 21). As Clark points out, 'most mainstream literary critics, it must be said, are oblivious to the Anthropocene and its challenge', a sentiment that carries over into Ghosh's lament that 'contemporary literature finds it . . . hard to deal with climate change' and other forms of anthropogenic change, due to 'the peculiar forms of resistance that climate change presents to what is now regarded as serious fiction' (Clark 2015: 51; Ghosh 2016: 8).

Arguably, such 'resistance' to representation is a universal rather than a specifically literary problem of anthropogenic change (see Rust, Monani and Cubitt 2016). There is currently no single academic discipline, in the sciences or the humanities, that has successfully invoked the gravity of anthropogenic change in a manner that poses an effective challenge to our capitalist consumer perspective on the world and our place in it. The data is there but it is difficult to take it all in, for as Timothy Morton points out in his influential study *Hyperobjects: Philosophy and Ecology after the End of the World* (2013), the problem with 'hyperobjects' like global warming is that there is no specific 'object' one can clearly identify. Accordingly, as Clark states it, 'the most prominent feature of the Anthropocene [is that] there is no simple or unitary object *directly* to confront, or delimit, let alone to "fix" or to "tackle"' (2015: 10). In the case of global warming, then, we are never able to see the 'object' in its totality:

> I only see brief patches of this gigantic object as it intersects with my world. The brief patch I call *hurricane* destroys the infrastructure of New Orleans. The brief patch I call *drought* burns the plains of Russia and the Midwestern United States to a crisp. The back of my neck itches with yesterday's sunburn. (Morton 2013: 70–2)

Anthropogenic change like global warming is therefore at one and the same time vast and monumental as well as insidious. Anthropogenic change, wherever we meet it and in whatever form, is always simultaneously too much and too little. It is therefore no wonder that individual academic disciplines – and certainly individual observers – struggle to register, comprehend and represent such change. Consequently, as Roy Scranton remarks in his direly titled *Learning to Die in the Anthropocene: Reflections on the End of a Civilization* (2015):

> In order for us to adapt to this strange new world, we're going to need more than scientific reports and military policy. We're going to need new myths and new stories, a new conceptual understanding of reality, and a new relationship to the deep polyglot traditions of human culture that carbon-based capitalism has vitiated through commodification and assimilation. (2015: 19)

The problem, as Scranton sees it, is that at present we are at a loss as to what exactly such 'myth and new stories' may be, and in what form and what media we are to shape them.

It is at this critical juncture that contemporary literature takes up a curious position of potential future promise and apparent gridlock. Ghosh suggests that 'the currents of global warming [are] too wild to be navigated in the accustomed barques of narration' and that if 'certain literary forms are unable to negotiate these torrents, then they will have failed' (2016: 8). Prevalent literary forms emerged and developed through a worldview of the environment and materialism that simply is not compatible with the world as we (are beginning to) know it today, hence it is ill equipped to deal with anthropogenic change on a massive scale, Ghosh argues. Accordingly, Trexler adds, 'novels composed in the Anthropocene challenge received literary functions, such as character, setting, milieu, class, time, and representation', leading to the sort of conclusion espoused by Clark, namely that the 'Anthropocene names a newly recognized context that entails a chastening recognition of the limits of cultural representation as a force of change' (Trexler 2015: 16; Clark 2015: 21). In this, all three critics seem to suggest, lies the potential for change, in that literature may paradoxically also find itself in the position of offering the expansive narrative that other forms of 'cultural representation' have as yet failed to do. They thus all to some extent make a call for 'a mode of critical reading newly sensitized by the demands of the Anthropocene' (Clark 2015: 181), which is to say a mode of reading that can perhaps begin to 'encourage more intelligent and sustainable engagements with vibrant matter and lively things' that diverges from 'our earth-destroying fantasies of conquest and consumption' (Bennett 2010: viii–ix).

The question, of course, is *how* to carry out such readings in practice. 'The Anthropocene is not an easy story to tell', Tobias Menely and Jesse Oak Taylor acknowledge in their introduction to *Anthropocene Reading: Literary History in Geologic Times* (2017: 4). Yet for that very reason this is potentially a highly exciting time for the field (if not necessarily for the planet) in that the 'Anthropocene provides an opportunity for literary studies to test and transform its methods by examining how the symbolic domain might, or might not, index a historicity that exceeds the human social relation and encompasses planetary flows of energy and matter' (Menely and Taylor 2017: 5). To some extent, and as one genre in particular has proven particularly rich in examples of this – namely science fiction – such change has in fact been under way for some time, thus offering a counterpoint to the literary trends that Ghosh, Trexler and Clark are otherwise critiquing. In the following, I will therefore pursue the 'indexing' suggested by Menely and Taylor through the lens of the sort of speculative fiction that Trexler and Ghosh identify as being the earliest genres to pick up on anthropogenic change like global warming. While Ghosh identifies a range of other speculative genres, like fantasy and horror, as having the potential to 'confront the centrality of the improbable' (2016: 23) in which he finds the realist novel to be severely lacking, it is science fiction in particular that has over the past decade or so taken centre stage in discussions on anthropogenic change. Not only has the genre seen the birth of the hugely popular subgenre of climate fiction, 'resolutely contemporary and dedicated to creating new narratives adequate to current conditions' (Irr 2017: n.p.), it has also been forcefully argued that 'the Anthropocene itself can usefully be understood as a Science Fiction trope' (Heise 2016: 18). While acknowledging that other speculative genres can offer useful perspectives on anthropogenic change that the realist novel cannot,[3] I will in the following continue this trend by examining not just how science fiction can be employed to engage with 'the challenge of how to understand the alien, how to convey experience from a non-anthropocentric view', but also how science fiction has problematised 'the shift toward a capitalist economy that increasingly regards the world as resource, and toward a rationalised conception of the universe that turns everything into object for the human subject' (Vint 2010: 14, 26). As a genre preoccupied with the future – like the finitude and scarcity of dystopias, but also the seeming limitlessness of utopias – science fiction is uniquely positioned to reimagine and redirect the question of resources in terms other than human privilege and entitlement. In the following, we shall look more closely at the question of scarcity and depletion as they are imagined in the genres of apocalyptic and dystopian fictions and the question of endings.

Spending the Future: Science Fiction, Dystopian Fiction and Apocalyptic Fiction

Once we begin to view anthropogenic change through the specific lens of *resources*, future tense and the notion of an end become significant:

as the world is perceived in terms of use, the notion of finitude and future depletion of a given source of matter inevitably appears on the horizon. We see this first of all in the general division of the world into renewable and non-renewable resources. Coal is at present a far more abundantly available resource than oil, promising a couple of hundred years more use at given rates of consumption. Solar power, on the other hand, is considered renewable and virtually infinite. In fact, however, no resource can ever be considered truly renewable. In comparison to the time estimate on the remaining oil in the world (say fifty more years) and coal (say two hundred more years), the amount of solar energy available for consumption is of a different order of magnitude (at least a couple of billion years) but not infinite. At some point, the sun will fizzle out, too, and humanity – if it still exists – will have to locate some alternative source of energy. Once we think of the world in terms of resources, then, we inescapably also begin to think about scarcity and, ultimately, of an end.

This is vividly illustrated in the most hotly debated of such contemporary discussions, namely that of peak oil. Through the advent of a range of novel technologies, oil was itself the instigator of 'an end', namely of the age of coal as steam-driven trains and ships were replaced with cars and planes. With the imminent or perhaps already happening event of so-called peak oil, we are witnessing yet another shift of energy regimes. Importantly, this is a shift that may be far more disruptive than that of coal to oil. Indeed, as Stephanie LeMenager asks in *Living Oil: Petroleum Culture in the American Century* (2014): 'Can the category of the human persist, practically speaking, without such forms indebted to fossil fuels?' (LeMenager 2014: 6). With so much invested in oil as a way of life, to the extent that we are seemingly willing to toss all other concerns aside as long as the oil keeps flowing, we are at present witnessing 'an unprecedented devotion, even love' (LeMenager 2014: 4) for oil as we go ever deeper, ever more extreme (fracking) and ever further (the Arctic, the deep sea). How will we react when this former love of ours passes on? Will we grudgingly accept the potential limitations forced upon our daily lives by the disappearance of the material that gave us plastics, cars and jet flight? Or will the world as we know it descend into war-torn chaos and existential crisis? Judging by the titles of books on peak oil that include the word 'crisis', 'collapse' or 'apocalypse' in their titles (see for instance, Winter 2006; Ruppert 2010; Schneider-Mayerson 2015), there seems to be a widespread belief that the collapse of the age of oil may cast us all back in the dark ages, literally and figuratively speaking. As we at present have no clear idea of what is to replace oil as our main source of portable energy, the ever-closer future of a world bereft of oil has generated a vast amount of speculation about the physical as well as the sociological, psychological and ethical ramifications of an oil-starved world.

While oil is currently the most visible and urgently debated of soon-to-be-depleted resources, other forms of matter are also becoming scarce. Indeed, as journalist Richard Heinberg has phrased it, we are heading towards not only peak oil but 'peak everything' (Heinberg 2007), whether it is that of fish (Costa and Chilese 2014), mushrooms (Tsing 2015), or even something as basic as the water we drink (Shiva 2016) or the air we breathe.[4] In addition to the most dominant discipline of petrocultural studies, recent years have seen the emergence of a range of other resource-related critical fields such as critical animal studies, critical plant studies and blue humanities. While such critical fields have much to offer in terms of disentangling what LeMenager terms 'the regional frame' (2014: 13) as of the specifics of a given kind of matter, much is to be gained from reading widely as well as specifically. Petrocultural studies has in recent years shed as much needed light on both the local and global problems of the oil industry, for instance, as on the capitalist system as a whole through regional-specific iterations of oil extraction (Barrett and Worden 2014; Wilson, Carlson and Szeman 2017), yet the broader lens made available by energy humanities (Szeman and Boyer 2017; Smil 2017) offers perspectives on human extraction and consumption of energy that petrocultural studies alone cannot hope to provide. A broader 'reading for resources' can thus perhaps provide perspectives that, in tandem with readings of specific types of resources (from oil over wood and coal and on to bees and fish), may help shed light on larger, structural problems pertaining to an Anthropocene world that go beyond the implications of any one given resource, particularly so when considered in the light of depletion and endings.

And so we return to the question of endings considered through futurity. Considered broadly, it is significant that polemical non-fiction texts on diminishing resources of the present, oil and otherwise, share many traits with science fiction, and particularly so that of post-apocalyptic fiction. As political scientist Claire P. Curtis remarks in *Postapocalyptic Fiction and the Social Contract* (2012), the speculative post-apocalyptic tale can therefore be a useful means to rethink the present:

> There is a kind of fictional realism to the postapocalyptic account because it takes us from where we are now to a place we can easily imagine being. It then uses that space to think about *how* it is we really want to live. (2012: 6)

In effect, post-apocalyptic narrative literally and figuratively questions *what matter matters*. Whether it is in novels, in films, computer games or television, the governing question of survival in such tales intimately ties in the acquisition of brute matter (e.g. food, water, oil) with ethical imperatives of the limits to which one would go simply to keep on living. This is illustrated, for instance, by Cormac McCarthy's novel *The Road* (2006), one of a handful of post-apocalyptic texts analysed in depth by Curtis. In the book, a father and a son travel across a post-apocalyptic America in constant search of food and shelter. In their desperate search for salvage in a world increasingly bereft of resources or renewal of any kind, the reader is again and again made painfully aware of just how much supposedly essential human characteristics like kindness and empathy are directly dependent upon surplus caloric energy rather than any inherent traits of the human mind and/or soul. Indeed, the central premise of the book is not so much the futuristic rendering of a world gone wrong as much as the question of ethics and its dependence upon material surplus. As the book unfolds, and the father is forced to take increasingly violent measures to gather and protect their resources, we witness a constant tug of war between the father, whose sole purpose in life is to ensure the survival of his son ('My job is to take care of you'; McCarthy 2007: 65), and the young boy who insists that mere physical survival is not sufficient to live a full human life.

Reimagining the present in the light of a post-apocalyptic future, the genre thus typically asks of us, the readers in the present, what we would value most (in a speculative future) once scarcity sets in. If faced with the dilemma of running short on matter X, Y or Z, what would we choose over the other? Even more poignantly, if we wanted matter X, but had to take it from someone else, by violence or other means, would we be willing and able to do without, or would we forcibly take it from those who are weaker than us? 'Postapocalyptic stories have always had a lot to say about where we're headed if we don't right our wrongs. They warn us about our reliance on fossil fuels, our abuse of the environment, and where those will lead us', science fiction writer Kameron Hurley tells us (2016: 85). In this, they function as a potential corrective to our current relation to, and use of, resources that we may deplete in the future. Yet they also force us to reconsider just how much matter matters in the present, even for seemingly immaterial and ephemeral matters such as 'ethics', 'civilisation' and 'culture'. The post-apocalyptic genre is thus split – but also converges – along an axis of material want, ethical concern and cultural meaning. To quote the *Guardian*'s George Monbiot, post-apocalyptic fiction like *The Road* reminds us that: 'our dependence on biological production remains absolute. Civilisation is just a russeting on the skin of the biosphere, never immune from being rubbed against the sleeve of environmental change' (Monbiot 2007: n.p.). After centuries of trying to escape the weight of the world through rational thought and a Cartesian dualism of (human) mind over matter, such speculative fictions can help pose

> a challenge to some of the most basic assumptions that have underpinned the modern world, including its normative sense of the human and its beliefs about human agency, but also regarding its practices such as the ways we labor on, exploit, and interact with nature. (Coole and Frost 2010: 4)

Questioning human privilege and the supposed right of humankind to exploit the Earth for its own benefit, reading such texts through resources can help us redirect and undermine such assumptions even as it employs the very human notion of 'use' in the first place.

Going back to the perspective of science fiction in general rather than the genre specifics particular to post-apocalyptic fiction, Ghosh identifies what he sees as two problematic aspects of the genre, namely those of futurity and alterity. To Ghosh, the otherworldliness and the future tense of science fiction disqualifies the genre as an effective tool for writing about a present in which the new normal is abnormal in that it is 'uncanny', 'improbable' and 'grotesque'. It is also, Ghosh argues, somehow all too familiar in such moments of alterity that 'we recognize something that we had turned away from: that is to say, the presence and proximity of nonhuman interlocuters' (2016: 30). For if any genre is concerned with alterity and the nonhuman, surely it is science fiction: 'SF is in some central sense about the encounter with difference', hence it 'is a form of cultural discourse . . . that involves a world-view differentiated in one way or another from the actual world in which its readers live' (Roberts 2003: 28; 2007: 2). Yet that is of course also precisely what Ghosh finds so problematic with the genre, namely the insistence of a worldview differentiated from 'the actual world'.

The question, though, is whether the Anthropocene can perhaps best be described as 'a world-view differentiated'. Hauntingly familiar yet otherworldly strange, perhaps the Anthropocene can 'actually' be most fully represented through a temporality and an ontology that is fluid and unbound by the restrictions of 'serious fiction'. First of all, the Anthropocene examined through the lens of resources is inextricably intermeshed with the notion of futurity and of the central ontological split of a cycle/status quo of sustainability and renewability versus that of endings, depletion and finitude. The potential of science fiction to present to us a 'world-view differentiated' of the catastrophic consequences of our use and consumption of matter, as of the manner in which our constantly increasing needs have irrevocably changed the environment, is perhaps therefore a case of reality being stranger than fiction; which is another way of saying that maybe Ghosh got his argument upside down. Rather than make the genre fit reality, perhaps reality finally fits the genre. With 'the actual world' turning out to be both familiar and strange, serious 'realist' fiction may not be all that realistic anymore, at least not as long as it refuses to reimagine the present through different temporalities and otherworldly worlds. Much of the environmental damage we are currently witnessing is, after all, not the result of our actions now, yesterday or even a year or a decade ago. Indeed, it is to some extent not 'ours' at all, in that cause and effect often involves a time lag of decades if not centuries, and that individual action in the present can be hard to link to the net result of the combined action of billions of people acting now and in the past.

In order to fully represent the effects of peak oil, for instance, both its end date and the damaging effects of a century's worth of emissions, one needs to look at the present through decades if not centuries of resource extraction and consumption, by others long dead as well as people yet to be born. The actions of people living in the past as well as in the future, collectively and individually, should ideally be incorporated with the specific subjective position of our (own) present. In such an endeavour, science fiction offers us advantages of scale and temporality as well as of nonhuman matter(s) that 'serious fiction', stubbornly sticking to the present (or at most a distinctly human past) and to a privileged human perspective, does not. Through science fiction, a genre that has 'from its very beginnings ... given us stories about how technoscience is making us strange to ourselves', hence also the means 'to think through the genuine encounter with difference', we can perhaps more fully grapple with the fact 'that the human has always coevolved, coexisted, or collaborated with the nonhuman – and that the human is characterized precisely by this indistinction from the nonhuman' (Hollinger 2011: 270; Easterbrook 2011: 384; Grusin 2015: ix–x).

Winding Up and Gearing Down: Spending and Expenditure in *The Windup Girl*

Hailed as a successor to influential cyberpunk writer William Gibson (1948–), the author of the seminal *Neuromancer* (1984) and the coiner of the word 'cyberspace', American science fiction writer Paolo Bacigalupi's authorship revolves around concerns shared with Gibson: namely capitalism, corporate power and the growth of urban megacities. In contrast to Gibson, however, whose focus is on the near future and (mostly) on technology that could conceivably be constructed within a couple of decades, Bacigalupi's fictive worlds are more speculative both in setting and technology. This is particularly the case in his debut *The Windup Girl* (2009), but also in the young adult novels *Ship Breaker* (2010) and *The Drowned Cities* (2012), in which we are treated to a mix of cyberpunk derivative genres like springpunk (also known as clockpunk), biopunk and agripunk in a fusion of retro-futurism and futurism proper.[5] With *The Water Knife* (2015), however, which takes place in a drought-ridden near-future version of the American Southwest, Bacigalupi has been moving into territory more akin to Gibson's, which is to say technologies and settings that could conceivably happen within a couple of decades. Common to all his fiction, however, regardless of the degree of their speculative qualities, is a focus on a world radically altered and impoverished by climate change, by diminishing resources, whether it is water (*The Water Knife*), oil (*Ship Breaker* and *The Drowned Cities*) or 'natural' biology like seeds, fruits and animals unmodified by human hand (*The Windup Girl*). As dystopian fiction dealing with a society characterised by scarcity and partial rather than complete system collapse, 'the world of the Windup stories focuses . . . on energy sources and their depletion, a topic, Bacigalupi argues, that garners too little interest from sf' (Schmeink 2016: 79), hence it is as good a place as any to begin to locate Žižek's 'apocalyptic zero-point' of the global capitalist system, or Fisher's 'capitalist realist apocalypse' discussed at the beginning of this chapter.

Set in a future in which global warming has flooded many of the world's former metropolises, and published at the end of the first decade of the twenty-first century, *The Windup Girl* has grown to become a modern biopunk classic of a world in which 'hypercapitalism has brought about a commodification of any and all life on earth' (Schmeink 2016: 75). With the disappearance of New York, Rangoon, Mumbai and New Orleans between the waves, 'the time when petroleum was cheap and men and women crossed the globe in hours instead of weeks' are long gone, too (Schmeink 2016: 24). Some former urban megacities, like Bangkok in which the book is set, still stand; but only precariously, just barely managing to keep the waters at bay. This is a world in which fossil fuels have either been depleted or banned and replaced with various forms of biological or 'windup' technologies that are supposed to be less harmful to the atmosphere. Rather than coal and oil, we find 'genehacked animals' like the elephantine 'megodonts' that provide 'energy for conveyor lines and venting fans and manufacturing machinery' (Bacigalupi 2009: 13). Repurposed waste is burnt off in 'methane composters' so that 'kink springs' can be charged with kinetic energy and released at a later date, while gene-manipulated food is engineered to contain the highest amount of calories, thus most effectively fuelling the teeming masses of human labour that have once again become a mainstay of the global economy (2010: 32, 302). Finally, we have the titular 'windups', bio-engineered posthumans (tellingly referred to as 'New People') designed to deliver the most efficient work per calorie ratio invested in them through superior strength, enhanced immune systems and extra limbs.

This is thus, to some extent, a world 'dominated by energy production after the depletion of fossil fuels, returned to a state as it was before the Anthropocene' (Schmeink 2016: 79), but with a distinct sense of irreversibility due to depletion of any and all conceivable resources, as of a slate of technologies that are both futuristic (advanced gene technologies and the invention of androids) and nostalgic (the almost Victorian obsession with springs and mechanics). In the world of *The Windup Girl*, as in the earlier short stories 'The Calorie Man' (2005) and 'Yellow Card Man' (2006), set in the Windup universe, we see the end point of Moore's hypothesis as presented in *Capitalism in the Web of Life* that this chapter opened with, namely that we are currently witnessing the clash of 'the finite character of the biosphere and the infinite character of capital's demand' (2015: 112). With capitalism based on 'endless accumulation', it is a system dependent on the 'extension of capitalist power to new, uncommodified spaces' (Moore 2015: 63), a practice that could be sustained as long as there was space left to commodify, but presently proving exceedingly difficult to uphold. As argued by Moore elsewhere, 'Capitalism has been able to outrun the rising costs of production by co-producing manifold Cheap Nature strategies, locating, creating, mapping, and quantifying natures external to capitalism but within reach of its power. Today there is nowhere to run' (2016: 114). This is literally so the case in 'The Calorie Man' (2005), in which the eponymous character of the title is unsuccessfully trying to outrun the reach of the multinational calorie companies that rule the world, but it is figuratively so also the case for capitalism itself. While still operative as the single most dominant global system, capitalism as envisioned by Bacigalupi in the Windup world has come to an impasse, struggling to survive in a world it has itself been instrumental in dismantling on every level. Having expanded to the point of cataclysmic collapse through a series of endings (animal extinction, loss of plant diversity, the weather system, the depletion/impossibility of fossil fuels), the world has seen the end of what Moore terms Cheap Nature, the era beginning in the long sixteenth century and ending at some point in the not too far future of Bacigalupi's text in what his characters refer to as the end and eventual regression of 'the Expansion'.

As if to confirm Jameson's statement about the end of the world being easier to imagine than the end of capitalism, it seems capitalism itself is, however, unwilling to concede defeat even as its central tenet has been sabotaged by none other than its own operative procedures played out in extremis. As one of Bacigalupi's characters muses when confronted with an employee of a Western calorie company, such representatives of capitalism appear 'too stupid to have possibly taken over the world once, let alone twice. That they succeeded in the Expansion and then – after the energy collapse beat them back to their own shores – that they returned again' seem not only improbably but outright 'supernatural' (Bacigalupi 2009: 40). This is, of course, absolutely to the point in that capitalism has at this point turned supernatural – not only in that it continues to refuse limits and boundaries of the natural even after the world of Cheap Nature has ended, but also that seeing as nature is no more, it now needs to go beyond and over ('super') nature in order to reaffirm itself and its principles in a post-natural world. In its lack of distinction between different forms of resources and a breakdown into calories pure and simple, the Windup world is an impoverished world in which everything seems to have run its course, and certainly Capitalism's reliance on 'a mode of distinction that presumed separation' (Moore 2016: 87) between human and nature, useful and useless, goods and waste.

Late capitalism as we know it in its twenty-first-century variant thus goes on about its business much as usual in the Windup universe. For while globalisation has to some extent been hampered by a lack of mobility due to the depletion of oil, the world continues to be governed by globally expansive corporations with names like 'AgriGen' and 'PurCal', so-called calorie companies whose gene-manipulated agriculture the world depends on for its continued survival and progress. 'The shift from petroleum to "calories" as a leading world trade commodity is shown to consolidate the power of corporations rather than undermine them', and by setting his novel in Bangkok rather than, say, London or Los Angeles, 'Bacigalupi transfers our present day Global South from periphery to center' and thereby 'complicates the idea of the Global North as the primary, if not the exclusive, engine of development for global economics' (Donelly 2014: 161; Hageman 2012: 285). Bacigalupi's critique of capital, however, goes beyond the present's unfair distribution of power in which consumption of the planet's resources is vastly skewed, whether through national and regional inequalities or corporate monopolies. Similarly, the account of the damaging effects of unbridled capitalism's exploitation of Cheap Nature as it is presented in *The Windup Girl* is framed not solely as nostalgic lament but to some extent as liberating. As one of the characters, Gibbons, informs us, we should not regret the passing of nature as we once knew it: 'Don't cling too tightly to what is natural. . . . *We* are nature. Our every tinkering is nature, our every biological striving. We are what we are, and the world is ours' (2009: 344). In this, Gibbons cherishes a fully Anthropocene world, even if such a state of affairs might paradoxically mean the passing of the human too: 'Nature has become something new. It is ours now, truly. And if our creation devours us, how poetic will that be?' (2009: 350). Having served its purpose and time on the evolutionary ladder, it is time for humanity (and our anthropocentric worldview) to recede in order to allow the post- and nonhuman (and their respective worldviews) to flourish.

While there are many such instances of 'poetic justice' threatening the extinction of 'the human' throughout *The Windup Girl*, the eponymous heroine of the book is the most obvious example of the eventual demise of our species, as 'nature' as we once knew it. Reminiscent of the 'replicant' Pris of Ridley Scott's *Blade Runner* (1982) as well as a range of other beautiful yet lethal cinematic robot-women going all the way back to Fritz Lang's Maria of *Metropolis* (1927), Bacigalupi's inclusion of a female posthuman protagonist undoubtedly addresses issues of gender as well as the status of the nonhuman. Forced to work in a sex club and engineered so as to achieve orgasm regardless of her own desires, the windup girl obviously brings issues of gender and sex to the fore, not least when she finally rebels and, in another bout of poetic justice, starts punishing those who formerly abused her. It is as 'the potential instigator of a post-human world', however, that the windup girl provides us with 'the text's most fundamental solution to the problem of capital: the destructions of humans brought on by their own meddling with ecological systems' (Donnelly 2014: 166–7). As the novel nears its conclusion, it is hinted that the end of the human race may be near and that, 'Someday, perhaps, all people will be New People and you will look back on us as we now look back on the poor Neanderthals' (Bacigalupi 2009: 505). In this, the conclusion of the novel seems to be in accord with critical posthumanist thought that 'criticize[s] human-centred (anthropocentric) ways of understanding life and reality' and 'does not see the human as the centre of all things' (Roden 2015: 10; Nayar 2014: 5). For while the conclusion is ambivalent with regard to the eventual outcome, it certainly seems to employ the posthuman as 'a generative tool to help us re-think the basic unit of reference for the human in the bio-genetic age known as "anthropocene",' in that 'it forces us to rethink our taken-for-granted modes of human experience' that we are not otherwise capable of discerning (Braidotti 2013: 5; Wolfe 2010: xxv).

The windup girl is the most obvious and, due to her human form and shape, recognisable of posthuman 'generative tools' presented to us in *The Windup Girl*. Acting as readily decoded cipher for a rich science fiction tradition of cyborgs, robots and replicants, it is, however, not in the familiar body of the rather human posthuman of the windups (the 'New People'), but in distinctly nonhuman forms of being that 'this novel exemplifies the interconnectedness of all beings through disease and death' that leads to the novel's perhaps most salient point, namely that all 'bodies' are dirty (Hageman 2012: 293). For in the *The Windup Girl*, bodies are not only everywhere but *in* everywhere; human bodies, posthuman and nonhuman bodies, organic or non-organic bodies, political or social bodies constantly 'intra-act', as Karen Barad would phrase it (Barad 2007).[6] 'Bodies dominate this text as sites of dirt, mutation and calorie use; they are hence nodes of potential change in exchanges with a grimy environment', in effect addressing 'spatially microscopic phenomena and ecological scales of temporal duration, as well as questions about human agency in relation to these very large and very small processes' (Sullivan 2012: 521; Selisker 2015: 501). In such a world, the human body, and the human body politic, is but one of many actors on a playing field on which the human matters very little. Or rather, it is a world in which that which is distinctly human – set apart from the animal, the bacterial and the material, indeed of the entirety of creation – is hardly significant or distinct at all.

In presenting a world to his readers in which everything, and everyone, can be reduced to a number (of calories) that can be sold to the highest bidder, *The Windup Girl* may at first seem to imply a world thoroughly governed by (human) capital and an anthropocentric worldview. Yet, in another sense, we are treated to a world that, viewed solely through the perspective of resource extraction and consumption, has been 'used up', only to present us with 'the strange limbo of those left in the wreckage of American modernity' (Hicks 2016: 146). Like the retro-technology of clockwork and springs on which much of the kinetic technology of the novel relies, the planet has virtually ground almost to a halt, at least in the sense that all that which was formerly deemed 'natural' has now been spent. Whether it is through melting poles and rising temperatures and waters, of humanly induced disease and pollution, or of bodies themselves – bacterial, animal, human, posthuman and planetary – nothing remains in *The Windup Girl* that has not in some way or other been modified by human behaviour, whether on purpose or by accident. Yet this is nevertheless a world in which the human (and human capital) is just barely keeping ahead of the curve. Constantly trying to rewind the clock on the sort of reckless consumption that has led to rising seas and temperatures, super-adaptive bacterial, vegetable, animal and posthuman species, 'the human' in, Bacigalupi's world, is seemingly on the edge of an inevitable and self-imposed extinction.

Ultimately, Bacigalupi tasks his readers with imagining the consequences of 'spending' the planet. 'Cheap nature' has run out, as has, it seems, the brief but vastly disruptive age of human mastery of matter. Something else, it is obvious, must take their place, but it is unclear what. Resource fiction like *The Windup Girl* thus ultimately asks the question: who gets to spend the future and what will it look like? Yet it also makes clear to us the 'unhappy limitation on the future growth of wealth' that drives home not only the uncomfortable truth of 'what is at stake: our ability to live on planet Earth, to have a future as a civilization' (Canavan 2014: 9), but also of the potential redundancy of the human observer placed in an 'environment' outside of 'us'. Indeed, what science fiction texts like Bacigalupi's are so apt at portraying is that the distinction between humanity and the rest of creation, nature and culture, consumer and resource never has been, nor ever will be, separate. In this, Bacigalupi's texts asks whether, as Fisher puts it in counterpoint to Jameson, there is indeed 'no alternative' to capitalism? Or if can we 'develop strategies against a Capital which presents itself as ontologically, as well as geographically, ubiquitous' (Fisher 2009: 77)? For while reading literature like *The Windup Girl* is unlikely to fundamentally and miraculously change the reader's basic assumption regarding resource use overnight, or fully reorient an anthropocentric worldview, it nevertheless asks vital questions regarding consumption, collapse and depletion in a manner that at very least may make us question what might happen at the other side of Žižek's 'apocalyptic zero-point' and Fisher's 'capitalist realist apocalypse'.

Notes

1. For some recent examples of this apocalyptic trend, see, for example, Diamond (2005), Homer-Dixon (2006), Heinberg (2007), Skrimshire (2010),

Žižek (2010), Klare (2012), Emmott (2014), Klein (2014), Dahlberg, Rubin and Vendelø (2016), Danowski and Castro (2017).
2. See Moore (2016), Haraway (2015) and Malm (2016) for compelling arguments as to why Capitalocene is to be preferred over Anthropocene. As admitted by T. J. Demos in *Against the Anthropocene: Visual Culture and Environment Today*, a thinker otherwise strongly critical of the term, 'the term Anthropocene is likely here to stay' – if for nothing else but the fact that it is now so widely employed even if it is arguably also problematic (Demos 2017: 85).
3. See, for instance, *Gothic in the Anthropocene: Dark Scenes from Damaged Earth* (2020), edited by Justin D. Edwards, Rune Graulund and Johan Höglund.
4. The company Aethaer is at the time of writing offering five different jars of '580ml of naturally occurring, clean fresh air', including Summerset, Dorset and Wales (www.aethaer.com/).
5. For more on the difficulty of genre-coding of *The Windup Girl*, see Hageman (2012: 301, n.4).
6. As Barad explains, 'in contrast to the usual "interaction," which assumes that there are separate individual agencies that precede their interaction, the notion of intra-action recognizes that distinct agencies do not precede, but rather emerge through, their intra-action' (2007: 33).

References

Bacigalupi, Paolo (2005), 'The calorie man', in Paolo Bacigalupi, *Pump Six and Other Stories*, San Francisco: Nightshade Books.
Bacigalupi, Paolo (2009), *The Windup Girl*, London: Orbit.
Barad, Karen (2007), *Meeting the Universe Halfway: Quantum Physics and the Entanglement of Matter and Meaning*, Durham, NC: Duke University Press.
Barrett, Ross and Daniel Worden (eds) (2014), *Oil Culture*, Minneapolis: University of Minnesota Press.
Bennett, Jane (2010), *Vibrant Matter: A Political Ecology of Things*, Durham, NC: Duke University Press.
Bonneuil, Christophe and Jean-Baptiste Fressoz (2016), *The Shock of the Anthropocene*, London and New York: Verso.
Braidotti, Rosi (2013), *The Posthuman*, Cambridge: Polity Press.
Canavan, Gerry (2014), 'Introduction: if this goes on', in Gerry Canavan and Kim Stanley Robinson (eds), *Green Planets: Ecology and Science Fiction*, Middletown, CT: Wesleyan University Press, pp. 1–24.
Clark, Timothy (2015), *Ecocriticism on the Edge: The Anthropocene as a Threshold Concept*, London: Bloomsbury.
Coole, Diana and Samantha Frost (2010), 'Introducing the new materialisms', in Diana Coole and Samantha Frost (eds), *New Materialisms: Ontology, Agency, and Politics*, Durham, NC: Duke University Press, pp. 1–43.

Costa, Mariarossa Dalla and Monica Chilese (2014), *Our Mother Ocean: Enclosure, Commons, and the Global Fishermen's Movement*, New York: Common Notions.
Curtis, Claire P. (2012), *Postapocalyptic Fiction and the Social Contract*, London: Lexington Books.
Dahlberg, Rasmus, Olivier Rubin and Morten Thanning Vendelø (eds) (2016), *Disaster Research: Multidiscinplinary and International Perspectives*, Abingdon: Routledge.
Danowski, Déborah and Eduardu Viveiros de Castro (2017), *The Ends of the World*, Cambridge: Polity Press.
Demos, T. J. (2017), *Against the Anthropocene: Visual Culture and Environment Today*, Berlin: Sternberg Press.
Diamond, Jared (2005), *Collapse: How Societies Choose to Fail or Survive*, London: Penguin.
Donnelly, Sean (2014), 'Peak oil imagining in Cormac McCarthy's *The Road* and Paolo Bacigalupi's *The Windup Girl*', *English Academy Review*, 31: 2, pp. 156–69.
Easterbrook, Neil (2011), 'Ethics and alterity', in Mark Bould, Andrew M. Butler, Adam Roberts and Sherryl Vint (eds), *The Routledge Companion to Science Fiction*, London and New York: Routledge, pp. 382–92.
Edwards, Justin D., Rune Graulund and Johan Höglund (eds) (2020), *Gothic in the Anthropocene: Dark Scenes from Damaged Earth*, Minneapolis: University of Minnesota Press.
Emmett, Robert S. and David E. Nye (2017), *The Environmental Humanities: A Critical Introduction*, Cambridge, MA: MIT Press.
Emmott, Stephen (2014), *10 Billion*, London: Penguin.
Fisher, Mark (2009), *Capitalist Realism: Is There No Alternative?* London: Zer0 Books.
Flannery, Tim (2000), *The Future Eaters*, Sydney: Reed New Holland.
Ghosh, Amitav (2016), *The Great Derangement: Climate Change and the Unthinkable*, Chicago and London: University of Chicago Press.
Grusin, Richard (2015), 'Introduction', in Richard Grusin (ed.), *The Nonhuman Turn*, Minneapolis and London: University of Minneapolis Press.
Hageman, Andrew (2012), 'The challenge of imagining ecological futures: Paolo Bacigalupi's *The Windup Girl*', *Science Fiction Studies*, 39: 2.
Haraway, Donna (2015), 'Anthropocene, Capitolocene, Plantationocene, Cthulhucene: making kin', *Environmental Humanities*, 6, pp. 159–65.
Heinberg, Richard (2007), *Peak Everything: Waking up to the Century of Decline in the Earth's Resources*, Forest Row: Clairview.
Heise, Ursula K. (2016), *Imagining Extinction: The Cultural Meaning of Endangered Species*, Chicago: University of Chicago Press.
Hicks, H. J. (2016), *The Post-Apocalyptic Novel in the Twenty-First Century: Modernity Beyond Salvage*, London and New York: Palgrave Macmillan.
Hollinger, Veronica (2011), 'Posthumanism and cyborg theory', in Mark Bould, Andrew M. Butler, Adam Roberts and Sherryl Vint (eds), *The*

Routledge Companion to Science Fiction, London and New York: Routledge, pp. 267–78.
Homer-Dixon, Thomas (2006), *The Upside of Down: Catastrophe, Creativity, and the Renewal of Civilisation*, London: Souvenir Press.
Hurley, Kameron (2016), *The Geek Feminist Revolution*, New York: Tor.
Irr, Caren (2017), 'Climate fiction in English', in Paula Rabinowitz (ed.), *Oxford Research Encyclopedia of Literature*. DOI: 10.1093/acrefore/9780190201098.013.4.
Jameson, Fredric (2003), 'Future city', *New Left Review*, 21, pp. 65–79.
Klare, Michael T. (2012), *The Race for What's Left: The Global Scramble for the World's Last Resources*, New York: Metropolitan Books.
Klein, Naomi (2014), *This Changes Everything: Capitalism vs. the Climate*, New York: Simon & Schuster.
LeMenager, Stephanie (2014), *Living Oil: Petroleum Culture in the American Century*, Oxford: Oxford University Press.
Leopold, Aldo (1968), *A Sand County Almanac*, London: Oxford University Press.
Malm, Andreas (2016), *Fossil Capital: The Rise of Steam Power and the Roots of Global Warming*, London and New York: Verso.
McCarthy, Cormac (2007), *The Road*, London: Picador.
Menely, Tobias and Jesse Oak Taylor (2017), 'Introduction', in Tobias Menely and Jesse Oak Taylor (eds), *Anthropocene Reading: Literary History in Geologic Times*, University Park: Pennsylvania State University Press, pp. 1–24.
Monbiot, George (2007), 'Civilisation ends with a shutdown of human concern. Are we there already?'. www.theguardian.com/commentisfree/2007/oct/30/comment.books (last accessed 4 May 2017).
Moore, Jason W. (2015), *Capitalism in the Web of Life: Ecology and the Accumulation of Capital*, London and New York: Verso.
Moore, Jason W. (2016), 'The rise of cheap nature', in Jason W. Moore (ed.), *Anthropocene or Capitalocene: Nature, History, and the Crisis of Capitalism*, Oakland, CA: Kairos, pp. 78–115.
Morton, Timothy (2013), *Hyperobjects: Philosophy and Ecology after the End of the World*, Minneapolis: University of Minnesota Press.
Nayar, Pramod K. (2014), *Posthumanism*, Cambridge: Polity Press.
Roberts, Adam (2003), *Science Fiction*, London and New York: Routledge.
Roberts, Adam (2007), *The History of Science Fiction*, Basingstoke: Palgrave Macmillan.
Robertson, Benjamin R. (2018), *None of This is Normal: The Fiction of Jeff Vandermeer*, Minneapolis: University of Minnesota Press.
Roden, David (2015), *Posthuman Life: Philosophy at the Edge of the Human*, London and New York: Routledge.
Ruppert, Michael C. (2010), *Confronting Collapse: The Crisis of Energy & Money in a Post Peak Oil World*, White River Junction, VT: Chelsea Green Publishing.

Rust, Stephen, Salma Monani and Sean Cubitt (eds) (2016), *Ecomedia: Key Issues*, London: Routledge.

Schmeink, Lars (2016), *Biopunk Dystopias: Genetic Engineering, Society, and Science Fiction*, Liverpool: Liverpool University Press.

Schneider-Mayerson, Matthew (2015), *Peak Oil: Apocalyptic Environmentalism and Libertarian Political Culture*, Chicago: Chicago University Press.

Scranton, Roy (2015), *Learning to Die in the Anthropocene: Reflections on the End of a Civilization*, San Francisco: City Lights Books.

Selisker, Scott (2015), '"Stutter-stop flash-bulb strange": GMOs and the aesthetics of scale in Paolo Bacigalupi's *The Windup Girl*', *Science Fiction Studies*, 42: 3, pp. 500–18.

Shaviro, Steven (2015), 'Consequences of panpsychism', in Richard Grusin (ed.), *The Nonhuman Turn*, Minneapolis and London: University of Minneapolis Press, pp. 19–44.

Shiva, Vandana (2016), *Water Wars: Privatization, Pollution, and Profit*, Berkeley: North Atlantic Books.

Skrimshire, Stefan (ed.) (2010), *Future Ethics: Climate Change and Apocalyptic Imagination*, London and New York: Continuum.

Smil, Vaclav (2017), *Energy and Civilization: A History*, Cambridge, MA: MIT Press.

Sullivan, Heather I. (2012), 'Dirt theory and material ecocriticism', *Interdisciplinary Studies in Literature and Environment*, 19: 3, pp. 515–31.

Szeman, Imre and Dominic Boyer (eds) (2017), *Energy Humanities: An Anthology*, Baltimore: Johns Hopkins University Press.

Trexler, Adam (2015), *Anthropocene Fictions: The Novel in a Time of Climate Change*, Charlottesville: University of Virginia Press.

Tsing, Anna Lowenhaupt (2015), *The Mushroom at the End of the World: On the Possibility of Life in Capitalist Ruins*, Princeton: Princeton University Press.

Vint, Sherryl (2010), *Animal Alterity: Science Fiction and the Question of the Animal*, Liverpool: Liverpool University Press.

White, Lynn Jr. (1996), 'The historical roots of our ecological crisis', in Cheryll Glotfelty and Harold Fromm (eds), *The Ecocriticism Reader: Landmarks in Literary Ecology*, Athens: University of Georgia Press, pp. 3–14.

Wilson, Sheena, Adam Carlson and Imre Szeman (eds) (2017), *Petrocultures: Oil, Politics, Culture*, Montreal: McGill-Queen's University Press.

Winter, Mick (2006), *Peak Oil Prep: Three Things You Can Do to Prepare for Peak Oil, Climate Change, and Economic Collapse*, Napa, CA: Westsong Publishing.

Wolfe, Cary (2010), *What is Posthumanism?* Minneapolis and London: University of Minnesota Press.

Žižek, Slavoj (2010), *Living in the End Times*, London and New York: Verso.

CHAPTER 10

Dry Ontology and Finance Capitalism: A Material–Affective Reading of Financial Crisis Fiction

Martin Karlsson Pedersen

Introduction: The Realist Financial Crises Novel and Post-anthropocentric Theory

The financial crisis in 2007/8 has, from a literary and novelistic point of view, been very productive. As Alex Preston – novelist, financial commentator and former employee of a big financial firm – remarks in a 2011 review of another financial novel, Robert Harris's *The Fear Index*: 'Literature has done well out of the financial crisis. . . . We now have an array of highly convincing novels set against the world of high finance, a domain previously underexplored in fiction' (Preston: 2011b).[1]

Alison Shonkwiler has highlighted the realist financial novel's depiction of financial money – what in Marxist terms is called 'fictitious capital' (M–M')[2] – as a particular dynamic between the abstract and the concrete, the fictitious/imaginary and the material. Digitalised financial money expresses an abstract process of self-valorisation that has become detached from material reality (Shonkwiler 2017: xiv; see also Shaw 2015: 3). But, by the same token, this form of abstraction and detachment, as represented in the financial novels, becomes another kind of 'material agency' that affects individuals and society in very tangible and concrete ways (for instance, the correlation between the volatility in stock market signs and work relations [unemployment] and austerity policies).

Many financial novels dramatise and therefore make visible the otherwise fetishised and blurred gap between structure – financial markets, institutions and financial money – and subjectivity – the subject-position as trader, hedge fund and portfolio manager (work), husband and wife (family), white male and female (gender and race), and so on. These novels demonstrate what Shonkwiler emphasises as a crucial aspect of the process and logic of contemporary financialisation: how it 'specialize[s] in putting distance between the concrete effects and the structural violence of an abstract value that is measured by nothing but the stock market' (2017: xxv).[3]

Taking my point of departure from financial capitalism as a violent interaction between abstraction and concreteness, or the affective relation between financial money as abstract and non-referential signs and information and the human body, I want to show how this aspect of the contemporary realist financial novel can be fruitfully analysed through a post-anthropocentric perspective on capitalistic and financial reality.

More particularly, through an material–affective reading of *This Bleeding City* (2010), by Alex Preston, I will demonstrate how the novel depicts an affective encounter between human bodies and nonhuman bodies of financial signs that produces an ontological reality of human disconnection and isolation. This depiction of reality resonates with theories of financialisation, emphasising the increasingly individualised and foreclosed vision and feeling of the future (Haiven 2014: 106). I thus seek to show how the novel depicts and engages with the reality of financial subjectivity.

In order to approach the material–affective side of the contemporary financial novel, I propose to read it in dialogue with a post-anthropocentric way of thinking about contemporary capitalism as found in the post-autonomist Marxism of Maurizio Lazzarato and Franco 'Bifo' Berardi. My primary focus later in the chapter will be on the ontological thinking of Berardi, but here I will briefly set the stage for this later section using some key insights from Lazzarato, thereby highlighting the post-anthropocentric tendencies in Berardi's thoughts.[4]

Through the concept of 'semio-capitalism'[5], Berardi and Lazzarato in different ways underline the dominant role and interconnected reality of subjectivity (human) and digital information technologies (nonhuman) in production (info-commodities) and creation of surplus value. If capitalism thrives on the creativity, knowledge, general skills and constant cognitive work and attention of the human, it can only do so through complicated and extensive machinery and digital information technologies. In other words: in order to understand the production of subjectivity and the capture of social life itself as value-producing for capital (Genosko 2016: 103), we need a dual perspective, according to Lazzarato. As he puts it: 'Capitalism owes its efficacy and power to the fact that it joins two heterogeneous dimensions of subjectivity – the molar and the molecular, individual and pre-individual, representational and pre-representational (or post-representational)' (Lazzarato 2014: 31). Capitalism's production of subjectivity thus consists of what Lazzarato (following Deleuze and Guattari) describes as 'social subjection' and 'machinic enslavement' (2014: 23–54; Genosko 2016: 105), but what I will likewise call an 'anthropocentric' and 'post-anthropocentric' perspective and interconnected dynamic.

Through this opposition Lazzarato postulates two different ways in which to grasp the relation between subject and object or the interaction between the cognitive worker and the digital machinery and information. From the anthropocentric perspective of 'social subjection', the subject and object is understood as a dualism based on use and functionality, that is, based on an ontological distinction. Through a conscious and individuated way, the subject uses the object-machinery as 'the "means" or mediation of his actions or use' (2014: 26). Social subjection likewise equips the individuated subject with a specific subject-position and subjectivity as a signifying reality (identity, sex, body, profession, nationality and so on) (2014: 12).

In opposition to this dualist reality, the post-anthropocentric perspective of 'machinic enslavement' underlines the entanglement of the subject and object, the human and nonhuman as part of complex machinic assemblages (2014: 13, 30). In this reality, the dualism of subject and object collapses and the individual becomes a dividual: 'The dividual does not stand opposite machines or make use of an external object; the dividual is contiguous with machines' (2014: 26). What this means is that the dualism of subject and object and the notions of individuality, consciousness and representation (language as signifying) are broken down and the co-shaping reality of the nonhuman is emphasised: 'Non-humans contribute just as humans do to defining the framework and conditions of action. One always acts within an assemblage, a collective, where machines, objects, and signs are at the same time "agents"' (2014: 30). This post-anthropocentric or 'machinic centric' way of thinking[6] allows for an understanding of financial reality and money-signs as a nonhuman agency co-shaping human subjectivity and its affective reality. For both Lazzarato and Berardi, the financial system is an example per excellence of 'machinic enslavement', where the individual is 'no longer instituted as an "individuated subject," "economic subject" (human capital, entrepreneur of the self)', but instead the subject is 'considered a gear, a cog, a component part in the "business" and "financial system" assemblages' (2014: 25).

In the financial system, the economic subject or financial trader is therefore no longer just in a position of power and control. The trader's subjectivity is a 'machinic subjectivity' (2014: 97) and part of a human–machine assemblage of interconnected computer networks, data banks and a constant flow of signs. The financial trader-subjectivity thus is not an individual subject who makes rational choices but one who is entangled in and constituted by the nonhuman reality of non-signifying signs and machines (algorithms, computerisation, digital networks and so on):

> Instead of a rational subject who controls information and his choices, *homo economicus* is a mere terminal of asignifying, symbolic, and signifying semiotics and of non-linguistic constituents which for the most part escape awareness. We are not only well beyond the individualism and rationality of *homo economicus*, we have moved beyond 'cognitive capitalism'. (2014: 99–100)

A significant part of understanding Lazzarato and Berardi's analysis of financial reality as 'machinic enslavement' lies in the concept of asignifying semiotics (Lazzarato 2014: 40, 62; Genosko 2016: 105). In moving beyond 'cognitive capitalism', Lazzarato underlines how financial money-signs, or 'info-signs', to use Berardi's term, is predicated on a different (asignifying) semiotics, one that emphasises what signs do instead of what they mean. Asignifying signs such as financial ratings, money-signs and stock market indices are devoid of meaning and referentiatlity. They act directly on the real that is the social and human body and produce different affective realities (2014: 40–1).

This way of thinking goes beyond the human subject, consciousness and semiotic representation as the predominant foundation for understanding the production of subjectivity and the conditions for human action. The nonhuman – machines, objects and asignifying signs – constitute, just as other humans do, the condition of possibility for action, thinking, feeling and affective reality. In this way, both Lazzarato and Berardi move beyond the 'linguistic turn' and a logocentric account of signs, and provide a useful way of addressing the aforementioned material effects and affective reality of abstract money-signs.

Situating my own analysis of Preston's *This Bleeding City* within this post-antropocentric perspective and framework, my 'material–affective approach' shows the historical specificity of the financial novel and its dramatisation of financial reality seen from a particular 'inside' perspective. It directs our attention to the machinic–human assemblage and bodily-affective side of the production (or destruction) of the financial subject. In the financial novel of Alex Preston, this is expressed in becoming-trader subjectivity of our main protagonist Charlie. In embodying the subject-position as a trader in a hedge fund company, Charlie experiences an immersion in a particular assemblage of trader – screen/computer, financial markets, networks and data flow. This position both enforces him as a powerful, male subject placed in the centre of the world (The City/London) and, at the same time, it de-subjectivises him by dismantling his grip on reality, his relations to other people, and himself.

In order to further outline my material–affective approach to the contemporary realist financial novel, I will pursue my argument in three parts. First, I will focus specifically on the question of literary realism and how the affective and bodily dimension of financial capitalism should be seen in the historical context of the uses of realistic modes of representation in the contemporary novel. I will here follow Fredric Jameson's mapping of realism as an antinomy between affect and narration, or between representation and signification and non-signification. This line of historical thought leads to the second part, where I again will take up and specify the post-anthropocentric perspectives within post-autonomist Marxism's analysis of 'semio-capitalism', and focus on Berardi's ontology of affective info-signs and the material encounter between human bodies and immaterial, financial logics and signs. Lastly, I will approach Alex Preston's novel *This Bleeding City* from this material–affective angle, and show the affective reality of financial capitalism experienced from the subject-position of the trader.

Financial Realism, Ontology and Affect

Since the beginning of the twenty-first century, there has been a growing recognition of a realist tendency in the Anglo-American novel's depiction of capitalism in general and the post-financial and economic crisis in 2007/8 more specifically (see earlier footnote). From a post-anthropocentric perspective – or what he designates as 'creatureliness' – Arne De Boever has proposed a concept of 'financial realism' that highlights how this genre 'records . . . the reality of finance, governed by digital agents and centred around immaterial speculative instruments like derivatives, mortgages and insurance policies' (De Boever 2015: 33). De Boever is especially interested in Robert Harris's *Fear Index*, where Harris depicts the autonomous agency of algorithmic life and the affective reality of fear and panic. Through his reading of Harris's novel, De Boever raises pertinent questions concerning the relation between nonhuman agency and literary realism and posits that Harris's novel should not be read as science fiction, but instead viewed as 'new' kind of realism.

In continuation of De Boever's inquiry, I want to address this combination of nonhuman agency and literary realism in the context of more 'traditional' financial realist novels like Preston's *This Bleeding City*[7] and ask how they negotiate this ontological question of nonhuman and human agency. I posit that financial realism and ontology is to be understood fundamentally through a basic analytical dualism[8] between subject and object, human and nonhuman (nature, machine), agency and social structure – not to be confused with philosophical or metaphysical dualism. This kind of literary realist dualism is what Georg Lukács and Raymond Williams call a balance between subject and object (Lukács 2007 [1938]; Williams 1980). It is predicated on the notion of ontological non-conflation: that is, subject and object, human and nonhuman are not reducible to each other. This kind of ontology is therefore not 'flat' or non-hierarchic (see Bennett 2010 and Lazzarato 2014, both following Deleuze and Guattari) but instead, more accurately, it is conceptualised as 'deep' and hierarchised, as reality becomes stratified into levels with different causal powers. The tendency of contemporary literary financial realism to push towards the 'less anthropocentric', as Harry Levin once put it (Levin 1966: 249), and to foreground an objective financial reality is not equivalent to a complete effacement of the human as distinctly human (consciousness, goal and purpose).

On the contrary, what is at stake in the financial novel's ontology is a depiction of a financial reality where the human and nonhuman conflation only happens in glimpses or in parts of reality. The overall ontology of the novel is such that the interaction between human and nonhuman bodies has a bearing on the production of subjectivity, and on the conscious life and actions of our human protagonist, in such a way that it ultimately sets him ontologically apart from the nonhuman financial and machinic reality. Or, to put it in the vocabulary of Lazzarato, the novel still upholds that the production of subjectivity lies in the (contradictory) dynamism between 'social subjection' and 'machinic enslavement'.

In my account of financial realism there is a dynamic relationship and (potential) contradiction between a post-anthropocentric reality and the financial novel's human-centred reality underlining both the integration and separation between human and machines. In my analysis, I will emphasise the post-anthropocentric perspective within a human-centred reality and follow the implication of this perspective for understanding the financial subject. Or, rather: although I will focus on the nonhuman reality as one that co-shapes human subjectivity, Preston's novel resists and evades a wholesale Lazzaratian and Berardian post-anthropocentric analysis. My material–affective approach thus raises a more modest question: can we develop an understanding of literary financial realism that takes this basic dynamism of post-anthropocentric and anthropocentric perspectives on reality into account?

From this dynamic or dialectical (contradictory) way of looking at financial realism and ontology – anthropocentric (subjection or subject-position, consciousness and representation) in relation to post-anthropocentric (machinic enslavement, asignyfying signs, body and affect) – I think we can connect this tension to Jameson's more recent theorisation on literary realism where he emphasises the relation between affect and reality. Jameson posits – from a temporal angle (Jameson 2013: 10) – 'narration' and 'affect' as the internal antinomy and twin forces and sources of realism, or a conflict between representation and signification over and against non-signifying description and bodily sensation.

Fredric Jameson's account of realism in *The Antinomies of Realism* (2013) is useful to broaden the question of realism and affect historically[9] and situate the discussion of financial realism, ontology and nonhuman agency in a specific literary-realist tradition. With it, he provides basic literary tools for analysing the dual reality and function of narration and affect in the genre of the realist novel. I will ultimately use Jameson's account as a way of going beyond his discussion of the bourgeois body to the financial body and financial realism. To clarify this antinomy in the realist novel, let us consider briefly an interpretation of the overall conflict and then examine more closely the specific temporality of affect.

First, Jameson reinterprets the traditional (narratological) distinction between narration and description, and points to the ideological fact that realism 'holds together' these two ways of representing reality in a contradictory – that is, dialectical and therefore unresolvable – way (2013: 6–7), or, as he puts it: 'they are never reconciled, never fold back into one another in some ultimate reconciliation and identity' (2013: 11). The narration/narrating of reality through the chronology of past, present and future is always countered by and in conflict with another form of temporality related to affect and bodily movements. This antinomy of realism is a conflict that allows for an understanding of the human subject as an affective body, which can be seen to be at odds with the subject that develops over time and who searches for the realisation of its ideals, goals and self-recognition. The two different modes of mediation – narration and affect – are two different ways of depicting the human subject and its relation to itself, other people and the outer, objective reality: an affective/bodily relation and a discursive (consciousness) relation.

This leads to the second point: the specific temporality of affect and the notion of intensity. When Jameson is talking about affect, he invokes a well-known distinction in affect theory between emotion and affect (see, for example, Massumi 2015), that is, between conscious states (nameable) and bodily feelings (potentially 'nameless'). The body makes possible all sorts of emotional states and feelings due to its constant movement, sensation and 'openness'. Some of these are conscious ('nameable') but many are outside the discursive field. They are just registered and experienced intensely, and not (necessarily) clearly articulated or articulable (which is relative to historical circumstances).

The notion of intensity emphasises the temporal aspect of affect; Jameson calls it 'affect's chromaticism' (2013: 38), where '[a]ffect becomes the very chromaticsm of the body itself' (2013: 42). Jameson uses the musical concept of chromaticism to stress the temporality of an 'eternal present', and the question of intensity thus becomes another kind of temporal registering; 'that is, the capacity of affect to be registered according to a range of volume, from minute to deafening, without losing its quality and determination' (2013: 36). Affect has to do with these shifting states of intensity, which take place on another kind of temporal scale than the narrative of past, present and future. It is premised on the body's affective capacity, which means that the realist depiction of affect – the 'stopping' of the narrative representation or narration of the subject (its actions, roles, positions, values, past, memories and so on, in other words, meanings and significations) and the 'emergence' of a description of a different bodily temporality – heightens our attention to the shifts and change of bodily states experienced as a shift in intensity: 'the sliding scale of the incremental, in which each infinitesimal moment differentiates itself from the last by a modification of tone and an increase or diminution of intensity' (2013: 42).

What is at stake here is therefore realism's sensitivity in registering affect as bodily sensations and movements (up and down, high and low) in a minute and unpredictable way, that is, as a qualitative change or transition. There is a difference between the body, its movement and experience of intensity, and the signifying–subjectifyng processes of conscious articulation or nameable states (see also Anderson 2016). But because of realism's inherently historical nature, the question of the body likewise becomes a question of the changing depictions of the body and its affective states.[10] In other words, the changing encounters between historically different bodies – human and nonhuman – produce changes in affective states experienced through different scales and moments of intensity.

From Jameson's account of narration and affect, and from the post-anthropocentric perspective of Lazzarato on the production of subjectivity, I return to contemporary financial realism, and specifically the financial body and its affective reality. Fundamental to the realism of financial novels is the way they make visible how financialisation and financial capitalism work affectively; how financial abstraction has real, material and bodily consequences through the interaction and potential submersion of human and nonhuman, machinic bodies.

In the next part of the chapter I will use the historical-specific analysis of Franco 'Bifo' Berardi to outline a theory of affect and the body under financial capitalism. For both Berardi and Preston, a fundamental metaphor for describing the financial reality of uncertainty, information-overflow and digital signs is dryness. I will therefore point to a common ontological way of depicting reality that I will call a 'dry ontology': the drying up of the human ability to touch and connect.

Franco Berardi, Info-Signs and Dry Ontology

Through Berardi's analysis of 'semio-capitalism' I will continue the post-anthropocentric perspective on financial capitalism already begun in the introduction. Following the concept of asignifying semiotics and the free floating of financial signs, I will highlight two aspects of what Berardi sees as the bodily reality of the 'cognitariat':[11] first, the post-modernisation of the economy[12] and the excess of signs, and second, the historical emergence of a dry ontology and the disconnection of human bodies.

Berardi poses the question: what does it mean, affectively, to live in an economy that has turned into a hyper-reality?[13] What are the consequences when money as sign has lost its referentiality (to things, commodities) and representational meaning: 'Whereas in industrial capitalism's past it [money as sign] was a referential sign, representing a certain quantity of physical things, today it is a self-referential sign, that has acquired the power of both mobilizing and dismantling the social forces of production' (Berardi 2017: 149). In the age of semio-capitalism where the production of information ('info-labor') has become hegemonic, we, according to Berardi, should not see material goods but semiotic signs as the primary means of creating value. The digitalisation of the 'infosphere' and the 'elimination of the concrete usefulness of products' has resulted in an acceleration in the creation of surplus value, which means that signs are being produced and circulate at an ever-growing speed (2011: 93; 2017: 156). This process of abstraction (disembodiment) and acceleration has real and affective consequences. It produces a reality in which the overflow and excess of signs (digital money-signs, info-signs) overstimulate the body and the brain ('the embodied mind'). It produces a crisis of attention that is also a crisis of affect:

> In the sphere of semio-capitalism, if you want to increase productivity, what you have to do is accelerate the infosphere, the environment where information races toward the brain. What happens, then, to our brain – to the social brain? Cognition takes time. Think of what attention is. Attention is the activation of physical reactions in the brain, and also of emotional, affective reactions. Attention cannot be infinitely accelerated. (2012: 97)

In this acceleration and excess of information, where the process of valorisation has been emancipated from the real production of useful things (M–M'), the 'real world' is being physically destroyed: the physical world of bodies (humans, things, resources) is being destroyed or 'cancelled out' so that the circulation of financial flows can accelerate (2012: 104–5). This perpetual encounter (through production and consumption) with 'immaterial signs' effectuates an overload of information that pressures the subject's capacity for attention. In economic terms, attention becomes a scarce resource[14] and the scarcity hereof is, for Berardi, understood as an 'affective reaction', that is, a bodily and material limit to this overload acceleration. It leads to a bodily and mental 'state of collapse' (2012: 94).

What the analysis of the post-modernisation of the economy leads to is precisely to show how info-signs, as nonhuman bodies, affect and effect human bodies, and how money as self-referential signs work as agential power in 'dismantling the social forces of production'. The financial crisis has made this fact clear through its destruction of the lives of millions of people. This destructive aspect of financial capitalism leads to my second point: abstraction, acceleration and excess of financial money-signs are creating a new kind of affective and bodily reality: a dry ontology.

The abstractness and 'immateriality' of financial signs have material and affective consequences in the way that they dissolve human bodily interaction. The financial trader or info-producer and consumer encounters a 'techno-linguistic machine that is the financial web [is] acting as a living organism and its mission is drying up the world' (2012: 26). This 'drying up of the world' – the exploitation and capture of human bodies (attention time and physical and mental exhaustion), isolation and the impossibility of more permanent human-bodily encounters – is both linguistic and sensuous:

> Human beings conjoin thanks to their ability to linguistically and sensuously interact ... Sensibility is the ability of human beings to communicate what cannot be said with words. Being available to conjunction, the social organism is open to affections, sensuous comprehension and social solidarity ... Sensibility is also the faculty that allows us to enter into relation with entities not composed of our matter, not speaking our language, and not reducible to the communication of discrete, verbal or digital signs. (2012: 121)

What the financial 'techno-linguistic machine' does as a nonhuman actor or force, 'a living organism', is to dry up human sensibility and affective openness. The consequences of finance capitalism or 'semio-capitalism' is, in other words, an elimination of positive and possible affective encounters between human beings. It prevents the bodily and linguistic 'conjunction', that is, of ways of connecting; of the experience of solidarity; of the presence of the body of the other and a non-verbal and physical experience of belonging.

This dry ontology – where non-referential or asignifying signs penetrate the brain–body of the financial subject or cognitive worker more generally – is characterised by an affective reality of uncertainty arising from the fact that life under 'semio-capitalism' has become in a particular way 'precarious'. As Berardi puts it:

> When the relation between the signifier and the signified is no longer guaranteed by the presence of the body, my affective relation to the world starts to be disturbed. My relation to the world becomes functional, operational – faster, if you will, but precarious. This is the point where precariousness starts. At the point of disconnection between language and the body. (2012: 102)

This precarious life produces a new kind of alienation, typical for the situation of the cognitive worker. The separation from other affective human bodies, the disconnection or 'virtualization of social relations', produces certain emotional effects that become characteristic of this new alienation: '[it] takes the form of psychic suffering, panic, depression, and a suicidal tide. This is the affective character of the first generation of people who have learned more words from a machine than from the mother' (2012: 141).[15] The separation of body and language means the loss of language as 'potency'[16] and the word as 'a factor in the conjunction of affective bodies' (2012: 19). Language has been reduced to a mere function to facilitate disembodied and accelerating communication, and is primarily operating as a 'connector of signifying functions transcodified by the economy' (2012: 19). The violence inherent in the dry ontology of financial reality is thus semiotic (and not linguistic) and machinic: The human body–brain becomes hardwired into an information flow of non-referential or asignifying signs that causes the destruction and collapse of the individual and social body. The exploited and degraded body of the cognitariat inhibits the production of subjectivity (for instance, the collective cognitive worker) and in the last instance restricts potentiality of signification that is creative power and potency.

A Material–Affective Reading of Alex Preston's *This Bleeding City*

In one of his financial columns in the *New Statesman,* Alex Preston writes about his life and experience during the stock market panic of autumn 2008, and comments on his and other traders' job as 'one of pattern recognition: to sift through information and judge between the incidental and the meaningful. The best in the business seem to make these judgements at the level of instincts' (Preston: 2011a). In one way, it is this kind of financial reality, 'to sift through information' in the search for capital gain, which Preston has sought to depict in his novel *This Bleeding City* (2010), but this time through its material and bodily-affective consequences – that is, in the encounter between money as abstraction and the concreteness of the body of the financial subject.

Like other financial novelists, Preston writes from an insider's experience and knowledge of the financial system. This is a common feature of what Shaw designates as 'crunch lit': the narrative use of 'fictionalized, insider protagonists operating at the heart of the financial industries' (Shaw 2015: 61). In Preston's novel, the homodiegetic narrator – Charlie Wales – gives it a certain 'voyeuristic perspective on this period of the panic' (2015: 61). The novel is, in its realism, concerned with the 'I' – the financial subject or individual – as a narrating and experiencing 'I' that tries to understand himself, his own development and the financial reality around him. The novel opens with Charlie's critique aimed at his own generation as well at earlier generations who never gave warning of possible failures and mistakes:

> Forever looking ahead, rarely pausing to savour bright moments, I raced forward. We all did. ... In the headlong rush towards experience we blasted ourselves away from our youth, towards the future of wrinkled disappointment. But no one stopped to tell us that we should be sucking it all in, searing the images onto our memories, baking the emotions into our hearts. Because soon it would be all that we had. (Preston 2010: 1)

It is a melancholy critique with a very Berardian flavour: Charlie and his generation trusted in a future that never materialised. This affective reality of trust is a way to make sense of the world (on this point see also Shaw 2015: 63), or, to put it differently, it directs our attention to the fact that Charlie's decisions and expectations are formed through a certain mood or affective relation to the world (see also Anderson 2016). The overall mood of the novel is one of distrust and it permeates both Charlie's conscious reflections and his bodily-affective sensation in the novel.

The novel oscillates between two modes of depicting the reality of finance capitalism. On the one hand, there is conscious (character) and self-conscious (character as narrator) reflection on the financialised reality. The homodiegetic narration means that narrator and reader know what is going to happen (what Shaw calls the novel's use of 'dramatic irony'; 2015: 64) and the narrator/Charlie self-consciously reflects on why the future turned out the way it did. This mode of self-conscious reflection includes the character-narrator Charlie's ongoing thoughts and concerns regarding his own desires and longings, his relationship to his friends, his precarious job, and later on his marriage to Vero, and so on.

On the other hand, another aspect of financial reality is being depicted through the financial body and its affects. This physical and bodily reality gradually undermines and dismantles Charlie's trust in the future. My contention is that Preston's novelistic depiction of life in the midst of finance capitalism is in many respects akin to Berardi's analysis: he depicts the affective encounter between finance money and human bodies as the same kind of affective dryness or disconnection.

Early on, we witness how finance money is pulling at Charlie's mind and body as he displays a kind of money-earning desire fostered by the workings of the financial sector; not a slow, steady increase, but instead the logic of 'fast money', of acceleration and speed: 'I had but one desire – to become swiftly, splendidly rich' (Preston 2010: 7). It is the money of finance that influences the movement of the body, his desire; this is what drives him to the city. It affects him through the promise of a 'gilded existence' in the future and by becoming the precarious cognitarian or 'cheap, hungry labour':

> Our entire social circle was going into the City. The Stock markets had risen manically all the time we were studying, and the banks and brokers, insurance companies and law firms saw graduates as a source of cheap, hungry labour. The pact was clear – give us your twenties and we will make sure you don't have to work in your forties. There were stories of recent graduates receiving

million-pound bonuses. . . . I would earn more in a year than my father had earned in his life, secure Vero and a gilded existence, buy my future with my youth. (2010: 7–8)

This is one way that finance money works in its disembodied and accelerated movement ('The Stock markets had risen manically') as a nonhuman body: it forces on Charlie a desire for a certain feeling of existence in the world. This time-binding relationship, 'buy my future with my youth', is rooted in certain 'affective expectations' (the imagination of affective relations) of how to move through the world, of what the encounter and connection between I and the World could feel like:

> I longed to live with the light touch that our friends at Edinburgh achieved, longed to move with the same soft padding foot through the world, unconscious and uncaring of the weight of life lived pressed close against cold necessity. I wanted to offer Vero that existence, hold out to her the future of thoughtless spending and uncaring extravagance that I knew she coveted. (2010: 7)

This desire for an encounter with the world through a 'light touch', to move with the 'soft padding foot' and yearning for the sensation of 'weightlessness', is paramount because it is related to love and the permanent connection between bodies. It is a desire for a certain kind of affirmative connectivity and attachment, a frictionless life where nothing is hindering their movement. This light touch and weightless life is both premised on and becomes almost in itself akin to the excess of abstract money: an abstract depiction of life, abstracted from the 'cold necessity' and 'the weight of life', free-floating, without care or a physical-material world that holds the body down. The body is almost ethereal as a soul.

This initial expectation of a future where love and connectedness between Charlie and Vero can happen and a permanent encounter can take hold becomes almost ironic, even sinister, in that it is precisely the opposite that happens. In order for Charlie to become rich and 'rise' to this kind of affective life with Vero, he must submit himself to his work as a trader in the financial industry. What I have described as a desire for the lightness of the body – 'a body left unravaged by time' (2010: 68) – must now be seen in stark contrast to Charlie's actual, affective encounter with the nonhuman body of financial signs devoid of referentiality (financial money and information). Preston's novel makes visible the reality of the financial body and how the body is affected by its encounter with the financial reality of an excess of numbers and money.

There are three central aspects in the novel of this registering of the financial body: (1) the excess of signs and the feeling of invincibility, (2) the reality of dryness and the oscillation between connection and disconnection, and (3) the ending and a sense of non-movement and entrapment (static future).

First, what Charlie encounters in his hedge fund workplace as a trader is the force of numbers, a pull and pressure from the nonhuman body of money-signs: 'there was something heady and compulsive about the numbers' (2010: 117). In its sheer quantitative amount, its excess, it gives rise to a feeling of 'invincibility' due to a bodily sensation of being 'in the middle' and the recognition of order or symmetry: 'But it was hard not to feel invincible sometimes, when I saw patterns in the markets, felt things aligning, sensed the strange magic of capital flows with me sitting in the middle with unique vision, able to see the mechanism of the great machine of capitalism' (2010: 117).

What Preston earlier in his financial column described as 'pattern recognition', we now see him flesh out. Using the familiar metaphor between eye and cognition, the novel depicts how the vision of patterns gives Charlie a sense of invincibility, almost omnipotence ('unique vision') and control: that he is mastering the 'great machine of capitalism'. But this position and potency of being in power is marked by another more sensuous and illusive moment when Charlie encounters 'the strange magic of capital flows'. Charlie – in trying to describe his feeling of invincibility – depicts the sensation of the flow of signs as something almost irrational and beyond economic and conscious calculation. He is sensing something that he is calling 'strange magic'. It is the bodily feeling of invincibility and not the purely cognitive (seeing, interpreting and controlling). Charlie is sensing something out of his control. Does Charlie in this passage 'misinterpret' his senses, so that he gives the eye privilege over the rest of his body's movement, sensation and reaction to the excess of money-signs? The nonhuman body of excessive signs is alluring, it captivates and draws him in. The position becomes reversed as the feeling of being 'in the middle' is not predicated on perfect vision or potency, but on impotence and being 'spellbound' by the excess of money-signs.

The irrationalism and pre-conscious reality becomes more visible when the financial crisis hits. As Charlie narrates the constant shift in the emotions of financial subjects, he seems positioned at a distance:

> I listened to these men and the rapid oscillation between hope and despair, greed and fear in their voices, and I thought to myself how the market is just a reflection of the psychologies of the traders who operate within it . . . The flight from mindless exuberance to blind panic had swept away any rational middle ground. (2010: 179)

Charlie is not gripped by panic. Instead his critical thought reflects on how the financial system works in an all too human and flawed way, 'how the market is just a reflection of the psychologies of the traders'. What before was magical has now become mundane or anthropocentric. Charlie – recognising a pattern – understands the problem: it is the lack of a rational position or the system's lack of grounding such a position. But this selfsame position of the narrator – able to view, listen and judge from a position of power – is contrasted with Charlie's own aforementioned bodily embeddedness in the situation itself. This is the Jamesonian conflict between affect and narration, or the Lazzaratian between subjection and machinic enslavement, now depicted as one between human disempowerment and machinic empowerment. Here is how it differs from Lazzarato's or Berardi's conflict: it is when the market becomes all too human – as it does in a financial crisis – that the sense of impotence and powerlessness sets in. But when 'the great machine' is working, when Charlie finds himself 'in the middle', tuned in to the flow of signs and part of the rhythm of the machine, he feels invincible and powerful. In this way, the novel exhibits a 'classic' dichotomy between human imperfection and machinic perfection: the financial crisis reveals the human behind the sign in contrast to the sign detached from an all too human reality. In this sense, the becoming-trader of Charlie is equal to becoming machine-like. But these two positions of either the machinic-submerged feeling of power or the distanced awareness of human irrationality is contrasted with a third experience and sensation of financial reality.

This leads to the second aspect and – following Berardi's line of thought – the question: what does this world of numbers and money-signs devoid of material referents (things, commodities) do to the human possibility of 'conjunction'. In Charlie's conversation with Jo (one of the women he tries to have a relationship with), he states: 'Maybe I should spend more time with people, Jo. I sit every day and look at numbers, wade deeply through abstractions. Sometimes I barely speak to another human for days. The only person I used to speak to in the office has just killed herself' (2010: 215), and Jo replies: 'People disappear into the numbers, lose themselves in the symbols of their success, the relentless drive for more' (2010: 215).

Preston makes visible the conflicts we saw in Berardi's theoretical analysis and how the abstract reality of finance and numbers produce human disconnection, isolation and suicide. The human sensibility – sensuous and linguistic – is being destroyed by the overflow and excess of signs, so many that one can 'disappear into the numbers'. When

Charlie later in the novel looks at his dead co-worker's desk, his comment resembles Berardi's: 'and I thought of all the dry abstract days spent worrying about the markets' (2015: 253). The (historical) financial ontology of dryness mirrors that which is drying up: life or the possibility of creating and maintaining meaningful conjunctions in the midst of an excess of numbers and the lonely cognitarian work of 'wad[ing] deeply through abstractions' (2015: 253). The detachment of signs from the 'real', physical world (abstraction) correlates with the disconnection of human, bodily encounters, that is, a world of sterility. The dry and abstract ontology of financial capitalism produces a feeling of fear as a result of a heightened awareness and sensation of the movement of the body that borders on a state of near collapse:

> At work, I sat at my desk and felt the blood move in my veins. My hands grew cool and my breathing quickened at the memory of my blind flight towards the hospital, clutching at my heaving heart. The pattern of my fear was layered, textured, complex. As the markets moved around me, as the portfolio managers yelled for coffee and slammed the phones into cradles and threw paper planes at one another, I sat entirely still and felt the fear creeping upon me once again. Madison looked at me, at first with friendship, then concern, then, as I ignored her and stared only ahead of myself, into the electronic depths of my computer, hostility. (2010: 77)

Again we have the bodily positioning of Charlie in the middle of it all, 'as the markets moved around me', but now he feels the opposite of invincibility. This emotional distress is predicated on the physical registering of the body's internal movements – 'felt the blood move in my veins' – and on the lack of human connectivity as he sits staring 'into the electronic depths of my computer'. Charlie registers the 'pattern of my fear' and not the digital information, making the obvious suggestion that his fear is correlated to the volatility of the markets, and his inability to control his body's movement seems to point to his inability to handle the markets. He has, in this passage, almost collapsed into himself, bodily and emotionally: 'sat entirely still and felt the fear creeping upon'.

Preston contrasts this dryness of the financial world and emotional fear with moments of positive bodily encounters and affects, centred on the physicality of natural bodies. The conversation between Jo and Charlie above is immediately countered by the tangible touch of the rain and of a human hand: 'A light drizzle had begun to fall and it smudged the lights around us, caressed Jo's hair and her face, fell upon my hand as it lay upon Jo's shoulder as we made our way down Hanbury Street and then left onto the row of imposing old houses' (2010: 215). This passage captures another kind of bodily entanglement: the physicality of rain that maps out a sensuous movement, from the caress of the rain to the hand on the shoulder that also caresses. This is the real world of physical touch and tangibility, not the light touch of the gilded future. These encounters between 'natural elements' and human bodies become moments of reconnectivity, where escape from the 'dry abstract days' seems possible.

Later in the novel, this dryness is contrasted with the encounter between water and human bodies of connectivity, when Charlie walks down the seafront with Vero and his father:

> and the October waves were grey and violent, falling down on the pebbles and then sucking back out, churning and spewing around the struts of the pier. Vero stood holding her belly and felt the full force of the wind upon her, and tears came to her eyes, and my father strode up behind her and put his arms around her, and they faced out to sea at the end of the pier and shouted into the wind. (2010: 313)

Again, there is a bodily 'rhythm' to this passage: first, the physicality of the sea and the waves (as bodies in motion), then the human body watching and then the entanglement and encounter with the force of the wind and tears coming from the body, and the voice shouting and mixing with the sound of the wind, 'into the wind'. All this seems to make possible or encourage – as the right atmosphere or affective climate – human encounters: how the father 'strode up behind her and put his arms around her': the tangibility of the rain, the waves, the wind seem to allow affirmative moments of touching and being touched, that is, moments of conjunction. Vero's pregnancy and fertility stands in contrast to the sterility and suicidal nature of the dry financial ontology.

This leads to the last aspect of the financial body: entrapment and non-movement. This is related to the manoeuverability of the body in a very specific sense: the way that Charlie does not seem to be able to escape London (he does leave temporarily but returns). Tying in with the beginning of the novel, the desire for money and the 'weightless existence' come to be linked to a kind of non-movement and a feeling of being trapped: 'We were all stranded, all of us trapped by London and money. All of us waiting for life to begin' (2010: 17). The entrapment (bodily, emotional and imaginative) likewise becomes associated with dissatisfaction and distrust as the more general feeling of existence, which resonates with the aforementioned feeling of fear. As Charlie says to a stripper (again a disconnection):

> I think maybe all jobs are like that. They pay you just enough to keep you working, just enough to stop you saying fuck it all and taking off into the sunset. Or maybe that's just something to do with our stage of capitalism. That, no matter how much you earn, the cost of things that seem essential for a decent existence

is enough to keep us running on the wheel. We are programmed to feel dissatisfied with what we have. That we are meant to feel miserable and that the only way out is to achieve some mythical level of wealth that will allow us to escape. (2010: 106)

Here Charlie's 'entrapment' precedes a reflexive rationality and consciousness and resonates on a deeper bodily and affective level. It demonstrates, as has already been shown, how the promise of future wealth, the exposure to the logic of financial money and its 'speediness' becomes a bodily investment, something that can no longer be changed. Entrapment becomes a binding of the affective capability: not being able to get out, move away. This is perhaps most striking in the way the novel ends, with Charlie again in the City, a lost marriage and (almost) a lost child behind him, at his office:

> here is a mark on the wall of my office . . . I pick up my trenchcoat, feel the heaviness of it as I lay it over my arm. I move closer and the mark seems to grow larger as I step towards it. Finally I am pressed against the wall, my face hard on the cool white plaster, and I realize that the mark is a full stop. (2010: 335)

This last scene in many ways contrasts with the opening depiction of an affective state and bodily movement of the 'light touch'. The feeling of the heaviness of the raincoat, the solidity of the wall and its hard surface and the final 'full stop'. This end of movement becomes a musing on the end of bodily conjunctions, and, in this sense, of affectivity and sensibility: Charlie is up against the wall, there is no exit and no entry, no future, no movement, no possibility for change, no hope. Here is the hard reality of a future that never came, and the inescapable, affective consequences of the dryness of finance capitalism. The force of abstractness and excess of money-signs has emptied the body and mind of any hope of future happiness and human conjunction. A few pages earlier, his tone is clarified but cannot hide the reality of permanent loneliness: 'It is the simplicity of the markets that appeal to me now. The clarity of the balance sheet, the logic of profit and loss. And I try to lead a life that is equally straightforward' (2010: 331). Clarity, simplicity and straightforwardness all seem to gesture towards a life without any possibility of being affected by and affecting other human beings. It suggests that the violent effects on the human body have become internalised as a permanent condition and state of mind. Subjectivity has become financialised in a different way – not in the potency of financial masculinity and invincibility, but in a resigned yet content way where life is as calculable as a balance sheet and predictable as a machine.

Notes

1. On the realist financial novel tendency, see Shaw (2015), De Boever (2015), Shonkwiler (2017) and McClanahan (2018). Shonkwiler and La Berge (2014) broaden the scope and talk about 'capitalist realism' as a new tendency in the post-millennial novel.
2. The basic Marxian formula for describing the process of abstraction where money begets more money without the need for or intermission of commodities and labour time (M–C–M'); see Berardi (2012).
3. For a further description of the violence of financial capitalism see Marazzi (2010) and McClanahan (2018).
4. In this way, I bypass some of the accusations that Lazzarato makes of the theories of 'cognitive capitalism' that could include certain aspects of Berardi's work.
5. For an exposition of the concept of 'semio-capitalism' and a comparison of Lazzarato and Berardi, see Genosko (2016: 91–117). I will throughout be using the terms 'semio-capitalism' and 'financial capitalism' interchangeably, referring to the same reality of financial abstraction, human–machine interaction and asignifying money-signs; see Genosko (2016: 91–117).
6. For a clear exposition of 'machinic centric' thinking, see Dyer-Witheford and de Peuter (2009).
7. But also other novels of the same realist kind, for instance Adam Haslett's *Union Atlantic* (2010), Jonathan Dee's *The Privileges* (2010) and Christina Alger's *The Darlings* (2012), to mention just a few. See also footnote 1 for references.
8. Analytical dualism means a distinction between subject and object not predicated on metaphysical or philosophical dualism but on the conception that although human subjects are rooted in material reality, like objects they possess properties that make a difference, in particular questions of goals, agency and conscious intention and self-reflection (Archer 1998).
9. 'Once we enter a discussion of affect and the body we also enter the realm of history, and we must necessarily think historically' (Jameson 2013: 34).
10. What I have just outlined as Jameson's reflections on realism has been formulated in a general way. What interests Jameson specifically, though, is the relation between affective styles of mid-century music, paintings and literature and the 'historic emergence of the bourgeois body' (Jameson 2013: 42).
11. This term designates what Berardi calls 'the cognitive proletariat', 'cognitive labor' or 'semio-workers': the workers that are involved in the Internet economy or the digitalised network of the global economy (Berardi 2011: 82–3). What Berardi wants to emphasise is 'the material (I mean physical, psychological, neurological) disease of the workers'. When I am talking about the financial subject and body in Preston's novel, it is a kind of sub-category to Berardi's overall categorisation, that is, human beings particularly situated in the financial system. Furthermore, the relationship

between 'financialization' and the 'cognitariat' means the re-emergence of a (new) kind of 'precariousness' (Berardi 2011: 89–92; 2015: 138–42) and a particular affective, emotional and mental situation of work under financial capitalism.
12. What is telling is how the realist financial novels challenge this abstraction, as I mentioned at the beginning, and the way that abstraction becomes visible through its material and bodily affect and violence. The question of reality is thus not framed solely in the context of what is real and unreal, what is referential and non-referential. The question is what real and material effects the sign, devoid of referential meaning, has on the human body, and what effects and affects it has on the subject's social reality and its relation to other people.
13. See Baudrillard (2006) [1981]), the numerous references to Baudrillard in Berardi (2012), and Genosko (2016).
14. See also Boutang (2011: 72–5) for a further elaboration of the economic analysis of attention time and affect as a prerequisite of value-creation.
15. For more on Berardi and the relationship between financial reality, affect and panic, see De Boever (2015).
16. For a further description of the conflict between potency and the current age of impotence – that is to say, the lack or latency of a possible solidarity among disembodied, cognitive workers – see Berardi (2017) and Genosko (2016: 102). For a specific comment on financial reality and masculine power and potency, see Haiven (2014: 122).

References

Anderson, Ben (2016), 'Neoliberal affects', *Progress in Human Geography*, 40: 6, pp. 734–53.
Archer, Margaret (1998), 'Introduction: realism in the social sciences', in Margaret Archer, Roy Bhaskar, Andrew Collier, Tony Lawson and Alan Norrie (eds), *Critical Realism – Essentiel Readings*, New York: Routledge, pp. 189–206.
Baudrillard, Jean (2006) [1981], *Simulacra and Simulation*, Ann Arbor: University of Michigan Press.
Bennett, Jane (2010), *Vibrant Matter: A Political Ecology of Things*, Durham, NC: Duke University Press.
Berardi, Franco 'Bifo' (2011), *After the Future*, Chico, CA: AK Press.
Berardi, Franco 'Bifo' (2012), *The Uprising: On Poetry and Finance*, Los Angeles: Semiotext(e).
Berardi, Franco 'Bifo' (2015), *Heroes*, New York: Verso.
Berardi, Franco 'Bifo' (2017), *Futurability*, New York: Verso.
Boutang, Yann Moulier (2011), *Cognitive Capitalism*, Malden, MA: Polity Press.
De Boever, Arne (2015), 'Creatures of panic', *European Journal of English Studies*, 19: 1, pp. 24–38.

Dyer-Witheford, Nick and Greig de Peuter (2009), *Games of Empire: Global Capitalism and Video Games*, Minneapolis: University of Minnesota Press.
Genosko, Gary (2016), *Critical Semiotics*, New York: Bloomsbury.
Haiven, Max (2014), *Crisis of Imagination, Crisis of Power*, New York: Zed Books.
Jameson, Fredric (2013), *The Antinomies of Realism*, New York: Verso.
La Berge, Claire Leigh and Alison Shonkwiler (2014), 'Introduction', in Alison Shonkwiler and Claire Leigh La Berge (eds), *Reading Capitalist Realism*, Iowa City: University of Iowa Press.
Lazzarato, Maurizio (2014), *Signs and Machines*, Los Angeles: Semiotext(e).
Levin, Harry (1966), *Refractions*, New York: Oxford University Press.
Lukács, Georg (2007) [1938], 'Realism in the balance', in Theodor Adorno, Walter Benjamin, Ernst Bloch, Bertolt Brecht and Georg Lukács, *Aesthetics and Politics*, New York: Verso, pp. 27–59.
Marazzi, Christian (2010), *The Violence of Financial Capitalism*, Los Angeles: Semiotext(e).
Massumi, Brian (2015), 'Navigating movements', in Brian Massumi, *The Politics of Affect*, Cambridge: Polity Press, pp. 1–46.
McClanahan, Annie (2018), *Dead Pledges*, Stanford: Stanford University Press.
Preston, Alex (2010), *This Bleeding City*, London: Faber & Faber.
Preston, Alex (2011a), 'Panic stalks the square mile', *New Statesman*, 15 August 2011.
Preston, Alex (2011b), 'Dog-eat-dog morality', *New Statesman*, 2 October 2011.
Shaw, Katy (2015), *Crunch Lit*, London: Bloomsbury.
Shonkwiler, Alison (2017), *The Financial Imaginary*, Minneapolis: University of Minnesota Press.
Shonkwiler, Alison and Claire Leigh La Berge (eds), *Reading Capitalist Realism*, Iowa City: University of Iowa Press.
Williams, Raymond (1980), 'Realism and the contemporary novel', in Raymond Williams, *The Long Revolution*, Harmondsworth: Penguin, pp. 300–19.

CHAPTER 11

The Work of Art in the Age of Capitalist Realism: Materiality/Aura/Apocalypse

Maurizia Boscagli

> Nowadays a political exit from capitalism seems unthinkable, as, in the new technical and anthropological framework, political decision is replaced by automatic governance. Therefore the end of capitalism tends to be imaginable only as the end of civilization itself.
>
> Franco Berardi, *Futurability*, 2017

> We will only escape from the major crisis of our era through the articulation of a nascent subjectivity, a constantly mutating *socius*, and an environment in the process of being reinvented.
>
> Félix Guattari, *The Three Ecologies*, 2000

> I was familiar with material things that seemed to have taken on a kind of magical power as a result of a monetizable signature . . . But this was incredibly rare . . . to encounter an object liberated from that logic. What was the word for that liberation? *Apocalypse? Utopia?*. . .
>
> Ben Lerner, *10:04*, 2014

Living at the time of the Anthropocene, the time of the Sixth Great Extinction, cannot but elicit apocalyptic feelings. The sense of the end, if we consider the condition of existence of thousands of species under the present environmental crisis, necessarily defines the contemporary zeitgeist. Climate change and its threat have recently become an impellent and everyday experience for everybody (I am writing from southern California, where extreme heat, floods and fires have become the 'new normal').

The sense of an ending, and speculations about a future that appears to be more and more out of reach, have become the trademark issues of the present. (Lousley 2017; Cazdyn and Szeman 2014; Harvey 1996; Hulme 2011; Weisman 2010) Yet in the twentieth and twenty-first centuries the question of the future also has another resonance, this time economic and social. In the 1970s, with their song 'No Future', the Sex Pistols, for example, expressed anger and angst against their condition as a 'lost generation', destined to a non-future of unemployment, marginality and poverty. This condition was embraced and made visible by the punk movement and its culture of nihilism. Margaret Thatcher's coming to power in 1979 Britain, in step with Reaganomics in the United States, inaugurated the neoliberal era. One of Thatcher's famous *dicta*, 'There is no alternative', to what her government and its policies had put in place, continues to inform the present. (Harvey 2007) Now a different world, a different way of living, even the possibility of resistance, are presented as unthinkable to masses of people who live in conditions of unemployment, exploitation, loss of financial security, climate emergency and depression. In the face of this economic, environmental and cultural scenario, it is more than ever necessary to imagine a different reality, capable of transforming apocalypse into utopia, and moving us towards the possible, rather than towards despair, so that a different relationship to one another and to the nonhuman might help to reconfigure, as Félix Guattari suggests in one of the epigraphs to this chapter, both subjectivity and politics. At the time of the postpolitical, as the apocalyptic becomes central to the neoliberal imaginary (Emmelhainz 2016: 3, 5), politics needs to be reconfigured as well: praxis can also become poiesis, a semiotic and poetic making, a fabulation that, through art and literature, narrates collectivity into existence, rebuilding community in political terms in the face of disaster. If capitalist realism, as Mark Fisher calls it (Fisher 2009: 2), presents us with only one reality, and only one homogeneous experience of it, we need to move beyond realism and open ourselves to forms of re-enchantment and historico-narrative experimentalism that free 'what is' from its neoliberal caption, and turn instead to the unexpected and the uncalculated.

The idea of co-constructing the common with others, and of narrating a different reality into existence through poiesis, are central to the text on which my discussion here will concentrate, Ben Lerner's *10:04* (2014), a novel set in New York at the time of climate disaster. Because of its focus on life at the time of Hurricane Sandy, futurity and the condition of *anthropos*, as well as on the meaning and value of aesthetics, Lerner's novel directly engages with current discussions of ecocriticism, the posthuman and neoliberalism. As a meditation on the meaning of literature, and as a story about living at the time of an announced catastrophe, *10:04* works as a form of cognitive mapping of the present and as a blueprint for survival. As such, the tone of its narrative changes from apocalyptic to utopian. This is a special type of utopia, different from the non-place of the utopian writing tradition (Jameson et al. 2016; Jameson 2004): rather, Lerner proposes a realised here-and-now utopia, that waits to be made visible through literary poiesis and the illuminations that, unexpectedly, flash in the dark landscape of black-out New York in 2012. The language and the concepts that Lerner's novel invokes to talk of futurity and apocalypse are Walter Benjamin's, and Benjamin's critique of modernity, historical time and the aura are important metatexts for Lerner's work. Both Benjamin and Lerner acknowledge a decline of experience. For Benjamin, in the early twentieth century, the decline is caused by the accelerated tempo and the shocks of technological modernity. For Lerner, the subject's incapability to feel shock and be shocked is produced by the contemporary culture of sedation, total calculability and resignation to what is, in which we find ourselves immersed today (Berardi 2017; Sturken 2007).

In this context, the subject of Western philosophical tradition, the rational agent of modernity who establishes its power and selfhood through the caesura between subject and object, culture and nature, human and nonhuman, animate and non-animate, enters a deep crisis, if not the beginning of its own extinction. This crisis is registered and celebrated in the figure of the cyborg Donna Haraway theorises in her work since her 1982 *The Cyborg Manifesto*, or in the concept of hybridity that Bruno Latour analyses in his critique of the divide between nature and culture (Latour 1991, 2004). Focused on this very crisis of the subject, Lerner's novel is a reflection on art, mortality and a postindividual future at the time of environmental and neoliberal disaster. In the novel the subject is in turn questioned, interrogated, dismantled and only partially recuperated. The fact that the protagonist is presented as an ill body makes it impossible to view him as the all-powerful and self-sufficient self; he is unable to sustain the old dichotomy of subject and object. Yet *10:04* offers both a representation *and* a critique of the posthuman. Even though the organic and the inorganic switch place more than once (the city is continually depicted as a living organism, for example), the novel does not completely move away from human individuality, albeit an individuality gone awry in the solipsism, isolation and claimed self-sufficiency of the neoliberal self. Neither does this self melt apocalyptically into nature or catastrophe. If the subject temporarily dissolves in *10:04*, it does so only in order to create new forms of collectivity and a new political subjectivity. In this sense, Lerner's novel is trying to outline the path to a possible politics, or a politics of the possible, even, after the posthuman.

One of the most damaging cultural effects of neoliberalism, together with the idea that 'there is no alternative', is the notion that we live at the time of post-politics, when 'the localized non collective forms of resistance appear to be always already inefficient and ineffectual' (Emmelhainz 2016: 9). For this reason, the move towards collectivity, even what the narrator calls 'bad collectivity' (in the book, those created by bedbugs and by Challenger jokes), is extremely important both for Lerner and for contemporary critical theorists. In the following section, in order to contextualise my discussion of the novel, I turn to some relevant interventions in the discourse of environmental and neoliberal apocalypse, from Franco Berardi to Donna Haraway, to conclude with Félix Guattari's theorisation of the three ecologies. The second part of the chapter will be dedicated to a critical analysis of *10:04* in the light of Walter Benjamin's concept of historical time as *Jetztzeit*.

Guattari's theory is key for my discussion as it recognises both art and literature as privileged spaces of dissent from, and contestation of, what capitalism proposes as the only possible reality. As Guattari suggests, the aesthetic ruptures the homogeneity of the contemporary semiosphere, opening new vistas in the regime of the visible established by Enlightenment modernity. Through moments of illumination, brought by newly auratic objects as well as by 'totaled' artworks, Lerner tries to make space for another possible reality, so that the novel provides a road map for navigating the contemporary scene beyond both apocalyptic catastrophism and an unjustified optimism.

Apocalypse Now

Contemporary apocalyptic discourse is articulated as part of a triangulation of elements that work in synergy, and that include the posthuman and the future. The question of the ending – of time, of life, of the planet – emerges on two different and related planes: the environmental and the sociopolitical. In the present global scene, there are plenty of reasons for thinking apocalyptically, and critics do so both in ecocriticism and in the humanities. The threat of future disasters and the experience of those which have already taken place is unavoidable. As T. J. Demos points out, following Christian Parenti's analysis,

> population growth, resource consumption, habitat transformation, greenhouse-gas-driven climate change . . . the world faces a near future of intensified global warming, desertification, acidification of the seas, and the precipitation of a mass species extinction event, the intensity and the scale of which has not yet been witnessed in 65 million years. (Demos 2013: 3; Parenti 2011)

This all too real vision of coming disaster is not simply centred on 'nature'. The notion of nature, as Timothy Morton and other critics affirm, has been replaced by 'the mesh', the weaving of 'infinite connections and infinitesimal differences in lichen, fungus, bacteria, endosymbiosis or symbiosis within organisms' (Morton 2010: 29–30). This interacting of different orders of reality ('material, economic, technological') (Apter 2013: 134) draws its discursive force from 'system environmentalism': 'The material sciences, cybernetics, network theory, and distributive computation' (Apter 2013: 30). The vitalism of this world does not exclude catastrophe: its 'dark ecology' (Morton 2018) juxtaposes with the catastrophism of sci-fi (Apter 2013: 134). This rather gloomy and apocalyptic projection of the future determines the melancholia and depression, and I would add, a sense of paralysis, that characterises what Emily Apter calls 'planetary dysphoria'. On a planet 'conceived as an environmental death trap', she asserts, the only possible affect is depression, recognised here as 'an ecological embodiment of the death drive' (Apter 2013: 40).

Posthumous life, an afterlife 'located in the temporality of the future aftermath' (Weinstein and Colebrook 2017: 4), excludes any vestiges of the human, turning instead to the inhuman. 'What could life without the human mean?', speculate Jaime Weinstein and Claire Colebrook (2017: 3). This prospect of the future without 'man', which Michel Foucault projected decades ago, this vision of the posthumous as apocalyptic and cosmic antihumanism, can assume at times an almost millenarist tone. The prospective of the future 'illegibility' of any human impact on environmental reality, although highly possible, indeed echoes the futuristic and catastrophic tone of sci-fi, particularly dystopian sci-fi, and leaves out of the picture the social and political aspect of life. As is possible in a sci-fi or fantasy text, the concept of the posthumous allows the theorist to skip the fundamental and extremely urgent question of what to do now, how to face the present conditions, including – but not only – environmental ones, in which people find themselves situated globally. Thinking about life before life, or life after life, as the discourse of the posthumous invites us to do, misses one specific temporality, that of the here and now, the *hic et nunc* of political life.

For a full understanding of life today, we need to take into account the double register of the contemporary discourse of the end: the ecocritical discussion of the human as life, on the one hand, without forgetting the neoliberal maximisation and financialisation of life itself, of nature; and of the human for profit, on the other. Both critical discourses hinge, and clash upon, the question of human agency, and the capability of the subject to change reality rather than just being changed by, and as, 'nature'. Regarding an exclusively biological understanding of the human as organism, we need to ask if the posthuman (non) subject is still provided with critical capacity and with voice against the noise that meaning and communication have become (Byung-Chul Han 2017). It is by theorising the social dimension of the posthuman that this critical capability, this possible agency, can be envisioned and recognised.

For Franco Berardi, the erosion and erasure of the human is visible in neoliberalism's *Homo oeconomicus*. This non-subject is at the centre of 'the digital financial era of semiocapital' (Berardi 2019: 6), in which the calculating, technical reason of Enlightenment is now taken to a new level of intensity. It must be pointed out that Berardi is not trying to resurrect *anthropos*, the individual subject of Western tradition: rather, he is interested in the general intellect, in the collectivity and its capability to create the commons. In a time without any project, any collective plan of action towards a shared, common ideal, we cannot just move towards a future utopia. Rather we need to move towards praxis at the very moment when any concrete political solution to capitalism's contradictions seems unthinkable. Nihilism and a sense of impotence are the most widespread affects at this point (2019: 33). Yet hope is still on Berardi's radar: 'Will the human mind imagine a human, postapocalyptic form of life? Will a new idea of humanism emerge from the wreckage of humanism?' (2019: 115). His call to reinvent a future beyond the apocalypse demands the reimagining of a commons through empathy and solidarity.

Donna Haraway, in *Staying with the Trouble. Making Kin in the Chthulucene*, likewise asks: 'How can we write at times of urgency, without the self-indulging and self-fulfilling myths of apocalypse?' (Haraway 2016: 1). Confronted with the disasters of the Anthropocene, we cannot be indifferent or take refuge in escapism; rather, we must learn to be present, to 'stay with the trouble' in order to 'stir potent responses to devastating events, as well as to settle troubled waters and rebuild quiet places' (2016: 1). 'To live and die well' in these troubled times, Haraway, like Berardi, looks towards the commons, and invites us to join forces and make unheard of alliances with 'oddkin'. Sympoiesis, making with, becomes the way to go beyond individualism, now unsuitable as a political, philosophical and scientific tool for living, as well as for confronting and changing reality. Echoing Berardi's historical materialist focus, she chooses to speak of the Capitalocene, instead of the Anthropocene. In her analysis, Haraway refuses the hypothesis of any *causa prima*:

> The Capitalocene was relationally made and not by a secular Godlike *Anthropos*, a law of history, the machine itself as a Demon who we call modernity. The Capitalocene must be relationally unmade, in order to compose in material-semiotic SF patterns and stories something more liveable. (2016: 50)

While we are asked to embrace realistically what is and stay with the trouble, Haraway foregrounds the power of semiosis and story-making as important tools for imagining differently: 'to affirm on the ground collectives capable of inventing new practices of imagination, resistance, revolt, repair or mourning, and of living and dying well' (2016: 51). This 'other world', so urgently needed, cannot be reached through an attitude that chooses as its alternatives despair or optimism, or even less through a recasting of the idea of progress, as an automatic movement towards a better world and the need to work at it.

Haraway founds her critique of the posthuman and of apocalyptic futurity on the necessity of making 'oddkin', of thinking and acting collectively through new entanglements with unexpected partners; they also call upon us to imagine a different future through different narrations of the present, against the sense of impotence and almost fatalistic resignation that forty years of neoliberalism have produced. The point for critical theory, then, is not to ask what comes after the human or the posthumous, but rather, what can the posthuman and the posthumous do? What praxis, and poiesis, can it put in place? How can new figurations of the subject take in, critically, the scenario in which we live? What can they do to help us understand and change the human, political and planetary conjuncture of these times? How can critique be reclaimed, beyond the need for a subject position 'outside' and 'above' the fray, knowing that there is no transcending what is, and that we can speak only from a terraneous space which the human shares with all their oddkin, animate and inanimate? How can fabulation, telling stories, as Haraway claims, become a call for the subject to imagine reality? That is, how can poiesis become a new form of critique?

The power of the aesthetic occupies a particular space in Félix Guattari's analysis. In *The Three Ecologies* (2000), through the concept of *ecosophy*, Guattari invites us to reflect upon the current crisis transversally, in terms of the social, the environmental and the mental, individual order. Ecology, he notes, is not simply a narrow interest in nature; rather, ecology 'questions the whole of subjectivity and capitalist power formations, whose sweeping progress cannot be guaranteed to continue as it has for the past decade' (2000: 35). These three orders of reality continually intersect in the present moment to produce a new type of subjectivity, no longer founded on individuality but rather on singularity. Guattari's posthuman subject abandons the sense of unitary subjectivity that characterised the modern self, and rather recognises all the singularities, all the extra-individual threads that make us the subject we think we are.

From the viewpoint of my own inquiry, here the most striking moment of Guattari's ecosophical perspective is his incitement to leave aside scientific paradigms and turn rather to the aesthetic as the most relevant source of experience, or better, as the space where experience can emerge and be remade anew. The aesthetic is posed as a privileged channel for the new and the non-calculable.

Through the transversality of his mode of thinking, focused on the complex panorama of intersecting planes that make contemporary reality, as well as through his focus on the aesthetic, Guattari pursues every kind of dissonance and dissent, as a means to recover the singularity of 'the world of childhood, love, art, as well as everything associated with anxiety, madness, pain, death, and the feeling of being lost in the cosmos' (2000: 33). These extraordinary states, akin to the aesthetic as they are, work against the state of sedation and the acquiescent disposition demanded of the contemporary subject. 'The rupture of meaning' (2000: 33), the unmaking of the logic of the capitalist semiosphere and our impotence *vis-à-vis* the historico-environmental catastrophe of these times, pass through the dissent and dissonance articulated by literature and art, so that the aesthetic becomes key to signifying, narrating and imagining differently. In Lerner's novel this rupture of meaning is configured in the terms of Benjamin's *Jetztzeit*. The 'now time' that, in Benjamin's view, cuts across the teleological continuum of history, provides a utopian and yet here-and now new sense of temporality, beyond the temporality of the apocalypse. Lerner learns from Benjamin, so that, through its multiple and dissonant temporalities, *10:04* establishes literary poiesis as a possible form of political, collective praxis.

How Matter Comes to Time

Dark ecology oozes through despair. Being realistic is always refreshing. Depression is the most accurate way of experiencing the current ecological disaster. It's better than wishful thinking.
Timothy Morton, *The Ecological Thought*, 2010

Art has to offer more than stylized despair.
Ben Lerner, *10:04*, 2014

Lerner's novel proposes a way out of the neoliberal and environmental apocalypse scenario, by imagining an alternative to what *is* through a futurity already inscribed in the present. The model for this configuration of the future is the concept of *Jetztzeit*, 'now time', that Benjamin elaborates in 'Theses on the Philosophy of History' (Benjamin 1968 [1940]). Benjamin's view of history and of the aura permeates Lerner's writing: flashes of illumination, a key concept for Benjamin, make reality auratic again. Even Paul Klee's painting of 'the angel of history', captioned by a famous line from 'Theses', is reproduced in *10:04*.

Benjamin's *Jetztzeit*, like the appearance of the aura in Lerner's novel, signals a moment of rupture (Benjamin 1968; Bratu Hansen 2008), 'a present which is not a transition, but in which time stands still and has come to a stop', 'grasping and holding the historical image as it flares up briefly' (Benjamin 1968: 263). Appearing at moments of danger as 'a sign of the messianic cessation of happening, a revolutionary chance in the fight for the oppressed past' (1968: 263), 'now time' makes visible in a flash the presence and the history of the vanquished, whose memory would otherwise disappear in the history written by the victors. The auratic moments and objects that punctuate *10:04* evoke Benjamin's concepts both of illumination and of 'now time'. As a response to the impotence and the paralysis produced by the apocalyptic imagination, the aura in Lerner's novel returns to make visible the possible, to shock us awake, and stands as an attempt to survive and overturn the solipsism, isolation and decline of experience put in place by late capitalism. It is from this process of re-enchantment that a different reality can be glimpsed, and a critical voice can emerge against the noise of neoliberal doxa. The flashing of 'now time' and the portentous illumination that a non-teleological sense of history allows are captured by Lerner through his protagonist's capability to 'see' common objects, everyday materiality – to become auratic. These objects are transfigured at a different type of historical emergency, the coming of a hurricane. It is this experience, at the same time elating and threatening, that produces both narrative and dissent, and provides us with a different way of looking at reality, and with an alternative to capitalist realism. Through its use of the aura *10:04* points to, or perhaps simply dreams up, the possibility of futurity, and thus opens the horizon of the thinkable once again.

With its complex architecture, Ben Lerner's novel *10:04* tells about life in 'the sinking metropolis', New York in 2011 and 2012, at the moment when two hurricanes, Irene and Sandy respectively, destroyed parts of Long Island and New Jersey. The novel also offers a precise snapshot of the condition of the subject at the time of environmental and socio-experiential decline. The protagonist, an alter ego of the author, is a successful writer. As we discover later, the book he is writing is the very novel we are reading and holding in our hands. Not only is Lerner writing a novel about writing fiction, but *10:04* contains several narratives: the protagonist writes a book on the extinction of dinosaurs with a young Ecuadorian boy he is mentoring, his first vicarious encounter with paternity; he reprints 'The Golden Vanity', the story Lerner actually published in the *New Yorker*; he plans, and starts writing, a new novel about fraudulence and a fake correspondence with famous authors; later, during his residence in Marfa, Texas, he changes his mind and, instead of the novel, he writes a Whitmanesque poem (Colman 2018; Preston 2015; Kunzru 2014; Blair 2015; Temple 2017).

In *10:04* the subject, no matter how damaged and changed, endures. The novel makes clear that there is a difference between renouncing human exceptionalism and mastery over nature in order to become enmeshed into posthuman interconnectivity, and becoming the networked and exploited non-subject in the fully calculable and calculated culture of the neoliberal algorithm, the already captioned reality where the understanding of one's predicament in order to change it is blocked. Against dark ecology and its ethos of despair and depression, Lerner seems to suggest, we need to start again from a different subject position. Equally distant from the Enlightenment understanding of the human, this new subjectivity is, in fact, what the human had been all along: a Latourian quasi-subject quasi object (Latour 1991), entangled with other species, with both the animate and the inanimate, centred on corporeality and its precariousness, unexceptional, post-Darwinian; political, bent towards the collective, and capable of critique, of recognising, that is, the conjuncture in which it lives and works in order to change it. This recognition is not the bird's-eye view acquired by the masterful gaze of Western humanism: it can only be, as Michel de Certeau argues in another context, regarding different perceptions of the city, a view from the ground (De Certeau 2011 [1984]), a voice from the place we already inhabit, rather than from an inexistent space outside. This is a key point of contention for New Materialists and critics of the posthuman, who claim that critique is not possible at the time of natureculture and of the all-encompassing culture of late capitalism. It seems that things can change only through an apocalyptic rupture, or through a utopian projection of an Eden-to-come. Lerner's novel makes a decisive intervention in this problematic and proposes a way out of the neoliberal and environmental apocalypse scenario, by imagining an alternative to what *is* through a futurity already inscribed in the present.

At the time of impending disaster, reality becomes charged with a sense of a future, rather than a past, in the present that dispels the idea of apocalypse. The possibility of survival, or at least of affirming one's presence before disappearing, is announced by the visibility of the aura and the auratic object, paradoxically set off by the very imminence of the catastrophe. Reality simultaneously contains at least two parallel orders of temporality, which further multiply in the novel: apocalyptic time (for example, the bleak future of underwater, submerged New York) is pitted against biological time (the protagonist's heart condition), and both are compared to 'the strange duration of the literary' (2014: 34). Lerner is particularly interested in time freed from systems of calculation, from schedules and deadlines:

> Something like the feel of a childhood snow day when time was emancipated from institutions, when the snow seemed like a technology for defending time, or like defeated time itself falling from the sky, each glittering ice particle an instant gifted back from your routine. (2014: 18)

This notion of defeated time is the opposite of technological time, busy with capitalist valorisation. The double-tracked temporality of the novel becomes clearly perceptible the night of the announced Hurricane Irene, when Alex and the narrator find themselves in a Whole Foods supermarket, almost ransacked by the panicked customers. The coming storm has already created an exceptional situation of emergency that produces human connection: strangers start communicating and commenting on the weather on buses and in the subway. 'The air excited by foreboding and something else' (2014: 19) announces an exceptional moment, when a portentous event takes place: in Whole Foods the narrator picks up a container of instant coffee that appears somehow transfigured in his eyes. Like the few items left on the shelves, the container seemed to be 'a little changed, a little charged' (2014: 18). This line invokes the Hasidic belief that in the world to come, 'everything will be just as it is here ... Everything will be as it is now, just a little different'. In this instance, the mundane routine of shopping is defamiliarised by the appearance of the aura, a strange radiance that surrounds the coffee can, and makes visible, in a sort of Marxist sublime, the past of the commodity:

> It was as if the social relations that produced the object in my hand began to glow within it as if they were threatened, stirred inside the packaging, lending a certain aura – the majesty and murderous stupidity of that organization of time and space and fuel and labour becoming visible in the commodity itself now that planes were grounded and the highways were starting to close. (2014: 219)

For a moment, the coffee container becomes 'the emissary of a world to come', where 'everything will be as it is now, only a little different'. He concludes: 'What normally felt like the only possible world became one among many, its meaning everywhere up for grabs, however briefly, in the passing commons of a train, in a container of tasteless coffee' (2014: 19). At a moment of emergency, reality becomes transfigured into the marvellous that both Benjamin and the Surrealist recognise in the everyday.

When the narrator touches the coffee container, the aura becomes the threshold to a multidimensional sphere of many, yet to emerge, possible worlds. However, as the commodity loses its lustre, his auratic experience, or the ephemeral perception of the radiant, multitemporal objects, fades. So does another auratic experience, the narrator's perception of the surrounding, everyday world as a live organism: for example, the way the city, through its 'intensities', vibrates 'at one frequency' with the narrator's body, does not last. At other times, the possibility of the auratic experience depends on the actualisation of the announced future; because certain moments of illumination had been enabled by a future that had never arrived and they could not be remembered, they fade, as if they had never happened. The excitement and exceptionality of the never-happened future is lost, and with it the possibility of memory, of remembering, and even experiencing, what the aura announced and illuminated. Nevertheless, this fleeting illumination lets us infer the existence of another possible world.

The most visionary of these revelatory moments of auratic experience through materiality takes place in Marfa, Texas, where the protagonist temporarily moves to write his new book. The high moment of his time in Marfa is his visit to the Chinati Foundation, and his encounter with Donald Judd's sculptures. When in New York, the narrator had never been interested in Judd's work, in the artist's 'desire to overcome the distinction between art and life, an insistence on literal objects in real space' (2014: 178) which 'could be found at Costco, Home Depot, or Ikea'. The literal object is merely real. Yet, when the setting sun is reflected in the aluminium surface of Judd's boxes, the protagonist's perspective changes. The division between reality and art collapses: 'The work was set in time, changing quickly because the light was changing, the dry grasses going gold in it . . . all combined to collapse my sense of inside and outside, a power that the work never had for me in New York' (2014: 179). In this moment, not only does the temporality of the here and now become shot through with the temporality of the present-future, but the space of art and that of reality seem to merge. Lerner, however, is not invested in the collapse of these two orders of time, space and materiality. Rather, he is interested in the tension, what he terms 'the flickering', between them. Art can make reality auratic and more surprising, and vice versa: the relationship of art and reality is presented as a dialectic at a standstill, with no resolution. The moment is ecstatic; however, with another dialectical turn, Lerner tells us that the boxes are situated in the vicinity of 'a refashioned artillery shed that had once held German prisoners of war' (2014: 178). The sculptures appear now to the narrator as coffins, and the installation as a memorial. The auratic vista he just enjoyed now clashes with 'a gesture towards tragedy that was literally uncontainable, or a tragedy that, since some of the "coffins" internally reflected the landscape outside of the shed, had itself come to contain the world' (2014: 180). Finally, the dialectical relation through which a harmonised view of the natural and the auratic is pitted against the tragic and the historical is reabsorbed into the momentary simultaneity of different temporalities, not only the present:

> it was also tuned to an inhuman, geological duration, lava flows and sills, aluminium expanding as the planet warms. As the boxes crimsoned and darkened with the sunset, I felt all those orders of temporality – the biological the historical, the geological – combine and interfere, and then dissolve. (2014: 180)

This sense of deeply falling into different temporalities, together with the sense of 'falling out of time' in Marfa, is both embraced and feared by the narrator as perhaps the darker side of the posthuman – the fear of being erased by a space and time out of bounds. In this perspective, the narrator's gesture of looking at time on his own phone during the screening of Christian Marklay's art installation *The Clock* (2000) is highly significant. As with Judd's boxes, Marklay's film is art set to time, or we could say, rather, time set to art. The film is de facto a clock and it stands as the ultimate collapse of real and fictional time. As a montage of thousands of film clips edited in a way that they are actually shown in real time, *The Clock* synchronises time outside and inside the theatre. As the protagonist affirms, 'I watched time in *The Clock* but I was not in it' (2014: 54), and by checking the time on his phone he breaks the spell of the perfect integration of reality and fiction: 'The distance had not collapsed for me' (2014: 51). With these words the narrator affirms the distance from the perfect suture of time and Time, and reclaims a form of critical faculty, thus refusing the incantatory integration of reality and fiction.

If the novel can be read as an attempt at cognitive mapping of life in the city at the time of disaster, the result of this effort is not the reconstruction of totality. Reality and fiction, present and future, need to correspond, but not to coincide. They remain connected through a flickering tension, since the only possible 'apocalypse' is not a millenarist overturning of history, but rather a new world where 'everything is the same as it is now, only a little different'. Just as the bourgeois homogeneous time, with its faith in progress, is interrupted by the *Jetztzeit* in Benjamin's materialist messianism, the homogeneous temporality of the apocalypse in contemporary dark ecological narratives is interrupted in the novel both by the appearance of the auratic object, and, in the case of *The Clock* scene, by the narrator keeping his own time.

The man who checks his phone at Marklay's film is in fact a new type of subject: this narrator has a defective sense of proprioception, which hinders his capability to recognise the position of his body in space. As a consequence, he lacks stereognosis, 'the capacity to form a mental image of the overall shape of what I touch' (2014: 6). Even more, he has lost the capacity to 'integrate that information into a larger picture, I cannot read the realistic fiction the world appears to be' (2014: 7). While he can no longer claim through his senses the mastery over his inhabited space, and with this mastery the power that the subject of Western tradition had possessed, thanks to this disability, the protagonist can, instead, perceive and recognise auratic objects and phenomena. How should we assess the return of the aura in hypertechnological late modernity, at the time of disaster and of the neoliberal alleged end of the possible? Through the image of a re-enchanted, portentous reality, *10:04* takes its stance against the contemporary culture of sedation. Radiant materiality, as much as the 'indeterminate objects' of the Institute for Totaled Art, punctuate and puncture capitalist realism, and as such open unexpected vistas within reality. This neo-auratic dimension which Lerner makes visible in his novel is neither an index of the sacred, nor a cipher of the individual artistic genius. Beyond apocalypse *and* utopia, the aura, for Lerner, is a messianic announcement of an already existing future, obscured by what is sold to us as 'what is'. It is, as I will show in the next section, the announcement of a different version, or narrative of reality, and at the same time a possible affirmation of a collectivity-to-come, of the possibility of connecting with others, of solidarity and praxis: in other words, the aura becomes an announcement of the possibility, once again, of politics.

How Literature Comes to Matter

So, as we lurch into the future, in this blietzkrieg of idiocy, Facebook 'likes', fascist marches, fake-news coups, and what looks like a race towards extinction – what's literature's place? What counts as literature?

Arundathy Roy, 'Literature Provides Shelter,
That's What We Need', 2019

Generating a child is one of the images of futurity that circulate in *10:04*. At a certain point, the narrator has an imaginary conversation with Camila, his yet-to-be-born baby

> 'Why reproduce if you think the world is ending?' she asks. To which he answers, 'Because the world is always ending for all of us and if one begins to withdraw from the possibilities of experience then no one would take any of the risks involved with love. And love has to be harnessed to the political.' (2014: 94)

In the book, the possibilities opened up by experience and taking risks, as well as the act of turning love into a venue for politics, are connected to poiesis, 'making' as a particular form of political praxis: creating a dissonant voice through literature. The novel tries to work out via aesthetics a possible path to politics at the time of the postpolitical. Like Haraway and Guattari, Lerner believes in the power of stories, and in the necessity to narrate reality differently, against the received doxa and unidirectional semiotics of neoliberalism. The aesthetic *can*, and must, become a channel for the political. For Guattari, as we have seen, the aesthetic is a channel for dissensus, a means not only for staying with, but for creating trouble. In *10:04* both materiality and aesthetics contribute strongly to providing a space for the possible, for a 'now time' that may cut through either a too optimistic, or too catastrophic, view of reality.

When the narrator invites one of the protesters from the Occupy Movement into his apartment for laundry and a shower, he reflects upon his own lack of familiarity 'with this brand of making, of poiesis', that is, for political commitment (2014: 46). Yet he is scathing of Brooklynites' 'boutique biopolitics, in which spending obscene sums and endless hours on stylised food preparation somehow enabled the conflation of self-care and political radicalism' (2014: 46–7). He even finds his own politics too self-indulgent and thus makes his plans:

> What you need to do is to harness the self-love you are hypostatizing as offspring, as the next generation of you, and let it branch out horizontally into the possibility of a transpersonal revolutionary subject in the present, and co-construct a world in which moments can be something other than elements of profit. (2014: 47)

In this passage the narrator seems to overcome his individualism to project the possibility of a post-capitalist world.

This world of aesthetical-political moments is rendered tangible in the novel by its greatest trope: the works collected in the Institute of Totaled Art. With the excuse of opening a special gallery, Alena, the protagonist's girlfriend, convinces the most important insurer of art in the United States to loan her some works of 'totaled art', damaged paintings and sculptures which are kept in a deposit in Long Island. These are works by famous artists, which, ruined, have 'zero value' (2014: 129). Now 'indeterminate objects', as the narrator calls them, they are the exact opposite of Judd's sculptures, which are presented as 'literal objects' later in the book. While Judd's boxes are objects you can find in Costco or Ikea, but, like the ready-made, are 'ennobled' by the artist's name, totaled art is art that reverts to valueless objecthood. As such it loses its financial value and becomes a tactile harbinger of a different sphere of valorisation, thus undergoing the same process as the dusty ex-commodities of the Parisian arcades that seduced both the Surrealists and Benjamin. The smashing of an already broken sculpture by Jeff Koons fills the protagonist with an uncontainable joy: 'It was wonderful to see an icon of art world commercialism and valorized stupidity shattered; it was wonderful to touch the pieces with their metallic finish, to see the hollow interior of a work of wilful superficiality' (2014: 133). The value of Koons's dog, or of Cartier-Bresson's incomplete tryptic, can no longer be translated into a system of equivalences, a system of which the narrator is acutely aware. 'The tryptic changed from being very valuable to carrying zero value without undergoing what was to me any perceptible material transformation, it was the same, only totally different' (2014: 133). This unchanged quality of the work of art after its devaluation makes visible the arbitrariness and meaningless of the capitalist system of value, in the first place, when applied to art. The pieces in the Institute for Totaled Art reverse the logic of branding, 'whether for Damien Hirst or for Louis Vuitton' (2014: 133). This is 'redeemed art, saved from something, saved for something':

> I was familiar with material things that seemed to have taken on a kind of magical power as a result of a monetizable signature ... But it was incredibly rare – I remembered the jar of instant coffee the night of the storm – to encounter an object liberated from that logic. What was the word for that liberation? *Apocalypse? Utopia?* (2014: 133)

The work of art that has shed its financial value and managed to survive 'the fetishism of the market' becomes for the narrator 'an object from the future where there was some other regime of value than the tyranny of price': 'it was art before or after capital' (2014: 134). This encounter with the damaged work of art is key: it signals a moment of rupture with the allegedly unbreakable logic of capital, and frees the aura from its shackles, so that it can speak the language of the possible.

The narrator's own poiesis, his 'making' of reality and politics through literature, works in synergy with this devalued art and the book's celebration of newly auratic everyday materiality. This is its bid to envision a world made of multiple possibilities. Literature, the very writing in *10:04* itself, functions as a magnifying lens, capable of illuminating an alternative dimension. By foregrounding an imperfect suture between fiction and capitalist reality, aesthetic temporality and real time, Lerner's protagonist and alter ego manages never to fall into this vertiginous, and, again, apocalyptic, space. When, watching *The Clock*, he looks at the time on his phone, rather than becoming absorbed into the incantatory dimension of the film, he looks at the clips as an instigation to write: 'As I made and unmade a variety of overlapping narratives out of its found footage, I felt acutely how many different days could be built out of a day, felt more possibilities than determinism, the utopian glimmer of fiction' (2014: 54).

This writer, who reclaims a voice and a story to narrate, is nevertheless no longer the autotelic subject of Western tradition (Buck-Morss 1992). Centred on a precarious, ill and dysfunctional corporeality, the protagonist's body cannot draw boundaries between itself and what lies outside of him. Nonetheless he does not disappear: rather than retrenching under the carapace of the God-like authorial position of the creator, the origin of the narrative, the protagonist practises a 'palimpsestic plagiarism'. When asked, during an academic presentation, how he became a poet, he replies that it was because of Ronald Reagan's speech after the tragedy of the Challenger space shuttle. The speech, we read, was written by Peggy Noonan, who, in turn, plagiarised a poem by John Gillespie Magee, who plagiarised another poem by G. W. M. Dunn: Reagan, it turns out, is merely an echo at the end of a long series of plagiarists. Nonetheless this palimpsest consists of a text which becomes many, and 'moves through bodies and time, a collective song with no single origin . . . the way a star, from an earthly perspective, is often survived by its own light' (2014: 114). Literature, the poem Reagan quoted, and speech in general, become a way to make meaning, and to make it available to a collectivity:

> I think I became a poet because of Ronald Reagan and Peggy Noonan. The way they used poetic language to integrate a terrible event and its image back into a framework of meaning, the way transpersonality of prosody constituted a community: poets were the unacknowledged legislators of the world, it seemed to me. (2014: 116)

The irony of the *dictum* of Percy Bysshe Shelley being fulfilled by the right-wing Reagan and by his speechwriter is of course not lost on the narrator.

However, even a late imperial plagiarism by Reagan, it turns out, can muster in the author a sense of the collective potential of aesthetics.

Thus, while he resists becoming dissolved in the collapse of reality and fiction, of apocalypse or utopia, the narrator wishes to 'melt and become part of a collectivity in the making' (2014: 108). This urban-based multitudinous collectivity which he dreams up through a phrase of Walt Whitman is figured by a view of Manhattan and 'its innumerable illuminated windows . . . the material signature of a collective person who did not yet exist; a still uninhabited second person plural to whom all arts . . . were addressed' (2014: 108). This new urban experience of the sublime announces 'beyond calculation, the intimation of community'. In this moment, Lerner's narrator affirms the purpose of artistic production: to become 'one of the artists who momentarily made bad forms of collectivity figures of its possibility a propriocentric flicker in advance of the communal body' (2014: 108).

In *10:04*, through its traffic with the aura, matter comes to literature in order to signify another possible reality, so that literature comes to matter, becomes newly important as the place where this reality can be elaborated and narrated. This is more than a *consolatio literaturae*: writing becomes a project, a way to plan a new collectivity and its future.

Fabulation, literature as poiesis, is a form of making. Yet the narrator of *10:04* must continually confront his deauthorised position and his precarity as a member of the human species in the face of an announced apocalypse. In this context, literature becomes the locus where the catastrophic reality of the present and the possibility of another time are kept in tension. *10:04* affirms that it is important to search for the flashes of 'now time', as moments whose memory is always already inscribed in the present. Yet the novel also affirms the need to retell the past in order to illuminate the present. This is what happens at the very end. Hurricane Sandy has reached New York, and Alex and the narrator set out on foot to cross a blacked-out Lower Manhattan to reach Brooklyn. In the last two pages, the tense of the narrative changes from the past to the future. This occurs after the narrator starts channelling parts of Reagan's speech, but with a very different ending: 'The moon is high in the sky and you can see its light on the water. I want to say something to the schoolchildren of America' (2014: 239). The future that is presented here is made by Alex's and the narrator's mundane gestures, stopping to eat in a sushi restaurant, and listening to the conversation of a couple at the next table. But while Reagan's speech ends with the ethos of individual heroism ('The future does not belong to the fainthearted: it belongs to the brave. The Challenger crew was pulling us into the future, and we'll continue to follow them') (2014: 16), Lerner concludes instead with the image of another disaster, the hurricane, but also with Whitman's words, that announce solidarity, empathy and a new, possible collectivity: 'I am with you, and I know how it is' (2014: 240).

Past utopia and the apocalypse, what is left? The ecocritic Teresa Shewry's answer is 'hope', against both apocalyptic and utopian thinking: 'Hope involves apprehension of the future in terms of an openness, an uncertainty, without which hope would not be required' (Shewry 2015). Shewry makes clear that hope is not escapism, and 'cannot erase losses' (2015: 17). Although hope is also part of the reparative toolbox that *10:04* provides, Lerner's novel calls us to understand hope as less of a loose-end concept and rather as encoded in the possible that contemporary auratic materiality and its narrativisation in literature make available. Our call, as Italo Calvino affirms in a different context, at the end of *Invisible Cities*, is to recognise the possible, and make it endure.

At the end of his book *Dark Ecology*, after examining the dismal environmental panorama in which we live, Timothy Morton suggests, with a slightly delirious flare, and a vitalistic and orgiastic tone: 'Let's pour the oil of death on the troubled waters of agrilogistics. Let's disco' (Morton 2018: 162). Lerner's novel suggests something different, perhaps less glam, definitely more challenging. He spurs us to look for others, human and not, in order to create new entanglements and new collectivities. He asks us to think politically, in order to live and die well with each other, to use Haraway's words. The task at hand is to retell in the future tense the stories we live by, and that allow us to understand how we live; to imagine a different plot for those stories, and work, and play, towards a different conclusion.

References

Apter, Emily (2013), 'Planetary dysphoria', *Third Text*, 27: 1, pp. 131–41.
Benjamin, Walter (1968) [1940], 'Theses on the philosophy of history', in Walter Benjamin, *Illuminations*, trans. Harry Zohn, New York: Schocken Books.
Berardi, Franco (2017), *Futurability: The Age of Impotence and the Horizon of Possibility*, London: Verso.
Berardi, Franco (2019), *The Second Coming*, Cambridge: Polity Press.
Blair, Elaine (2015), 'So, this is how it works', *London Review of Books* (4 January), 37: 4.
Bratu Hansen, Miriam (2008), 'Benjamin's aura', *Critical Inquiry*, 34 (Winter), pp. 337–75.

Buck-Morss, Susan (1992), 'Aesthetics and anaesthetics: Walter Benjamin's art work essayreconsidered', *October*, 62, pp. 3–41.
Cazdyn Eric and Imre Szeman (2014), *After Globalization*, Malden, MA: Wiley Blackwell.
Colman, Adam (2018), *New Uses for Failure: Ben Lerner's 10:04*, New York: A Fiction Advocate Book.
De Certeau, Michel (2011) [1984], *The Practice of the Everyday*, trans. Steven Randall, Berkeley: University of California.
Demos T. J. (2013), 'Contemporary art and the politics of ecology', *Third Text*, 27: 1, pp. 1–9.
Emmelhainz, Irmgard (2016), 'Self-Destruction or insurrection, or how to lift the earth above all that has died', *e-flux journal* # 87, December. www.e-flux.com/journal/87/169041/self-destruction-as-insurrection-or-how-to-lift-the-earth-above-all-that-has-died/ (last accessed 9 June 2020).
Fisher, Mark (2009), *Capitalist Realism*, London: Zer0 Books.
Guattari, Félix (2000), *The Three Ecologies*, trans. Ian Pindar and Paul Sutton, New York: Continuum.
Han, Byung-Chul (2017), *In the Swarm: Digital Perspectives*, trans. Erik Butler, Cambridge, MA: MIT Press.
Haraway, Donna (2016), *Staying with the Trouble: Making Kin in the Chthulucene*, Durham, NC: Duke University Press.
Harvey, David (1996), *Justice, Nature, and the Geography of Difference*, London: Blackwell.
Harvey, David (2007), *Brief History of Neoliberalism*, Oxford: Oxford University Press.
Hulme, Mike (2011), 'Reducing the future to climate: a story of climate determinism and reductionism', *Osiris*, 26: 1, pp. 245–66.
Jameson, Fredric (2004), 'The politics of utopia', *New Left Review* (January–February), 25.
Jameson, Fredric et al. (2016), *An American Utopia: Dual Power and the Universal Army*, London: Verso.
Kunzru, Harry (2014), 'Impossible mirrors', *New York Times*, 5 September.
Latour, Bruno (1991), *We Have Never Been Modern*, trans. Catherine Porter, Cambridge, MA: Harvard University Press.
Latour, Bruno (2004), *The Politics of Nature: How to Bring the Sciences into Democracy*, trans. Catherine Porter, Cambridge, MA: Harvard University Press.
Lerner, Ben (2014), *10:04*, New York: Farrar, Straus and Giroux.
Lousley, Cheryl (2017), 'Global futures past: our common futures, postcolonial times and world ecologies', *Resilience*, 4: 2–3, pp. 21–42.
Morton, Timothy (2010), *The Ecological Thought*, Cambridge, MA: Harvard University Press.
Morton, Timothy (2018), *Dark Ecology: For A Logic of Future Coexistence*, New York: Columbia University Press.

Parenti, Christian (2011), *Tropics of Chaos: Climate Change and the New Geography of Violence*, New York: W. W. Norton.
Preston, Alex (2015), '*10:04* by Ben Lerner – a great writer, a great novel', *The Guardian*, 4 January.
Roy, Arundathy (2019), 'Literature provides shelter, that's what we need', *The Guardian*, 20 May.
Shewry, Teresa (2015), *Hope at Sea: Possible Ecologies in Oceanic Literature*, Minneapolis: University of Minnesota Press.
Sturken, Marita (2007), *Tourists of History. Memory, Kitsch and Consumerism from Oklahoma City to Ground Zero*, Durham, NC: Duke University Press.
Weinstein, Jaime, and Claire Colebrook (eds) (2017), *Posthumous: Theorizing Beyond the Posthuman*, New York: Columbia University Press.
Weisman, Alan (2010), *The World Without Us*, London: Picador.

AFTERWORD

Woodenness – The (Palm) Heart of the Matter

Timothy Morton

The chapters in this volume are in the urgent business of changing the past, by reinterpreting it in such a way as to make the future possible, which is to say, the possibility that things might be different. We do not at all have a moment for being wooden, that is, caught in sclerotic patterns of behaviour. Around the world right now, societies seem hell-bent on making things more sclerotic. Automation is not scary because of artificial intelligence. Automaton is scary because it causes the past to eat the future. Facial recognition software is based on white supremacist geometry from the eugenics period in the United States. The inevitable results are, for example, what happened when Google beta-tested their version of the software: it recognised black people as gorillas. Racism is baked into the software, no matter what the beliefs of those who use it. Automation, which is a better word for what used to be called 'nature', 'destiny', 'fate', seems to be something we should just stare at in wonder, rather than something to intervene in actively. Life turns into wood turns into helicopter gunships.

I might have called this afterword 'Hylicity' because the Greek for 'matter' (*hyle*) is the Greek for 'wood' – an ecologically significant overlap between actual trees and human 'civilised' attitudes to trees, as in Pope's 'Windsor Forest' (1713) where the narrator invites us to look at the forest as so many battleships waiting to be constructed. This is exactly the salivating sentiment expressed in what the director of the corporation in *Avatar* (2009) says, displaying the quantities of the mineral Unobtainium that reside under the Home Tree of the Indigenous people: 'Just look at all that cheddar.' But instead I am calling the afterword 'Woodenness', in part because it sounds funny and less pretentious. And also because it gathers a lot of extra meanings, about artificiality, 'stiffness' in style, just going through the motions, mechanisms. In other words, it melts together things ('nature', 'art'; artifice, spontaneity; machine, organism) that are kept apart, also with (destructive) ecological consequences.

Many materialisms seem woodenly keen on dissolving things into smaller or simpler components. Take scientism, for example, a set of beliefs based on concepts from science, generally taken to be the default ideas about what exists. Scientism is almost the opposite of science, which is statements about patterns in data, verified by various kinds of institution. Scientism generally holds that things are made of atoms, and that these atoms are more real than the things they comprise. Hydrogen atoms are more real than cows. The very idea that there is only one form of materialism tends to be scientistic – there is materialism, which is true, which means that small things are more real than larger things; and there is everything else, which is nonsense. We have all felt beaten up and beaten down by the rhetoric of Richard Dawkins, a statistician, not a biologist, who has popularised ways of feeling right and smart about what is called 'materialism'.

And there is the physics variant, with its New Age popular cultural shadings, that involves quantum theory. According to this kind of materialism, the small things are not really real either, so that what results from the pincer movement of reduction to atomic structures and reduction of those structures to effects of measurement (the Standard Model of quantum theory), should more accurately be called *immaterialism* not materialism. This has generated a slew of idealist New Age interpretations, along the lines of 'I can make anything into anything with the power of my mind' (Arntz, Chasse and Vicente 2004).

Graham Harman has called the technique *duomining*, or 'undermining' and 'overmining' at once (Harman 2013): undermining, which means that small things such as quarks are more real than medium-sized things such as bottles of milk; overmining, which means that it is the measurer or the perceiver that makes a thing real, just as a conductor 'realises' a piece of music. To exist is to be a measured tiny thing: that is the Standard Model of quantum theory (the Copenhagen Interpretation of 1920), which happily for more ambitious materialists is coming under pressure these days. Undermining reduces things to their parts. Overmining reduces things to how they are measured, perceived, discursively 'produced', eaten . . . it is the most popular post-Kantian way of reducing things and it is rampant in 'theory' class in the humanities. It seems more sophisticated than scientistic reductionism (undermining), which is just medieval ontology smuggled into the modern age, as Descartes and Kant had already pointed out in their different ways. But in the post-Kantian consensus, access to a thing is what makes it real or 'realises' it. There are all kinds of varieties: Spirit makes things real (Hegel), human economic relations make things real (Marx), will to power makes things real (Nietzsche), *Dasein* makes things real (Heidegger), German *Dasein* makes things really really real (also Heidegger). Things become blank screens, a fate probably worse than that of being Aristotelian clay or putty that you can manipulate as you wish. At least there is something there already. But if (for example) for Marx a potato does not exist until a human being has farmed and picked and eaten and possibly sold one or two, planet Earth is in trouble, just as it is in trouble in capitalist economic theory which regards anything outside of human economic relations as 'externals'.

The 'new materialism', as it has been called in the noisy record store of ideas, seems to be significantly opposed to these kinds of materialism in all kinds of ways. What one finds are varied emphases on the thingliness of things, and, very promisingly, studies of how things interpenetrate. From an ecological perspective, the work of Stacy Alaimo in this region cannot be underestimated, for her concept of transcorporeality is powerful indeed (Alaimo 2010), as Laura Oulanne's chapter in this volume makes clear. What is being said here is aesthetic – it is about the physicality of a thing, its liquidity, permeability, movement. That does not mean at all that what is being said is superficial. There is a politics of the aesthetic, and in a sense politics as such just is aesthetic, as the extreme right exploits and the left, committed to blowing up the aesthetic for that reason, ignores at its peril. If my decision to associate with such and such a being is political rather than moral, then it has to do with the same kinds of decision that an artist makes when she chooses to use red rather than yellow paint right there on that canvas, next to the orange. Materialism in this sense is not very much about matter as an unformatted flux. A better word might be *physiography*, the writing of the physical. If only such a word existed.

'Mattering' is a deft play on words but quite a thin concept. If all that matters is mattering – in other words, the sheer fact of significance at all – then I can say anything about anything. Or the systems theory variant, 'making a difference'. Making a difference is what words, socks, politicians and quarks do. But the real issue with mattering and making a difference is that they are about observers. You make a difference *for* someone, you matter *to* someone. There has to be a field of meaningfulness already in place, always already, for that kind of difference-making to be recognisable. There has already got to be some 'matter' for things to matter.

Even if we subtract 'human subjects' and allow saws and quantum fields to mark things as significant, we are faced with something like this problem. If an electron matters because it has released energy in the form of light, it is mattering because it has been excited by some energy and because it is about to have an effect, say by splashing onto the retina of a human couch potato watching their favourite show on an LCD screen. Lots of things already 'matter' – there might be an infinite regress, in an unpleasant way: mattering all the way down, leading to puzzling questions about teleology – what came before all the mattering? Did not something have to matter in the first place, and for what (or whom)?

Intrinsic to matter, then, is what in this afterword is called hylicity, the quality of being matter at all, 'in the first place'. It is relational. Matter is matter-for, and has nothing to do with what is really said in, for example, Karen Barad's theory of intra-activity. Hylicity, as it were, is wooden. It is a construct. That does not mean that hydrogen and snails do not exist. That means that they do, but the notion that they are *matter* in particular might, according to vanilla forms of Western logic, mean that they are raw materials or standing-reserve, and sometimes it is possible to distinguish between these categories, in what is called (rather wishfully) late capitalism. Oil corporations treat oil as a reserve of raw materials for fuels and plastics (and so much more), conveniently located under our feet, if only we could find the right intensity of drill bit and abolish some regulations about common land. Palm trees are for their tasty hearts.

This kind of matter is 'formless': somewhat oxymoronically, everything must have some kind of shape, even if it is hard to describe mathematically. Mr Spock traffics in this kind of woodenness when he says (on more than one occasion) that what he is seeing on the view screen is 'pure matter devoid of form' (Dugan 1968; see also Laycock 1972 and Denkel 2007: 188–94). John Lennon sings about it: 'Yellow matter custard / Dripping from a dead dog's eye' (The Beatles 1967). Matter in the Lennon sense is indeed a kind of custard (*Oxford English Dictionary*: 'matter', n.19.b.). Spock's sense of seemingly physical matter is closer to the sense of 'matter' as content as opposed to rhetorical 'form' (*Oxford English Dictionary*: 'matter', n.9.a.). It is an Aristotelian habit to think that matter is like 'unformed' clay, formatted in a certain shape, say a cup, and stamped with accidental properties like colour. The 'matter' of the cup in a sense is both the physical cup and what the cup 'actually is', which for Aristotle is its form (there can be plastic and ceramic and ... cups, no matter what they are made of) and function (telos, in this case, drinking from them).

What it 'actually is' is inevitably what it is for a human being, a 'human subject' as we somewhat grandly like to say, with a kind of deference to the subjectification process in the form of a monarch or ideology or consumer objects, or *objet petit a* in Lacanian. Brexit Britain wants its passports back, which used to say 'Subject of her Majesty the Queen' on the front. So it is a strange, deferential grandeur, this notion of subjection as a noble thing, totally different from being a mute inert 'object'. This obviously alienated being who likes to think they are the one authentic person in the universe, this human subject, constructs in whatever way the clay as a cup. And some philosophers join in: it is not really a cup until you have drunk from it; it is not really a cup until you have named it; it is not really a cup without a cup discourse that supports the way cupness manifests in the twentieth century. The cup all by itself is long gone, or did not even exist – and as for the clay, how convenient, it has been totally disappeared in this logic.

But the clay had a form that was altered to make the cup, which will end up in a garbage dump and then in Earth's crust, as part of the layer that is the signal of what geology calls the Anthropocene. This is the longest-lasting kind of cup, this distributed garbage, bits of handle, powder, hard-to-discern glazes . . . If lasting long, remaining the same, aka the metaphysics of presence, is really something we believe in, we should think of cups as broken garbage dust rather than visualising a cylinder we can drink from. The cup-for-humans was just a tiny blip, precisely because the for-humans logic forgot about clay (the past) and garbage (the future), and imposed a present on the clay that was simply a human-scaled present. Whoever controls the imposition of the ruler that determines what *present* means (a femtosecond if you are a quantum physicist, a decade of a century if you are a historian) is what we call 'in charge'. Colonialism, reduced to simplicity, is the oppressive imposition of one group's temporality on another.

The subject is decentred, dethroned: that is what subjectum, 'thrown under', means. But the decentring process is weaponised to exclude all nonhuman life forms (and others, all that 'crude inert matter') – even 'cattle', which are four legged (cows) or abjected objectified two-legged (women, 'chattels') or standing-reserve ('capital') versions of yellow-matter custard dripping from a dead dog's eye (*Oxford English Dictionary*: 'cattle', n.1.).

In 1997 the somewhat appropriately named Yve-Alain Bois and Rosalind Kraus published *Formless*, a book about this topic in visual art. Drawing on George Bataille's concept of the *informe*, *Formless* catalogues visual art that appears to draw or otherwise to illustrate or display this concept. The trouble with that is that when you look at a work of art, you are looking at this work of art, not that one, and this work of art and not that banana in a brown paper bag that you brought into the gallery to snack on. Already, in the distinction between the artwork and the banana, there is a question of form: the artwork is not the banana, and you can tell, because happily you do not put the artwork in your mouth (unless it is made of chocolate – but then you might get arrested). The formless must always be some kind of form that does not matter to us in quite the same way as something more shapely to our human eyes. The concept is entirely anthropocentric. A fly landing on the artwork would bestow upon it the form of a landing pad. But that does not mean that this 'formless' artwork is just anything that any human, or any life form if you oppose anthropocentrism, or any being at all if you are employing OOO, could make of it. Otherwise there would be no way to tell the difference between something by Louise Bourgeois and something by Robert Rauschenberg, when obviously there are very significant differences.

Bataille's epigraph says it all: the formless is what has 'no rights', what can be 'squashed everywhere, like a spider or an earthworm' (Bois and Kraus 1997: 1). So that is nice and clear. The formless is whatever resides on or over the periphery of anthropocentric vision, treated as raw materials, or as classical capitalist economic theory puts it, 'externals'. How to talk about what is said in the somewhat record-store-label-like term *matter* without implying a fatal formlessness, while avoiding the obviously imperialist, racist and misogynist (and so on: the language of the powerful) senses of form as wedded to telos or function, as in Aristotle? A broken, gnarly runway is still a runway. As Karin Sellberg puts it in this volume, 'embodiment and identity emerge out of a continual reconditioning of connective events and experiences'. Which means that telos is out of the question – everything is being remixed too much for a steady goal to be held in mind.

It would be interesting to do a thought experiment on the deformation of a thing. At what point could one rightly claim that it was now something different? Perhaps the easiest material to hand is supplied by good old language. This is the deconstructive problem that Derrida puts this way: what is the difference between a letter and a squiggle? When do random-seeming marks, like the scuff marks on a formica tabletop, end up looking like language? Marlene Karlsson Marcussen's chapter makes a number of very salient observations about this.

Perhaps, argues Derrida, there is always-already in place a kind of language, an attentiveness to meaningfulness and an array of marks that designate marks as meaningful: the 're-mark'. The word is poised nicely between a physical thing (a 'mark'), a semiotic thing ('mark' as 'notation') and a correlationist gaze, that of the 'realiser' (the one who 'remarks'). The fact that literature as such is a central topic of this book – matters.

Return to the scratches on the table. How to see them as language? For example, I might put a speech bubble around them. Then the scratches might become speech: we would not know what it was saying, but we would know *that* it is saying something or other. Is this not the charm of the Peanuts character Woodstock? Woodstock, Snoopy's avian chum, speaks on the page in little vertical scratches within speech bubbles, scratches that resemble the tufts of lawn around Snoopy's kennel. Since Woodstock and what he says and how Charles Schulz drew him are finite – since Woodstock is not an apple pie – there should be a moment at which the grass-speech ceases to look like speech. But where? Can we ever determine exactly?

And this raises a still deeper question. How much does a thing have to scratch the table for something like a scratch to appear at all, in the first place? When should we start caring about what happens to a thing? Rune Graulund lays out the stakes eloquently here, when he states, 'the human body, and the human body politic, is but one of many actors on a playing field on which the human matters very little. Or rather . . . that which is distinctly human – set apart from the animal, the bacterial and the material, indeed of the entirety of creation – is hardly significant or distinct at all'.

Perhaps ambiguity is an *accuracy signal*. Consider going to the eye doctor. The doctor tries various lenses, then, at some point, she arrives at a stage at which she says, 'Is it number one? Or number two? Number one? Or number two?', while varying the lenses back and forth. You have a choice between two equally good prescriptions. And this is as good as it gets, because lenses are flawed and doctors are flawed and you are flawed and optometry is flawed . . . and so on. You have an ambiguous decision to make. This has nothing to do with vagueness. This is very very specific and sharp.

What does that mean, the moment at the optician's? It means you have an accurate prescription. Ambiguity is an accuracy signal.

Perhaps the best thing to learn from this is that 'matter' is ambiguous. No amount of systems theory about emergent properties of processes will be able to pinpoint the exact moment when a squiggle becomes an /x/ or a /y/. We assume ambiguity to be in the eye of the beholder. But standard quantum theory tells us that the ground state of a thing, not influenced by anything else (near to absolute zero in a vacuum), is a trembling, quivering movement not caused by mechanical pushing, something more like dancing than getting from A to B, something without a telos.

There is a form, a specific frequency: there are no transparent oceans of energy, all states of matter have a colour or a flavour, figuratively speaking, just like everyone has an accent, except from the position of power where one can claim that one speaks properly without one – in which case one would be inaudible. At their ground state, things are moving and still at the same time, and this property of things can now be observed in objects far, far larger than those traditional quantum theory deals with, by factors of billions (O'Connell et al. 2010: 697–703). And this suggests in turn that the idea that there is a Newtonian world at all, a world of ping-pong balls bopping against each other in a void, might be an illusion entirely (Safavi-Naeini et al. 2012).

Why should matter *matter*, to be valuable to us? Surely the difference that makes a difference, as systems theory likes to say, depends on an inscribable surface and sets of rules that the theory takes for granted without examining them. How many grains of sand make a heap? None, if you keep staring at it and asking a simplistic question. You will never determine exactly when it stops being a number of individual grains and starts being a heap. The logic used here, based on section gamma of Aristotle's metaphysics and its law of non-contradiction, is too wooden. It means, in the end, that there are no such things as heaps of anything, which is great news for progress.

But this does not mean there are no heaps. There had better be heaps, because ecological beings of all sizes, from a single life form to a meadow to the whole biosphere, are heaps of things that are not them. We had better be holists. And we had better not have a criterion for when a certain amount of grass and insects and trees and water starts to be something that matters. We just might not want to be the sort of holist for whom the thing that matters is the whole above its parts, as if the whole were more real than them – or, for that matter, a neoliberal insistence that things like society are illusions that emerge from lots of people doing similar things in a similar place.

One cannot determine in advance whether this thing I am reading right now is a squiggle or a letter. And it gets better – or worse, depending on how you see it. Matter might matter, or it might not, and this might not depend on someone observing or measuring, or something observing or measuring for that matter, if you will pardon the pun. This quivering between being a squiggle and being a letter should be carefully conserved, because the relative motion between matter and mattering is what makes meaning possible at all. It is not that things are not what they seem, or are just what they seem. Things are almost what they seem. Those clouds might look very like a whale, as Polonius says to Hamlet – they also almost look like clouds. This is almost an afterword to a remarkable book. This will almost have to do as the final sentence.

References

Alaimo, Stacy (2010), *Bodily Natures: Science, Environment, and the Material Self*, Indianapolis: Indiana University Press.
Arntz, William, Betsy Chasse and Mark Vicente (dirs) (2004), *What the Bleep Do We Know!?*, Samuel Goldwyn Films.
Beatles, The (1967), 'I Am the Walrus', *Magical Mystery Tour*, London: EMI.
Bois, Yves Alain and Rosalind Kraus (1997), *Formless: A User's Guide*, Cambridge, MA: MIT.
Cameron, David (dir.) (2009), *Avatar*, Los Angeles: 20th Century Fox.
Denkel, Arda (2007), *Object and Property*, Cambridge: Cambridge University Press.
Dugan, John T. (1968, first broadcast 9 February), 'Return to Tomorrow', *Star Trek*, Los Angeles: Desilu Productions.
Harman, Graham (2013), 'Undermining, overmining, and duomining: a critique', in Jenna Sutela (ed.), *ADD Metaphysics*, Helsinki: Aalto University Design Research Laboratory, pp. 40–9.
Laycock, Henry (1972), 'Some questions of ontology', *The Philosophical Review*, 81, pp. 3–42.
O'Connell, Aaron et al. (2010), 'Quantum ground state and single phonon control of a mechanical ground resonator', *Nature*, 464, pp. 697–703.
Oxford English Dictionary, Oxford: Oxford University Press, www.oed.com (last accessed 26 August 2019).
Pope, Alexander (1963 [1713]), 'Windsor Forest', in John Butt (ed.), *The Poems of Alexander Pope: A One-Volume Edition of the Twickenham Text, with Selected Annotations*, New York: Routledge.
Safavi-Naeini, Amir H., Jasper Chan, Jeff T. Hill, T. P. Mayer Alegre, Alex Krause and Oskar Painter (2012), 'Observation of quantum motion of a nanomechanical resonator', *Physical Review Letters*, art. 033602.

Index

'actant' (Bruno Latour), 11–12, 14–15, 112, 119
Actor Network Theory (ANT), 3, 11, 140
Aeolian *see* literary concepts
aesthetic *see* literary concepts
affect (and feeling/ emotional states), 2, 18, 22–4, 53–6, 65, 66, 75, 82, 89, 90n, 104, 123, 124, 132, 134, 137, 142–9, 149, 149n, 153–6, 158, 159–69, 173, 182–5, 187–8, 215–18, 220–32, 233n, 234n, 236, 240, 241, 243
  affect theory, 221, 223
  anxiety, 94, 101–2, 104
  see also affective materialities reading *under* reading (ways of); material–affective approach *under* reading (ways of)
agent/ agency
  human agency, 11, 21, 67, 74, 76, 82, 84, 96, 107n, 141, 154, 155, 159, 163, 166, 167, 168, 169, 187, 188, 202, 208, 210n, 219, 238, 241
  nonhuman agency, 1, 2, 3, 5, 11, 12, 13, 15, 18, 20, 22, 23, 33, 49, 50, 51, 64, 74, 76, 77, 80, 82, 86, 89n, 95, 96, 98, 99, 100, 103–6, 107n, 112, 113, 115, 116, 118, 126n, 141, 142, 154, 158, 162, 163, 166, 167, 168, 187, 188, 208, 210, 210n, 214, 216, 218–20, 223, 233n155, 241
  quasi-agent, 64
  see also 'actant'
Ahmed, Sara, 131, 148, 155, 156–7, 161, 165
aisthesis (sense-aesthetics), 22, 76, 78, 87, 89n, 90n
Alaimo, Stacy, 23, 89n, 143, 154, 163, 167, 259
  Exposed. Environmental Politics and Pleasures in Posthuman Times, 89
  see also trans-corporeality
Andersen, Hans Christian, 18, 22, 109–25, 126n
  A Poet's Bazar, 126n
  In Sweden, 121–2

Journey on Foot, 111, 126n
'Pen and Inkstand', 110, 113–14, 116–17, 120, 124
'The Darning Needle', 109
The Improvisatore, 111
'The Master and the Instruments', 117
'The New Century's Goddess', 123
'The Nightingale', 115
'The Shepherdess and the Chimney Sweep', 115
'The Steadfast Tin Soldier', 114, 119–21
'The Sweethearts', 119, 120, 121
animism, 94, 105
Anthropocene, the, 5, 20–1, 23, 63, 89n, 193–8, 200, 202, 205, 207–8, 210n, 236, 241–2, 261
  and climate change, 21, 63, 196, 204, 236, 237, 239; *see also* climate fiction *under* literary subgenres/ periods
  and global warming, 9, 109, 195–8, 204, 239
anthropocentrism/ human-centred, 2, 5, 6, 8, 10, 13, 17, 53, 60, 61, 66, 67, 74, 82, 86, 87, 97, 102, 104, 113, 114, 116, 122, 125, 134, 155, 156, 160, 163, 164, 169, 195, 207, 208, 209, 216, 219, 220, 229, 262; *see also* human exceptionalism; post-anthropocentric cultural constructionism
anthropomorphisation/ humanisation, 3, 17–18, 20, 22, 112, 115–16, 121
anti-anthropocentric *see* post-anthropocentric
'anti-realist' tradition (Graham Harman), 6
antihumanism, 240
apocalypse, 107n, 193–4, 198–202, 204, 209, 209n, 236–46, 249, 251–4; *see also* postapocalypse
'apocalyptic zero-point' (Slavoj Žižek), 193, 204
Aristotle, 117, 177, 259, 260, 262, 264
Armah, Ayi Kwei *see The Beautiful Ones Are Not Yet Born*
artificial intelligence, 257

asignification/ asignifying signs, 185, 217, 220, 222, 224, 225, 233n
'asignifying semiotics' (Lazzarato), 217
assemblage, 11, 15, 18, 49, 66, 68n, 87, 98, 99, 118–19, 154, 158, 160–1, 163, 216–18; *see also* Deleuze, Gilles; Latour, Bruno
aura/ auratic experience, 238, 239, 244, 246–9, 251–4
Axelrod, Steven Gould, 96, 100

Bacigalupi, Paolo, 23, 204–6, 209
  Ship Breaker, 204
  'The Calorie Man', 205
  The Drowned Cities, 204
  The Water Knife, 204
  The Windup Girl, 23, 194, 203–9, 210n
  'Yellow Card Man', 205
Banfield, Ann, 44, 68n
Barad, Karen, 5, 7–8, 59, 116, 126n, 140, 141, 154, 173, 187, 208, 210n, 260; *see also* intra-action; 'quantum dis/continuity'
Barnes, Djuna, 23, 153–7, 159–60, 162, 164–9
  'Dusie', 155–62, 165, 167, 170n
  'Finale', 155–6, 160, 162, 165, 167
  'How It Feels to be Forcibly Fed', 156, 164–8
  Nightwood, 168
Barthes, Roland, 32, 42
Bassnett, Susan, 96, 105
Bataille, George, 261, 262; *see also* 'informe'
The Beautyful Ones Are Not Yet Born (Armah, Ayi Kwei), 73–90
Beauvoir, Simone de, 138, 149n
  Le Deuxième Sexe, 132–4
Benjamin, Walter, 24, 181, 238, 239, 243–4, 247, 249, 251
  'Angel of History', 181, 188, 244
  see also 'jetztzeit'
Bennett, Jane, 4, 5, 11, 12, 14–15, 16, 17–18, 20, 49–50, 54, 74, 81, 82, 89n, 90n, 98, 99, 107n, 112, 114, 116–17, 118, 121, 140, 143, 154, 161, 162, 197, 219
  Vibrant Matter: A Political Ecology of Things, 11, 17, 49, 107n, 112, 140
  see also matter-realisms *under* realisms; nonsubjects; speculative onto-story; thing-power; vibrant matter
Berardi, Franco, 215, 216–18, 220, 222–4, 226, 229, 230, 233n, 234n, 236, 238, 239, 241; *see also* capitalism; Marxist criticism
Bergson, Henri, 11, 117

biology, 77, 82, 124, 126n, 202, 204, 207, 241, 246, 248, 258
body/ bodily being, 12, 81, 105, 138, 141, 153, 175
  body as flesh, 139–40, 142, 147
  see also intercorporeity; phenomenology; senses/ bodily perception
Boileau, Nicolas, 34, 35, 36
  Art Poétique, 34
Boscagli, Maurizia, 4, 5, 13, 18, 23, 24
  Stuff Theory. Everyday Objects, Radical Materialism, 18
  see also Capitalist Realism *under* realisms; stuff
Braidotti, Rosi, 5, 87, 88, 140, 148, 173, 180–1, 183, 185, 208; *see also* agential realism *under* realisms; life itself
Brandes, Georg, 112
Brooks, Peter, 33, 38
Brown, Bill, 4, 5, 12–13, 17, 18, 74, 84, 90n, 98; *see also* corporeal imagination
Butler, Judith, 4, 137–41, 149n
  Bodies That Matter, 141
  Gender Trouble, 137–8, 141

Calvino, Italo, 22, 52
  Invisible Cities, 254
  Mr Palomar, 51, 53–6, 60–1, 63–7, 68n
capitalism, 8, 11, 21, 23, 24, 73–5, 82, 83, 84, 88, 174, 193–8, 200, 204–7, 209, 215–18, 222–4, 226, 228, 230–2, 233n, 234n, 236–7, 239, 241–6, 249, 250–2, 259, 260, 262
  cognitive capitalism, 217, 233n;
    see also human subject/ subjectivity and capitalism
  'semio-capitalism' (Franco Berardi and Maurizio Lazzarato), 215, 218, 222–4, 233n
'capitalist realist apocalypse' (Mark Fisher), 194, 204, 209
Capitalocene, the, 193, 210n, 241–2
Carter, Angela, 23, 177, 178
  Wise Children, 23, 172–3, 176–80, 182–7, 189
Cartesian subject/ dualism, 6, 11, 97, 202;
  see also human subject/ subjectivity; subject-centrism; subject-object relations
Cartesian view on nature, 6
Cartier-Bresson, Henri, 251
Carver, Raymond, 21
Cheah, Pheng, 9
'Cheap Nature' (Jason Moore), 205–7, 209

Christianity, 110, 123–5
Cixous, Hélène, 135; *see also* écriture féminine *under* feminist literary criticism *under* reading (ways of)
Clark, Timothy, 4, 20–1, 63, 195–8; *see also* spatio-temporal scales *under* reading (ways of)
climate change *see* Anthropocene, the
Code, Lorraine, 149
cognition, 6, 19, 50, 54, 55, 68n, 99, 143, 154, 155, 215–17, 223–5, 228, 233n, 234n, 237, 248; *see also* cognitive capitalism, cognitive metaphor theory
cognitive metaphor theory, 155
Colebrook, Claire, 140, 142, 240
Coleridge, Samuel Taylor, 124
colonialism, 73, 79, 81, 89n, 137, 261
commodification, 18, 73, 195, 197, 204, 205, 206, 215, 222, 229, 233n, 246, 247, 251; *see also* Marxist criticism
'conatus' (Baruch de Spinoza), 11
consciousness, 1, 2, 6, 12, 81, 82, 85, 86, 89, 90n, 112, 119, 123, 136, 142, 161, 162, 167, 180, 181, 216, 217, 219, 220, 221, 232
constructionism/ sociocultural constructions, 3, 7, 10, 17, 82, 89n, 90n, 131, 138, 142, 147, 182–3, 185
Coole, Diana, 12, 15, 89n, 202
Copernicus, Nicolaus, 6, 9
'corporeal imagination' (Bill Brown), 74, 84, 173
correlation/ correlationism, 8, 113, 116, 126n, 175, 263
criticism *see* reading (ways of)
cultural constructionism *see* constructionism/ sociocultural constructions
Curtis, Claire P., 200, 201

'dark ecology' (Timothy Morton), 240, 243, 245, 254
Darwin, Charles, 9, 245
Dawkins, Richard, 258
De Boever, Arne, 218–19; *see also* financial realism *under* literary subgenres/ periods
de Certeau, Michel, 245
deconstruction, 4, 6, 9–10, 20, 32, 37, 125, 139, 142–3, 167, 262; *see also* Derrida, Jacques; Morton, Timothy; poststructuralism
defamiliarisation *see* defamiliarisation/ ostraneniye *under* literary concepts
Deleuze, Gilles, 6, 10, 11, 15–16, 80, 118, 140, 154, 161–2, 180, 185, 216, 219 and assemblage, 11, 15, 118, 154
see also asignification; immanence; impersonal vitality; meaning-effects and sense-effects *under* language
Demos, T. J., 210n, 239
der Tuin, Iris, 50, 149n, 173, 175, 179, 187, 188
Derrida, Jacques, 6, 9–10, 35, 75, 84, 142, 179, 183, 262
'différance', 10
'messianicity', 75
and teleology, 75
see also deconstruction
Descartes, René, 5, 6, 7, 10, 109, 258; *see also* Cartesian subject; Cartesian view on nature
différance see Derrida, Jacques
discourse, 8, 10, 25n, 32, 37, 40, 46, 57, 68n, 74, 76, 77, 79, 85, 116, 120, 125, 126n, 131, 132, 133, 135, 137–44, 148, 168, 183, 202, 221, 239, 240–1, 258, 261
'distributions of the sensible' (Jacques Rancière), 75–6, 80–3, 85–8
Dolphijn, Rick, 173, 175, 187, 188
Driesch, Hans, 11, 117
dualism, 11, 50, 110, 114, 118–19, 144, 166, 202, 216, 219, 233n
'duomining' (Graham Harman), 258; *see also* overmining; undermining

ecocriticism *see* literary theory/ schools of study
ecomimesis *see* literary concepts
'ecosophy' (Félix Guattari), 242–3
electromagnetism, 121–2, 123
emotions *see* affect
Enlightenment, the, 239, 241, 245
entanglement
 of art and matter, 124
 entangled realities, 8, 22, 149
 of harmony and dissonance, 123
 of human and nonhuman/ subject and object, 8, 22, 59, 149, 187, 216–17, 230–1, 242, 245, 254
 of matter and sociocultural meaning, 8, 14, 22, 25n
 of reading and material forces, 25n, 142
 of texts and life forms, 10, 14, 25n
 of theory and literature, 173, 189
 of time and matter, 23, 24, 172, 184–9
 see also agent/ agency; assemblage; corporeal imagination; human-human interrelations; human-nonhuman

interrelations; intercorporeity; intra-action; the mesh; object-object relations; oddkin; subject-object relations; quasi subject quasi object; sympoiesis; trans-corporeality
epistemology, 8, 52, 82, 87, 88, 114, 142, 143
Everything (David OReilly), 67

Fanon, Franz, 75, 143
Felski, Rita, 132, 133, 134, 149n, 154; see also surface reading *under* reading (ways of)
feminism, 3, 4, 8, 12, 22–3, 24, 131–49, 149n, 154–5, 169, 170n, 172–4, 176, 177, 179
  Écriture Féminine *see under* feminist literary criticism *under* reading (ways of)
  French feminist theory, 131–2, 135–7
  second wave feminism, 131–7, 141
  see also feminist literary criticism *under* reading (ways of); feminist literature *under* literary subgenres/ periods; feminist new materialism; gender criticism; gynocriticism *under* reading (ways of); postfeminism; queer theory
feminist new materialism, 4, 12, 131–2, 139–49
Fisher, Mark, 194, 204, 209, 237; *see also* Capitalist Realism *under* realisms; capitalist realist apocalypse
Flanagan, Matthew, 51
Formless (Yve-Alain Bois and Rosalind Kraus), 261–2
Freeman, Elizabeth, 173, 182–4, 185, 186–7, 188, 189
Freud, Sigmund, 9, 183
Frost, Samantha, 15, 89n, 202

The Gap of Time (Jeanette Winterson), 23, 172–3, 175–9, 181ᴸ–9
Garber, Marjorie, 172, 176, 178
gender criticism, 3, 8, 11, 23, 132–4, 137–9, 141, 143, 149n, 153, 156, 172–3, 178, 207, 214; *see also* feminism; misogyny; sexism; queer criticism
Genette, Gérard, 32, 57; *see also* summary *under* literary concepts
Ghosh, Amitav, 195
  The Great Derangement, 195, 196, 197–8, 202, 203
Gibson, William, 203, 204
Gilroy, Paul, 89n
global warming *see* Anthropocene, the
Greenblatt, Stephen, 176, 179–80

Greimas, Algirdas-Julien, 68n
Grosz, Elizabeth, 4, 140, 141
  Volatile Bodies, 141, 146, 149n
Guattari, Félix, 24, 118, 185, 216, 219, 236, 237, 239, 242–3, 250; *see also* asignification; ecosophy

Halberstam, Jack (Judith), 174–5, 176
Hamon, Philippe, 33–4, 35, 36, 41, 43
Haraway, Donna, 132, 140, 141, 144, 146, 148, 210n, 238, 239, 241, 242, 250, 254
  The Cyborg Manifesto, 238
  Staying with the Trouble. Making Kin in the Chthulucene, 241
  see also oddkin; sympoiesis
Harman, Graham, 4, 5, 6, 7, 8, 9, 11–14, 16, 18–19, 74, 77, 87, 90n, 95, 98–9, 106, 140, 142, 258
  Immaterialism, 5, 7, 14, 258
  Tool-Being: Heidegger and the Metaphysics of Objects, 98
  Weird Realism: Lovecraft and Philosophy, 19, 98, 99
  see also anti-realist tradition; duomining; immaterialism; mind-independent realism *under* realisms (philosophical); overmining; *The Speculative Turn*; surplus of reality; undermining; weird realism *under* realism (philosophical)
Harris, Robert, 214, 218
Harrison, Robert Pogue, 107n
Heaney, Seamus, 52
Hegel, G. W. F., 111, 126n, 259
Heiberg, Johan Ludvig, 111
Heidegger, Martin, 10, 12, 13, 24, 42, 95, 96–9, 100, 101, 102, 104, 106n, 107n, 259
  Being and Time, 96–7, 98, 102
  'Building Dwelling Thinking', 107n
  'Dasein', 97, 101, 102, 259
  'The Origin of the Work of Art', 96–7
  'The Thing', 107n
  tool-analysis, 13, 97, 98
  'What is Metaphysics?', 101
  work/ earth, 97–106
  see also phenomenology; withdrawnness/ self-receding nature of things
Heinberg, Richard, 200, 209n
Herman, David, 53–4
hermeneutics of suspicion, 134, 148
hermeneutics of trust, 134, 148
historical materialism, 89n, 90n, 241; *see also* Marxist materialism

Homo oeconomicus, 217, 241
human autonomy, 5, 45, 76, 102, 111, 115
human exceptionalism, 24, 89n, 104, 245
  as European construct, 89n
human-human interrelations/ human-human reality, 8, 21, 74, 81–2, 115, 160, 169; *see also* sociality
human-nonhuman interrelations
  as human and nonhuman relations/ relationships, 2, 3, 12, 109, 125, 163, 216
  as human and nonhuman divide/ division/ boundary/ hierarchy, 21, 66, 104, 113, 116, 219, 238
  as human and nonhuman interaction, 154–5
  see also human subject/ subjectivity; sociality
human subject/ subjectivity, 2, 4, 12, 17, 32–4, 45–6, 59–61, 63–4, 66, 81, 95, 100, 102, 111, 119, 139, 146, 153, 155–6, 158–60, 169, 194, 198, 216–17, 219–20, 233n, 260, 261
  and capitalism, 215–16
  and de-anthropocisation, 4, 12, 14
  economic subject, 216–17
  and interiority, 155–6, 158, 163
  intersubjectivity, 54–6
  see also Cartesian subject; human-human interrelations; nonhuman subjectivity *under* nonhuman/s
humanisation *see* anthropomorphisation
Hurley, Kameron, 201
Hutto, Daniel, 165
'hylicity' (Timothy Morton), 257, 260
'hyperobjects' (Timothy Morton), 5, 196

idealism, 6, 8–9, 111, 117, 124, 258
  as linguistic idealism, 8
  as Romantic idealism, 111, 117, 124
identity, 3, 85, 88, 97, 100, 132–3, 135, 138–9, 143, 148, 156, 172–3, 177, 180–1, 185, 216, 220, 262
  as gender identity, 133, 139, 156, 172
  as identity/ identitarian politics, 88, 173
ideology, 77, 88, 136, 261
immanence, 11, 116
'immaterialism' (Graham Harman), 5, 14, 258
immateriality, 8, 100, 102, 104, 110–11, 114, 117–19, 121, 218, 223; *see also* immaterialism
'impersonal vitality' (Gilles Deleuze), 11
'informe' (George Bataille), 261

Ingemann, Bernhard Severin, 122
inhuman *see* nonhuman/s
'intercorporeity' (Florence Chiew), 12, 76
'intra-action' (Karen Barad), 59, 154–6, 160, 163, 167, 169, 187, 208, 210n, 260
isomorphism, 116

Jameson, Frederic, 77, 193, 218, 220
'jetztzeit' (Walter Benjamin), 239, 243–4, 249
Johnson, Mark, 155, 159; *see also* cognitive metaphor theory

Kafka, Franz, 17
Kant, Immanuel, 5–11, 13, 117, 258–9
  '*Bildungstrieb*', 117
  thing-in-itself, 7
Kirby, Vicky, 5, 8, 140; *see also* prison-house of language
Kittay, Jeffrey, 35–6

Lakoff, George, 155, 159; *see also* cognitive metaphor theory
language, 2, 4–5, 8–10, 19–20, 22, 33, 35–9, 44–5, 49, 60, 74, 76, 78, 81–2, 89, 131, 135–6, 138, 141–4, 155, 163, 168–9, 176, 216, 224, 238, 252, 262–3
  language writing itself, 35
  linguistic idealism, 8
  literary language, 19, 22, 143, 163
  and 'meaning-effects' (Gilles Deleuze), 80
  and 'sense-effects' (Gilles Deleuze), 80–1
  sensuous language, 78
  see also figurative language *under* literary concepts, linguistic turn; prison-house of language; representation; semiotics/ signs; signification; signifier/ signified
Latour, Bruno, 11, 14, 119, 238, 245
  and assemblage, 11
  see also 'actant'; Actor Network Theory; quasi subject quasi object
Lawrence, D. H., 94
Lazarus, Neil, 75, 77, 82, 84
Lazzarato, Maurizio, 215–17, 219, 222, 229; *see also* capitalism; Marxist criticism
Lefebvre, Henri, 83
LeMenager, Stephanie, 199–200
Leopold, Aldo, 195
Lerner, Ben *see 10:04* (Ben Lerner)
Levine, Caroline, 51, 67
'life itself' (Rosi Braidotti), 87–8
linguistic constructions *see* constructionism/ sociocultural constructions

linguistic idealism *see* language
linguistic turn, 5, 8, 217
literary concepts
  'the Aeolian' (Timothy Morton), 40, 44, 126n; *see also* 'The Aeolian Harp' *under* Coleridge, Samuel Taylor
  aesthetic, 16–19, 41, 68n, 74–9, 87–8, 90n, 97, 99–100, 110, 112, 121, 125, 126n, 134–5, 137, 157–8, 164–5, 167, 173, 237, 239, 242–3, 250, 252–3, 259
  allegory, 64, 77–81, 90n, 112, 114–16, 124, 182, 188
  alliteration, 42
  allure, 19
  'ambient poetics' (Timothy Morton), 19–20, 31, 36–8, 40, 45, 126n
  ambiguity, 24, 120, 263
  anthropomorphisation, 17–18, 20, 112, 115–16, 121
  author, 4, 19, 23, 34, 36, 39, 44, 60, 111, 133–5, 172–4, 177–8, 189, 203–4, 245, 253: male authors, 133–5; *see also* gynocriticism *under* feminist literary criticism *under* reading (ways of)
  background/ foreground, 1, 12, 19–20, 22, 31–2, 36–9, 41, 44–6, 53–6, 60, 67, 68n, 80, 87, 106, 109, 156–7, 160–1, 164, 168, 219, 252
  character/ characterisation, 1, 4, 32–6, 40, 43, 46, 51–6, 58, 64, 66, 74–8, 83, 87, 89, 89n, 90n, 115, 117, 122, 143, 153, 155–9, 161–2, 168, 173–4, 177–8, 180, 182, 184–9, 197, 203, 205–7, 226, 243, 263
  defamiliarisation/ 'ostraneniye' (Viktor Shklovsky), 50, 58, 64, 67, 246
  description/ depiction, 1, 19, 22–4, 31–6, 38–46, 53–4, 58, 60, 66, 68n, 76–8, 80–2, 95, 98–9, 102, 155–60, 162–3, 165–7, 212, 215, 218–21, 227, 232: and narration/ narratology, 34, 43–4, 46, 156; as representation, 35–6, 40; sensuous, 43
  ecomimesis, 22, 43
  ekphrasis, 43
  fabula and *sjuzet*, 144
  focalisation, 67, 86–7
  imagery, 77, 79, 80, 100–4, 166–7, 249–50
  imagination, 17, 23, 54, 66–8, 74–5, 84–8, 107, 119, 143, 165, 169, 173, 227, 242–4
  'infra-ordinary', the (Georges Perec), 39–41, 46

irony, 123, 252
lyrical 'I', 95
metaphor, 42, 61, 68, 77–81, 124, 143, 153, 155–60, 163, 166–9, 222, 228
meta-textual representation/ representational status, 19, 35, 36, 40, 156
mimesis, 19, 40, 43
mise en abyme, 31, 36, 37, 38, 41, 44–6
narrative: narrativity, 53, 58, 68n; homodiegetic narration, 226; and rhythm, 53–68, 135, 140–7, 175, 229–31; slow narrative (Marco Carracciolo), 22, 49–69; visual narrative, 53, 68n; *see also* description *under* literary concepts; human subject/ subjectivity; Narratology *under* literary theory/ schools of study; tellability *under* literary concepts
narrator, 4, 19, 40–6, 55–6, 117, 120–4, 160–1, 173, 178, 225–9, 238, 257
onomatopoeia, 42, 56, 60
parable, 65, 117, 154, 161, 181
plot, 4, 33, 38, 43, 51–6, 114–15, 144, 154
point of view, 4, 18, 21, 33, 37, 61–3, 114, 138, 158, 195, 214: nonhuman, 37, 158, 195
reader, the, 34–46, 53–6, 60–1, 118, 142–3, 154, 159, 201, 209
realism, 80, 200, 218–22, 225, 233n, 237; *see also* financial realism *under* literary subgenres/ periods; weird realism *under* realisms (philosophical)
'the re-mark' (Timothy Morton), 41, 44–5, 263
'rendering' (Timothy Morton), 15, 20, 37, 40–1, 44, 143
rhetorical strategies, 19, 34, 37, 40, 42, 120, 121, 166, 260
scale, 21, 63–5, 88, 124, 197, 203, 208, 221–2
self-reflectivity, 37, 40, 45, 233n
sequentiality, 40, 44
setting/ milieu/ environment, 19, 20, 31–41, 46, 61, 78, 83, 87, 90, 99, 103, 113, 144, 184, 197, 204
sjuzet see fabula and *sjuzet under* literary concepts
Stimmung/ atmosphere, 231
stylistics, 35, 38, 42, 44, 52, 77, 125, 132, 158, 173, 257
'summary' (Gérard Genette), 57
suspense, 55
tellability, 53–7, 67

272 INDEX

literary concepts (*cont.*)
  text (materiality), 42, 90; *see also* textuality
  textuality, 3, 20, 37, 38
  theme, 3, 20, 37, 38
  timbral, 42
  title, 35, 41, 42, 45, 64, 75, 84, 85, 88, 117, 193, 196, 199, 205
  tone, 43, 221, 237, 240
  uncanniness (*Unheimlichkeit*), 101–2, 112, 220
  work of art (literature as), 37, 78, 79, 84, 97, 134, 239, 251, 261; *see also* work/ earth *under* Heidegger
  writing as thematised *see* self-reflectivity
  see also literary subgenres/ periods; literary theory/ schools of study; reading (ways of); realisms (philosophical)
literary subgenres/ periods
  agripunk, 204
  apocalyptic fiction, 200
  biopunk, 204
  cyberpunk, 203, 204
  fairy tale, 18, 110–25, 181
  fantasy, 148, 198
  feminist literature, 22
  financial crisis fiction, 214
  financial realism (Arne de Boever), 218–20
  futurism, 204
  graphic novel, 52, 53, 56, 60, 63, 65, 66; *see also* visual narrative *under* narrative *under* literary concepts
  horror, 99, 166, 198
  modernist literature, 22
  Oulipian novel, 39
  postcolonial literature, 4, 73
  retro-futurism, 204
  science fiction, 19, 198, 240
  springpunk, 204
  see also literary concepts; literary theory/ schools of study; reading (ways of); realisms (philosophical)
literary theory/ schools of study
  ecocriticism, 20, 37, 195, 239; *see also* scale spatio-temporal scales *under* reading (ways of)
  feminist literary theory, 23, 131, 132, 135–40
  Narratology, 22, 24, 31–4, 41, 43, 45, 55, 57, 67, 114
  New Formalism, 51
  and post-anthropocentric theory, 74, 89n
  postcolonial literary theory, 4, 22, 72, 77, 88, 143, 172
  see also Actor Network Theory (ANT); Assemblage Theory; deconstruction; feminist new materialism; hermeneutics of suspicion; hermeneutics of trust; historical materialism; literary concepts; literary subgenres/ periods; Marxist criticism; New Materialism; Object-Oriented Ontology; phenomenology; posthumanism; poststructuralism; reading (ways of); queer criticism; queer theory; realisms (philosophical); semiotics/ signs; structuralism; Thing Theory
Lorde, Audre, 167
Lovecraft, H. P., 19, 98, 99
Lowell, Robert, 93, 94
Lucas, Maja, 23, 143–7
Lukács, Georg, 219

Marx, Karl, 89n, 259; *see also* Marxist materialism; Marxist reading *under* reading (ways of)
Marxist criticism, 8, 75, 214
  'cognitariat' (Franco Berardi), 225
  'info-signs' (Franco Berardi), 218, 222
  'machinic enslavement' (Franco Berardi and Maurizio Lazzarato), 216, 217, 219, 220, 229
  see also capitalism; commodification
Marxist materialism, 90n; *see also* historical materialism
Massumi, Brian, 5, 86, 87, 143, 221
materiality, 3, 8, 15, 18, 35, 39, 42, 45, 49, 50, 53, 55, 64, 66, 67, 97, 99–100, 109–16, 131–2, 140–3, 147, 153, 154, 156, 161, 165, 166, 169, 194, 195, 223, 236, 244, 247–54
  and anti-materialism, 101; *see also* immaterialism
mattering, 259, 260, 265
McCarthy, Cormac, 201
McNaught, Jon, 22, 51–67
  Kingdom, 51–67
meaninglessness, 8, 9
mediality/ mediation, 17, 37, 44–6, 86, 216, 220
Meillassoux, Quentin, 8; *see also* correlationism
'the mesh' (Timothy Morton), 240
metaphysics, 78, 95, 101, 138, 144, 219, 261, 264

'metapoetic negotiation' (Torsten Bøgh Thomsen), 111, 113, 121
Merleau-Ponty, Maurice, 12, 140, 141; *see also* phenomenology
Millett, Kate, 136
misogyny, 134, 137, 262; *see also* gender criticism; sexism
modernity, 17, 110, 238, 239, 242; *see also* Enlightenment, the
Moi, Toril, 136, 149n
Moore, Jason, 106, 192, 193, 205, 210n; *see also* Cheap Nature
Morton, Timothy, 9, 10, 14–16, 19, 20, 24, 31, 36, 37, 39, 40–4, 46, 90n, 116, 126n, 196, 240, 254, 256
   'An Object-Oriented Defense of Poetry', 16, 20
   Dark Ecology, 254
   'Deconstruction and/ as Ecology', 37
   Ecology without Nature – Rethinking Environmental Aesthetics, 14, 19, 20, 40
   Hyperobjects, 196
   see also the Aeolian *under* literary concepts; ambient poetics *under* literary concepts; dark ecology; formally ecological *under* reading (ways of); hylicity; hyperobjects; the mesh; ontotheological claim; physiography; the re-mark *under* literary concepts; rendering *under* literary concepts; scientism; slow reading *under* reading (ways of); stuff; woodenness

natural science, 121–5, 168, 194, 196, 203, 240, 258
neoliberalism, 243
neurology, 124
New Materialism, 4–8, 12–16, 18, 22, 23, 25n, 50–1, 66, 67, 74, 76, 85, 89n, 99, 110, 113, 116, 118, 125, 131–3, 141–3, 149n, 154–5, 158–9, 172–3, 175–6, 179, 182, 185, 187, 188, 189, 245
   and feminist theory, 131, 132, 139, 141, 142; *see also* feminist new materialism
   and overlaps with/ differences from Object-Oriented Ontology, 4–7, 13–16, 22
   and queer theory, 131, 132, 139, 174, 183, 185
   see also agential realism *under* realisms (philosophical); assemblage; Barad, Karen; Bennett, Jane; Coole, Diana; Frost, Samantha; Kirby, Vicky; matter-realism *under* realisms (philosophical); Object-Oriented Ontology

Nietzsche, Friedrich, 11, 259
'No Future' (the Sex Pistols), 237
nonhuman/s
   nonhuman agency, 2–3, 5, 12, 18, 21–2, 76, 80, 82, 85–6, 89n, 154, 162, 216, 218–20; *see also* agent/ agency
   nonhuman reality, 3, 5, 7, 9, 16, 19–20, 78, 85, 111, 217, 219
   nonhuman subjectivity, 63
   nonhuman theory, 11
   nonhuman viewpoints *see* point of view *under* literary concepts
   as Other/ otherness, 3, 6–7, 81, 85, 89, 94, 149
   see also entanglement; human-nonhuman interrelations; non-subjects; perceptual attunement to the nonhuman *under* senses/ bodily perception
The Nonhuman Turn (Richard Grusin), 17
non-identity (Theodor Adorno), 75, 88
non-linguistic reality/ non-textual reality, 8–9, 217
non-relationality, 98–9, 102
'non-semantic signification' (Sten Moslund), 80
'non-subjects' (Jane Bennett), 13, 82; *see also* nonhuman/s; object

Oatley, Keith, 55
object agency *see* agent/ agency
Object-Oriented Ontology (OOO), 3–7, 9, 11–16, 18, 20, 22, 74, 85, 89n, 90n, 95, 98–9, 140, 262
   and criticism of Actor Network Theory, 11; *see also* overmining
   and essence, 13–14, 18, 102
   and overlaps with/ differences from New Materialism, 11–16; *see also* overmining
   and relationality/ non-relation, 13, 19, 95, 98–9
   see also Harman, Graham; mind-independent realism *under* realisms (philosophical); Morton, Timothy; New Materialism; object; object-object relations; object-oriented reading *under* reading (ways of); reductionism; weird realism *under* realisms (philosophical); withdrawnness/ self-receding nature of things
object-object relations, 2, 3, 7, 16, 18, 20, 21, 34, 35, 43, 45, 66, 84, 113
O'Connell, Hugh, 75, 77, 84, 85, 87, 264; *see also* weak utopia
'oddkin' (Donna Haraway), 241, 242; *see also* sympoiesis

ontology, 2, 3, 4, 7, 11, 12, 14, 17, 24, 74, 89n, 94–8, 102, 106n, 116–18, 125, 140, 172, 202, 218–20, 222–5, 230, 258
    anthropocentric, 97
    of the artwork, 97
    'dry ontology' (Martin Karlsson Pedersen), 214, 222, 224, 225
    flat, 11, 12, 14, 17, 116, 117, 118, 219
    'ontotheological claim' (Timothy Morton), 16
    of the thing, 98, 99, 100
Ørsted, Hans Christian, 121–3
otherness/ alterity, 85, 89, 94, 96, 202; see also uncanniness (Unheimlichkeit) under literary concepts
otherworldliness, 202, 203, 242; see also uncanniness (Unheimlichkeit) under literary concepts
'overmining' (Graham Harman), 7, 8, 13, 14, 90, 258; see also duomining; undermining

Peanuts (Charles Schulz), 263
Parenti, Christian, 239
Perec, Georges, 4, 31–47
    Espèces d'espaces, 39
    La Vie mode d'emploi, 39
    'Still Life/ Style Leaf', 31–47
    tentative d'epuisement d'un lieu parisien, 39
    see also infra-ordinary under literary concepts
Perloff, Marjorie, 94–5, 104–5
Phelan, James, 32, 33
phenomenology, 12, 15, 78, 87, 141, 154, 155, 156, 163, 164, 168, 169
    body-phenomenology (Maurice Merleau-Ponty), 12
    queer phenomenology, 154
    thing-phenomenology (Martin Heidegger), 13
Phillips, Robert, 93
'physiography' (Timothy Morton), 260
'planetary dysphoria' (Emily Apter), 240
Plath, Sylvia, 4, 22, 92–107
    Ariel, 94, 95
    'In Plaster', 96
    'Lady Lazarus', 93
    'Ocean 1212-W', 107n
    'Tulips', 92–107
Plato, 6
post-anthropocentric/ de-anthropocentric, 3–6, 9–12, 14, 16, 21–5, 31–5, 49, 75, 88, 89n, 95–7, 105–7, 160, 166, 169, 215–20

postapocalypse, 200–2, 241; see also apocalypse
postfeminism, 137; see also feminism
posthumanism, 110, 111, 113, 114, 126n, 207, 242
poststructuralism, 6, 8, 10, 25n, 135, 138, 140–2; see also deconstruction; structuralism
Preston, Alex, 214, 225
    This Bleeding City, 215, 217–19, 222, 225–30, 233n
'prison-house of language' (Vicky Kirby), 8

'quantum dis/continuity' (Karen Barad), 187
quantum theory, 258, 263–4
'quasi subject quasi object' (Bruno Latour), 245
queer criticism, 139, 173
    'queer interiorities' (Laura Oulannne), 153
    'queer narratology' (Susan Lanser), 173
    queer time, 172, 174–6, 179, 182
    see also feminism; literary theory/ schools of study, queer reading under reading (ways of)

Rancière, Jacques, 75–6, 87; see also distributions of the sensible
racism, 275
reading (ways of)
    'affective materialities reading' (Laura Oulanne), 154, 160, 169
    'aisthetic reading' (Sten Moslund), 34, 76, 78, 80, 82, 85, 101n
    allegorical, 64, 77–81, 90n, 112, 114–16, 124, 182, 188
    'carnacriticism' (Tobias Skiveren), 143, 148
    'concrete reading' (Marlene Marcussen), 40
    feminist literary criticism, 131–9, 142, 144, 147–8, 149n; Écriture Féminine, 135, 137, 148; see also Cixous, Hélène; gynocriticism; Showalter, Elaine
    Marxist reading, 75
    'material–affective approach' (Martin Karlsson Pedersen), 215, 217–18, 220
    matter-oriented reading, 45, 76, 78, 81
    narratological reading, 39
    post-anthropocentric reading, 4–5, 34, 40
    queer reading, 139, 169, 173
    reading as bodily experience, 42
    reading as 'formally ecological' (Timothy Morton), 37–8
    'reading for resources' (Rune Graulund), 23, 200

'responsive reading'/ 'close reading' (Eve Sedgwick), 173
semantic interpretation, 76
sequential/ temporal reading, 37
'slow reading' (Timothy Morton), 19
'slow reading' (Marco Caracciolo), 50–1, 60; *see also* slow narrative *under* narrative *under* literary concepts
'spatio-temporal scales' (Timothy Clark), 21
'subject-centric reading' (Michael Karlsson Pedersen), 93
'surface reading' (Rita Felski), 154
thing-oriented reading, 67, 95, 101, 103–4
see also literary concepts; literary subgenres/ periods; literary theory/ schools of study; realisms (philosophical)
Reagan, Ronald, 252
realisms (philosophical)
'agential realism' (Karen Barad), 5, 126n
'Capitalist Realism' (Mark Fisher), 237, 244, 249
'matter-realisms' (Rosi Braidotti), 5
'mind-independent' realism (Graham Harman), 18, 74
Speculative Realism, 3, 19, 140
'weird realism' (Graham Harman), 19, 98–9
see also realism *under* literary concepts
reductionism, 7, 15–16, 24, 80, 98, 258
religion, 110, 121, 125
representation, 2, 4, 6, 8, 10, 19–20, 22, 24, 32, 35–6, 40, 46, 74, 79, 89n, 90n, 94, 110, 116, 125, 140–2, 173, 196–7, 216–18, 220, 222, 238
and Capitalism, 216, 222
and consciousness, 6, 216–17, 220
cultural representation, 8, 21, 66, 140–2, 196–7
highly formalised, 66
linguistic representation, 6, 10, 217
symbolic representation, 79, 94
see also language; literary concepts; mediality/ mediation; semiotics/ signs; signification; signifier/signified
resources (energy), 54, 60, 82, 194–5, 198–222, 223
Rivera, Mayra, 132, 139–43, 145, 147
Romanticism, 23, 109–11, 123
Rosenthal, M. L., 93, 100, 106
Ryan, Marie-Laure, 32, 53

Sanders, Karin, 112–13
Saussure, Ferdinand de, 6, 8–10; *see also* signifier/ signified
Schelling, Friedrich von, 111, 126n
Schlegel, Friedrich, 111, 123
'scientism' (Timothy Morton), 258
Scranton, Roy, 196–7
Sedgwick, Eve Kosofsky, 139, 148, 149n, 173; *see also* responsive reading/ close reading *under* reading (ways of)
semiotics/ signs, 2, 6–10, 20–1, 33, 36, 38, 41, 46, 74, 79–80, 112, 121, 131, 136, 139, 158, 214–18, 220, 222–5, 227–30, 232, 233n, 234n, 237, 242, 244, 263; *see also* asignification; info-signs *under* Marxist criticism; non-semantic signification; semiotic inexhaustibility; signification; signifier/ signified
senses/ bodily perception, 6, 9, 12, 14, 22, 37, 43, 49–50, 52–4, 56, 58–61, 74–84, 86–9, 89n, 90n, 97–8, 121, 143, 145, 147, 158, 163–5, 224, 228–9, 231, 240–2, 247, 249
deceleration of perception, 50–1, 58, 60
'perceptual attunement to the nonhuman' (Marco Carraciolo), 49, 53, 56
pre-semantic bodily sensations, 80–1
synaesthesia, 59, 76
see also body; smell; sound; taste, touch; vision
sexism, 134; *see also* gender criticism; misogyny
Shakespeare, William, 172–3, 176–82, 184, 186–7
Shaviro, Steven, 5, 87, 195
Shklovsky, Viktor, 50, 58, 67n; *see also* defamiliarisation/ ostraneniye *under* literary concepts
Shonkwiler, Alison, 214–15, 233n
Showalter, Elaine, 134, 136, 149n
A Literature of Their Own, 134
see also gynocriticism *under* reading (ways of)
signification, 9, 80–1, 141, 181, 185, 218, 220–1, 225; *see also* language; signifier/ signified
signifier/ signified, 8, 143, 224; *see also* signification
'slow cinema' (Lutz Koepnick), 51
smell, 76–8, 81, 83, 90n
Snitow, Ann, 137–8
social constructionism *see* constructionism/ sociocultural constructions

sociality, 55
somatophobia, 131
sound, 42, 60, 76, 86–7, 123, 145, 158, 231, 264
   as sound image (Saussure), 8
'speculative onto-story' (Jane Bennett), 49
Speculative Realism *see* realisms (philosophical)
The Speculative Turn (Levi Bryant, Nick Srnicek and Graham Harman), 3, 6
Spinoza, Baruch de, 6, 10–11
structuralism, 8; *see also* poststructuralism
'stuff' (Maurizia Boscagli), 18
subject-centrism, 6, 21–2, 24, 33, 40, 45, 93, 98
subjectification, 261
subjectivity *see* human subject
subject-object relations, 18
   as binaries, 44, 50, 94, 104, 114, 119
'surplus of reality' (Graham Harman), 7, 77
surplus of thingness, 14
sympoiesis (Donna Haraway), 241; *see also* oddkin

tactility *see* touch
taste, 76, 78, 83, 90n, 104
teleology, 51, 75, 85, 260
textuality *see* literary concepts
Thatcher, Margaret, 237
theocentrism, 116
thing
   autonomy of, 119
   in Heidegger, 12–13, 42, 95, 97–102, 258
   self-receding nature, 22, 99
   semiotic inexhaustibility, 112, 121
   'things in themselves'/ 'thing-in-itself', 7, 13
   see also Object-Oriented Ontology; surplus of thingness, thing-power; thing-oriented reading *under* reading (ways of); thing-phenomenology *under* phenomenology; Thing Theory; thing world; withdrawnness/ self-receding nature of things
'thing-power' (Jane Bennett), 2, 5, 16, 49, 59, 74, 112, 166

Thing Theory, 3, 17–18, 74, 90n, 98; *see also* Brown, Bill; object; thing
thing world, 8, 82, 96, 99, 101–2
Thiong'o, Ngũgĩ wa, 74
touch, 1, 68n, 76, 78, 81, 115, 147, 159, 187–8, 222, 227, 230–1, 251
transcendence, 116
'trans-corporeality' (Stacy Alaimo), 146, 154, 160, 163, 166–8
Trexler, Adam, 195–8

'undermining' (Graham Harman), 7, 258; *see also* duomining; overmining
Unheimlich see uncannninness *under* literary concepts

'vibrant matter' (Jane Bennett), 2, 11–12, 14, 17–18, 49, 98, 107n, 112, 140, 154, 197
vision (bodily sense of), 60, 63, 68n, 76, 161

'weak utopia' (Hugh O'Connell), 77, 84–5, 87
Weinstein, Jaime, 240
Williams, Raymond, 219
Winterson, Jeanette *see The Gap of Time* (Jeanette Winterson)
withdrawnness/ self-receding nature of things, 10, 13–14, 80–1, 85, 87, 97–9, 105
Wright, Derek, 77
Wolfe, Cary, 126n, 208
'woodenness' (Timothy Morton), 257–8, 260, 264
Woods, Derek, 63
Woolf, Virgina, 17–18
   A Room of One's Own, 1
   'Modern Fiction', 174–5, 187
   The Waves, 1–3
worldliness, 94, 97, 101, 105

Young, Iris Marion, 154

Žižek, Slavoj, 193, 204, 209; *see also* apocalyptic zero-point

www.ingramcontent.com/pod-product-compliance
Lightning Source LLC
Chambersburg PA
CBHW060231240426
4367ICB00016B/2908

EU representative:
Easy Access System Europe
Mustamäe tee 50, 10621 Tallinn, Estonia
Gpsr.requests@easproject.com